This edition is dedicated to my girls. To my wife Jessica who has supported me for all of these years and to my daughter Josephine, who will support me when I'm too old to know what's going on.

—Scott

To my wife, Becky, without whom this adventure never would have begun.

—Ben

Contents at a Glance

Contents at a Glance

Contents

About the Authors

Scott Chacon is a cofounder and the CIO of GitHub and is also the maintainer of the Git homepage (`git-scm.com`). Scott has presented at dozens of conferences around the world on Git, GitHub and the future of work.

Ben Straub is a developer, long time contributor to Libgit2, holder of a Masters degree, international speaker and Git teacher, avid reader, lifelong explorer, and student of the art of making fine software. He lives with his wife and two children in Portland, Oregon.

About the Authors

Preface by Scott Chacon

Welcome to the second edition of *Pro Git*. The first edition was published over four years ago now. Since then a lot has changed and yet many important things have not. While most of the core commands and concepts are still valid today as the Git core team is pretty fantastic at keeping things backward compatible, there have been some significant additions and changes in the community surrounding Git. The second edition of this book is meant to address those changes and update the book so it can be more helpful to the new user.

When I wrote the first edition, Git was still a relatively difficult to use and barely adopted tool for the harder core hacker. It was starting to gain steam in certain communities, but had not reached anywhere near the ubiquity it has today. Since then, nearly every open source community has adopted it. Git has made incredible progress on Windows, in the explosion of graphical user interfaces to it for all platforms, in IDE support and in business use. The *Pro Git* of four years ago knows about none of that. One of the main aims of this new edition is to touch on all of those new frontiers in the Git community.

The Open Source community using Git has also exploded. When I originally sat down to write the book nearly five years ago (it took me a while to get the first version out), I had just started working at a very little known company developing a Git hosting website called GitHub. At the time of publishing there were maybe a few thousand people using the site and just four of us working on it. As I write this introduction, GitHub is announcing our 10 millionth hosted project, with nearly 5 million registered developer accounts and over 230 employees. Love it or hate it, GitHub has heavily changed large swaths of the Open Source community in a way that was barely conceivable when I sat down to write the first edition.

I wrote a small section in the original version of *Pro Git* about GitHub as an example of hosted Git which I was never very comfortable with. I didn't much like that I was writing what I felt was essentially a community resource and also talking about my company in it. While I still don't love that conflict of interests, the importance of GitHub in the Git community is unavoidable. Instead of an example of Git hosting, I have decided to turn that part of the book into more deeply describing what GitHub is and how to effectively use it. If you are going to learn how to use Git then knowing how to use GitHub will help you take part in a huge community, which is valuable no matter which Git host you decide to use for your own code.

The other large change in the time since the last publishing has been the development and rise of the HTTP protocol for Git network transactions. Most of the examples in the book have been changed to HTTP from SSH because it's so much simpler.

It's been amazing to watch Git grow over the past few years from a relatively obscure version control system to basically dominating commercial and open source version control. I'm happy that *Pro Git* has done so well and has also been able to be one of the few technical books on the market that is both quite successful and fully open source.

I hope you enjoy this updated edition of *Pro Git*.

Preface by Scott Chacon

Preface by Ben Straub

The first edition of this book is what got me hooked on Git. This was my introduction to a style of making software that felt more natural than anything I had seen before. I had been a developer for several years by then, but this was the right turn that sent me down a much more interesting path than the one I was on.

Now, years later, I'm a contributor to a major Git implementation, I've worked for the largest Git hosting company, and I've traveled the world teaching people about Git. When Scott asked if I'd be interested in working on the second edition, I didn't even have to think.

It's been a great pleasure and privilege to work on this book. I hope it helps you as much as it did me.

Preface by Ben Straub

CHAPTER 1

■ ■ ■

Getting Started

This chapter is about getting started with Git. We will begin at the beginning by explaining some background on version control tools, then move on to how to get Git running on your system and finally how to get it set up to start working with. At the end of this chapter you should understand why Git is around, why you should use it, and you should be all set up to do so.

About Version Control

What is "version control," and why should you care? Version control is a system that records changes to a file or set of files over time so that you can recall specific versions later. For the examples in this book you will use software source code as the files being version controlled, though in reality you can do this with nearly any type of file on a computer.

If you are a graphic or web designer and want to keep every version of an image or layout (which you would most certainly want to), a Version Control System (VCS) is a very wise thing to use. It allows you to revert files to a previous state, revert the entire project to a previous state, compare changes over time, see who last modified something that might be causing a problem, who introduced an issue and when, and more. Using a VCS also generally means that if you screw things up or lose files, you can easily recover. In addition, you get all this for very little overhead.

Local Version Control Systems

Many people's version-control method of choice is to copy files into another directory (perhaps a time-stamped directory, if they're clever). This approach is very common because it is so simple, but it is also incredibly error prone. It is easy to forget which directory you're in and accidentally write to the wrong file or copy over files you don't mean to.

To deal with this issue, programmers long ago developed local VCSs that had a simple database that kept all the changes to files under revision control.

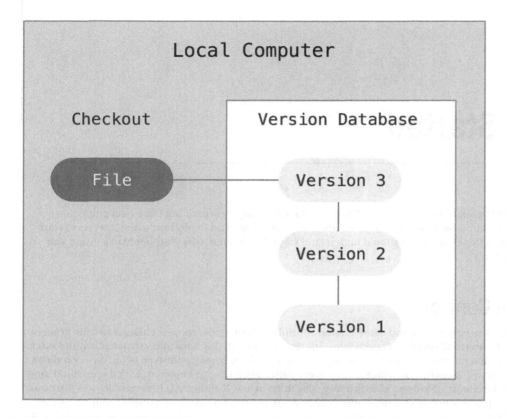

Figure 1-1. *Local version control*

One of the more popular VCS tools was a system called RCS, which is still distributed with many computers today. Even the popular Mac OS X operating system includes the rcs command when you install the Developer Tools. RCS works by keeping patch sets (that is, the differences between files) in a special format on disk; it can then re-create what any file looked like at any point in time by adding up all the patches.

Centralized Version Control Systems

The next major issue that people encounter is that they need to collaborate with developers on other systems. To deal with this problem, Centralized Version Control Systems (CVCSs) were developed. These systems, such as CVS, Subversion, and Perforce, have a single server that contains all the versioned files, and a number of clients that check out files from that central place. For many years, this has been the standard for version control.

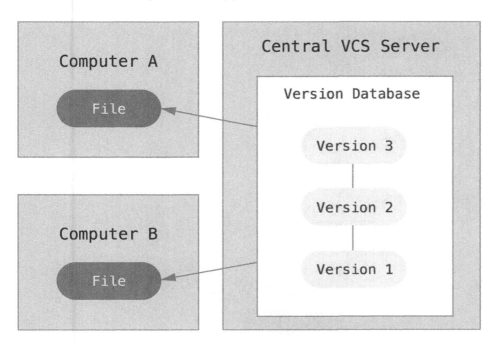

Figure 1-2. *Centralized version control*

This setup offers many advantages, especially over local VCSs. For example, everyone knows to a certain degree what everyone else on the project is doing. Administrators have fine-grained control over who can do what; and it's far easier to administer a CVCS than it is to deal with local databases on every client.

However, this setup also has some serious downsides. The most obvious is the single point of failure that the centralized server represents. If that server goes down for an hour, then during that hour nobody can collaborate at all or save versioned changes to anything they're working on. If the hard disk the central database is on becomes corrupted, and proper backups haven't been kept, you lose absolutely everything—the entire history of the project except whatever single snapshots people happen to have on their local machines. Local VCS systems suffer from this same problem—whenever you have the entire history of the project in a single place, you risk losing everything.

Distributed Version Control Systems

This is where Distributed Version Control Systems (DVCSs) step in. In a DVCS (such as Git, Mercurial, Bazaar, or Darcs), clients don't just check out the latest snapshot of the files—they fully mirror the repository. Thus if any server dies, and these systems were collaborating via it, any of the client repositories can be copied back up to the server to restore it. Every checkout is really a full backup of all the data.

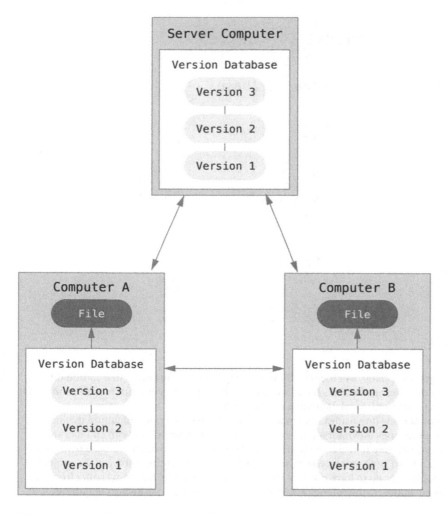

Figure 1-3. *Distributed version control*

Furthermore, many of these systems deal pretty well with having several remote repositories they can work with, so you can collaborate with different groups of people in different ways simultaneously within the same project. This allows you to set up several types of workflows that aren't possible in centralized systems, such as hierarchical models.

A Short History of Git

As with many great things in life, Git began with a bit of creative destruction and fiery controversy.

The Linux kernel is an open source software project of fairly large scope. For most of the lifetime of the Linux kernel maintenance (1991–2002), changes to the software were passed around as patches and archived files. In 2002, the Linux kernel project began using a proprietary DVCS called BitKeeper.

In 2005, the relationship between the community that developed the Linux kernel and the commercial company that developed BitKeeper broke down, and the tool's free-of-charge status was revoked. This prompted the Linux development community (and in particular Linus Torvalds, the creator of Linux) to develop their own tool based on some of the lessons they learned while using BitKeeper. Some of the goals of the new system were as follows:

- Speed
- Simple design
- Strong support for non-linear development (thousands of parallel branches)
- Fully distributed
- Able to handle large projects like the Linux kernel efficiently (speed and data size)

Since its birth in 2005, Git has evolved and matured to be easy to use and yet retain these initial qualities. It's incredibly fast, it's very efficient with large projects, and it has an incredible branching system for non-linear development (see Chapter 3).

Git Basics

So, what is Git in a nutshell? This is an important section to absorb, because if you understand what Git is and the fundamentals of how it works, then using Git effectively will probably be much easier for you. As you learn Git, try to clear your mind of the things you may know about other VCSs, such as Subversion and Perforce; doing so will help you avoid subtle confusion when using the tool. Git stores and thinks about information much differently than these other systems, even though the user interface is fairly similar, and understanding those differences will help prevent you from becoming confused while using it.

Snapshots, Not Differences

The major difference between Git and any other VCS (Subversion and friends included) is the way Git thinks about its data. Conceptually, most other systems store information as a list of file-based changes. These systems (CVS, Subversion, Perforce, Bazaar, and so on) think of the information they keep as a set of files and the changes made to each file over time.

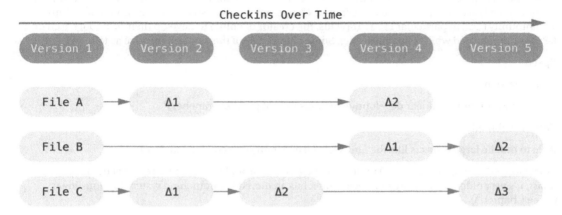

Figure 1-4. *Storing data as changes to a base version of each file*

Git doesn't think of or store its data this way. Instead, Git thinks of its data more like a set of snapshots of a miniature filesystem. Every time you commit, or save the state of your project in Git, it basically takes a picture of what all your files look like at that moment and stores a reference to that snapshot. To be efficient, if files have not changed, Git doesn't store the file again, just a link to the previous identical file it has already stored. Git thinks about its data more like a *stream of snapshots*.

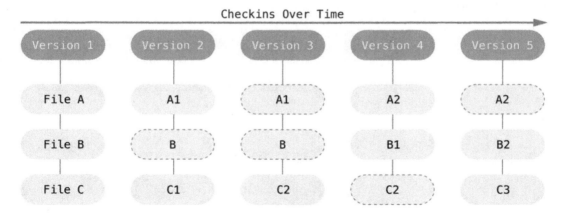

Figure 1-5. *Storing data as snapshots of the project over time*

This is an important distinction between Git and nearly all other VCSs. It makes Git reconsider almost every aspect of version control that most other systems copied from the previous generation. This makes Git more like a mini filesystem with some incredibly powerful tools built on top of it, rather than simply a VCS. We'll explore some of the benefits you gain by thinking of your data this way when we cover Git branching in Chapter 3.

Nearly Every Operation Is Local

Most operations in Git only need local files and resources to operate—generally no information is needed from another computer on your network. If you're used to a CVCS where most operations have that network latency overhead, this aspect of Git will make you think that the gods of speed have blessed Git with unworldly powers. Because you have the entire history of the project right there on your local disk, most operations seem almost instantaneous.

For example, to browse the history of the project, Git doesn't need to go out to the server to get the history and display it for you—it simply reads it directly from your local database. This means you see the project history almost instantly. If you want to see the changes introduced between the current version of a file and the file a month ago, Git can look up the file a month ago and do a local difference calculation, instead of having to either ask a remote server to do it or pull an older version of the file from the remote server to do it locally.

This also means that there is very little you can't do if you're offline or off VPN. If you get on an airplane or a train and want to do a little work, you can commit happily until you get to a network connection to upload. If you go home and can't get your VPN client working properly, you can still work. In many other systems, doing so is either impossible or painful. In Perforce, for example, you can't do much when you aren't connected to the server; and in Subversion and CVS, you can edit files, but you can't commit changes to your database (because your database is offline). This may not seem like a huge deal, but you may be surprised what a big difference it can make.

Git Has Integrity

Everything in Git is check-summed before it is stored and is then referred to by that checksum. This means it's impossible to change the contents of any file or directory without Git knowing about it. This functionality is built in to Git at the lowest levels and is integral to its philosophy. You can't lose information in transit or get file corruption without Git being able to detect it.

The mechanism that Git uses for this checksumming is called a SHA-1 hash. This is a 40-character string composed of hexadecimal characters (0–9 and a–f) and calculated based on the contents of a file or directory structure in Git. A SHA-1 hash looks something like this:

```
24b9da6552252987aa493b52f8696cd6d3b00373
```

You will see these hash values all over the place in Git because it uses them so much. In fact, Git stores everything in its database not by filename but by the hash value of its contents.

Git Generally Only Adds Data

When you do actions in Git, nearly all of them only add data to the Git database. It is hard to get the system to do anything that is not undoable or to make it erase data in any way. As in any VCS, you can lose or mess up changes you haven't committed yet; but after you commit a snapshot into Git, it is very difficult to lose, especially if you regularly push your database to another repository.

This makes using Git a joy because we know we can experiment without the danger of severely screwing things up.

The Three States

Now, pay attention. This is the main thing to remember about Git if you want the rest of your learning process to go smoothly. Git has three main states that your files can reside in: committed, modified, and staged. *Committed* means that the data is safely stored in your local database. *Modified* means that you have changed the file but have not committed it to your database yet. *Staged* means that you have marked a modified file in its current version to go into your next commit snapshot.

This leads us to the three main sections of a Git project: the Git directory, the working directory, and the staging area.

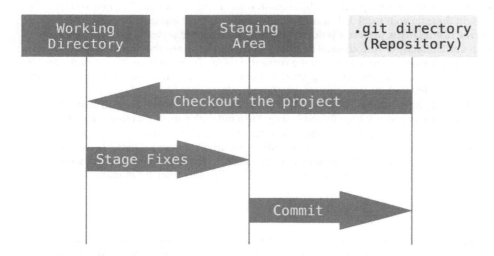

Figure 1-6. *Working directory, staging area, and Git directory*

The Git directory is where Git stores the metadata and object database for your project. This is the most important part of Git, and it is what is copied when you clone a repository from another computer.

The working directory is a single checkout of one version of the project. These files are pulled out of the compressed database in the Git directory and placed on disk for you to use or modify.

The staging area is a file, generally contained in your Git directory, that stores information about what will go into your next commit. It's sometimes referred to as the "index", but it's also common to refer to it as the staging area.

The basic Git workflow goes something like this:

1. You modify files in your working directory.

2. You stage the files, adding snapshots of them to your staging area.

3. You do a commit, which takes the files as they are in the staging area and stores that snapshot permanently to your Git directory.

If a particular version of a file is in the Git directory, it's considered committed. If it's modified but has been added to the staging area, it is staged. And if it was changed since it was checked out but has not been staged, it is modified. In Chapter 2, you'll learn more about these states and how you can either take advantage of them or skip the staged part entirely.

The Command Line

There are a lot of different ways to use Git. There are the original command line tools, and there are many graphical user interfaces of varying capabilities. For this book, we will be using Git on the command line. For one, the command line is the only place you can run all Git commands – most of the GUIs only implement some subset of Git functionality for simplicity. If you know how to run the command line version, you can probably also figure out how to run the GUI version, while the opposite is not necessarily true. Also, while your choice of graphical client is a matter of personal taste, all users will have the command-line tools installed and available.

So we will expect you to know how to open Terminal in Mac or Command Prompt or Powershell in Windows. If you don't know what we're talking about here, you may need to stop and research that quickly so that you can follow the rest of the examples and descriptions in this book.

Installing Git

Before you start using Git, you have to make it available on your computer. Even if it's already installed, it's probably a good idea to update to the latest version. You can either install it as a package or via another installer, or download the source code and compile it yourself.

■ **Note**   This book was written using Git version 2.0.0. Though most of the commands we use should work even in ancient versions of Git, some of them might not or might act slightly differently if you're using an older version. Since Git is quite excellent at preserving backward compatibility, any version after 2.0 should work just fine.

Installing on Linux

If you want to install Git on Linux via a binary installer, you can generally do so through the basic package-management tool that comes with your distribution. If you're on Fedora for example, you can use yum:

```
$ yum install git
```

If you're on a Debian-based distribution like Ubuntu, try apt-get:

```
$ apt-get install git
```

For more options, there are instructions for installing on several different Unix flavors on the Git website, at http://git-scm.com/download/linux.

Installing on Mac

There are several ways to install Git on a Mac. The easiest is probably to install the Xcode command line tools. On Mavericks (10.9) or above you can do this simply by trying to run git from the Terminal the very first time. If you don't have it installed already, it will prompt you to install it.

If you want a more up-to-date version, you can also install it via a binary installer. An OSX Git installer is maintained and available for download at the Git website, at http://git-scm.com/download/mac.

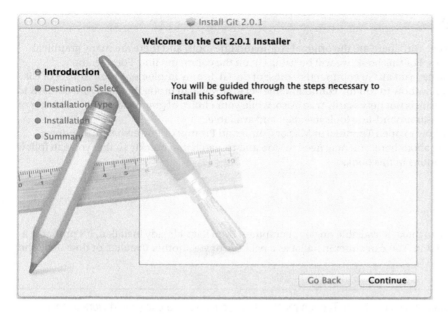

Figure 1-7. *Git OS X Installer*

You can also install it as part of the GitHub for Mac install. Their GUI Git tool has an option to install command line tools as well. You can download that tool from the GitHub for Mac website, at `http://mac.github.com`.

Installing on Windows

There are also a few ways to install Git on Windows. The most official build is available for download on the Git website. Just go to `http://git-scm.com/download/win` and the download will start automatically. Note that this is a project called Git for Windows (also called msysGit), which is separate from Git itself; for more information on it, go to `http://msysgit.github.io/`.

Another easy way to get Git installed is by installing GitHub for Windows. The installer includes a command line version of Git as well as the GUI. It also works well with Powershell, and sets up solid credential caching and sane CRLF settings. We'll learn more about those things a little later, but suffice it to say they're things you want. You can download this from the GitHub for Windows website, at `http://windows.github.com`.

Some people may instead find it useful to install Git from source, because you'll get the most recent version. The binary installers tend to be a bit behind, though as Git has matured in recent years, this has made less of a difference.

If you do want to install Git from source, you need to have the following libraries that Git depends on: `curl`, `zlib`, `openssl`, `expat`, and `libiconv`. For example, if you're on a system that has `yum` (such as Fedora) or `apt-get` (such as a Debian-based system), you can use one of these commands to install all of the dependencies:

```
$ yum install curl-devel expat-devel gettext-devel \
    openssl-devel zlib-devel

$ apt-get install libcurl4-gnutls-dev libexpat1-dev gettext \
    libz-dev libssl-dev
```

When you have all the necessary dependencies, you can go ahead and grab the latest tagged release tarball from several places. You can get it via the Kernel.org site, at `https://www.kernel.org/pub/software/scm/git`, or the mirror on the GitHub web site, at https://github.com/git/git/releases. It's generally a little clearer what the latest version is on the GitHub page, but the kernel.org page also has release signatures if you want to verify your download.

Then, compile and install:

```
$ tar -zxf git-1.9.1.tar.gz
$ cd git-1.9.1
$ make configure
$ ./configure --prefix=/usr
$ make all doc info
$ sudo make install install-doc install-html install-info
```

After this is done, you can also get Git via Git itself for updates:

```
$ git clone git://git.kernel.org/pub/scm/git/git.git
```

First-Time Git Setup

Now that you have Git on your system, you'll want to do a few things to customize your Git environment. You should have to do these things only once on any given computer; they'll stick around between upgrades. You can also change them at any time by running through the commands again.

Git comes with a tool called git config that lets you get and set configuration variables that control all aspects of how Git looks and operates. These variables can be stored in three different places:

- /etc/gitconfig file: Contains values for every user on the system and all their repositories. If you pass the option --system to git config, it reads and writes from this file specifically.

- ~/.gitconfig or ~/.config/git/config file: Specific to your user. You can make Git read and write to this file specifically by passing the --global option.

- config file in the Git directory (that is, .git/config) of whatever repository you're currently using: Specific to that single repository.

Each level overrides values in the previous level, so values in .git/config trump those in /etc/gitconfig.

On Windows systems, Git looks for the .gitconfig file in the $HOME directory (C:\Users\$USER for most people). It also still looks for /etc/gitconfig, although it's relative to the MSys root, which is wherever you decide to install Git on your Windows system when you run the installer.

Your Identity

The first thing you should do when you install Git is to set your user name and e-mail address. This is important because every Git commit uses this information, and it's immutably baked into the commits you start creating:

```
$ git config --global user.name "John Doe"
$ git config --global user.email johndoe@example.com
```

Again, you need to do this only once if you pass the --global option, because then Git will always use that information for anything you do on that system. If you want to override this with a different name or e-mail address for specific projects, you can run the command without the --global option when you're in that project.

Many of the GUI tools will help you do this when you first run them.

Your Editor

Now that your identity is set up, you can configure the default text editor that will be used when Git needs you to type in a message. If not configured, Git uses your system's default editor, which is generally Vim. If you want to use a different text editor, such as Emacs, you can do the following:

```
$ git config --global core.editor emacs
```

■ **Note** Vim and Emacs are popular text editors often used by developers on Unix-based systems like Linux and Mac. If you are not familiar with either of these editors or are on a Windows system, you may need to search for instructions for how to set up your favorite editor with Git.

Checking Your Settings

If you want to check your settings, you can use the git config --list command to list all the settings Git can find at that point:

```
$ git config --list
user.name=John Doe
user.email=johndoe@example.com
color.status=auto
color.branch=auto
color.interactive=auto
color.diff=auto
...
```

You may see keys more than once, because Git reads the same key from different files (/etc/gitconfig and~/ .gitconfig, for example). In this case, Git uses the last value for each unique key it sees.

You can also check what Git thinks a specific key's value is by typing git config <key>:

```
$ git config user.name
John Doe
```

Getting Help

If you ever need help while using Git, there are three ways to get the manual page (manpage) help for any of the Git commands:

```
$ git help <verb>
$ git <verb> --help
$ man git-<verb>
```

For example, you can get the manpage help for the config command by running

```
$ git help config
```

These commands are nice because you can access them anywhere, even offline. If the manpages and this book aren't enough and you need in-person help, you can try the #git or #github channel on the Freenode IRC server (irc. freenode.net). These channels are regularly filled with hundreds of people who are all very knowledgeable about Git and are often willing to help.

Summary

You should have a basic understanding of what Git is and how it's different from the centralized version control system you may have previously been using. You should also now have a working version of Git on your system that's set up with your personal identity. It's now time to learn some Git basics.

CHAPTER 2

Git Basics

If you can read only one chapter to get going with Git, this is it. This chapter covers every basic command you need to do the vast majority of the things you'll eventually spend your time doing with Git. By the end of the chapter, you should be able to configure and initialize a repository, begin and stop tracking files, and stage and commit changes. We'll also show you how to set up Git to ignore certain files and file patterns, how to undo mistakes quickly and easily, how to browse the history of your project and view changes between commits, and how to push and pull from remote repositories.

Getting a Git Repository

You can get a Git project using two main approaches. The first takes an existing project or directory and imports it into Git. The second clones an existing Git repository from another server.

Initializing a Repository in an Existing Directory

If you're starting to track an existing project in Git, you need to go to the project's directory and type

```
$ git init
```

This creates a new subdirectory named .git that contains all your necessary repository files—a Git repository skeleton. At this point, nothing in your project is tracked yet. (See Chapter 11 for more information about exactly what files are contained in the .git directory you just created).

If you want to start version-controlling existing files (as opposed to an empty directory), you should probably begin tracking those files and do an initial commit. You can accomplish that with a few git add commands that specify the files you want to track, followed by a git commit:

```
$ git add *.c
$ git add LICENSE
$ git commit -m 'initial project version'
```

We'll go over what these commands do in just a minute. At this point, you have a Git repository with tracked files and an initial commit.

Cloning an Existing Repository

If you want to get a copy of an existing Git repository—for example, a project you'd like to contribute to—the command you need is git clone. If you're familiar with other VCS systems such as Subversion, you'll notice that the command is "clone" and not "checkout." This is an important distinction—instead of getting just a working copy, Git receives a full copy of nearly all data that the server has. Every version of every file for the history of the project is pulled down by default when you run git clone. In fact, if your server disk gets corrupted, you can often use nearly any of the clones on any client to set the server back to the state it was in when it was cloned (you may lose some server-side hooks and such, but all the versioned data would be there—see Chapter 4 for more details).

You clone a repository with git clone [url]. For example, if you want to clone the Git linkable library called libgit2, you can do so like this:

```
$ git clone https://github.com/libgit2/libgit2
```

That creates a directory named libgit2, initializes a .git directory inside it, pulls down all the data for that repository, and checks out a working copy of the latest version. If you go into the new libgit2 directory, you'll see the project files in there, ready to be worked on or used. If you want to clone the repository into a directory named something other than libgit2, you can specify that as the next command-line option:

```
$ git clone https://github.com/libgit2/libgit2 mylibgit
```

That command does the same thing as the previous one, but the target directory is called mylibgit.

Git has a number of different transfer protocols you can use. The previous example uses the https:// protocol, but you may also see git:// or user@server:path/to/repo.git, which uses the SSH transfer protocol. Chapter 4 will introduce all of the available options the server can set up to access your Git repository and the pros and cons of each.

Recording Changes to the Repository

You have a bona fide Git repository and a checkout or working copy of the files for that project. You need to make some changes and commit snapshots of those changes into your repository each time the project reaches a state you want to record.

Remember that each file in your working directory can be in one of two states: tracked or untracked. Tracked files are files that were in the last snapshot; they can be unmodified, modified, or staged. Untracked files are everything else—any files in your working directory that were not in your last snapshot and are not in your staging area. When you first clone a repository, all your files will be tracked and unmodified because you just checked them out and haven't edited anything.

As you edit files, Git sees them as modified, because you've changed them since your last commit. You stage these modified files and then commit all your staged changes, and the cycle repeats.

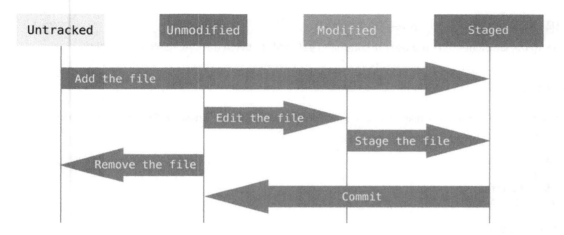

Figure 2-1. *The lifecycle of the status of your files*

Checking the Status of Your Files

The main tool you use to determine which files are in which state is the `git status` command. If you run this command directly after a clone, you should see something like this:

```
$ git status
On branch master
nothing to commit, working directory clean
```

This means you have a clean working directory—in other words, there are no tracked and modified files. Git also doesn't see any untracked files, or they would be listed here. Finally, the command tells you which branch you're on and informs you that it has not diverged from the same branch on the server. For now, that branch is always "master," which is the default; you won't worry about it here. Branches and references are discussed in detail in Chapter 3.

Let's say you add a new file to your project, a simple README file. If the file didn't exist before, and you run `git status`, you see your untracked file like so:

```
$ echo 'My Project' > README
$ git status
On branch master
Untracked files:
  (use "git add <file>..." to include in what will be committed)

	README

nothing added to commit but untracked files present (use "git add" to track)
```

You can see that your new README file is untracked, because it's under the "Untracked files" heading in your status output. Untracked basically means that Git sees a file you didn't have in the previous snapshot (commit); Git won't start including it in your commit snapshots until you explicitly tell it to do so. It does this so you don't accidentally begin including generated binary files or other files that you did not mean to include. You do want to start including README, so let's start tracking the file.

17

Tracking New Files

In order to begin tracking a new file, you use the command git add. To begin tracking the README file, you can run this:

```
$ git add README
```

If you run your status command again, you can see that your README file is now tracked and staged to be committed:

```
$ git status
On branch master
Changes to be committed:
  (use "git reset HEAD <file>..." to unstage)

    new file:   README
```

You can tell that it's staged because it's under the Changes to be committed heading. If you commit at this point, the version of the file at the time you ran git add is what will be in the historical snapshot. You may recall that when you ran git init earlier, you then ran git add (files)—that was to begin tracking files in your directory. The git add command takes a path name for either a file or a directory; if it's a directory, the command adds all the files in that directory recursively.

Staging Modified Files

Let's change a file that was already tracked. If you change a previously tracked file called "benchmarks.rb" and then run your git status command again, you get something that looks like this:

```
$ git status
On branch master
Changes to be committed:
  (use "git reset HEAD <file>..." to unstage)

    new file:   README

Changes not staged for commit:
  (use "git add <file>..." to update what will be committed)
  (use "git checkout -- <file>..." to discard changes in working directory)

    modified: benchmarks.rb
```

The benchmarks.rb file appears under a section named Changed but not staged for commit—which means that a file that is tracked has been modified in the working directory but not yet staged. To stage it, you run the git add command. git add is a multipurpose command—you use it to begin tracking new files, to stage files, and to do other things like marking merge-conflicted files as resolved. It may be helpful to think of it more as "add this content to the next commit" rather than "add this file to the project". Let's run git add now to stage the benchmarks.rb file, and then run git status again:

```
$ git add benchmarks.rb
$ git status
On branch master
```

```
Changes to be committed:
  (use "git reset HEAD <file>..." to unstage)

    new file:    README
    modified:    benchmarks.rb
```

Both files are staged and will go into your next commit. At this point, suppose you remember one little change that you want to make in benchmarks.rb before you commit it. You open it again and make that change, and you're ready to commit. However, let's run git status one more time:

```
$ vim benchmarks.rb
$ git status
On branch master
Changes to be committed:
  (use "git reset HEAD <file>..." to unstage)

    new file:    README
    modified:    benchmarks.rb

Changes not staged for commit:
  (use "git add <file>..." to update what will be committed)
  (use "git checkout -- <file>..." to discard changes in working directory)

    modified:    benchmarks.rb
```

What the heck? Now benchmarks.rb is listed as both staged *and* unstaged. How is that possible? It turns out that Git stages a file exactly as it is when you run the git add command. If you commit now, the version of benchmarks.rb as it was when you last ran the git add command is how it will go into the commit, not the version of the file as it looks in your working directory when you run git commit. If you modify a file after you run git add, you have to run git add again to stage the latest version of the file:

```
$ git add benchmarks.rb
$ git status
On branch master
Changes to be committed:
  (use "git reset HEAD <file>..." to unstage)

    new file:    README
    modified:    benchmarks.rb
```

Short Status

While the git status output is pretty comprehensive, it's also quite wordy. Git also has a short status flag so you can see your changes in a more compact way. If you run git status -s or git status --short you get a far more simplified output from the command.

```
$ git status -s
 M README
MM Rakefile
A  lib/git.rb
M  lib/simplegit.rb
?? LICENSE.txt
```

New files that aren't tracked have a ?? next to them, new files that have been added to the staging area have an A, modified files have an M and so on. There are two columns to the output—the left hand column indicates that the file is staged and the right hand column indicates that it's modified. So for example in that output, the README file is modified in the working directory but not yet staged, while the lib/simplegit.rb file is modified and staged. The Rakefile was modified, staged and then modified again, so there are changes to it that are both staged and unstaged.

Ignoring Files

Often, you'll have a class of files that you don't want Git to automatically add or even show you as being untracked. These are generally automatically generated files such as log files or files produced by your build system. In such cases, you can create a file listing patterns to match them named .gitignore. Here is an example .gitignore file:

```
$ cat .gitignore
*.[oa]
*~
```

The first line tells Git to ignore any files ending in ".o" or ".a"—object and archive files that may be the product of building your code. The second line tells Git to ignore all files that end with a tilde (~), which is used by many text editors such as Emacs to mark temporary files. You may also include a log, tmp, or pid directory; automatically generated documentation; and so on. Setting up a .gitignore file before you get going is generally a good idea so you don't accidentally commit files that you really don't want in your Git repository.

The rules for the patterns you can put in the .gitignore file are as follows:

- Blank lines or lines starting with # are ignored.

- Standard glob patterns work.

- You can end patterns with a forward slash (/) to specify a directory.

- You can negate a pattern by starting it with an exclamation point (!).

Glob patterns are like simplified regular expressions that shells use. An asterisk (*) matches zero or more characters; [abc] matches any character inside the brackets (in this case a, b, or c); a question mark (?) matches a single character; and brackets enclosing characters separated by a hyphen ([0-9]) matches any character between them (in this case 0 through 9). You can also use two asterisks to match nested directories; a/**/z would match a/z, a/b/z,a/b/c/z, and so on.

Here is another example .gitignore file:

```
# a comment - this is ignored
*.a        # no .a files
!lib.a     # but do track lib.a, even though you're ignoring .a files above
/TODO      # only ignore the root TODO file, not subdir/TODO
build/     # ignore all files in the build/ directory
doc/*.txt  # ignore doc/notes.txt, but not doc/server/arch.txt
```

■ **Tip** GitHub maintains a fairly comprehensive list of good .gitignore file examples for dozens or projects and languages at https://github.com/github/gitignore if you want a starting point for your project.

Viewing Your Staged and Unstaged Changes

If the git status command is too vague for you—you want to know exactly what you changed, not just which files were changed—you can use the git diff command. We'll cover git diff in more detail later, but you'll probably use it most often to answer these two questions: What have you changed but not yet staged? And what have you staged that you are about to commit? Although git status answers those questions very generally by listing the file names, git diff shows you the exact lines added and removed—the patch, as it were.

Let's say you edit and stage the README file again and then edit the benchmarks.rb file without staging it. If you run your git status command, you once again see something like this:

```
$ git status
On branch master
Changes to be committed:
  (use "git reset HEAD <file>..." to unstage)

    new file:   README

Changes not staged for commit:
  (use "git add <file>..." to update what will be committed)
  (use "git checkout -- <file>..." to discard changes in working directory)

    modified:   benchmarks.rb
```

To see what you've changed but not yet staged, type git diff with no other arguments:

```
$ git diff
diff --git a/benchmarks.rb b/benchmarks.rb
index 3cb747f..e445e28 100644
--- a/benchmarks.rb
+++ b/benchmarks.rb
@@ -36,6 +36,10 @@ def main
          @commit.parents[0].parents[0].parents[0]
        end

+       run_code(x, 'commits 1') do
+         git.commits.size
+       end
+
        run_code(x, 'commits 2') do
          log = git.commits('master', 15)
          log.size
```

That command compares what is in your working directory with what is in your staging area. The result tells you the changes you've made that you haven't yet staged.

If you want to see what you've staged that will go into your next commit, you can use git diff --staged. This command compares your staged changes to your last commit:

```
$ git diff --staged
diff --git a/README b/README
new file mode 100644
index 0000000..03902a1
```

```
--- /dev/null
+++ b/README
@@ -0,0 +1,4 @@
+My Project
+
+ This is my project and it is amazing.
+
```

It's important to note that git diff by itself doesn't show all changes made since your last commit—only changes that are still unstaged. This can be confusing, because if you've staged all your changes, git diff will give you no output.

For another example, if you stage the benchmarks.rb file and then edit it, you can use git diff to see the changes in the file that are staged and the changes that are unstaged:

```
$ git add benchmarks.rb
$ echo '# test line' >> benchmarks.rb
$ git status
On branch master
Changes to be committed:
  (use "git reset HEAD <file>..." to unstage)

    modified: benchmarks.rb

Changes not staged for commit:
  (use "git add <file>..." to update what will be committed)
  (use "git checkout -- <file>..." to discard changes in working directory)

    modified: benchmarks.rb
```

Now you can use git diff to see what is still unstaged:

```
$ git diff
diff --git a/benchmarks.rb b/benchmarks.rb
index e445e28..86b2f7c 100644
--- a/benchmarks.rb
+++ b/benchmarks.rb
@@ -127,3 +127,4 @@ end
 main()

 ##pp Grit::GitRuby.cache_client.stats
+# test line
```

and git diff --cached to see what you've staged so far:

```
$ git diff --cached
diff --git a/benchmarks.rb b/benchmarks.rb
index 3cb747f..e445e28 100644
--- a/benchmarks.rb
+++ b/benchmarks.rb
@@ -36,6 +36,10 @@ def main
          @commit.parents[0].parents[0].parents[0]
        end
```

```
+        run_code(x, 'commits 1') do
+          git.commits.size
+        end
+
         run_code(x, 'commits 2') do
           log = git.commits('master', 15)
           log.size
```

Committing Your Changes

Now that your staging area is set up the way you want it, you can commit your changes. Remember that anything that is still unstaged—any files you have created or modified that you haven't run git add on since you edited them—won't go into this commit. They will stay as modified files on your disk. In this case, let's say that the last time you ran git status, you saw that everything was staged, so you're ready to commit your changes. The simplest way to commit is to type git commit:

```
$ git commit
```

Doing so launches your editor of choice. (This is set by your shell's $EDITOR environment variable—usually vim or emacs, although you can configure it with whatever you want using the git config --global core.editor command as you saw in Chapter 1).

The editor displays the following text (this example is a Vim screen):

```
# Please enter the commit message for your changes. Lines starting
# with '#' will be ignored, and an empty message aborts the commit.
# On branch master
# Changes to be committed:
#       new file:   README
#       modified:   benchmarks.rb
#
~
~
~
".git/COMMIT_EDITMSG" 9L, 283C
```

You can see that the default commit message contains the latest output of the git status command commented out and one empty line on top. You can remove these comments and type your commit message, or you can leave them there to help you remember what you're committing. (For an even more explicit reminder of what you've modified, you can pass the -v option to git commit. Doing so also puts the diff of your change in the editor so you can see exactly what changes you're committing). When you exit the editor, Git creates your commit with that commit message (with the comments and diff stripped out).

Alternatively, you can type your commit message inline with the commit command by specifying it after a -m flag, like this:

```
$ git commit -m "Story 182: Fix benchmarks for speed"
[master 463dc4f] Story 182: Fix benchmarks for speed
 2 files changed, 2 insertions(+)
 create mode 100644 README
```

Now you've created your first commit! You can see that the commit has given you some output about itself: which branch you committed to (master), what SHA-1 checksum the commit has (463dc4f), how many files were changed, and statistics about lines added and removed in the commit.

Remember that the commit records the snapshot you set up in your staging area. Anything you didn't stage is still sitting there modified; you can do another commit to add it to your history. Every time you perform a commit, you're recording a snapshot of your project that you can revert to or compare to later.

Skipping the Staging Area

Although it can be amazingly useful for crafting commits exactly how you want them, the staging area is sometimes a bit more complex than you need in your workflow. If you want to skip the staging area, Git provides a simple shortcut. Adding the -a option to the git commit command makes Git automatically stage every file that is already tracked before doing the commit, letting you skip the git add part:

```
$ git status
On branch master
Changes not staged for commit:
  (use "git add <file>..." to update what will be committed)
  (use "git checkout -- <file>..." to discard changes in working directory)

    modified: benchmarks.rb

no changes added to commit (use "git add" and/or "git commit -a")
$ git commit -a -m 'added new benchmarks'
[master 83e38c7] added new benchmarks
 1 file changed, 5 insertions(+), 0 deletions(-)
```

Notice how you don't have to run git add on the "benchmarks.rb" file in this case before you commit.

Removing Files

To remove a file from Git, you have to remove it from your tracked files (more accurately, remove it from your staging area) and then commit. The git rm command does that, and also removes the file from your working directory so you don't see it as an untracked file the next time around.

If you simply remove the file from your working directory, it shows up under the "Changed but not updated" (that is, unstaged) area of your git status output:

```
$ rm grit.gemspec
$ git status
On branch master
Changes not staged for commit:
  (use "git add/rm <file>..." to update what will be committed)
  (use "git checkout -- <file>..." to discard changes in working directory)

    deleted: grit.gemspec

no changes added to commit (use "git add" and/or "git commit -a")
```

Then, if you run `git rm`, it stages the file's removal:

```
$ git rm grit.gemspec
rm 'grit.gemspec'
$ git status
On branch master
Changes to be committed:
  (use "git reset HEAD <file>..." to unstage)

    deleted: grit.gemspec
```

The next time you commit, the file will be gone and no longer tracked. If you modified the file and added it to the index already, you must force the removal with the `-f` option. This is a safety feature to prevent accidental removal of data that hasn't yet been recorded in a snapshot and that can't be recovered from Git.

Another useful thing you may want to do is to keep the file in your working tree but remove it from your staging area. In other words, you may want to keep the file on your hard drive but not have Git track it anymore. This is particularly useful if you forgot to add something to your `.gitignore` file and accidentally added it, like a large log file or a bunch of `.a` compiled files. To do this, use the `--cached` option:

```
$ git rm --cached README
```

You can pass files, directories, and file-glob patterns to the `git rm` command. That means you can do things such as

```
$ git rm log/\*.log
```

Note the backslash (\) in front of the *. This is necessary because Git does its own filename expansion in addition to your shell's filename expansion. This command removes all files that have the `.log` extension in the `log/` directory. Or, you can do something like this:

```
$ git rm \*~
```

This command removes all files that end with ~.

Moving Files

Unlike many other VCS systems, Git doesn't explicitly track file movement. If you rename a file in Git, no metadata is stored in Git that tells it you renamed the file; however, Git is pretty smart about figuring that out after the fact. We'll deal with detecting file movement a bit later.

Thus it's a bit confusing that Git has a `mv` command. If you want to rename a file in Git, you can run something like:

```
$ git mv file_from file_to
```

and it works fine. In fact, if you run something like this and look at the status, you'll see that Git considers it a renamed file:

```
$ git mv README.md README
$ git status
On branch master
Changes to be committed:
  (use "git reset HEAD <file>..." to unstage)

    renamed: README.md -> README
```

However, this is equivalent to running something like this:

```
$ mv README.md README
$ git rm README.md
$ git add README
```

Git figures out that it's a rename implicitly, so it doesn't matter if you rename a file that way or with the mv command. The only real difference is that mv is one command instead of three—it's a convenience function. More important, you can use any tool you like to rename a file, and address the add/rm later, before you commit.

Viewing the Commit History

After you have created several commits, or if you have cloned a repository with an existing commit history, you'll probably want to look back to see what has happened. The most basic and powerful tool to do this is the git log command.

These examples use a very simple project called simplegit. To get the project, run

```
git clone https://github.com/schacon/simplegit-progit
```

When you run git log in this project, you should get output that looks something like this:

```
$ git log
commit ca82a6dff817ec66f44342007202690a93763949
Author: Scott Chacon <schacon@gee-mail.com>
Date:   Mon Mar 17 21:52:11 2008 -0700

    changed the version number

commit 085bb3bcb608e1e8451d4b2432f8ecbe6306e7e7
Author: Scott Chacon <schacon@gee-mail.com>
Date:   Sat Mar 15 16:40:33 2008 -0700

    removed unnecessary test

commit a11bef06a3f659402fe7563abf99ad00de2209e6
Author: Scott Chacon <schacon@gee-mail.com>
Date:   Sat Mar 15 10:31:28 2008 -0700

    first commit
```

By default, with no arguments, git log lists the commits made in that repository in reverse chronological order—that is, the most recent commits show up first. As you can see, this command lists each commit with its SHA-1 checksum, the author's name and e-mail, the date written, and the commit message.

Many different options to the git log command are available to show you exactly what you're looking for. Here, we'll show you some of the most popular.

One of the more helpful options is -p, which shows the difference introduced in each commit. You can also use -2, which limits the output to only the last two entries:

```
$ git log -p -2
commit ca82a6dff817ec66f44342007202690a93763949
Author: Scott Chacon <schacon@gee-mail.com>
Date:   Mon Mar 17 21:52:11 2008 -0700

    changed the verison number

diff --git a/Rakefile b/Rakefile
index a874b73..8f94139 100644
--- a/Rakefile
+++ b/Rakefile
@@ -5,7 +5,7 @@ require 'rake/gempackagetask'
 spec = Gem::Specification.new do |s|
     s.platform  =   Gem::Platform::RUBY
     s.name      =   "simplegit"
-    s.version   =   "0.1.0"
+    s.version   =   "0.1.1"
     s.author    =   "Scott Chacon"
     s.email     =   "schacon@gee-mail.com"
     s.summary   =   "A simple gem for using Git in Ruby code."

commit 085bb3bcb608e1e8451d4b2432f8ecbe6306e7e7
Author: Scott Chacon <schacon@gee-mail.com>
Date:   Sat Mar 15 16:40:33 2008 -0700

    removed unnecessary test

diff --git a/lib/simplegit.rb b/lib/simplegit.rb
index a0a60ae..47c6340 100644
--- a/lib/simplegit.rb
+++ b/lib/simplegit.rb
@@ -18,8 +18,3 @@ class SimpleGit
      end

 end
-
-if $0 == __FILE__
-  git = SimpleGit.new
-  puts git.show
-end
\ No newline at end of file
```

This option displays the same information but with a `diff` directly following each entry. This is very helpful for code review or to quickly browse what happened during a series of commits that a collaborator has added. You can also use a series of summarizing options with `git log`. For example, if you want to see some abbreviated stats for each commit, you can use the `--stat` option:

```
$ git log --stat
commit ca82a6dff817ec66f44342007202690a93763949
Author: Scott Chacon <schacon@gee-mail.com>
Date:   Mon Mar 17 21:52:11 2008 -0700

    changed the verison number

 Rakefile | 2 +-
 1 file changed, 1 insertion(+), 1 deletion(-)

commit 085bb3bcb608e1e8451d4b2432f8ecbe6306e7e7
Author: Scott Chacon <schacon@gee-mail.com>
Date:   Sat Mar 15 16:40:33 2008 -0700

    removed unnecessary test

 lib/simplegit.rb | 5 -----
 1 file changed, 5 deletions(-)

commit a11bef06a3f659402fe7563abf99ad00de2209e6
Author: Scott Chacon <schacon@gee-mail.com>
Date:   Sat Mar 15 10:31:28 2008 -0700

    first commit

 README          |  6 ++++++
 Rakefile        | 23 +++++++++++++++++++++++
 lib/simplegit.rb | 25 +++++++++++++++++++++++++
 3 files changed, 54 insertions(+)
```

As you can see, the `--stat` option prints below each commit entry a list of modified files, how many files were changed, and how many lines in those files were added and removed. It also puts a summary of the information at the end.

Another really useful option is `--pretty`. This option changes the log output to formats other than the default. A few prebuilt options are available for you to use. The `oneline` option prints each commit on a single line, which is useful if you're looking at a lot of commits. In addition, the `short`, `full`, and `fuller` options show the output in roughly the same format but with less or more information, respectively:

```
$ git log --pretty=oneline
ca82a6dff817ec66f44342007202690a93763949 changed the verison number
085bb3bcb608e1e8451d4b2432f8ecbe6306e7e7 removed unnecessary test
a11bef06a3f659402fe7563abf99ad00de2209e6 first commit
```

The most interesting option is `format`, which allows you to specify your own log output format. This is especially useful when you're generating output for machine parsing—because you specify the format explicitly, you know it won't change with updates to Git:

```
$ git log --pretty=format:"%h - %an, %ar : %s"
ca82a6d - Scott Chacon, 6 years ago : changed the version number
085bb3b - Scott Chacon, 6 years ago : removed unnecessary test
a11bef0 - Scott Chacon, 6 years ago : first commit
```

Table 2-1 lists some of the more useful options that format takes.

Table 2-1. *Useful Options for* `git log --pretty=format`

Option	Description of Output
%H	Commit hash
%h	Abbreviated commit hash
%T	Tree hash
%t	Abbreviated tree hash
%P	Parent hash
%p	Abbreviated parent hash
%an	Author name
%ae	Author e-mail
%ad	Author date (format respects the –date= option
%ar	Author date, relative
%cn	Committer name
%ce	Committer e-mail
%cd	Committer date
%cr	Committer date, relative
%s	Subject

You may be wondering what the difference is between *author* and *committer*. The author is the person who originally wrote the work, whereas the committer is the person who last applied the work. So, if you send in a patch to a project and one of the core members applies the patch, both of you get credit—you as the author, and the core member as the committer. We'll cover this distinction a bit more in Chapter 5.

The `oneline` and `format` options are particularly useful with another `log` option called `--graph`. This option adds a nice little ASCII graph showing your branch and merge history:

```
$ git log --pretty=format:"%h %s" --graph
* 2d3acf9 ignore errors from SIGCHLD on trap
*   5e3ee11 Merge branch 'master' of git://github.com/dustin/grit
|\
| * 420eac9 Added a method for getting the current branch.
* | 30e367c timeout code and tests
* | 5a09431 add timeout protection to grit
```

```
*  | e1193f8 support for heads with slashes in them
|/
*  d6016bc require time for xmlschema
*  11d191e Merge branch 'defunkt' into local
```

This type of output will become more interesting as we go through branching and merging in the next chapter.

Those are only some simple output-formatting options to git log – there are many more. Table 2-2 lists the options we've covered so far, as well as some other common formatting options that may be useful, along with how they change the output of the log command.

Table 2-2. *Common Options to* git log

Option	Description
-p	Show the patch introduced with each commit.
--stat	Show statistics for files modified in each commit.
--shortstat	Display only the changed/insertions/deletions line from the --stat command.
--name-only	Show the list of files modified after the commit information.
--name-status	Show the list of files affected with added/modified/deleted information as well.
--abbrev-commit	Show only the first few characters of the SHA-1 checksum instead of all 40.
--relative-date	Display the date in a relative format (for example, "2 weeks ago") instead of using the full date format.
--graph	Display an ASCII graph of the branch and merge history beside the log output.
--pretty	Show commits in an alternate format. Options include oneline, short, full, fuller, and format (where you specify your own format).

Limiting Log Output

In addition to output-formatting options, git log takes a number of useful limiting options—that is, options that let you show only a subset of commits. You've seen one such option already—the -2 option, which shows only the last two commits. In fact, you can do -<n>, where n is any integer to show the last n commits. In reality, you're unlikely to use that often, because Git by default pipes all output through a pager so you see only one page of log output at a time.

However, the time-limiting options such as --since and --until are very useful. For example, this command gets the list of commits made in the last two weeks:

```
$ git log --since=2.weeks
```

This command works with lots of formats—you can specify a specific date like "2008-01-15", or a relative date such as "2 years 1 day 3 minutes ago".

You can also filter the list to commits that match some search criteria. The --author option allows you to filter on a specific author, and the --grep option lets you search for keywords in the commit messages. (Note that if you want to specify both author and grep options, you have to add --all-match or the command will match commits with either).

Another really helpful filter is the -S option that takes a string and only shows the commits that introduced a change to the code that added or removed that string. For instance, if you wanted to find the last commit that added or removed a reference to a specific function, you could call:

```
$ git log --Sfunction_name
```

The last really useful option to pass to git log as a filter is a path. If you specify a directory or filename, you can limit the log output to commits that introduced a change to those files. This is always the last option and is generally preceded by double dashes (--) to separate the paths from the options.

Table 2-3 lists these and a few other common options for your reference.

Table 2-3. *Options to Limit the output of git log*

Option	Description
-(n)	Show only the last *n* commits
--since, --after	Limit the commits to those made after the specified date
--until, --before	Limit the commits to those made before the specified date
--author	Only show commits in which the author entry matches the specified string
--committer	Only show commits in which the committer entry matches the specified string
--grep	Only show commits with a commit message containing the string
-S	Only show commits adding or removing code matching the string

For example, if you want to see which commits modifying test files in the Git source code history were committed by Junio Hamano and were not merges in the month of October 2008, you can run something like this:

```
$ git log --pretty="%h - %s" --author=gitster --since="2008-10-01" \
  --before="2008-11-01" --no-merges -- t/
5610e3b - Fix testcase failure when extended attributes are in use
acd3b9e - Enhance hold_lock_file_for_{update,append}() API
f563754 - demonstrate breakage of detached checkout with symbolic link HEAD
d1a43f2 - reset --hard/read-tree --reset -u: remove unmerged new paths
51a94af - Fix "checkout --track -b newbranch" on detached HEAD
b0ad11e - pull: allow "git pull origin $something:$current_branch" into an unborn branch
```

Of the nearly 40,000 commits in the Git source code history, this command shows the 6 that match those criteria.

Undoing Things

At any stage, you may want to undo something. Here, we'll review a few basic tools for undoing changes that you've made. Be careful, because you can't always undo some of these undos. This is one of the few areas in Git where you may lose some work if you do it wrong.

One of the common undos takes place when you commit too early and possibly forget to add some files, or you mess up your commit message. If you want to try that commit again, you can run commit with the --amend option:

```
$ git commit –amend
```

This command takes your staging area and uses it for the commit. If you've made no changes since your last commit (for instance, you run this command immediately after your previous commit), then your snapshot will look exactly the same, and all you'll change is your commit message.

The same commit-message editor fires up, but it already contains the message of your previous commit. You can edit the message the same as always, but it overwrites your previous commit.

As an example, if you commit and then realize you forgot to stage the changes in a file you wanted to add to this commit, you can do something like this:

```
$ git commit -m 'initial commit'
$ git add forgotten_file
$ git commit --amend
```

You end up with a single commit—the second commit replaces the results of the first.

Unstaging a Staged File

The next two sections demonstrate how to wrangle your staging area and working directory changes. The nice part is that the command you use to determine the state of those two areas also reminds you how to undo changes to them. For example, let's say you've changed two files and want to commit them as two separate changes, but you accidentally type git add * and stage them both. How can you unstage one of the two? The git status command reminds you:

```
$ git add .
$ git status
On branch master
Changes to be committed:
  (use "git reset HEAD <file>..." to unstage)

    renamed:    README.md -> README
    modified:   benchmarks.rb
```

Right below the "Changes to be committed" text, it says use git reset HEAD <file>... to unstage. So, let's use that advice to unstage the benchmarks.rb file:

```
$ git reset HEAD benchmarks.rb
Unstaged changes after reset:
M        benchmarks.rb
$ git status
On branch master
Changes to be committed:
  (use "git reset HEAD <file>..." to unstage)

    renamed: README.md -> README

Changes not staged for commit:
  (use "git add <file>..." to update what will be committed)
  (use "git checkout -- <file>..." to discard changes in working directory)

    modified: benchmarks.rb
```

The command is a bit strange, but it works. The benchmarks.rb file is modified but once again unstaged.

■ **Note** While git reset *can* be a dangerous command if you call it with --hard, in this instance the file in your working directory is not touched. Calling git reset without an option is not dangerous—it only touches your staging area.

For now this magic invocation is all you need to know about the `git reset` command. We'll go into much more detail about what `reset` does and how to master it to do really interesting things in Git Reset.

Unmodifying a Modified File

What if you realize that you don't want to keep your changes to the `benchmarks.rb` file? How can you easily unmodify it—revert to what it looked like when you last committed (or initially cloned, or however you got it into your working directory)? Luckily, `git status` tells you how to do that, too. In the last example output, the unstaged area looks like this:

```
Changes not staged for commit:
  (use "git add <file>..." to update what will be committed)
  (use "git checkout -- <file>..." to discard changes in working directory)

    modified: benchmarks.rb
```

It tells you pretty explicitly how to discard the changes you've made. Let's do what it says:

```
$ git checkout -- benchmarks.rb
$ git status
On branch master
Changes to be committed:
  (use "git reset HEAD <file>..." to unstage)

    renamed: README.md -> README
```

You can see that the changes have been reverted.

■ **Important** It's important to understand that `git checkout -- [file]` is a dangerous command. Any changes you made to that file are gone—you just copied another file over it. Don't ever use this command unless you absolutely know that you don't want the file.

If you would like to keep the changes you've made to that file but still need to get it out of the way for now, we'll go over stashing and branching in Chapter 3—these are generally better ways to go.

Remember, anything that is *committed* in Git can almost always be recovered. Even commits that were on branches that were deleted or commits that were overwritten with an `--amend` commit can be recovered (see the section on data recovery). However, anything you lose that was never committed is likely never to be seen again.

Working with Remotes

To be able to collaborate on any Git project, you need to know how to manage your remote repositories. Remote repositories are versions of your project that are hosted on the Internet or network somewhere. You can have several of them, each of which generally is either read-only or read/write for you. Collaborating with others involves managing these remote repositories and pushing and pulling data to and from them when you need to share work. Managing remote repositories includes knowing how to add remote repositories, remove remotes that are no longer valid, manage various remote branches and define them as being tracked or not, and more. In this section, we'll cover some of these remote-management skills.

Showing Your Remotes

To see which remote servers you have configured, you can run the `git remote` command. It lists the shortnames of each remote handle you've specified. If you've cloned your repository, you should at least see origin—that is the default name Git gives to the server you cloned from:

```
$ git clone https://github.com/schacon/ticgit
Cloning into 'ticgit'...
remote: Reusing existing pack: 1857, done.
remote: Total 1857 (delta 0), reused 0 (delta 0)
Receiving objects: 100% (1857/1857), 374.35 KiB | 268.00 KiB/s, done.
Resolving deltas: 100% (772/772), done.
Checking connectivity... done.
$ cd ticgit
$ git remote
origin
```

You can also specify -v, which shows you the URLs that Git has stored for the shortname to be used when reading and writing to that remote:

```
$ git remote -v
Origin  https://github.com/schacon/ticgit (fetch)
Origin  https://github.com/schacon/ticgit (push)
```

If you have more than one remote, the command lists them all. For example, a repository with multiple remotes for working with several collaborators might look something like this.

```
$ cd grit
$ git remote -v
bakkdoor  https://github.com/bakkdoor/grit (fetch)
bakkdoor  https://github.com/bakkdoor/grit (push)
cho45     https://github.com/cho45/grit (fetch)
cho45     https://github.com/cho45/grit (push)
defunkt   https://github.com/defunkt/grit (fetch)
defunkt   https://github.com/defunkt/grit (push)
koke      git://github.com/koke/grit.git (fetch)
koke      git://github.com/koke/grit.git (push)
origin    git@github.com:mojombo/grit.git (fetch)
origin    git@github.com:mojombo/grit.git (push)
```

This means we can pull contributions from any of these users pretty easily. We may additionally have permission to push to one or more of these, though we can't tell that here.

Notice that these remotes use a variety of protocols; we'll cover more about this in Chapter 4.

Adding Remote Repositories

I've mentioned and given some demonstrations of adding remote repositories in previous sections, but here is how to do it explicitly. To add a new remote Git repository as a shortname you can reference easily, run `git remote add [shortname] [url]`:

```
$ git remote
origin
$ git remote add pb https://github.com/paulboone/ticgit
$ git remote -v
origin  https://github.com/schacon/ticgit (fetch)
origin  https://github.com/schacon/ticgit (push)
pb      https://github.com/paulboone/ticgit (fetch)
pb      https://github.com/paulboone/ticgit (push)
```

Now you can use the string pb on the command line in lieu of the whole URL. For example, if you want to fetch all the information that Paul has but that you don't yet have in your repository, you can run `git fetch pb`:

```
$ git fetch pb
remote: Counting objects: 43, done.
remote: Compressing objects: 100% (36/36), done.
remote: Total 43 (delta 10), reused 31 (delta 5)
Unpacking objects: 100% (43/43), done.
From https://github.com/paulboone/ticgit
 * [new branch]      master     -> pb/master
 * [new branch]      ticgit     -> pb/ticgit
```

Paul's master branch is now accessible locally as pb/master—you can merge it into one of your branches, or you can check out a local branch at that point if you want to inspect it. (We'll go over what branches are and how to use them in much more detail in Chapter 3).

Fetching and Pulling from Your Remotes

As you just saw, to get data from your remote projects, you can run:

```
$ git fetch [remote-name]
```

The command goes out to that remote project and pulls down all the data from that remote project that you don't have yet. After you do this, you should have references to all the branches from that remote, which you can merge in or inspect at any time.

If you clone a repository, the command automatically adds that remote repository under the name "origin." So, `git fetch origin` fetches any new work that has been pushed to that server since you cloned (or last fetched from) it. It's important to note that the `git fetch` command pulls the data to your local repository—it doesn't automatically merge it with any of your work or modify what you're currently working on. You have to merge it manually into your work when you're ready.

If you have a branch set up to track a remote branch (see the next section and Chapter 3 for more information), you can use the `git pull` command to automatically fetch and then merge a remote branch into your current branch. This may be an easier or more comfortable workflow for you; and by default, the `git clone` command automatically sets up your local master branch to track the remote master branch (or whatever the default branch is called) on the server you cloned from. Running `git pull` generally fetches data from the server you originally cloned from and automatically tries to merge it into the code you're currently working on.

Pushing to Your Remotes

When you have your project at a point that you want to share, you have to push it upstream. The command for this is simple: git push [remote-name] [branch-name]. If you want to push your master branch to your origin server (again, cloning generally sets up both of those names for you automatically), then you can run this to push any commits you've done back up to the server:

```
$ git push origin master
```

This command works only if you cloned from a server to which you have write access and if nobody has pushed in the meantime. If you and someone else clone at the same time and they push upstream and then you push upstream, your push will rightly be rejected. You'll have to pull down their work first and incorporate it into yours before you'll be allowed to push. See Chapter 3 for more detailed information on how to push to remote servers.

Inspecting a Remote

If you want to see more information about a particular remote, you can use the git remote show [remote-name] command. If you run this command with a particular shortname, such as origin, you get something like this:

```
$ git remote show origin
* remote origin
  Fetch URL: https://github.com/schacon/ticgit
  Push  URL: https://github.com/schacon/ticgit
  HEAD branch: master
  Remote branches:
    master                              tracked
    dev-branch                          tracked
  Local branch configured for 'git pull':
    master merges with remote master
  Local ref configured for 'git push':
    master pushes to master (up to date)
```

It lists the URL for the remote repository as well as the tracking branch information. The command helpfully tells you that if you're on the master branch and you run git pull, it will automatically merge in the master branch on the remote after it fetches all the remote references. It also lists all the remote references it has pulled down.

That is a simple example you're likely to encounter. When you're using Git more heavily, however, you may see much more information from git remote show:

```
$ git remote show origin
* remote origin
  URL: https://github.com/my-org/complex-project
  Fetch URL: https://github.com/my-org/complex-project
  Push  URL: https://github.com/my-org/complex-project
  HEAD branch: master
  Remote branches:
    master                              tracked
    dev-branch                          tracked
    markdown-strip                      tracked
    issue-43                            new (next fetch will store in remotes/origin)
    issue-45                            new (next fetch will store in remotes/origin)
    refs/remotes/origin/issue-11        stale (use 'git remote prune' to remove)
```

```
Local branches configured for 'git pull':
  dev-branch merges with remote dev-branch
  master     merges with remote master
Local refs configured for 'git push':
  dev-branch                 pushes to dev-branch         (up to date)
  markdown-strip             pushes to markdown-strip     (up to date)
  master                     pushes to master             (up to date)
```

This command shows which branch is automatically pushed to when you run git push while on certain branches. It also shows you which remote branches on the server you don't yet have, which remote branches you have that have been removed from the server, and multiple branches that are automatically merged when you run git pull.

Removing and Renaming Remotes

If you want to rename a reference you can run git remote rename to change a remote's shortname. For instance, if you want to rename pb to paul, you can do so with git remote rename:

```
$ git remote rename pb paul
$ git remote
origin
paul
```

It's worth mentioning that this changes your remote branch names, too. What used to be referenced at pb/master is now at paul/master.

If you want to remove a remote for some reason—you've moved the server or are no longer using a particular mirror, or perhaps a contributor isn't contributing anymore—you can use git remote rm:

```
$ git remote rm paul
$ git remote
origin
```

Tagging

Like most VCSs, Git has the ability to tag specific points in history as being important. Typically people use this functionality to mark release points (v1.0, and so on). In this section, you'll learn how to list the available tags, how to create new tags, and what the different types of tags are.

Listing Your Tags

Listing the available tags in Git is straightforward. Just type git tag:

```
$ git tag
v0.1
v1.3
```

This command lists the tags in alphabetical order; the order in which they appear has no real importance.

You can also search for tags with a particular pattern. The Git source repo, for instance, contains more than 500 tags. If you're only interested in looking at the 1.8.5 series, you can run this:

```
$ git tag -l 'v1.8.5*'
v1.8.5
v1.8.5-rc0
v1.8.5-rc1
v1.8.5-rc2
v1.8.5-rc3
v1.8.5.1
v1.8.5.2
v1.8.5.3
v1.8.5.4
v1.8.5.5
```

Creating Tags

Git uses two main types of tags: lightweight and annotated.

A lightweight tag is very much like a branch that doesn't change—it's just a pointer to a specific commit.

Annotated tags, however, are stored as full objects in the Git database. They're checksummed; contain the tagger name, e-mail, and date; have a tagging message; and can be signed and verified with GNU Privacy Guard (GPG). It's generally recommended that you create annotated tags so you can have all this information; but if you want a temporary tag or for some reason don't want to keep the other information, lightweight tags are available too.

Annotated Tags

Creating an annotated tag in Git is simple. The easiest way is to specify -a when you run the tag command:

```
$ git tag -a v1.4 -m 'my version 1.4'
$ git tag
v0.1
v1.3
v1.4
```

The -m specifies a tagging message, which is stored with the tag. If you don't specify a message for an annotated tag, Git launches your editor so you can type it in.

You can see the tag data along with the commit that was tagged by using the git show command:

```
$ git show v1.4
tag v1.4
Tagger: Ben Straub <ben@straub.cc>
Date:   Sat May 3 20:19:12 2014 -0700

my version 1.4

commit ca82a6dff817ec66f44342007202690a93763949
Author: Scott Chacon <schacon@gee-mail.com>
Date:   Mon Mar 17 21:52:11 2008 -0700

    changed the verison number
```

That shows the tagger information, the date the commit was tagged, and the annotation message before showing the commit information.

Lightweight Tags

Another way to tag commits is with a lightweight tag. This is basically the commit checksum stored in a file—no other information is kept. To create a lightweight tag, don't supply the -a, -s, or -m option:

```
$ git tag v1.4-lw
$ git tag
v0.1
v1.3
v1.4
v1.4-lw
v1.5
```

This time, if you run git show on the tag, you don't see the extra tag information. The command just shows the commit:

```
$ git show v1.4-lw
commit ca82a6dff817ec66f44342007202690a93763949
Author: Scott Chacon <schacon@gee-mail.com>
Date:   Mon Mar 17 21:52:11 2008 -0700

    changed the verison number
```

Tagging Later

You can also tag commits after you've moved past them. Suppose your commit history looks like this:

```
$ git log --pretty=oneline
15027957951b64cf874c3557a0f3547bd83b3ff6 Merge branch 'experiment'
a6b4c97498bd301d84096da251c98a07c7723e65 beginning write support
0d52aaab4479697da7686c15f77a3d64d9165190 one more thing
6d52a271eda8725415634dd79daabbc4d9b6008e Merge branch 'experiment'
0b7434d86859cc7b8c3d5e1dddfed66ff742fcbc added a commit function
4682c3261057305bdd616e23b64b0857d832627b added a todo file
166ae0c4d3f420721acbb115cc33848dfcc2121a started write support
9fceb02d0ae598e95dc970b74767f19372d61af8 updated rakefile
964f16d36dfccde844893cac5b347e7b3d44abbc commit the todo
8a5cbc430f1a9c3d00faaeffd07798508422908a updated readme
```

Now, suppose you forgot to tag the project at v1.2, which was at the "updated rakefile" commit. You can add it after the fact. To tag that commit, you specify the commit checksum (or part of it) at the end of the command:

```
$ git tag -a v1.2 9fceb02
```

You can see that you've tagged the commit:

```
$ git tag
v0.1
v1.2
v1.3
v1.4
v1.4-lw
v1.5

$ git show v1.2
tag v1.2
Tagger: Scott Chacon <schacon@gee-mail.com>
Date:   Mon Feb 9 15:32:16 2009 -0800

version 1.2
commit 9fceb02d0ae598e95dc970b74767f19372d61af8
Author: Magnus Chacon <mchacon@gee-mail.com>
Date:   Sun Apr 27 20:43:35 2008 -0700

    updated rakefile
...
```

Sharing Tags

By default, the git push command doesn't transfer tags to remote servers. You will have to explicitly push tags to a shared server after you have created them. This process is just like sharing remote branches—you can run git push origin [tagname].

```
$ git push origin v1.5
Counting objects: 14, done.
Delta compression using up to 8 threads.
Compressing objects: 100% (12/12), done.
Writing objects: 100% (14/14), 2.05 KiB | 0 bytes/s, done.
Total 14 (delta 3), reused 0 (delta 0)
To git@github.com:schacon/simplegit.git
 * [new tag]         v1.5 -> v1.5
```

If you have a lot of tags that you want to push up at once, you can also use the --tags option to the git push command. This transfers all your tags that are not already there to the remote server.

```
$ git push origin --tags
Counting objects: 1, done.
Writing objects: 100% (1/1), 160 bytes | 0 bytes/s, done.
Total 1 (delta 0), reused 0 (delta 0)
To git@github.com:schacon/simplegit.git
 * [new tag]         v1.4 -> v1.4
 * [new tag]         v1.4-lw -> v1.4-lw
```

Now, when someone else clones or pulls from your repository, they will get all your tags as well.

Git Aliases

Before we finish this chapter on basic Git, there's just one little tip that can make your Git experience simpler, easier, and more familiar: aliases. We won't refer to them or assume you've used them later in the book, but you should probably know how to use them.

Git doesn't automatically infer your command if you type it in partially. If you don't want to type the entire text of each of the Git commands, you can easily set up an alias for each command using git config. Here are a couple of examples you may want to set up:

```
$ git config --global alias.co checkout
$ git config --global alias.br branch
$ git config --global alias.ci commit
$ git config --global alias.st status
```

This means that, for example, instead of typing git commit, you just need to type git ci. As you go on using Git, you'll probably use other commands frequently as well; don't hesitate to create new aliases.

This technique can also be very useful in creating commands that you think should exist. For example, to correct the usability problem you encountered with unstaging a file, you can add your own unstage alias to Git:

```
$ git config --global alias.unstage 'reset HEAD --'
```

This makes the following two commands equivalent:

```
$ git unstage fileA
$ git reset HEAD fileA
```

This seems a bit clearer. It's also common to add a last command, like this:

```
$ git config --global alias.last 'log -1 HEAD'
This way, you can see the last commit easily:
```

```
$ git last
commit 66938dae3329c7aebe598c2246a8e6af90d04646
Author: Josh Goebel <dreamer3@example.com>
Date:    Tue Aug 26 19:48:51 2008 +0800

    test for current head

    Signed-off-by: Scott Chacon <schacon@example.com>
```

As you can tell, Git simply replaces the new command with whatever you alias it for. However, maybe you want to run an external command, rather than a Git subcommand. In that case, you start the command with a ! character. This is useful if you write your own tools that work with a Git repository. We can demonstrate by aliasing git visual to run gitk:

```
$ git config --global alias.visual "!gitk"
```

Summary

At this point, you can do all the basic local Git operations—creating or cloning a repository, making changes, staging and committing those changes, and viewing the history of all the changes the repository has been through. Next, we'll cover Git's killer feature: its branching model.

## CHAPTER 3

Git Branching

Nearly every VCS has some form of branching support. Branching means you diverge from the main line of development and continue to do work without messing with that main line. In many VCS tools, this is a somewhat expensive process, often requiring you to create a new copy of your source code directory, which can take a long time for large projects.

Some people refer to Git's branching model as its "killer feature," and it certainly sets Git apart in the VCS community. Why is it so special? The way Git branches is incredibly lightweight, making branching operations nearly instantaneous, and switching back and forth between branches generally just as fast. Unlike many other VCSs, Git encourages workflows that branch and merge often, even multiple times in a day. Understanding and mastering this feature gives you a powerful and unique tool and can entirely change the way that you develop.

Branching in a Nutshell

To really understand the way Git does branching, we need to take a step back and examine how Git stores its data.

As you may remember from Chapter 1, Git doesn't store data as a series of changesets or differences, but instead as a series of snapshots.

When you make a commit, Git stores a commit object that contains a pointer to the snapshot of the content you staged. This object also contains the author's name and email, the message that you typed, and pointers to the commit or commits that directly came before this commit (its parent or parents): zero parents for the initial commit, one parent for a normal commit, and multiple parents for a commit that results from a merge of two or more branches.

To visualize this, let's assume that you have a directory containing three files, and you stage them all and commit. Staging the files checksums each one (the SHA-1 hash we mentioned in Chapter 1), stores that version of the file in the Git repository (Git refers to them as blobs), and adds that checksum to the staging area:

```
$ git add README test.rb LICENSE
$ git commit -m 'initial commit of my project'
```

When you create the commit by running git commit, Git checksums each subdirectory (in this case, just the root project directory) and stores those tree objects in the Git repository. Git then creates a commit object that has the metadata and a pointer to the root project tree so it can re-create that snapshot when needed.

Your Git repository now contains five objects: one blob for the contents of each of your three files, one tree that lists the contents of the directory and specifies which file names are stored as which blobs, and one commit with the pointer to that root tree and all the commit metadata.

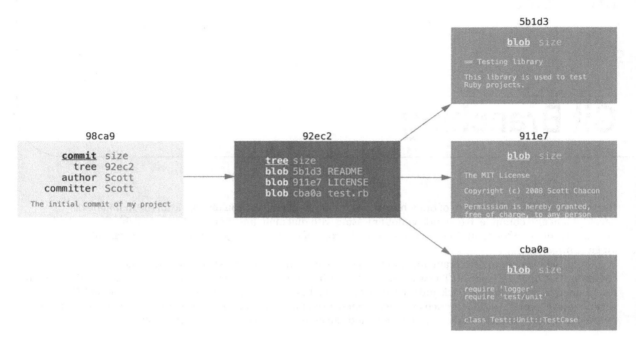

Figure 3-1. *A commit and its tree*

If you make some changes and commit again, the next commit stores a pointer to the commit that came immediately before it.

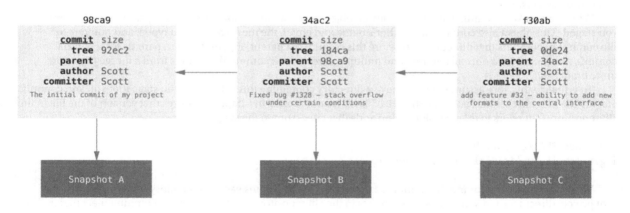

Figure 3-2. *Commits and their parents*

A branch in Git is simply a lightweight movable pointer to one of these commits. The default branch name in Git is master. As you start making commits, you're given a master branch that points to the last commit you made. Every time you commit, it moves forward automatically.

■ **Note** The "master" branch in Git is not a special branch. It is exactly like any other branch. The only reason nearly every repository has one is that the `git init` command creates it by default and most people don't bother to change it.

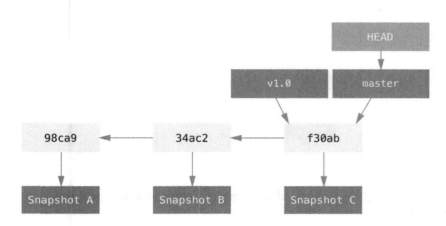

Figure 3-3. *A branch and its commit history*

Creating a New Branch

What happens if you create a new branch? Well, doing so creates a new pointer for you to move around. Let's say you create a new branch called testing. You do this with the `git branch` command:

```
$ git branch testing
```

This creates a new pointer at the same commit you're currently on.

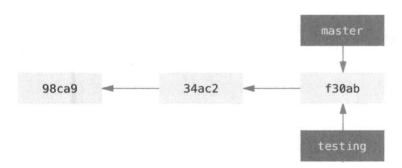

Figure 3-4. *Two branches pointing into the same series of commits*

How does Git know what branch you're currently on? It keeps a special pointer called HEAD. Note that this is a lot different than the concept of HEAD in other VCSs you may be used to, such as Subversion or CVS. In Git, this is a pointer to the local branch you're currently on. In this case, you're still on master. The `git branch` command only created a new branch—it didn't switch to that branch.

Figure 3-5. *HEAD pointing to a branch*

You can easily see this by running a simple `git log` command that shows you where the branch pointers are pointing. This option is called `--decorate`.

```
$ git log --oneline --decorate
f30ab (HEAD, master, testing) add feature #32 - ability to add new
34ac2 fixed bug #1328 - stack overflow under certain conditions
98ca9 initial commit of my project
```

You can see the "master" and "testing" branches that are right there next to the f30ab commit.

Switching Branches

To switch to an existing branch, you run the `git checkout` command. Let's switch to the new testing branch:

```
$ git checkout testing
```

This moves HEAD to point to the `testing` branch.

Figure 3-6. *HEAD points to the current branch*

What is the significance of that? Well, let's do another commit:

```
$ vim test.rb
$ git commit -a -m 'made a change'
```

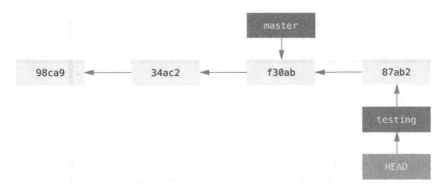

Figure 3-7. *The HEAD branch moves forward when a commit is made*

This is interesting, because now your testing branch has moved forward, but your master branch still points to the commit you were on when you ran git checkout to switch branches. Let's switch back to the master branch:

```
$ git checkout master
```

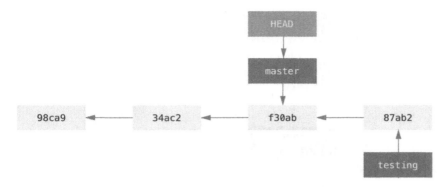

Figure 3-8. *HEAD moves when you checkout*

That command did two things. It moved the HEAD pointer back to point to the master branch, and it reverted the files in your working directory to the snapshot that master points to. This also means the changes you make from this point forward will diverge from an older version of the project. It essentially rewinds the work you've done in your testing branch so you can go in a different direction.

SWITCHING BRANCHES CHANGES FILES IN YOUR WORKING DIRECTORY

It's important to note that when you switch branches in Git, files in your working directory will change. If you switch to an older branch, your working directory will be reverted to look like it did the last time you committed on that branch. If Git cannot do it cleanly, it will not let you switch at all.

Let's make a few changes and commit again:

```
$ vim test.rb
$ git commit -a -m 'made other changes'
```

Now your project history has diverged. You created and switched to a branch, did some work on it, and then switched back to your main branch and did other work. Both of those changes are isolated in separate branches: you can switch back and forth between the branches and merge them when you're ready. And you did all that with simple branch, checkout, and commit commands.

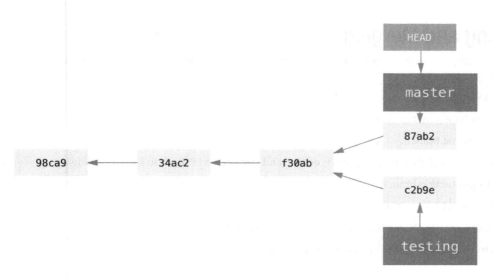

Figure 3-9. *Divergent history*

You can also see this easily with the git log command. If you run `git log --oneline --decorate --graph --all` it will print the history of your commits, showing where your branch pointers are and how your history has diverged.

```
$ git log --oneline --decorate --graph --all
* c2b9e (HEAD, master) made other changes
| * 87ab2 (testing) made a change
|/
* f30ab add feature #32 - ability to add new formats to the
* 34ac2 fixed bug #1328 - stack overflow under certain conditions
* 98ca9 initial commit of my project
```

Because a branch in Git is in actuality a simple file that contains the 40 character SHA-1 checksum of the commit it points to, branches are cheap to create and destroy. Creating a new branch is as quick and simple as writing 41 bytes to a file (40 characters and a newline).

This is in sharp contrast to the way most older VCS tools branch, which involves copying all the project's files into a second directory. This can take several seconds or even minutes, depending on the size of the project, whereas in Git the process is always instantaneous. Also, because we're recording the parents when we commit, finding a proper merge base for merging is automatically done for us and is generally very easy to do. These features help encourage developers to create and use branches often.

Let's see why you should do so.

Basic Branching and Merging

Let's go through a simple example of branching and merging with a workflow that you might use in the real world. You'll follow these steps:

1. Do work on a web site.

2. Create a branch for a new story you're working on.

3. Do some work in that branch.

At this stage, you'll receive a call that another issue is critical and you need a hotfix. You'll do the following:

4. Switch to your production branch.

5. Create a branch to add the hotfix.

6. After it's tested, merge the hotfix branch, and push to production.

7. Switch back to your original story and continue working.

Basic Branching

First, let's say you're working on your project and have a couple of commits already.

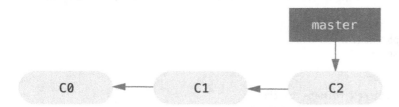

Figure 3-10. *A simple commit history*

You've decided that you're going to work on issue #53 in whatever issue-tracking system your company uses. To create a branch and switch to it at the same time, you can run the `git checkout` command with the -b switch:

```
$ git checkout -b iss53
Switched to a new branch "iss53"
```

This is shorthand for:

```
$ git branch iss53
$ git checkout iss53
```

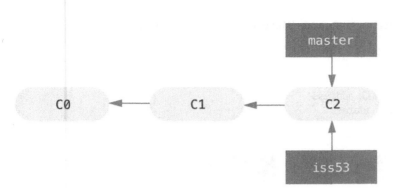

Figure 3-11. *Creating a new branch pointer*

You work on your web site and do some commits. Doing so moves the iss53 branch forward, because you have it checked out (that is, your HEAD is pointing to it):

```
$ vim index.html
$ git commit -a -m 'added a new footer [issue 53]'
```

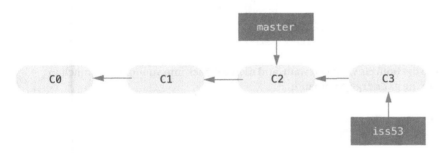

Figure 3-12. *The iss53 branch has moved forward with your work*

Now you get the call that there is an issue with the web site, and you need to fix it immediately. With Git, you don't have to deploy your fix along with the iss53 changes you've made, and you don't have to put a lot of effort into reverting those changes before you can work on applying your fix to what is in production. All you have to do is switch back to your master branch.

However, before you do that, note that if your working directory or staging area has uncommitted changes that conflict with the branch you're checking out, Git won't let you switch branches. It's best to have a clean working state when you switch branches. There are ways to get around this (namely, stashing and commit amending) that we'll cover later on. For now, let's assume you've committed all your changes, so you can switch back to your master branch:

```
$ git checkout master
Switched to branch 'master'
```

At this point, your project working directory is exactly the way it was before you started working on issue #53, and you can concentrate on your hotfix. This is an important point to remember: when you switch branches, Git resets your working directory to look like it did the last time you committed on that branch. It adds, removes, and modifies files automatically to make sure your working copy is what the branch looked like on your last commit to it.

Next, you have a hotfix to make. Let's create a hotfix branch on which to work until it's completed:

```
$ git checkout -b hotfix
Switched to a new branch 'hotfix'
$ vim index.html
$ git commit -a -m 'fixed the broken email address'
[hotfix 1fb7853] fixed the broken email address
 1 file changed, 2 insertions(+)
```

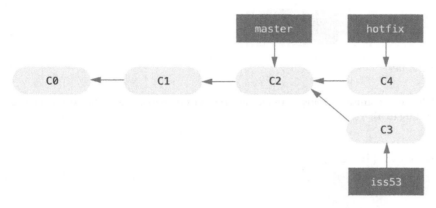

Figure 3-13. *Hotfix branch based on* master

You can run your tests, make sure the hotfix is what you want, and merge it back into your master branch to deploy to production. You do this with the git merge command:

```
$ git checkout master
$ git merge hotfix
Updating f42c576..3a0874c
Fast-forward
 index.html | 2 ++
 1 file changed, 2 insertions(+)
```

You'll notice the phrase "fast-forward" in that merge. Because the commit pointed to by the branch you merged in was directly upstream of the commit you're on, Git simply moves the pointer forward. To phrase that another way, when you try to merge one commit with a commit that can be reached by following the first commit's history, Git simplifies things by moving the pointer forward because there is no divergent work to merge together—this is called a *fast-forward*.

Your change is now in the snapshot of the commit pointed to by the master branch, and you can deploy the fix.

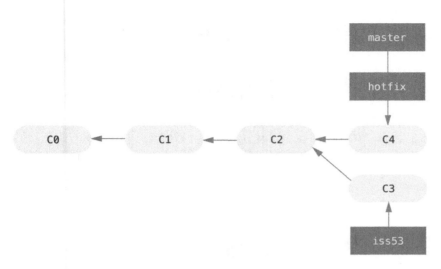

Figure 3-14. *master is fast-forwarded to* hotfix

After your super-important fix is deployed, you're ready to switch back to the work you were doing before you were interrupted. However, first you'll delete the hotfix branch, because you no longer need it—the master branch points at the same place. You can delete it with the -d option to git branch:

```
$ git branch -d hotfix
Deleted branch hotfix (3a0874c).
```

Now you can switch back to your work-in-progress branch on issue #53 and continue working on it.

```
$ git checkout iss53
Switched to branch "iss53"
$ vim index.html
$ git commit -a -m 'finished the new footer [issue 53]'
[iss53 ad82d7a] finished the new footer [issue 53]
1 file changed, 1 insertion(+)
```

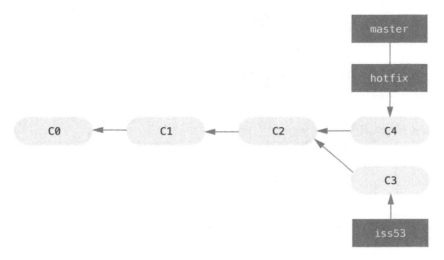

Figure 3-15. *Work continues on iss53*

It's worth noting here that the work you did in your hotfix branch is not contained in the files in your iss53 branch. If you need to pull it in, you can merge your master branch into your iss53 branch by running git merge master, or you can wait to integrate those changes until you decide to pull the iss53 branch back into master later.

Basic Merging

Suppose you've decided that your issue #53 work is complete and ready to be merged into your master branch. In order to do that, you'll merge in your iss53 branch, much like you merged in your hotfix branch earlier. All you have to do is check out the branch you want to merge into and then run the git merge command:

```
$ git checkout master
Switched to branch 'master'
$ git merge iss53
Merge made by the 'recursive' strategy.
README |    1 +
1 file changed, 1 insertion(+)
```

This looks a bit different than the hotfix merge you did earlier. In this case, your development history has diverged from some older point. Because the commit on the branch you're on isn't a direct ancestor of the branch you're merging in, Git has to do some work. In this case, Git does a simple three-way merge, using the two snapshots pointed to by the branch tips and the common ancestor of the two.

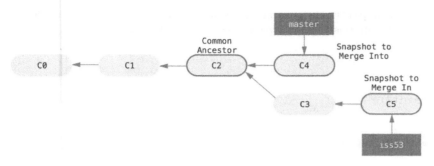

Figure 3-16. *Three snapshots used in a typical merge*

Instead of just moving the branch pointer forward, Git creates a new snapshot that results from this three-way merge and automatically creates a new commit that points to it. This is referred to as a merge commit, and is special in that it has more than one parent.

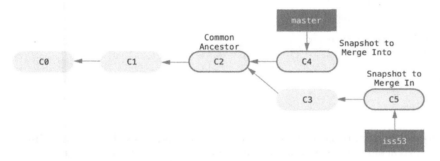

Figure 3-17. *A merge commit*

It's worth pointing out that Git determines the best common ancestor to use for its merge base; this is different than older tools like CVS or Subversion (before version 1.5), where the developer doing the merge had to figure out the best merge base for themselves. This makes merging a heck of a lot easier in Git than in these other systems.

Now that your work is merged in, you have no further need for the iss53 branch. You can close the ticket in your ticket-tracking system, and delete the branch:

```
$ git branch -d iss53
```

Basic Merge Conflicts

Occasionally, this process doesn't go smoothly. If you changed the same part of the same file differently in the two branches you're merging, Git won't be able to merge them cleanly. If your fix for issue #53 modified the same part of a file as the hotfix, you'll get a merge conflict that looks something like this:

```
$ git merge iss53
Auto-merging index.html
CONFLICT (content): Merge conflict in index.html
Automatic merge failed; fix conflicts and then commit the result.
```

Git hasn't automatically created a new merge commit. It has paused the process while you resolve the conflict. If you want to see which files are unmerged at any point after a merge conflict, you can run git status:

```
$ git status
On branch master
You have unmerged paths.
  (fix conflicts and run "git commit")

Unmerged paths:
  (use "git add <file>..." to mark resolution)

    both modified: index.html

no changes added to commit (use "git add" and/or "git commit -a")
```

Anything that has merge conflicts and hasn't been resolved is listed as unmerged. Git adds standard conflict-resolution markers to the files that have conflicts, so you can open them manually and resolve those conflicts. Your file contains a section that looks something like this:

```
<<<<<<< HEAD:index.html
<div id="footer">contact : email.support@github.com</div>
=======
<div id="footer">
 please contact us at support@github.com
</div>
>>>>>>>iss53:index.html
```

This means the version in HEAD (your master branch, because that was what you had checked out when you ran your merge command) is the top part of that block (everything above the =======), while the version in your iss53 branch looks like everything in the bottom part. To resolve the conflict, you have to either choose one side or the other or merge the contents yourself. For instance, you might resolve this conflict by replacing the entire block with this:

```
<div id="footer">
please contact us at email.support@github.com
</div>
```

This resolution has a little of each section, and the <<<<<<<, =======, and >>>>>>>lines have been completely removed. After you've resolved each of these sections in each conflicted file, run git add on each file to mark it as resolved. Staging the file marks it as resolved in Git.

If you want to use a graphical tool to resolve these issues, you can run git mergetool, which fires up an appropriate visual merge tool and walks you through the conflicts:

```
$ git mergetool

This message is displayed because 'merge.tool' is not configured.
See 'git mergetool --tool-help' or 'git help config' for more details.
'git mergetool' will now attempt to use one of the following tools:
opendiff kdiff3 tkdiff xxdiff meld tortoisemerge gvimdiff diffuse diffmerge ecmerge p4merge
araxis bc3 codecompare vimdiff emerge
Merging:
index.html
```

```
Normal merge conflict for 'index.html':
  {local}: modified file
  {remote}: modified file
Hit return to start merge resolution tool (opendiff):
```

If you want to use a merge tool other than the default (Git chose opendiff in this case because the command was run on a Mac), you can see all the supported tools listed at the top after one of the following tools. Just type the name of the tool you'd rather use.

■ **Note** If you need more advanced tools for resolving tricky merge conflicts, we cover more on merging later.

After you exit the merge tool, Git asks you whether the merge was successful. If you tell the script that it was, it stages the file to mark it as resolved for you. You can run git status again to verify that all conflicts have been resolved:

```
$ git status
On branch master
All conflicts fixed but you are still merging.
  (use "git commit" to conclude merge)

Changes to be committed:

    modified: index.html
```

If you're happy with that, and you verify that everything that had conflicts has been staged, you can type git commit to finalize the merge commit. The commit message by default looks something like this:

```
Merge branch 'iss53'

Conflicts:
    index.html
#
# It looks like you may be committing a merge.
# If this is not correct, please remove the file
#        .git/MERGE_HEAD
# and try again.

# Please enter the commit message for your changes. Lines starting
# with '#' will be ignored, and an empty message aborts the commit.
# On branch master
# All conflicts fixed but you are still merging.
#
# Changes to be committed:
#        modified: index.html
#
```

You can modify that message with details about how you resolved the merge if you think it would be helpful to others looking at this merge in the future—why you did what you did, if it's not obvious.

Branch Management

Now that you've created, merged, and deleted some branches, let's look at some branch-management tools that will come in handy when you begin using branches all the time.

The git branch command does more than just create and delete branches. If you run it with no arguments, you get a simple listing of your current branches:

```
$ git branch
  iss53
* master
  testing
```

Notice the * character that prefixes the master branch: it indicates the branch that you currently have checked out (i.e., the branch that HEAD points to). This means that if you commit at this point, the master branch will be moved forward with your new work. To see the last commit on each branch, you can run git branch -v:

```
$ git branch -v
  iss53   93b412c fix javascript issue
* master  7a98805 Merge branch 'iss53'
  testing 782fd34 add scott to the author list in the readmes
```

The useful --merged and --no-merged options can filter this list to branches that you have or have not yet merged into the branch you're currently on. To see which branches are already merged into the branch you're on, you can run git branch --merged:

```
$ git branch --merged
  iss53
* master
```

Because you already merged in iss53 earlier, you see it in your list. Branches on this list without the * in front of them are generally fine to delete with git branch -d; you've already incorporated their work into another branch, so you're not going to lose anything.

To see all the branches that contain work you haven't yet merged in, you can run git branch --no-merged:

```
$ git branch --no-merged
  testing
```

This shows your other branch. Because it contains work that isn't merged in yet, trying to delete it with git branch -d will fail:

```
$ git branch -d testing
error: The branch 'testing' is not fully merged.
If you are sure you want to delete it, run 'git branch -D testing'.
```

If you really do want to delete the branch and lose that work, you can force it with -D, as the helpful message points out.

Branching Workflows

Now that you have the basics of branching and merging down, what can or should you do with them? In this section, we'll cover some common workflows that this lightweight branching makes possible, so you can decide if you would like to incorporate it into your own development cycle.

Long-Running Branches

Because Git uses a simple three-way merge, merging from one branch into another multiple times over a long period is generally easy to do. This means you can have several branches that are always open and that you use for different stages of your development cycle; you can merge regularly from some of them into others.

Many Git developers have a workflow that embraces this approach, such as having only code that is entirely stable in their master branch—possibly only code that has been or will be released. They have another parallel branch named develop or next that they work from or use to test stability—it isn't necessarily always stable, but whenever it gets to a stable state, it can be merged into master. It's used to pull in topic branches (short-lived branches, like your earlier iss53 branch) when they're ready, to make sure they pass all the tests and don't introduce bugs.

In reality, we're talking about pointers moving up the line of commits you're making. The stable branches are farther down the line in your commit history, and the bleeding-edge branches are farther up the history.

Figure 3-18. *A linear view of progressive-stability branching*

It's generally easier to think about them as work silos, where sets of commits graduate to a more stable silo when they're fully tested.

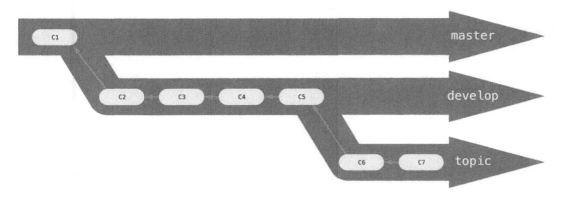

Figure 3-19. *A "silo" view of progressive-stability branching*

You can keep doing this for several levels of stability. Some larger projects also have a proposed or pu (proposed updates) branch that has integrated branches that may not be ready to go into the next or master branch. The idea is that your branches are at various levels of stability; when they reach a more stable level, they're merged into the branch above them. Again, having multiple long-running branches isn't necessary, but it's often helpful, especially when you're dealing with very large or complex projects.

Topic Branches

Topic branches, however, are useful in projects of any size. A topic branch is a short-lived branch that you create and use for a single particular feature or related work. This is something you've likely never done with a VCS before because it's generally too expensive to create and merge branches. But in Git it's common to create, work on, merge, and delete branches several times a day.

You saw this in the last section with the iss53 and hotfix branches you created. You did a few commits on them and deleted them directly after merging them into your main branch. This technique allows you to context-switch quickly and completely – because your work is separated into silos where all the changes in that branch have to do with that topic, it's easier to see what has happened during code review and such. You can keep the changes there for minutes, days, or months, and merge them in when they're ready, regardless of the order in which they were created or worked on.

Consider an example of doing some work (on master), branching off for an issue (iss91), working on it for a bit, branching off the second branch to try another way of handling the same thing (iss91v2), going back to your master branch and working there for a while, and then branching off there to do some work that you're not sure is a good idea (dumbidea branch). Your commit history will look something like this:

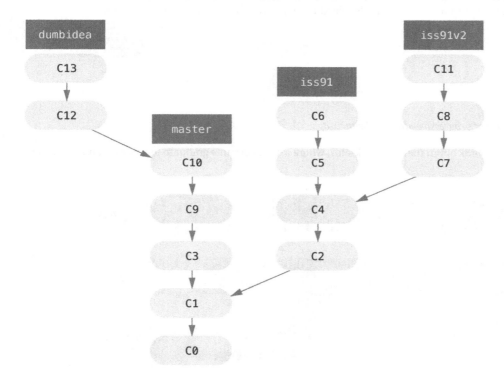

Figure 3-20. *Multiple topic branches*

Now, let's say you decide you like the second solution to your issue best (iss91v2); and you showed the dumbidea branch to your coworkers, and it turns out to be genius. You can throw away the original iss91 branch (losing commits C5 and C6) and merge in the other two. Your history then looks like this:

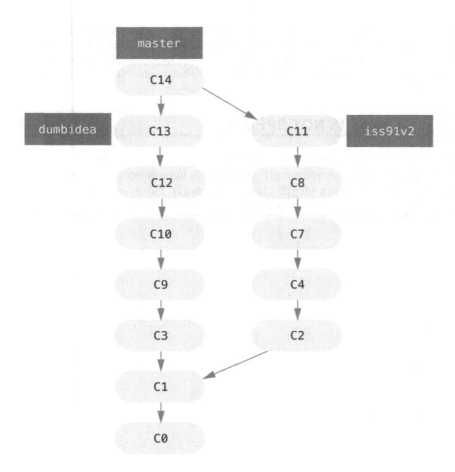

Figure 3-21. *History after merging dumbidea and iss91v2*

We will go into more detail about the various possible workflows for your Git project in Chapter 5, so before you decide which branching scheme your next project will use, be sure to read that chapter.

It's important to remember when you're doing all this that these branches are completely local. When you're branching and merging, everything is being done only in your Git repository—no server communication is happening.

Remote Branches

Remote branches are references (pointers) to the state of branches in your remote repositories. They're local branches that you can't move; they're moved automatically for you whenever you do any network communication. Remote branches act as bookmarks to remind you where the branches on your remote repositories were the last time you connected to them.

They take the form (remote)/(branch). For instance, if you wanted to see what the master branch on your origin remote looked like as of the last time you communicated with it, you would check the origin/master branch. If you were working on an issue with a partner and they pushed up an iss53 branch, you might have your own local iss53 branch; but the branch on the server would point to the commit at origin/iss53.

This may be a bit confusing, so let's look at an example. Let's say you have a Git server on your network at git.ourcompany.com. If you clone from this, Git's clone command automatically names it origin for you, pulls down all its data, creates a pointer to where its master branch is, and names it origin/master locally. Git also gives you your own local master branch starting at the same place as origin's master branch, so you have something to work from.

"ORIGIN" IS NOT SPECIAL

Just like the branch name "master" does not have any special meaning in Git, neither does "origin". While "master" is the default name for a starting branch when you run git init which is the only reason it's widely used, "origin" is the default name for a remote when you run git clone. If you run git clone -o booyah instead, then you will have booyah/master as your default remote branch.

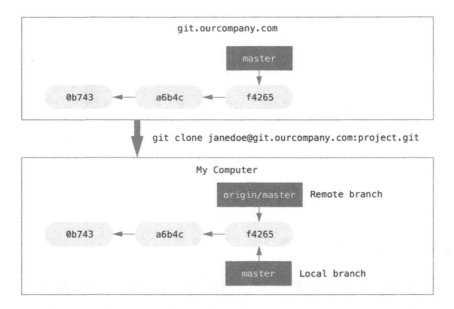

Figure 3-22. *Server and local repositories after cloning*

If you do some work on your local master branch, and, in the meantime, someone else pushes to git.ourcompany.com and updates its master branch, then your histories move forward differently. Also, as long as you stay out of contact with your origin server, your origin/master pointer doesn't move.

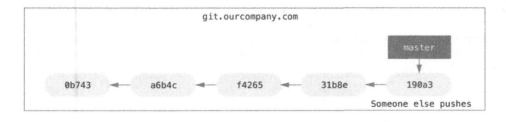

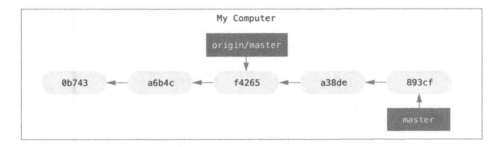

Figure 3-23. *Local and remote work can diverge*

To synchronize your work, you run a `git fetch origin` command. This command looks up which server "origin" is (in this case, it's `git.ourcompany.com`), fetches any data from it that you don't yet have, and updates your local database, moving your `origin/master` pointer to its new, more up-to-date position.

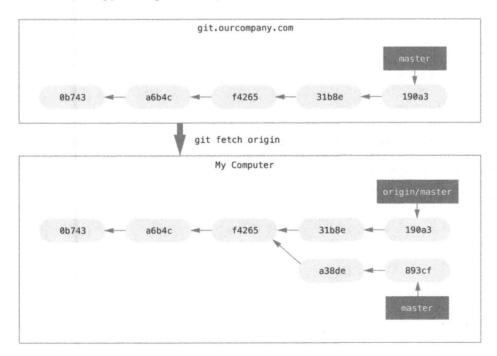

Figure 3-24. *git fetch updates your remote references*

To demonstrate having multiple remote servers and what remote branches for those remote projects look like, let's assume you have another internal Git server that is used only for development by one of your sprint teams. This server is at git.team1.ourcompany.com. You can add it as a new remote reference to the project you're currently working on by running the git remote add command as we covered in Chapter 2. Name this remote teamone, which will be your shortname for that whole URL.

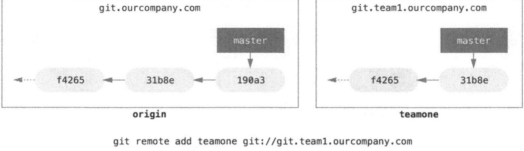

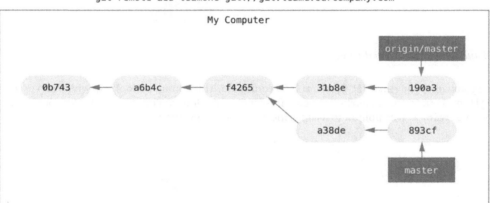

Figure 3-25. *Adding another server as a remote*

Now, you can run git fetch teamone to fetch everything the remote teamone server has that you don't have yet. Because that server is a subset of the data your origin server has right now, Git fetches no data but sets a remote branch called teamone/master to point to the commit that teamone has as its master branch.

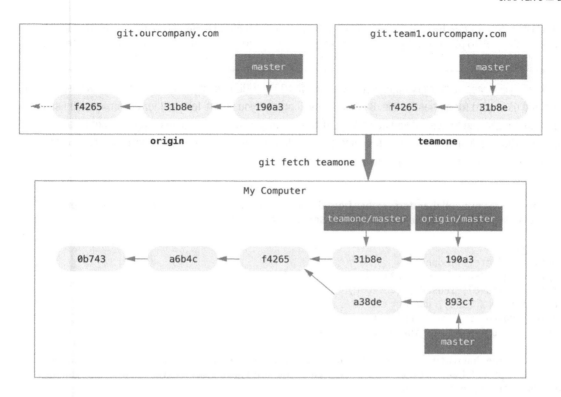

Figure 3-26. *Remote tracking branch for teamone/master*

Pushing

When you want to share a branch with the world, you need to push it up to a remote that you have write access to. Your local branches aren't automatically synchronized to the remotes you write to – you have to explicitly push the branches you want to share. That way, you can use private branches for work you don't want to share, and push up only the topic branches you want to collaborate on.

If you have a branch named `serverfix` that you want to work on with others, you can push it up the same way you pushed your first branch. Run `git push (remote) (branch)`:

```
$ git push origin serverfix
Counting objects: 24, done.
Delta compression using up to 8 threads.
Compressing objects: 100% (15/15), done.
Writing objects: 100% (24/24), 1.91 KiB | 0 bytes/s, done.
Total 24 (delta 2), reused 0 (delta 0)
To https://github.com/schacon/simplegit
 * [new branch]      serverfix -> serverfix
```

This is a bit of a shortcut. Git automatically expands the `serverfix` branchname out to `refs/heads/serverfix:refs/heads/serverfix`, which means, "Take my serverfix local branch and push it to update the remote's serverfix branch." We'll go over the `refs/heads/` part in detail in Chapter 11, but you can generally leave it off. You can also do `git push origin serverfix:serverfix`, which does the same thing – it says, "Take my serverfix and make it the remote's serverfix." You can use this format to push a local branch into a remote branch that is named differently. If you didn't want it to be called serverfix on the remote, you could instead run git push origin serverfix:awesomebranch to push your local serverfix branch to the awesomebranch branch on the remote project.

■ **Note**   Don't type your password every time. If you're using an HTTPS URL to push over, the Git server will ask you for your username and password for authentication. By default it will prompt you on the terminal for this information so the server can tell if you're allowed to push. If you don't want to type it every single time you push, you can set up a "credential cache." The simplest is just to keep it in memory for a few minutes, which you can easily set up by running git config --global credential.helper cache.

The next time one of your collaborators fetches from the server, they will get a reference to where the server's version of serverfix is under the remote branch origin/serverfix:

```
$ git fetch origin
remote: Counting objects: 7, done.
remote: Compressing objects: 100% (2/2), done.
remote: Total 3 (delta 0), reused 3 (delta 0)
Unpacking objects: 100% (3/3), done.
From https://github.com/schacon/simplegit
 * [new branch] serverfix -> origin/serverfix
```

It's important to note that when you do a fetch that brings down new remote branches, you don't automatically have local, editable copies of them. In other words, in this case, you don't have a new serverfix branch—you only have an origin/serverfix pointer that you can't modify.

To merge this work into your current working branch, you can run git merge origin/serverfix. If you want your own serverfix branch that you can work on, you can base it off your remote branch:

```
$ git checkout -b serverfix origin/serverfix
Branch serverfix set up to track remote branch serverfix from origin.
Switched to a new branch 'serverfix'
```

This gives you a local branch that you can work on that starts where origin/serverfix is.

Tracking Branches

Checking out a local branch from a remote branch automatically creates what is called a "tracking branch" (or sometimes an "upstream branch"). Tracking branches are local branches that have a direct relationship to a remote branch. If you're on a tracking branch and type git push, Git automatically knows which server and branch to push to. Also, running git pull while on one of these branches fetches all the remote references and then automatically merges in the corresponding remote branch.

When you clone a repository, it generally automatically creates a master branch that tracks origin/master. That's why git push and git pull work out of the box with no other arguments. However, you can set up other tracking branches if you wish—ones that track branches on other remotes, or don't track the master branch. The simple case is the example you just saw, running git checkout -b [branch] [remotename]/[branch]. This is a common enough operation that git provides the --track shorthand:

```
$ git checkout --track origin/serverfix
Branch serverfix set up to track remote branch serverfix from origin.
Switched to a new branch 'serverfix'
```

To set up a local branch with a different name than the remote branch, you can easily use the first version with a different local branch name:

```
$ git checkout -b sf origin/serverfix
Branch sf set up to track remote branch serverfix from origin.
Switched to a new branch 'sf'
```

Now, your local branch sf will automatically push to and pull from origin/serverfix.

If you already have a local branch and want to set it to a remote branch you just pulled down, or want to change the upstream branch you're tracking, you can use the -u or --set-upstream-to option to git branch to explicitly set it at any time.

```
$ git branch -u origin/serverfix
Branch serverfix set up to track remote branch serverfix from origin.
```

UPSTREAM SHORTHAND

When you have a tracking branch set up, you can reference it with the @{upstream} or @{u} shorthand. So if you're on the master branch and it's tracking origin/master, you can say something like git merge @{u} instead of git merge origin/master if you want.

If you want to see what tracking branches you have set up, you can use the -vv option to git branch. This lists your local branches with more information, including what each branch is tracking and whether your local branch is ahead, behind or both.

```
$ git branch -vv
  iss53     7e424c3 [origin/iss53: ahead 2] forgot the brackets
  master    1ae2a45 [origin/master] deploying index fix
* serverfix f8674d9 [teamone/server-fix-good: ahead 3, behind 1] this should do it
  testing   5ea463a trying something new
```

So here we can see that our iss53 branch is tracking origin/iss53 and is "ahead" by two, meaning that we have two commits locally that are not pushed to the server. We can also see that our master branch is tracking origin/master and is up to date. Next we can see that our serverfix branch is tracking the server-fix-good branch on our teamone server and is ahead by three and behind by one, meaning that there is one commit on the server we haven't merged in yet and three commits locally that we haven't pushed. Finally we can see that our testing branch is not tracking any remote branch.

It's important to note that these numbers are only since the last time you fetched from each server. This command does not reach out to the servers, it's telling you about what it has cached from these servers locally. If you want totally up to date ahead and behind numbers, you'll need to fetch from all your remotes right before running this. You could do that like this: $ git fetch --all; git branch -vv.

Pulling

While the git fetch command will fetch down all the changes on the server that you don't have yet, it will not modify your working directory at all. It will simply get the data for you and let you merge it yourself. However, there is a command called git pull which is essentially a git fetch immediately followed by a git merge in most cases. If you have a tracking branch set up as demonstrated in the last section, either by explicitly setting it or by having it created for you by the clone or checkout commands, git pull will look up what server and branch your current branch is tracking, fetch from that server and then try to merge in that remote branch.

Generally it's better to simply use the fetch and merge commands explicitly as the magic of git pull can often be confusing.

Deleting Remote Branches

Suppose you're done with a remote branch—say you and your collaborators are finished with a feature and have merged it into your remote's master branch (or whatever branch your stable codeline is in). You can delete a remote branch using the --delete option to git push. If you want to delete your serverfix branch from the server, you run the following:

```
$ git push origin --delete serverfix
To https://github.com/schacon/simplegit
 - [deleted]         serverfix
```

Basically all this does is remove the pointer from the server. The Git server will generally keep the data there for a while until a garbage collection runs, so if it was accidentally deleted, it's often easy to recover.

Rebasing

In Git, there are two main ways to integrate changes from one branch into another: the merge and the rebase. In this section you'll learn what rebasing is, how to do it, why it's a pretty amazing tool, and in what cases you won't want to use it.

The Basic Rebase

If you go back to an earlier example from our Basic Merging section, you can see that you diverged your work and made commits on two different branches.

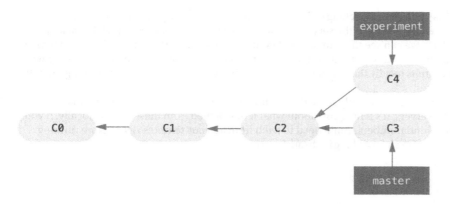

Figure 3-27. *Simple divergent history*

The easiest way to integrate the branches, as we've already covered, is the merge command. It performs a three-way merge between the two latest branch snapshots (C3 and C4) and the most recent common ancestor of the two (C2), creating a new snapshot (and commit).

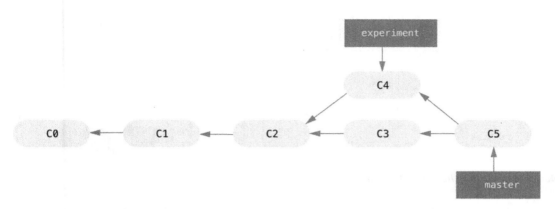

Figure 3-28. *Merging to integrate diverged work history*

However, there is another way: you can take the patch of the change that was introduced in C4 and reapply it on top of C3. In Git, this is called *rebasing*. With the rebase command, you can take all the changes that were committed on one branch and replay them on another one.

In this example, you'd run the following:

```
$ git checkout experiment
$ git rebase master
First, rewinding head to replay your work on top of it...
Applying: added staged command
```

It works by going to the common ancestor of the two branches (the one you're on and the one you're rebasing onto), getting the diff introduced by each commit of the branch you're on, saving those diffs to temporary files, resetting the current branch to the same commit as the branch you are rebasing onto, and finally applying each change in turn.

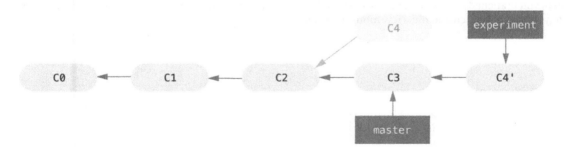

Figure 3-29. *Rebasing the change introduced in C3 onto C4*

At this point, you can go back to the master branch and do a fast-forward merge.

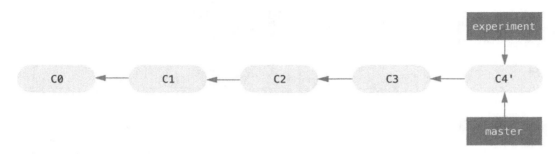

Figure 3-30. *Fast-forwarding the master branch*

Now, the snapshot pointed to by C3' is exactly the same as the one that was pointed to by C5 in the merge example. There is no difference in the end product of the integration, but rebasing makes for a cleaner history. If you examine the log of a rebased branch, it looks like a linear history: it appears that all the work happened in series, even when it originally happened in parallel.

Often, you'll do this to make sure your commits apply cleanly on a remote branch – perhaps in a project to which you're trying to contribute but that you don't maintain. In this case, you'd do your work in a branch and then rebase your work onto origin/master when you were ready to submit your patches to the main project. That way, the maintainer doesn't have to do any integration work—just a fast-forward or a clean apply.

Note that the snapshot pointed to by the final commit you end up with, whether it's the last of the rebased commits for a rebase or the final merge commit after a merge, is the same snapshot—it's only the history that is different. Rebasing replays changes from one line of work onto another in the order they were introduced, whereas merging takes the endpoints and merges them.

More Interesting Rebases

You can also have your rebase replay on something other than the rebase target branch. Take a history like Figure 3-31, for example. You branched a topic branch (server) to add some server-side functionality to your project, and made a commit. Then, you branched off that to make the client-side changes (client) and committed a few times. Finally, you went back to your server branch and did a few more commits.

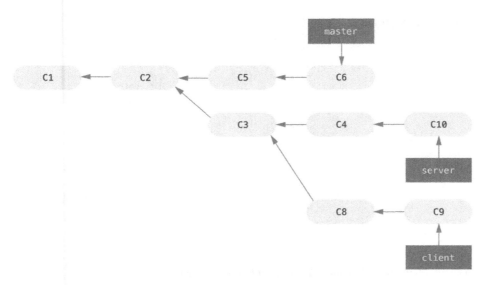

Figure 3-31. *A history with a topic branch off another topic branch*

Suppose you decide that you want to merge your client-side changes into your mainline for a release, but you want to hold off on the server-side changes until it's tested further. You can take the changes on client that aren't on server (C8 and C9) and replay them on your master branch by using the --onto option of git rebase:

```
$ git rebase --onto master server client
```

This basically says, "Check out the client branch, figure out the patches from the common ancestor of the client and server branches, and then replay them onto master." It's a bit complex, but the result is pretty cool.

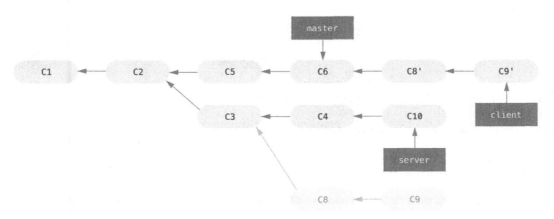

Figure 3-32. *Rebasing a topic branch off another topic branch*

Now you can fast-forward your master branch:

```
$ git checkout master
$ git merge client
```

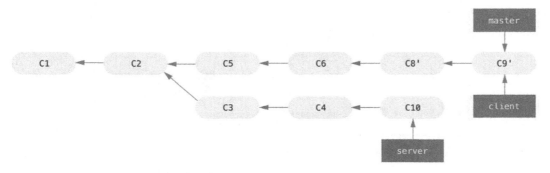

Figure 3-33. *Fast-forwarding your master branch to include the client branch changes*

Let's say you decide to pull in your server branch as well. You can rebase the server branch onto the master branch without having to check it out first by running git rebase [basebranch] [topicbranch]—which checks out the topic branch (in this case, server) for you and replays it onto the base branch (master):

```
$ git rebase master server
```

This replays your server work on top of your master work.

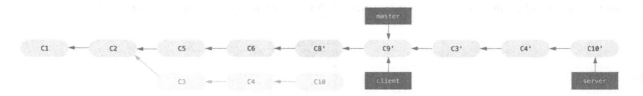

Figure 3-34. *Rebasing your server branch on top of your master branch*

Then, you can fast-forward the base branch (master):

```
$ git checkout master
$ git merge server
```

You can remove the client and server branches because all the work is integrated and you don't need them anymore.

```
$ git branch -d client
$ git branch -d server
```

Figure 3-35. *Final commit history*

The Perils of Rebasing

Ahh, but the bliss of rebasing isn't without its drawbacks, which can be summed up in a single line:

Do not rebase commits that exist outside your repository.

If you follow that guideline, you'll be fine. If you don't, people will hate you, and you'll be scorned by friends and family.

When you rebase stuff, you're abandoning existing commits and creating new ones that are similar but different. If you push commits somewhere and others pull them down and base work on them, and then you rewrite those commits with `git rebase` and push them up again, your collaborators will have to re-merge their work and things will get messy when you try to pull their work back into yours.

Let's look at an example of how rebasing work that you've made public can cause problems. Suppose you clone from a central server and then do some work off that.

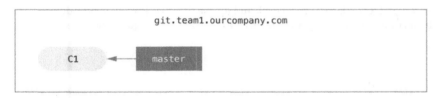

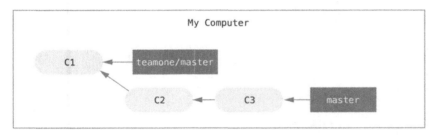

Figure 3-36. *Clone a repository, and base some work on it*

Now, someone else does more work that includes a merge, and pushes that work to the central server. You fetch them and merge the new remote branch into your work.

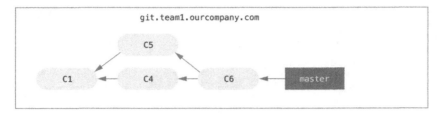

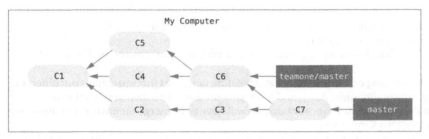

Figure 3-37. *Fetch more commits, and merge them into your work*

Next, the person who pushed the merged work decides to go back and rebase their work instead; they do a `git push --force` to overwrite the history on the server. You then fetch from that server, bringing down the new commits.

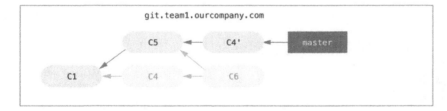

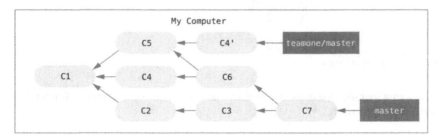

Figure 3-38. *Someone pushes rebased commits, abandoning commits you've based your work on*

Now you're both in a pickle. If you do a `git pull`, you'll create a merge commit which includes both lines of history.

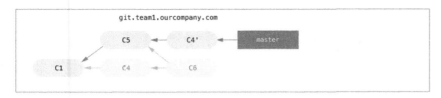

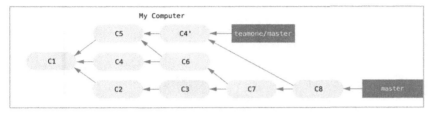

Figure 3-39. You merge in the same work again into a new merge commit

If you run a `git log` when your history looks like this, you'll see two commits that have the same author, date, and message, which will be confusing. Furthermore, if you push this history back up to the server, you'll reintroduce all those rebased commits to the central server, which can further confuse people. It's pretty safe to assume that the other developer doesn't want C4 and C6 to be in the history; that's why she rebased in the first place.

Rebase When You Rebase

If you do find yourself in a situation like this, Git has some further magic that might help you out. If someone on your team force pushes changes that overwrite work that you've based work on, your challenge is to figure out what is yours and what they've rewritten.

It turns out that in addition to the commit SHA checksum, Git also calculate a checksum that is based just on the patch introduced with the commit. This is called a "patch-id."

If you pull down work that was rewritten and rebase it on top of the new commits from your partner, Git can often successfully figure out what is uniquely yours and apply them back on top of the new branch.

For instance, in the previous scenario, if instead of doing a merge when we're at Figure 3-38, abandoning commits you've based your work on we run `git rebase teamone/master`, Git will:

- Determine what work is unique to our branch (C2, C3, C4, C6, C7)

- Determine which are not merge commits (C2, C3, C4)

- Determine which have not been rewritten into the target branch (just C2 and C3, since C4 is the same patch as C4')

- Apply those commits to the top of `teamone/master`

So instead of the result seen in Figure 3-39, we would end up with something more like Figure 3-40.

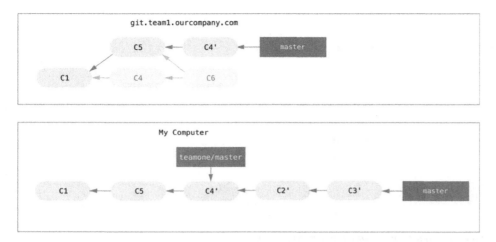

Figure 3-40. *Rebase on top of force-pushed rebase work*

This only works if C4 and C4' that your partner made are almost exactly the same patch. Otherwise the rebase won't be able to tell that it's a duplicate and will add another C4-like patch (which will probably fail to apply cleanly, since the changes would already be at least somewhat there).

You can also simplify this by running a `git pull --rebase` instead of a normal `git pull`. Or you could do it manually with a `git fetch` followed by a `git rebase teamone/master` in this case.

If you are using `git pull` and want to make `--rebase` the default, you can set the `pull.rebase` config value with something like `git config --global pull.rebase true`.

If you treat rebasing as a way to clean up and work with commits before you push them, and if you only rebase commits that have never been available publicly, then you'll be fine. If you rebase commits that have already been pushed publicly, and people may have based work on those commits, then you may be in for some frustrating trouble, and the scorn of your teammates.

If you or a partner does find it necessary at some point, make sure everyone knows to run `git pull --rebase` to try to make the pain after it happens a little bit simpler.

Rebase vs. Merge

Now that you've seen rebasing and merging in action, you may be wondering which one is better. Before we can answer this, let's step back a bit and talk about what history means.

One point of view on this is that your repository's commit history is a record of what actually happened. It's a historical document, valuable in its own right, and shouldn't be tampered with. From this angle, changing the commit history is almost blasphemous; you're lying about what actually transpired. So what if there was a messy series of merge commits? That's how it happened, and the repository should preserve that for posterity.

The opposing point of view is that the commit history is the story of how your project was made. You wouldn't publish the first draft of a book, and the manual for how to maintain your software deserves careful editing. This is the camp that uses tools like rebase and filter-branch to tell the story in the way that's best for future readers.

Now, to the question of whether merging or rebasing is better: hopefully you'll see that it's not that simple. Git is a powerful tool, and allows you to do many things to and with your history, but every team and every project is different. Now that you know how both of these things work, it's up to you to decide which one is best for your particular situation.

In general the way to get the best of both worlds is to rebase local changes you've made but haven't shared yet before you push them in order to clean up your story, but never rebase anything you've pushed somewhere.

Summary

We've covered basic branching and merging in Git. You should feel comfortable creating and switching to new branches, switching between branches, and merging local branches. You should also be able to share your branches by pushing them to a shared server, working with others on shared branches, and rebasing your branches before they are shared. Next, we'll cover what you'll need to run your own Git repository-hosting server.

CHAPTER 4

■ ■ ■

Git on the Server

At this point, you should be able to do most of the day-to-day tasks for which you'll be using Git. However, in order to do any collaboration in Git, you'll need to have a remote Git repository. Although you can technically push changes to and pull changes from individuals' repositories, doing so is discouraged because you can fairly easily confuse what they're working on if you're not careful. Furthermore, you want your collaborators to be able to access the repository even if your computer is offline—having a more reliable common repository is often useful. Therefore, the preferred method for collaborating with someone is to set up an intermediate repository that you both have access to, and push to and pull from that.

Running a Git server is fairly straightforward. First, you choose which protocols you want your server to communicate with. The first section of this chapter will cover the available protocols and the pros and cons of each. The next sections will explain some typical setups using those protocols and how to get your server running with them. Last, we'll go over a few hosted options, if you don't mind hosting your code on someone else's server and don't want to go through the hassle of setting up and maintaining your own server.

If you have no interest in running your own server, you can skip to the last section of the chapter to see some options for setting up a hosted account and then move on to the next chapter, where we discuss the various ins and outs of working in a distributed source control environment.

A remote repository is generally a *bare repository*—a Git repository that has no working directory. Because the repository is only used as a collaboration point, there is no reason to have a snapshot checked out on disk; it's just the Git data. In the simplest terms, a bare repository is the contents of your project's `.git` directory and nothing else.

The Protocols

Git can use four major protocols to transfer data: Local, HTTP, Secure Shell (SSH), and Git. Here we'll discuss what they are and in what basic circumstances you would want (or not want) to use them.

Local Protocol

The most basic is the *Local protocol*, in which the remote repository is in another directory on disk. This is often used if everyone on your team has access to a shared filesystem such as an NFS mount, or in the less likely case that everyone logs in to the same computer. The latter wouldn't be ideal, because all your code repository instances would reside on the same computer, making a catastrophic loss much more likely.

If you have a shared mounted filesystem, then you can clone, push to, and pull from a local file-based repository. To clone a repository like this or to add one as a remote to an existing project, use the path to the repository as the URL. For example, to clone a local repository, you can run something like this:

```
$ git clone /opt/git/project.git
```

Or you can do this:

```
$ git clone file:///opt/git/project.git
```

Git operates slightly differently if you explicitly specify `file://` at the beginning of the URL. If you just specify the path, Git tries to use hardlinks or directly copy the files it needs. If you specify `file://`, Git fires up the processes that it normally uses to transfer data over a network which is generally a lot less efficient method of transferring the data. The main reason to specify the `file://` prefix is if you want a clean copy of the repository with extraneous references or objects left out—generally after an import from another version-control system or something similar (see Chapter 10 for maintenance tasks). We'll use the normal path here because doing so is almost always faster.

To add a local repository to an existing Git project, you can run something like this:

```
$ git remote add local_proj /opt/git/project.git
```

Then, you can push to and pull from that remote as though you were doing so over a network.

The Pros

The pros of file-based repositories are that they're simple and they use existing file permissions and network access. If you already have a shared filesystem to which your whole team has access, setting up a repository is very easy. You stick the bare repository copy somewhere everyone has shared access to and set the read/write permissions as you would for any other shared directory. We'll discuss how to export a bare repository copy for this purpose in the next section "Getting Git on a Server".

This is also a nice option for quickly grabbing work from someone else's working repository. If you and a co-worker are working on the same project and he wants you to check something out, running a command like `git pull /home/john/project` is often easier than him pushing to a remote server and you pulling down.

The Cons

The cons of this method are that shared access is generally more difficult to set up and reach from multiple locations than basic network access. If you want to push from your laptop when you're at home, you have to mount the remote disk, which can be difficult and slow compared to network-based access.

It's also important to mention that this isn't necessarily the fastest option if you're using a shared mount of some kind. A local repository is fast only if you have fast access to the data. A repository on NFS is often slower than the repository over SSH on the same server, allowing Git to run off local disks on each system.

The HTTP Protocols

Git can communicate over HTTP in two different modes. Prior to Git 1.6.6 there was only one way it could do this, which was very simple and generally read-only. In version 1.6.6 a new, smarter protocol was introduced that involved Git being able to intelligently negotiate data transfer in a manner similar to how it does over SSH. In the last few years, this new HTTP protocol has become very popular since it's simpler for the user and smarter about how it communicates. The newer version is often referred to as the "Smart" HTTP protocol and the older way as "Dumb" HTTP. We'll cover the newer "Smart" HTTP protocol first.

Smart HTTP

The "Smart" HTTP protocol operates very similarly to the SSH or Git protocols but runs over standard HTTP/S ports and can use various HTTP authentication mechanisms, meaning it's often easier on the user than something like SSH, because you can use things like username/password basic authentication rather than having to set up SSH keys.

It has probably become the most popular way to use Git now, because it can be set up to both serve anonymously like the `git://` protocol, and can also be pushed over with authentication and encryption like the SSH protocol. Instead of having to set up different URLs for these things, you can now use a single URL for both. If you try to push and the repository requires authentication (which it normally should), the server can prompt for a username and password. The same goes for read access.

In fact, for services like GitHub, the URL you use to view the repository online (for example, `https://github.com/schacon/simplegit[]`) is the same URL you can use to clone and, if you have access, push over.

Dumb HTTP

If the server does not respond with a Git HTTP smart service, the Git client will try to fall back to the simpler Dumb HTTP protocol. The Dumb protocol expects the bare Git repository to be served like normal files from the web server. The beauty of the Dumb HTTP protocol is the simplicity of setting it up. Basically, all you have to do is put a bare Git repository under your HTTP document root and set up a specific post-update hook, and you're done. At that point, anyone who can access the web server under which you put the repository can also clone your repository. To allow read access to your repository over HTTP, do something like this:

```
$ cd /var/www/htdocs/
$ git clone --bare /path/to/git_project gitproject.git
$ cd gitproject.git
$ mv hooks/post-update.sample hooks/post-update
$ chmod a+x hooks/post-update
```

That's all. The post-update hook that comes with Git by default runs the appropriate command (git update-server-info) to make HTTP fetching and cloning work properly. This command is run when you push to this repository (over SSH perhaps); then, other people can clone via something like

```
$ git clone https://example.com/gitproject.git
```

In this particular case, we're using the /var/www/htdocs path that is common for Apache setups, but you can use any static web server—just put the bare repository in its path. The Git data is served as basic static files (see Chapter 10 for details about exactly how it's served).

Generally you would either choose to run a read/write Smart HTTP server or simply have the files accessible as read-only in the Dumb manner. It's rare to run a mix of the two services.

The Pros

We'll concentrate on the pros of the Smart version of the HTTP protocol.

The simplicity of having a single URL for all types of access and having the server prompt only when authentication is needed makes things very easy for the end user. Being able to authenticate with a username and password is also a big advantage over SSH, since users don't have to generate SSH keys locally and upload their public key to the server before being able to interact with it. For less sophisticated users, or users on systems where SSH is less common, this is a major advantage in usability. It is also a very fast and efficient protocol, similar to the SSH one.

You can also serve your repositories read-only over HTTPS, which means you can encrypt the content transfer; or you can go so far as to make the clients use specific signed SSL certificates.

Another nice thing is that HTTP/S are such commonly used protocols that corporate firewalls are often set up to allow traffic through these ports.

The Cons

Git over HTTP/S can be a little trickier to set up compared to SSH on some servers. Other than that, there is very little advantage that other protocols have over the Smart HTTP protocol for serving Git.

If you're using HTTP for authenticated pushing, providing your credentials is sometimes more complicated than using keys over SSH. There are however several credential caching tools you can use, including Keychain access on OSX and Credential Manager on Windows, to make this pretty painless.

The SSH Protocol

A common transport protocol for Git when self-hosting is over SSH. This is because SSH access to servers is already set up in most places—and if it isn't, it's easy to do. SSH is also an authenticated network protocol; and because it's ubiquitous, it's generally easy to set up and use.

To clone a Git repository over SSH, you can specify `ssh://`URL like this:

```
$ git clone ssh://user@server:project.git
Or you can not specify a protocol - Git assumes SSH if you aren't explicit:
$ git clone user@server:project.git
```

You can also not specify a user, and Git assumes the user you're currently logged in as.

The Pros

The pros of using SSH are many. First, SSH is relatively easy to set up—SSH daemons are commonplace, many network admins have experience with them, and many OS distributions are set up with them or have tools to manage them. Next, access over SSH is secure—all data transfer is encrypted and authenticated. Last, like the HTTP/S, Git, and Local protocols, SSH is efficient, making the data as compact as possible before transferring it.

The Cons

The negative aspect of SSH is that you can't serve anonymous access of your repository over it. People must have access to your machine over SSH to access it, even in a read-only capacity, which doesn't make SSH access conducive to open source projects. If you're using it only within your corporate network, SSH may be the only protocol you need to deal with. If you want to allow anonymous read-only access to your projects and also want to use SSH, you'll have to set up SSH for you to push over but something else for others to fetch over.

The Git Protocol

Next is the Git protocol. This is a special daemon that comes packaged with Git; it listens on a dedicated port (9418) that provides a service similar to the SSH protocol, but with absolutely no authentication. In order for a repository to be served over the Git protocol, you must create the `git-export-daemon-ok` file—the daemon won't serve a repository without that file in it—but other than that there is no security. Either the Git repository is available for everyone to clone or it isn't. This means that there is generally no pushing over this protocol. You can enable push access; but given the lack of authentication, if you turn on push access, anyone on the Internet who finds your project's URL could push to your project. Suffice it to say that this is rare.

The Pros

The Git protocol is often the fastest network transfer protocol available. If you're serving a lot of traffic for a public project or serving a very large project that doesn't require user authentication for read access, it's likely that you'll want to set up a Git daemon to serve your project. It uses the same data-transfer mechanism as the SSH protocol but without the encryption and authentication overhead.

The Cons

The downside of the Git protocol is the lack of authentication. It's generally undesirable for the Git protocol to be the only access to your project. Generally, you'll pair it with SSH or HTTPS access for the few developers who have push (write) access and have everyone else use git:// for read-only access. It's also probably the most difficult protocol to set up. It must run its own daemon, which requires xinetd configuration or the like, which isn't always a walk in the park. It also requires firewall access to port 9418, which isn't a standard port that corporate firewalls always allow. Behind big corporate firewalls, this obscure port is commonly blocked.

Getting Git on a Server

Now we'll cover setting up a Git service running these protocols on your own server.

■ **Note** Here we'll be demonstrating the commands and steps needed to do basic, simplified installations on a Linux-based server, though it's also possible to run these services on Mac or Windows servers too. Actually setting up a production server within your infrastructure will certainly entail differences in security measures or operating system tools, but hopefully this will give you the general idea of what's involved.

To initially set up any Git server, you have to export an existing repository into a new bare repository—a repository that doesn't contain a working directory. This is generally straightforward to do. To clone your repository to create a new bare repository, you run the clone command with the --bare option. By convention, bare repository directories end in .git, like so:

```
$ git clone --bare my_project my_project.git
Cloning into bare repository 'my_project.git'...
done.
```

You should now have a copy of the Git directory data in your my_project.git directory. This is roughly equivalent to something like

```
$ cp -Rf my_project/.git my_project.git
```

There are a couple of minor differences in the configuration file; but for your purpose, this is close to the same thing. It takes the Git repository by itself, without a working directory, and creates a directory specifically for it alone.

Putting the Bare Repository on a Server

Now that you have a bare copy of your repository, all you need to do is put it on a server and set up your protocols. Let's say you've set up a server called git.example.com that you have SSH access to, and you want to store all your Git repositories under the /opt/git directory. Assuming that /opt/git exists on that server, you can set up your new repository by copying your bare repository over:

```
$ scp -r my_project.git user@git.example.com:/opt/git
```

At this point, other users who have SSH access to the same server that has read-access to the /opt/git directory can clone your repository by running.

```
$ git clone user@git.example.com:/opt/git/my_project.git
```

If a user SSHs into a server and has write access to the /opt/git/my_project.git directory, they will also automatically have push access.

Git will automatically add group write permissions to a repository properly if you run the git init command with the --shared option.

```
$ ssh user@git.example.com
$ cd /opt/git/my_project.git
$ git init --bare --shared
```

You see how easy it is to take a Git repository, create a bare version, and place it on a server to which you and your collaborators have SSH access. Now you're ready to collaborate on the same project.

It's important to note that this is all you need to do to run a useful Git server to which several people have access—just add SSH-able accounts on a server, and stick a bare repository somewhere that all those users have read and write access to. You're ready to go—nothing else needed.

In the next few sections, you'll see how to expand to more sophisticated setups. This discussion includes not having to create user accounts for each user, adding public read access to repositories, setting up web UIs, using the Gitosis tool, and more. However, keep in mind that to collaborate with a couple of people on a private project, all you need is an SSH server and a bare repository.

Small Setups

If you're a small outfit or are just trying out Git in your organization and have only a few developers, things can be simple for you. One of the most complicated aspects of setting up a Git server is user management. If you want some repositories to be read-only to certain users and read/write to others, access and permissions can be a bit more difficult to arrange.

SSH Access

If you have a server to which all your developers already have SSH access, it's generally easiest to set up your first repository there, because you have to do almost no work (as we covered in the last section). If you want more complex access control type permissions on your repositories, you can handle them with the normal filesystem permissions of the operating system your server runs.

If you want to place your repositories on a server that doesn't have accounts for everyone on your team whom you want to have write access, then you must set up SSH access for them. We assume that if you have a server with which to do this, you already have an SSH server installed, and that's how you're accessing the server.

There are a few ways you can give access to everyone on your team. The first is to set up accounts for everybody, which is straightforward but can be cumbersome. You may not want to run adduser and set temporary passwords for every user.

A second method is to create a single git user on the machine, ask every user who is to have write access to send you an SSH public key, and add that key to the ~/.ssh/authorized_keys file of your new git user. At that point, everyone will be able to access that machine via the git user. This doesn't affect the commit data in any way—the SSH user you connect as doesn't affect the commits you've recorded.

Another way to do it is to have your SSH server authenticate from an LDAP server or some other centralized authentication source that you may already have set up. As long as each user can get shell access on the machine, any SSH authentication mechanism you can think of should work.

Generating Your SSH Public Key

That being said, many Git servers authenticate using SSH public keys. To provide a public key, each user in your system must generate one if they don't already have one. This process is similar across all operating systems. First, you should check to make sure you don't already have a key. By default, a user's SSH keys are stored in that user's ~/.ssh directory. You can easily check to see whether you have a key already by going to that directory and listing the contents:

```
$ cd ~/.ssh
$ ls
authorized_keys2  id_dsa        known_hosts
config            id_dsa.pub
```

You're looking for a pair of files named something like id_dsa or id_rsa and a matching file with a .pub extension. The .pub file is your public key, and the other file is your private key. If you don't have these files (or you don't even have a .ssh directory), you can create them by running a program called ssh-keygen, which is provided with the SSH package on Linux/Mac systems and comes with the MSysGit package on Windows:

```
$ ssh-keygen
Generating public/private rsa key pair.
Enter file in which to save the key (/home/schacon/.ssh/id_rsa):
Created directory '/home/schacon/.ssh'.
Enter passphrase (empty for no passphrase):
Enter same passphrase again:
Your identification has been saved in /home/schacon/.ssh/id_rsa.
Your public key has been saved in /home/schacon/.ssh/id_rsa.pub.
The key fingerprint is:
d0:82:24:8e:d7:f1:bb:9b:33:53:96:93:49:da:9b:e3 schacon@mylaptop.local
```

First it confirms where you want to save the key (.ssh/id_rsa), and then it asks twice for a passphrase, which you can leave empty if you don't want to type a password when you use the key.

Now, each user that does this has to send their public key to you or whoever is administrating the Git server (assuming you're using an SSH server setup that requires public keys). All they have to do is copy the contents of the .pub file and e-mail it. The public keys look something like this:

```
$ cat ~/.ssh/id_rsa.pub
ssh-rsa AAAAB3NzaC1yc2EAAAABIwAAAQEAklOUpkDHrfHY17SbrmTIpNLTGK9Tjom/BWDSU
GPl+nafzlHDTYW7hdI4yZ5ew18JH4JW9jbhUFrviQzM7xlELEVf4h9lFX5QVkbPppSwg0cda3
Pbv7kOdJ/MTyBlWXFCR+HAo3FXRitBqxiX1nKhXpHAZsMciLq8V6RjsNAQwdsdMFvSlVK/7XA
t3FaoJoAsncM1Q9x5+3VOWw68/eIFmb1zuUFljQJKprrX88XypNDvjYNby6vw/PbOrwert/En
mZ+AW4OZPnTPI89ZPmVMLuayrD2cE86Z/il8b+gw3r3+1nKatmIkjn2so1d01QraTlMqVSsbx
NrRFi9wrf+M7Q== schacon@mylaptop.local
```

For a more in-depth tutorial on creating an SSH key on multiple operating systems, see the GitHub guide on SSH keys at https://help.github.com/articles/generating-ssh-keys.

Setting Up the Server

Let's walk through setting up SSH access on the server side. In this example, you'll use the authorized_keys method for authenticating your users. We also assume you're running a standard Linux distribution like Ubuntu. First, you create a git user and a .ssh directory for that user.

```
$ sudo adduser git
$ su git
$ cd
$ mkdir .ssh
```

Next, you need to add some developer SSH public keys to the authorized_keys file for that user. Let's assume you've received a few keys by e-mail and saved them to temporary files. Again, the public keys look something like this:

```
$ cat /tmp/id_rsa.john.pub
ssh-rsa AAAAB3NzaC1yc2EAAAADAQABAAABAQCB007n/ww+ouN4gSLKssMxXnBOvf9LGt4L
ojG6rs6hPB09j9R/T17/x4lhJAOF3FR1rP6kYBRsWj2aThGw6HXLm9/5zytK6Ztg3RPKK+4k
Yjh6541NYsnEAZuXzOjTTyAUfrtU3Z5E003C4oxOj6HOrfIF1kKI9MAQLMdpGW1GYEIgS9Ez
Sdfd8AcCIicTDWbqLAcU4UpkaX8KyGlLwsNuuGztobF8m72ALC/nLF6JLtPofwFBlgc+myiv
O7TCUSBdLQlgMVOFq1I2uPWQOkOWQAHukEOmfjy2jctxSDBQ220ymjaNsHT4kgtZg2AYYgPq
dAv8JggJICUvax2T9va5 gsg-keypair
```

You just append them to your authorized_keys file:

```
$ cat /tmp/id_rsa.john.pub >> ~/.ssh/authorized_keys
$ cat /tmp/id_rsa.josie.pub >> ~/.ssh/authorized_keys
$ cat /tmp/id_rsa.jessica.pub >> ~/.ssh/authorized_keys
```

Now, you can set up an empty repository for them by running git init with the --bare option, which initializes the repository without a working directory:

```
$ cd /opt/git
$ mkdir project.git
$ cd project.git
$ git init --bare
Initialized empty Git repository in /opt/git/project.git/
```

Then, John, Josie, or Jessica can push the first version of their project into that repository by adding it as a remote and pushing up a branch. Note that someone must shell onto the machine and create a bare repository every time you want to add a project. Let's use gitserver as the hostname of the server on which you've set up your git user and repository. If you're running it internally, and you set up DNS for gitserver to point to that server, then you can use the commands pretty much as is:

```
# on Johns computer
$ cd myproject
$ git init
$ git add.
```

```
$ git commit -m 'initial commit'
$ git remote add origin git@gitserver:/opt/git/project.git
$ git push origin master
```

At this point, the others can clone it down and push changes back up just as easily:

```
$ git clone git@gitserver:/opt/git/project.git
$ vim README
$ git commit -am 'fix for the README file'
$ git push origin master
```

With this method, you can quickly get a read/write Git server up and running for a handful of developers.

You should note that currently all these users can also log in to the server and get a shell as the "git" user. If you want to restrict that, you will have to change the shell to something else in the passwd file.

You can easily restrict the git user to only doing Git activities with a limited shell tool called git-shell that comes with Git. If you set this as your git user's login shell, then the git user can't have normal shell access to your server. To use this, specify git-shell instead of bash or csh for your user's login shell. To do so, you'll likely have to edit your /etc/passwd file:

```
$ sudo vim /etc/passwd
```

At the bottom, you should find a line that looks something like this:

```
git:x:1000:1000::/home/git:/bin/sh
```

Change /bin/sh to /usr/bin/git-shell (or run which git-shell to see where it's installed). The line should look something like this:

```
git:x:1000:1000::/home/git:/usr/bin/git-shell
```

Now, the git user can only use the SSH connection to push and pull Git repositories and can't shell onto the machine. If you try, you'll see a login rejection like this:

```
$ ssh git@gitserver
fatal: Interactive git shell is not enabled.
hint: ~/git-shell-commands should exist and have read and execute access.
Connection to gitserver closed.
```

Now Git network commands will still work just fine but the users won't be able to get a shell. As the output states, you can also set up a directory in the "git" user's home directory that customizes the git-shell command a bit. For instance, you can restrict the Git commands that the server will accept or you can customize the message that users see if they try to SSH in like that. Run git help shell for more information on customizing the shell.

Git Daemon

Next we'll set up a daemon serving repositories over the "Git" protocol. This is common choice for fast, unauthenticated access to your Git data. Remember that because it's not an authenticated service, anything you serve over this protocol is public within it's network.

If you're running this on a server outside your firewall, it should only be used for projects that are publicly visible to the world. If the server you're running it on is inside your firewall, you might use it for projects that a large number of people or computers (continuous integration or build servers) have read-only access to, when you don't want to have to add an SSH key for each.

In any case, the Git protocol is relatively easy to set up. Basically, you need to run this command in a daemonized manner:

```
git daemon --reuseaddr --base-path=/opt/git/ /opt/git/
```

`--reuseaddr` allows the server to restart without waiting for old connections to time out, the `--base-path` option allows people to clone projects without specifying the entire path, and the path at the end tells the Git daemon where to look for repositories to export. If you're running a firewall, you'll also need to punch a hole in it at port 9418 on the box you're setting this up on.

You can daemonize this process a number of ways, depending on the operating system you're running. On an Ubuntu machine, you can use an Upstart script. So, in the following file

```
/etc/event.d/local-git-daemon
```

you put this script:

```
start on startup
stop on shutdown
exec /usr/bin/git daemon \
    --user=git --group=git \
    --reuseaddr \
    --base-path=/opt/git/ \
    /opt/git/
respawn
```

For security reasons, it is strongly encouraged to have this daemon run as a user with read-only permissions to the repositories—you can easily do this by creating a new user `git-ro` and running the daemon as them. For the sake of simplicity we'll simply run it as the same git user that Gitosis is running as.

When you restart your machine, your Git daemon will start automatically and respawn if it goes down. To get it running without having to reboot, you can run this:

```
initctl start local-git-daemon
```

On other systems, you may want to use `xinetd`, a script in your `sysvinit` system, or something else—as long as you get that command daemonized and watched somehow.

Next, you have to tell Git which repositories to allow unauthenticated Git server-based access to. You can do this in each repository by creating a filename `git-daemon-export-ok`.

```
$ cd /path/to/project.git
$ touch git-daemon-export-ok
```

The presence of that file tells Git that it's okay to serve this project without authentication.

Smart HTTP

We now have authenticated access through SSH and unauthenticated access through git://, but there is also a protocol that can do both at the same time. Setting up Smart HTTP is basically just enabling a CGI script that is provided with Git called git-http-backend on the server.git commands, http-backend This CGI will read the path and headers sent by a git fetch or git push to an HTTP URL and determine if the client can communicate over HTTP (which is true for any client since version 1.6.6). If the CGI sees that the client is smart, it will communicate smartly with it, otherwise it will fall back to the dumb behavior (so it is backward compatible for reads with older clients).

Let's walk though a very basic setup. We'll set this up with Apache as the CGI server. If you don't have Apache setup, you can do so on a Linux box with something like this:

```
$ sudo apt-get install apache2 apache2-utils
$ a2enmod cgi alias env
```

This also enables the mod_cgi, mod_alias, and mod_env modules, which are all needed for this to work properly.

Next we need to add some things to the Apache configuration to run the git http-backend as the handler for anything coming into the /git path of your web server.

```
SetEnv GIT_PROJECT_ROOT /opt/git
SetEnv GIT_HTTP_EXPORT_ALL
ScriptAlias /git/ /usr/libexec/git-core/git-http-backend/
```

If you leave out GIT_HTTP_EXPORT_ALL environment variable, then Git will only serve to unauthenticated clients the repositories with the git-daemon-export-ok file in them, just like the Git daemon did.

Then you'll have to tell Apache to allow requests to that path with something like this:

```
<Directory "/usr/lib/git-core*">
    Options ExecCGI Indexes
    Order allow,deny
    Allow from all
    Require all granted
</Directory>
```

Finally you'll want to make writes be authenticated somehow, possibly with an Auth block like this:

```
<LocationMatch "^/git/.*/git-receive-pack$">
    AuthType Basic
    AuthName "Git Access"
    AuthUserFile /opt/git/.htpasswd
    Require valid-user
</LocationMatch>
```

That will require you to create a .htaccess file containing the passwords of all the valid users. Here is an example of adding a "schacon" user to the file:

```
$ htdigest -c /opt/git/.htpasswd "Git Access" schacon
```

There are tons of ways to have Apache authenticate users, you'll have to choose and implement one of them. This is just the simplest example we could come up with. You'll also almost certainly want to set this up over SSL so all this data is encrypted.

We don't want to go too far down the rabbit hole of Apache configuration specifics, since you could well be using a different server or have different authentication needs. The idea is that Git comes with a CGI called git http-backend that when invoked will do all the negotiation to send and receive data over HTTP. It does not implement any authentication itself, but that can easily be controlled at the layer of the web server that invokes it. You can do this with nearly any CGI-capable web server, so go with the one that you know best.

■ **Note**   For more information on configuring authentication in Apache, check out the Apache docs here: http://httpd.apache.org/docs/current/howto/auth.html.

GitWeb

Now that you have basic read/write and read-only access to your project, you may want to set up a simple web-based visualizer. Git comes with a CGI script called GitWeb that is sometimes used for this.

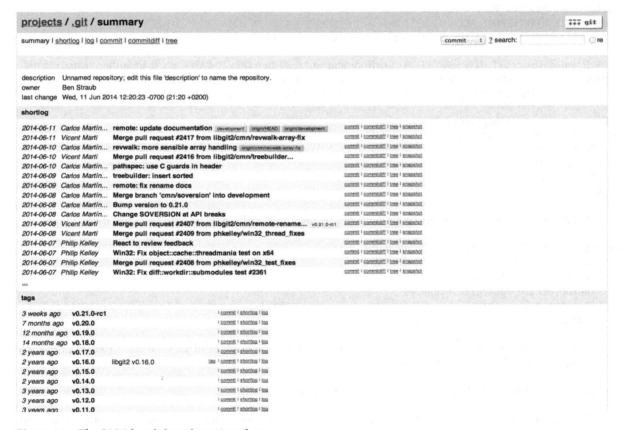

Figure 4-1.   *The GitWeb web-based user interface*

If you want to check out what GitWeb would look like for your project, Git comes with a command to fire up a temporary instance if you have a lightweight server on your system like lighttpd or webrick. On Linux machines, lighttpd is often installed, so you may be able to get it to run by typing git instaweb in your project directory. If you're running a Mac, Leopard comes preinstalled with Ruby, so webrick may be your best bet. To start instaweb with a non-lighttpd handler, you can run it with the --httpd option.

```
$ git instaweb --httpd=webrick
[2009-02-21 10:02:21] INFO  WEBrick 1.3.1
[2009-02-21 10:02:21] INFO  ruby 1.8.6 (2008-03-03) [universal-darwin9.0]
```

That starts up an HTTPD server on port 1234 and then automatically starts a web browser that opens on that page. It's pretty easy on your part. When you're done and want to shut down the server, you can run the same command with the --stop option:

```
$ git instaweb --httpd=webrick --stop
```

If you want to run the web interface on a server all the time for your team or for an open source project you're hosting, you'll need to set up the CGI script to be served by your normal web server. Some Linux distributions have a gitweb package that you may be able to install via apt or yum, so you may want to try that first. We'll walk through installing GitWeb manually very quickly. First, you need to get the Git source code, which GitWeb comes with, and generate the custom CGI script:

```
$ git clone git://git.kernel.org/pub/scm/git/git.git
$ cd git/
$ make GITWEB_PROJECTROOT="/opt/git" prefix=/usr gitweb
    SUBDIR gitweb
    SUBDIR ../
make[2]: `GIT-VERSION-FILE' is up to date.
    GEN gitweb.cgi
    GEN static/gitweb.js
$ sudo cp -Rf gitweb /var/www/
```

Notice that you have to tell the command where to find your Git repositories with the GITWEB_PROJECTROOT variable. Now, you need to make Apache use CGI for that script, for which you can add a VirtualHost:

```
<VirtualHost *:80>
    ServerName gitserver
    DocumentRoot /var/www/gitweb
    <Directory /var/www/gitweb>
        Options ExecCGI +FollowSymLinks +SymLinksIfOwnerMatch
        AllowOverride All
        order allow,deny
        Allow from all
        AddHandler cgi-script cgi
        DirectoryIndex gitweb.cgi
    </Directory>
</VirtualHost>
```

Again, GitWeb can be served with any CGI or Perl capable web server; if you prefer to use something else, it shouldn't be difficult to set up. At this point, you should be able to visit http://gitserver/ to view your repositories online.

GitLab

GitWeb is pretty simplistic though. If you're looking for a more modern, fully featured Git server, there are several open source solutions out there that you can install instead. As GitLab is one of the more popular ones, we'll cover installing and using it as an example. This is a bit more complex than the GitWeb option and likely requires more maintenance, but it is a much more fully featured option.

Installation

GitLab is a database-backed web application, so its installation is a bit more involved than some other git servers. Fortunately, this process is very well-documented and supported.

There are a few methods you can pursue to install GitLab. To get something up and running quickly, you can download a virtual machine image or a one-click installer from `https://bitnami.com/stack/gitlab`, and tweak the configuration to match your particular environment. One nice touch Bitnami has included is the login screen (accessed by typing **alt-→**); it tells you the IP address and default username and password for the installed GitLab.

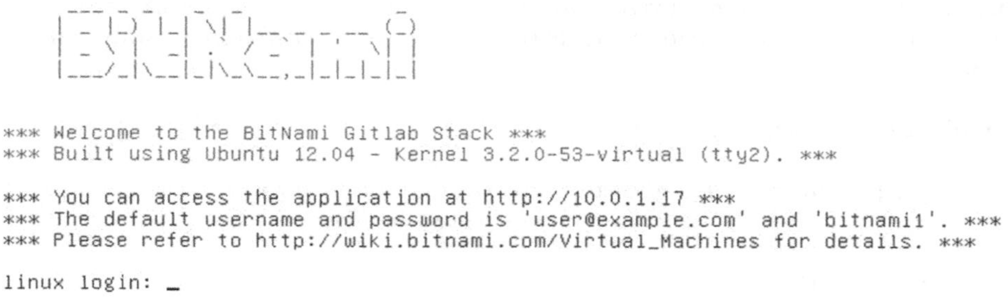

```
 |   |_) |_| \| |___ _ __ _(_)
 |  _ \ |  | | | \___ \ | | | | |
 |___/_| \_|_|\__,_|_|_|_|

*** Welcome to the BitNami Gitlab Stack ***
*** Built using Ubuntu 12.04 - Kernel 3.2.0-53-virtual (tty2). ***

*** You can access the application at http://10.0.1.17 ***
*** The default username and password is 'user@example.com' and 'bitnami1'. ***
*** Please refer to http://wiki.bitnami.com/Virtual_Machines for details. ***

linux login: _
```

Figure 4-2. *The Bitnami GitLab virtual machine login screen*

For anything else, follow the guidance in the GitLab Community Edition readme, which can be found at `https://gitlab.com/gitlab-org/gitlab-ce/tree/master`. There you'll find assistance for installing GitLab using Chef recipes, a virtual machine on Digital Ocean, and RPM and DEB packages (which, as of this writing, are in beta). There's also "unofficial" guidance on getting GitLab running with non-standard operating systems and databases, a fully-manual installation script, and many other topics.

Administration

GitLab's administration interface is accessed over the web. Simply point your browser to the hostname or IP address where GitLab is installed, and log in as an admin user. The default username is `admin@local.host`, and the default password is `5iveL!fe` (which you will be prompted to change as soon as you enter it). Once logged in, click the "Admin area" icon in the menu at the top right.

Figure 4-3. *The "Admin area" item in the GitLab menu*

Users

Users in GitLab are accounts that correspond to people. User accounts don't have a lot of complexity; mainly it's a collection of personal information attached to login data. Each user account comes with a namespace, which is a logical grouping of projects that belong to that user. If the user `jane` had a project named `project`, that project's URL would be `http://server/jane/project`.

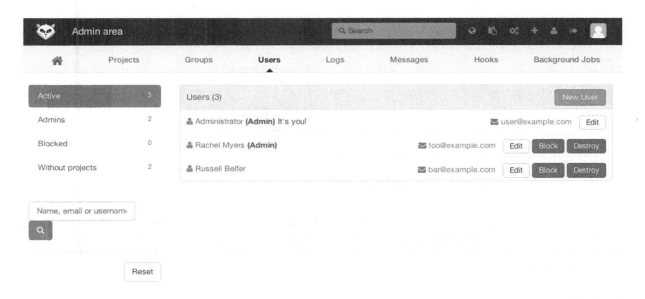

Figure 4-4. *The GitLab user administration screen*

Removing a user can be done in two ways. *Blocking* a user prevents them from logging into the GitLab instance, but all the data under that user's namespace will be preserved, and commits signed with that user's email address will still link back to their profile.

Destroying a user, on the other hand, completely removes them from the database and filesystem. All projects and data in their namespace are removed, and any groups they own will also be removed. This is obviously a much more permanent and destructive action, and its uses are rare.

Groups

A GitLab group is an assemblage of projects, along with data about how users can access those projects. Each group has a project namespace (the same way that users do), so if the group training has a project materials, its URL would be `http://server/training/materials`.

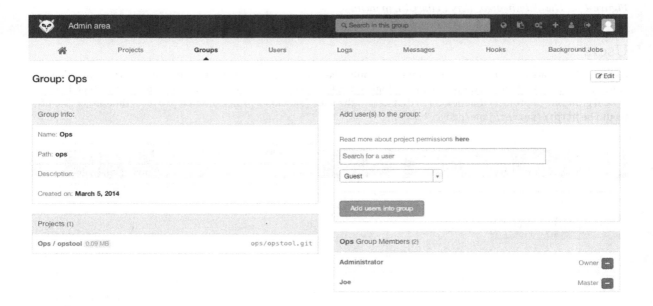

Figure 4-5. *The GitLab group administration screen*

Each group is associated with a number of users, each of which has a level of permissions for the group's projects and the group itself. These range from "Guest" (issues and chat only) to "Owner" (full control of the group, its members, and its projects). The types of permissions are too numerous to list here, but GitLab has a helpful link on the administration screen.

Projects

A GitLab project roughly corresponds to a single git repository. Every project belongs to a single namespace, either a user or a group. If the project belongs to a user, the owner of the project has direct control over who has access to the project; if the project belongs to a group, the group's user-level permissions will also take effect.

Every project also has a visibility level, which controls who has read access to that project's pages and repository. If a project is Private, the project's owner must explicitly grant access to specific users. An Internal project is visible to any logged-in user, and a Public project is visible to anyone. Note that this controls both git "fetch" access as well as access to the web UI for that project.

Hooks

GitLab includes support for hooks, both at a project or system level. For either of these, the GitLab server will perform an HTTP POST with some descriptive JSON whenever relevant events occur. This is a great way to connect your git repositories and GitLab instance to the rest of your development automation, such as CI servers, chat rooms, or deployment tools.

Basic Usage

The first thing you'll want to do with GitLab is create a new project. This is accomplished by clicking the + icon on the toolbar. You'll be asked for the project's name, which namespace it should belong to, and what its visibility level should be. Most of what you specify here isn't permanent, and can be re-adjusted later through the settings interface. Click Create Project, and you're done.

Once the project exists, you'll probably want to connect it with a local Git repository. Each project is accessible over HTTPS or SSH, either of which can be used to configure a Git remote. The URLs are visible at the top of the project's home page. For an existing local repository, this command will create a remote named `gitlab` to the hosted location:

```
$ git remote add gitlab https://server/namespace/project.git
```

If you don't have a local copy of the repository, you can simply do this:

```
$ git clone https://server/namespace/project.git
```

The web UI provides access to several useful views of the repository itself. Each project's home page shows recent activity, and links along the top will lead you to views of the project's files and commit log.

Working Together

The simplest way of working together on a GitLab project is by giving another user direct push access to the git repository. You can add a user to a project by going to the Members section of that project's settings, and associating the new user with an access level (the different access levels are discussed a bit in Groups). By giving a user an access level of Developer or above, that user can push commits and branches directly to the repository with impunity.

Another, more decoupled way of collaboration is by using merge requests. This feature enables any user that can see a project to contribute to it in a controlled way. Users with direct access can simply create a branch, push commits to it, and open a merge request from their branch back into master or any other branch. Users who don't have push permissions for a repository can "fork" it (create their own copy), push commits to that copy, and open a merge request from their fork back to the main project. This model allows the owner to be in full control of what goes into the repository and when, while allowing contributions from untrusted users.

Merge requests and issues are the main units of long-lived discussion in GitLab. Each merge request allows a line-by-line discussion of the proposed change (which supports a lightweight kind of code review), as well as a general overall discussion thread. Both can be assigned to users, or organized into milestones.

This section has focused mainly on the Git-related parts of GitLab, but it's a fairly mature system, and provides many other features that can help your team work together. These include project wikis, discussion "walls", and system maintenance tools. One benefit to GitLab is that, once the server is set up and running, you'll rarely need to tweak a configuration file or access the server via SSH; most administration and general usage can be accomplished through the in-browser interface.

Third Party Hosted Options

If you don't want to go through all of the work involved in setting up your own Git server, you have several options for hosting your Git projects on an external dedicated hosting site. Doing so offers a number of advantages: a hosting site is generally quick to set up and easy to start projects on, and no server maintenance or monitoring is involved. Even if you set up and run your own server internally, you may still want to use a public hosting site for your open source code—generally easier for the open source community to find and help you with.

These days, you have a huge number of hosting options to choose from, each with different advantages and disadvantages. To see an up-to-date list, check out the GitHosting page on the main Git wiki at https://git.wiki.kernel.org/index.php/GitHosting.

We'll cover using GitHub in detail in Chapter 6, as it is the largest Git host out there and you may need to interact with projects hosted on it in any case, but there are dozens more to choose from should you not want to set up your own Git server.

Summary

You have several options to get a remote Git repository up and running so that you can collaborate with others or share your work.

Running your own server gives you a lot of control and allows you to run the server within your own firewall, but such a server generally requires a fair amount of your time to set up and maintain. If you place your data on a hosted server, it's easy to set up and maintain; however, you have to be able to keep your code on someone else's servers, and some organizations don't allow that.

It should be fairly straightforward to determine which solution or combination of solutions is appropriate for you and your organization.

CHAPTER 5

■ ■ ■

Distributed Git

Now that you have a remote Git repository set up as a point for all the developers to share their code, and you're familiar with basic Git commands in a local workflow, you'll look at how to utilize some of the distributed workflows that Git affords you.

In this chapter, you'll see how to work with Git in a distributed environment as a contributor and an integrator. That is, you'll learn how to contribute code successfully to a project and make it as easy on you and the project maintainer as possible, and also how to maintain a project successfully with a number of developers contributing.

Distributed Workflows

Unlike Centralized Version Control Systems (CVCSs), the distributed nature of Git allows you to be far more flexible in how developers collaborate on projects. In centralized systems, every developer is a node working more or less equally on a central hub. In Git, however, every developer is potentially both a node and a hub—that is, every developer can both contribute code to other repositories and maintain a public repository on which others can base their work and which they can contribute to. This opens a vast range of workflow possibilities for your project and/or your team, so we'll cover a few common paradigms that take advantage of this flexibility. We'll go over the strengths and possible weaknesses of each design; you can choose a single one to use, or you can mix and match features from each.

Centralized Workflow

In centralized systems, there is generally a single collaboration model—the centralized workflow. One central hub, or repository, can accept code, and everyone synchronizes their work to it. A number of developers are nodes—consumers of that hub—and synchronize to that one place.

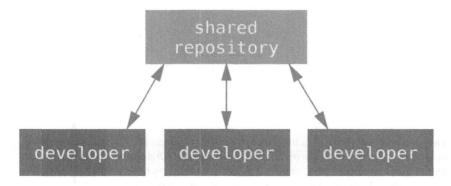

Figure 5-1. *Centralized workflow*

This means that if two developers clone from the hub and both make changes, the first developer to push their changes back up can do so with no problems. The second developer must merge in the first one's work before pushing changes up, so as not to overwrite the first developer's changes. This concept is as true in Git as it is in Subversion (or any CVCS), and this model works perfectly well in Git.

If you are already comfortable with a centralized workflow in your company or team, you can easily continue using that workflow with Git. Simply set up a single repository, and give everyone on your team push access; Git won't let users overwrite each other. Say John and Jessica both start working at the same time. John finishes his change and pushes it to the server. Then Jessica tries to push her changes, but the server rejects them. She is told that she's trying to push non–fast-forward changes and that she won't be able to do so until she fetches and merges. This workflow is attractive to a lot of people because it's a paradigm that many are familiar and comfortable with.

This is also not limited to small teams. With Git's branching model, it's possible for hundreds of developers to successfully work on a single project through dozens of branches simultaneously.

Integration-Manager Workflow

Because Git allows you to have multiple remote repositories, it's possible to have a workflow where each developer has write access to their own public repository and read access to everyone else's. This scenario often includes a canonical repository that represents the "official" project. To contribute to that project, you create your own public clone of the project and push your changes to it. Then, you can send a request to the maintainer of the main project to pull in your changes. The maintainer can then add your repository as a remote, test your changes locally, merge them into their branch, and push back to their repository. The process works as follows:

1. The project maintainer pushes to their public repository.

2. A contributor clones that repository and makes changes.

3. The contributor pushes to their own public copy.

4. The contributor sends the maintainer an e-mail asking them to pull changes.

5. The maintainer adds the contributor's repo as a remote and merges locally.

6. The maintainer pushes merged changes to the main repository.

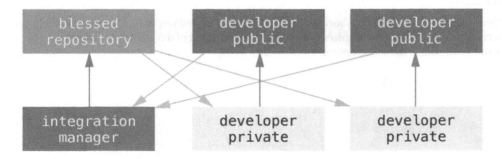

Figure 5-2. *Integration-manager workflow*

This is a very common workflow with hub-based tools such as GitHub or GitLab, where it's easy to fork a project and push your changes into your fork for everyone to see. One of the main advantages of this approach is that you can continue to work, and the maintainer of the main repository can pull in your changes at any time. Contributors don't have to wait for the project to incorporate their changes—each party can work at their own pace.

Dictator and Lieutenants Workflow

This is a variant of a multiple-repository workflow. It's generally used by huge projects with hundreds of collaborators; one famous example is the Linux kernel. Various integration managers are in charge of certain parts of the repository; they're called lieutenants. All the lieutenants have one integration manager known as the benevolent dictator. The benevolent dictator's repository serves as the reference repository from which all the collaborators need to pull. The process works like this:

1. Regular developers work on their topic branch and rebase their work on top of master. The master branch is that of the dictator.

2. Lieutenants merge the developers' topic branches into their master branch.

3. The dictator merges the lieutenants' master branches into the dictator's master branch.

4. The dictator pushes their master to the reference repository so the other developers can rebase on it.

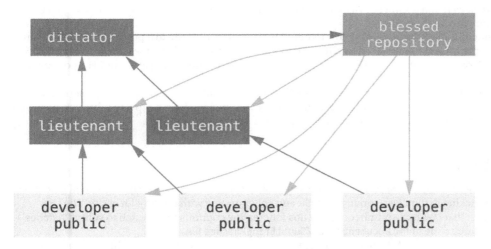

Figure 5-3. *Benevolent dictator workflow*

This kind of workflow isn't common, but can be useful in very big projects, or in highly hierarchical environments. It allows the project leader (the dictator) to delegate much of the work and collect large subsets of code at multiple points before integrating them.

Workflows Summary

These are some commonly used workflows that are possible with a distributed system like Git, but you can see that many variations are possible to suit your particular real-world workflow. Now that you can (hopefully) determine which workflow combination may work for you, we'll cover some more specific examples of how to accomplish the main roles that make up the different flows. In the next section, you'll learn about a few common patterns for contributing to a project.

Contributing to a Project

The main difficulty with describing how to contribute to a project is that there are a huge number of variations on how it's done. Because Git is very flexible, people can and do work together in many ways, and it's problematic to describe how you should contribute—every project is a bit different. Some of the variables involved are active contributor count, chosen workflow, your commit access, and possibly the external contribution method.

The first variable is active contributor count—how many users are actively contributing code to this project, and how often? In many instances, you'll have two or three developers with a few commits a day, or possibly less for somewhat dormant projects. For larger companies or projects, the number of developers could be in the thousands, with hundreds or thousands of commits coming in each day. This is important because with more and more developers, you run into more issues with making sure your code applies cleanly or can be easily merged. Changes you submit may be rendered obsolete or severely broken by work that is merged in while you were working or while your changes were waiting to be approved or applied. How can you keep your code consistently up to date and your commits valid?

The next variable is the workflow in use for the project. Is it centralized, with each developer having equal write access to the main codeline? Does the project have a maintainer or integration manager who checks all the patches? Are all the patches peer-reviewed and approved? Are you involved in that process? Is a lieutenant system in place, and do you have to submit your work to them first?

The next issue is your commit access. The workflow required in order to contribute to a project is much different if you have write access to the project than if you don't. If you don't have write access, how does the project prefer to accept contributed work? Does it even have a policy? How much work are you contributing at a time? How often do you contribute?

All these questions can affect how you contribute effectively to a project and what workflows are preferred or available to you. We'll cover aspects of each of these in a series of use cases, moving from simple to more complex; you should be able to construct the specific workflows you need in practice from these examples.

Commit Guidelines

Before we start looking at the specific use cases, here's a quick note about commit messages. Having a good guideline for creating commits and sticking to it makes working with Git and collaborating with others a lot easier. The Git project provides a document that lays out a number of good tips for creating commits from which to submit patches—you can read it in the Git source code in the `Documentation/SubmittingPatches` file.

First, you don't want to submit any whitespace errors. Git provides an easy way to check for this—before you commit, run `git diff --check`, which identifies possible whitespace errors and lists them for you.

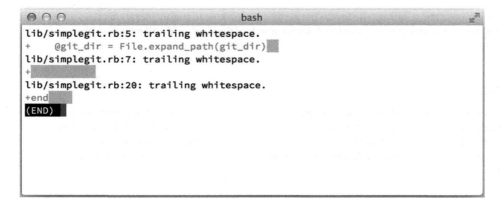

Figure 5-4. *Output of git diff -check*

If you run that command before committing, you can tell if you're about to commit whitespace issues that may annoy other developers.

Next, try to make each commit a logically separate changeset. If you can, try to make your changes digestible – don't code for a whole weekend on five different issues and then submit them all as one massive commit on Monday. Even if you don't commit during the weekend, use the staging area on Monday to split your work into at least one commit per issue, with a useful message per commit. If some of the changes modify the same file, try to use git add --patch to partially stage files. The project snapshot at the tip of the branch is identical whether you do one commit or five, as long as all the changes are added at some point, so try to make things easier on your fellow developers when they have to review your changes. This approach also makes it easier to pull out or revert one of the changesets if you need to later.

The last thing to keep in mind is the commit message. Getting in the habit of creating quality commit messages makes using and collaborating with Git a lot easier. As a general rule, your messages should start with a single line that's no more than about 50 characters and that describes the changeset concisely, followed by a blank line, followed by a more detailed explanation. The Git project requires that the more detailed explanation include your motivation for the change and contrast its implementation with previous behavior—this is a good guideline to follow. It's also a good idea to use the imperative present tense in these messages. In other words, use commands. Instead of "I added tests for" or "Adding tests for," use "Add tests for." Here is a template originally written by Tim Pope:

```
Short (50 chars or less) summary of changes

More detailed explanatory text, if necessary. Wrap it to
about 72 characters or so. In some contexts, the first
line is treated as the subject of an email and the rest of
the text as the body. The blank line separating the
summary from the body is critical (unless you omit the body
entirely); tools like rebase can get confused if you run
the two together.

Further paragraphs come after blank lines.

  - Bullet points are okay, too

  - Typically a hyphen or asterisk is used for the bullet,
    preceded by a single space, with blank lines in
    between, but conventions vary here
```

If all your commit messages look like this, things will be a lot easier for you and the developers you work with. The Git project has well-formatted commit messages—try running git log --no-merges there to see what a nicely formatted project-commit history looks like.

In the following examples, and throughout most of this book, for the sake of brevity this book doesn't have nicely formatted messages like this; instead, we use the -m option to git commit. Do as we say, not as we do.

Private Small Team

The simplest setup you're likely to encounter is a private project with one or two other developers. "Private," in this context, means closed-source—not accessible to the outside world. You and the other developers all have push access to the repository.

In this environment, you can follow a workflow similar to what you might do when using Subversion or another centralized system. You still get the advantages of things like offline committing and vastly simpler branching and merging, but the workflow can be very similar; the main difference is that merges happen client-side rather than on the server at commit time. Let's see what it might look like when two developers start to work together with a shared repository. The first developer, John, clones the repository, makes a change, and commits locally. (The protocol messages have been replaced with . . . in these examples to shorten them somewhat.)

```
# John's Machine
$ git clone john@githost:simplegit.git
Initialized empty Git repository in /home/john/simplegit/.git/
...
$ cd simplegit/
$ vim lib/simplegit.rb
$ git commit -am 'removed invalid default value'
[master 738ee87] removed invalid default value
 1 files changed, 1 insertions(+), 1 deletions(-)
```

The second developer, Jessica, does the same thing—clones the repository and commits a change:

```
# Jessica's Machine
$ git clone jessica@githost:simplegit.git
Initialized empty Git repository in /home/jessica/simplegit/.git/
...
$ cd simplegit/
$ vim TODO
$ git commit -am 'add reset task'
[master fbff5bc] add reset task
 1 files changed, 1 insertions(+), 0 deletions(-)
```

Now, Jessica pushes her work up to the server:

```
# Jessica's Machine
$ git push origin master
...
To jessica@githost:simplegit.git
   1edee6b..fbff5bc  master -> master
```
John tries to push his change up, too:

```
# John's Machine
$ git push origin master
To john@githost:simplegit.git
 ! [rejected] master -> master (non-fast forward)
error: failed to push some refs to 'john@githost:simplegit.git'
```

John isn't allowed to push because Jessica has pushed in the meantime. This is especially important to understand if you're used to Subversion, because you'll notice that the two developers didn't edit the same file. Although Subversion automatically does such a merge on the server if different files are edited, in Git you must merge the commits locally. John has to fetch Jessica's changes and merge them in before he will be allowed to push:

```
$ git fetch origin
...
From john@githost:simplegit
 + 049d078...fbff5bc master -> origin/master
```

At this point, John's local repository looks something like this:

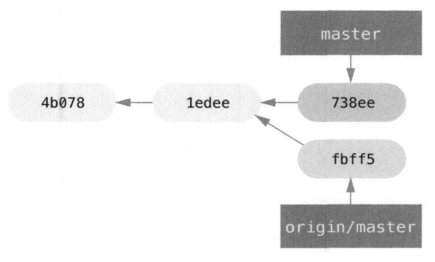

Figure 5-5. *John's divergent history*

John has a reference to the changes Jessica pushed up, but he has to merge them into his own work before he is allowed to push:

```
$ git merge origin/master
Merge made by recursive.
 TODO |    1 +
 1 files changed, 1 insertions(+), 0 deletions(-)
```

The merge goes smoothly. John's commit history now looks like this:

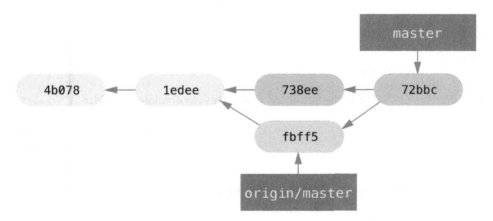

Figure 5-6. *John's repository after merging origin/master*

Now, John can test his code to make sure it still works properly, and then he can push his new merged work up to the server:

```
$ git push origin master
...
To john@githost:simplegit.git
   fbff5bc..72bbc59  master -> master
```

Finally, John's commit history looks like this:

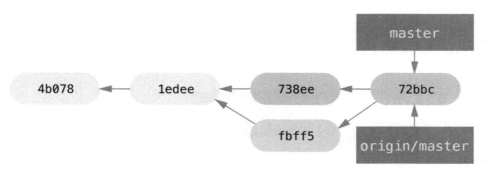

Figure 5-7. *John's history after pushing to the origin server*

In the meantime, Jessica has been working on a topic branch. She's created a topic branch called issue54 and done three commits on that branch. She hasn't fetched John's changes yet, so her commit history looks like this:

```
Jessica's topic branch.
Figure 5. Jessica's topic branch.
```

Jessica wants to sync up with John, so she fetches:

```
# Jessica's Machine
$ git fetch origin
...
From jessica@githost:simplegit
   fbff5bc..72bbc59  master -> origin/master
```

That pulls down the work John has pushed up in the meantime. Jessica's history now looks like this:

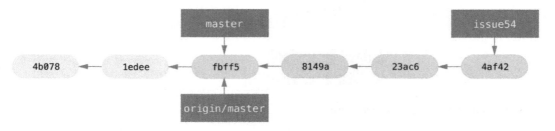

Figure 5-8. *Jessica's history after fetching John's changes*

Jessica thinks her topic branch is ready, but she wants to know what she has to merge into her work so that she can push. She runs git log to find out:

```
$ git log --no-merges issue54..origin/master
commit 738ee872852dfaa9d6634e0dea7a324040193016
Author: John Smith <jsmith@example.com>
Date:    Fri May 29 16:01:27 2009 -0700

   removed invalid default value
```

The issue54..origin/master syntax is a log filter that asks Git to only show the list of commits that are on the latter branch (in this case origin/master) that are not on the first branch (in this case issue54).

For now, we can see from the output that there is a single commit that John has made that Jessica has not merged in. If she merges origin/master, that is the single commit that will modify her local work.

Now, Jessica can merge her topic work into her master branch, merge John's work (origin/master) into her master branch, and then push back to the server again. First, she switches back to her master branch to integrate all this work:

```
$ git checkout master
Switched to branch "master"
Your branch is behind 'origin/master' by 2 commits, and can be fast-forwarded.
```

She can merge either origin/master or issue54 first—they're both upstream, so the order doesn't matter. The end snapshot should be identical no matter which order she chooses; only the history will be slightly different. She chooses to merge in issue54 first:

```
$ git merge issue54
Updating fbff5bc..4af4298
Fast forward
 README          |    1 +
 lib/simplegit.rb |    6 +++++-
 2 files changed, 6 insertions(+), 1 deletions(-)
```

No problems occur; as you can see it, was a simple fast-forward. Now Jessica merges in John's work (origin/master):

```
$ git merge origin/master
Auto-merging lib/simplegit.rb
Merge made by recursive.
 lib/simplegit.rb |    2 +-
 1 files changed, 1 insertions(+), 1 deletions(-)
```

Everything merges cleanly, and Jessica's history looks like this:

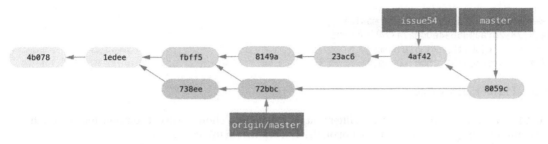

Figure 5-9. *Jessica's history after merging John's changes*

Now `origin/master` is reachable from Jessica's `master` branch, so she should be able to successfully push (assuming John hasn't pushed again in the meantime):

```
$ git push origin master
...
To jessica@githost:simplegit.git
   72bbc59..8059c15  master -> master
```

Each developer has committed a few times and merged each other's work successfully.

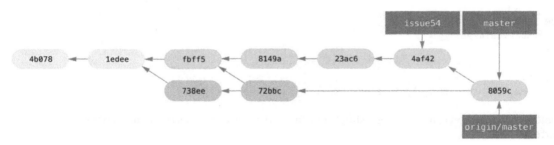

Figure 5-10. *Jessica's history after pushing all changes back to the server*

That is one of the simplest workflows. You work for a while, generally in a topic branch, and merge into your master branch when it's ready to be integrated. When you want to share that work, you merge it into your own master branch, then fetch and merge origin/master if it has changed, and finally push to the master branch on the server. The general sequence is something like this:

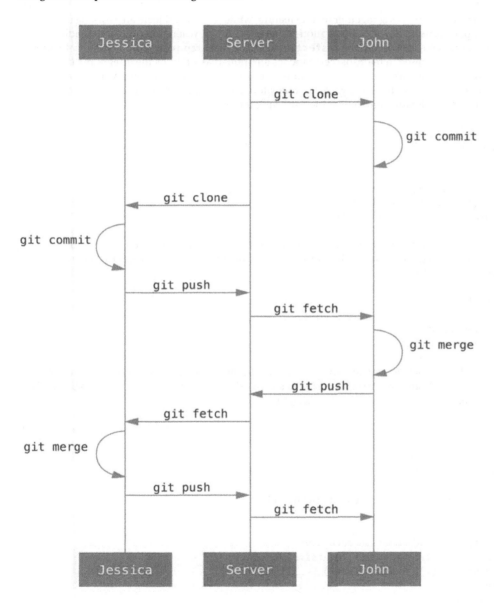

Figure 5-11. *General sequence of events for a simple multiple-developer Git workflow*

Private Managed Team

In this next scenario, you'll look at contributor roles in a larger private group. You'll learn how to work in an environment where small groups collaborate on features and then those team-based contributions are integrated by another party.

Let's say that John and Jessica are working together on one feature, while Jessica and Josie are working on a second. In this case, the company is using a type of integration-manager workflow where the work of the individual groups is integrated only by certain engineers, and the master branch of the main repo can be updated only by those engineers. In this scenario, all work is done in team-based branches and pulled together by the integrators later.

Let's follow Jessica's workflow as she works on her two features, collaborating in parallel with two different developers in this environment. Assuming she already has her repository cloned, she decides to work on featureA first. She creates a new branch for the feature and does some work on it there:

```
# Jessica's Machine
$ git checkout -b featureA
Switched to a new branch "featureA"
$ vim lib/simplegit.rb
$ git commit -am 'add limit to log function'
[featureA 3300904] add limit to log function
 1 files changed, 1 insertions(+), 1 deletions(-)
```

At this point, she needs to share her work with John, so she pushes her featureA branch commits up to the server. Jessica doesn't have push access to the master branch—only the integrators do—so she has to push to another branch in order to collaborate with John:

```
$ git push -u origin featureA
...
To jessica@githost:simplegit.git
 * [new branch] featureA -> featureA
```

Jessica e-mails John to tell him that she's pushed some work into a branch named featureA and he can look at it now. While she waits for feedback from John, Jessica decides to start working on featureB with Josie. To begin, she starts a new feature branch, basing it off the server's master branch:

```
# Jessica's Machine
$ git fetch origin
$ git checkout -b featureB origin/master
Switched to a new branch 'featureB'
```

Now, Jessica makes a couple of commits on the featureB branch:

```
$ vim lib/simplegit.rb
$ git commit -am 'made the ls-tree function recursive'
[featureB e5b0fdc] made the ls-tree function recursive
 1 files changed, 1 insertions(+), 1 deletions(-)
$ vim lib/simplegit.rb
$ git commit -am 'add ls-files'
[featureB 8512791] add ls-files
 1 files changed, 5 insertions(+), 0 deletions(-)
```

Jessica's repository looks like this:

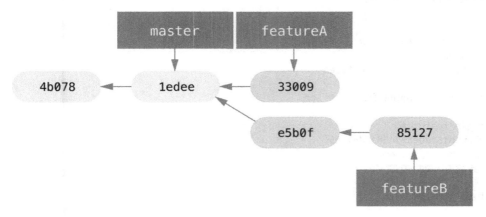

Figure 5-12. *Jessica's initial commit history*

She's ready to push up her work, but gets an e-mail from Josie that a branch with some initial work on it was already pushed to the server as featureBee. Jessica first needs to merge those changes in with her own before she can push to the server. She can then fetch Josie's changes down with git fetch:

```
$ git fetch origin
...
From jessica@githost:simplegit
 * [new branch] featureBee -> origin/featureBee
```

Jessica can now merge this into the work she did with git merge:

```
$ git merge origin/featureBee
Auto-merging lib/simplegit.rb
Merge made by recursive.
 lib/simplegit.rb |    4 ++++
 1 files changed, 4 insertions(+), 0 deletions(-)
```

There is a bit of a problem—she needs to push the merged work in her featureB branch to the featureBee branch on the server. She can do so by specifying the local branch followed by a colon (:) followed by the remote branch to the git push command:

```
$ git push -u origin featureB:featureBee
...
To jessica@githost:simplegit.git
   fba9af8..cd685d1  featureB -> featureBee
```

This is called a refspec. Also notice the -u flag; this is short for --set-upstream, which configures the branches for easier pushing and pulling later.

Next, John e-mails Jessica to say he's pushed some changes to the featureA branch and ask her to verify them. She runs a git fetch to pull down those changes:

```
$ git fetch origin
...
From jessica@githost:simplegit
   3300904..aad881d  featureA -> origin/featureA
```

Then, she can see what has been changed with git log:

```
$ git log featureA..origin/featureA
commit aad881d154acdaeb2b6b18ea0e827ed8a6d671e6
Author: John Smith <jsmith@example.com>
Date:   Fri May 29 19:57:33 2009 -0700

   changed log output to 30 from 25
```

Finally, she merges John's work into her own featureA branch:

```
$ git checkout featureA
Switched to branch "featureA"
$ git merge origin/featureA
Updating 3300904..aad881d
Fast forward
 lib/simplegit.rb |   10 +++++++++-
1 files changed, 9 insertions(+), 1 deletions(-)
```

Jessica wants to tweak something, so she commits again and then pushes this back up to the server:

```
$ git commit -am 'small tweak'
[featureA ed774b3] small tweak
 1 files changed, 1 insertions(+), 1 deletions(-)
$ git push
...
To jessica@githost:simplegit.git
   3300904..ed774b3  featureA -> featureA
```

Jessica's commit history now looks something like this:

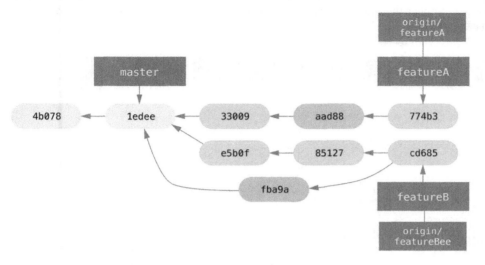

Figure 5-13. *Jessica's history after committing on a feature branch*

Jessica, Josie, and John inform the integrators that the featureA and featureBee branches on the server are ready for integration into the mainline. After the integrators merge these branches into the mainline, a fetch will bring down the new merge commit, making the history look like this:

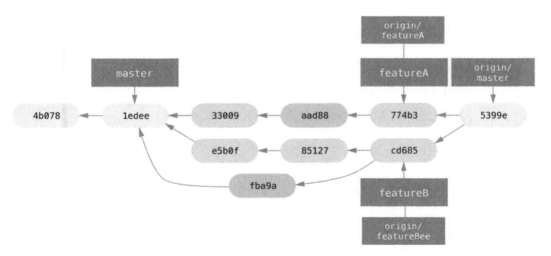

Figure 5-14. *Jessica's history after merging both her topic branches*

Many groups switch to Git because of this ability to have multiple teams working in parallel, merging the different lines of work late in the process. The ability of smaller subgroups of a team to collaborate via remote branches without necessarily having to involve or impede the entire team is a huge benefit of Git. The sequence for the workflow you saw here is something like this:

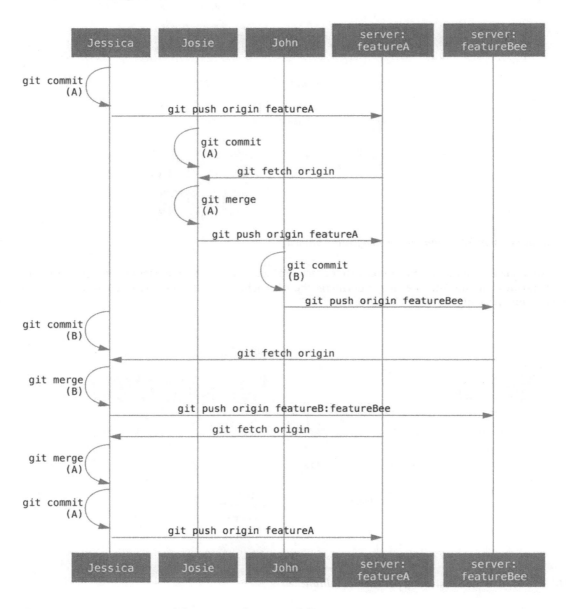

Figure 5-15. *Basic sequence of this managed-team workflow*

Public Project, Fork

Contributing to public projects is a bit different. Because you don't have the permissions to directly update branches on the project, you have to get the work to the maintainers some other way. This first example describes contributing via forking on Git hosts that support easy forking. Many hosting sites support this (including GitHub, BitBucket, Google Code, repo.or.cz, and others), and many project maintainers expect this style of contribution. The next section deals with projects that prefer to accept contributed patches via e-mail.

First, you'll probably want to clone the main repository, create a topic branch for the patch or patch series you're planning to contribute, and do your work there. The sequence looks basically like this:

```
$ git clone (url)
$ cd project
$ git checkout -b featureA
# (work)
$ git commit
# (work)
$ git commit
```

■ **Note**   You may want to use `rebase -i` to squash your work down to a single commit, or rearrange the work in the commits to make the patch easier for the maintainer to review.

When your branch work is finished and you're ready to contribute it back to the maintainers, go to the original project page and click the "Fork" button, creating your own writable fork of the project. You then need to add in this new repository URL as a second remote, in this case named `myfork`:

```
$ git remote add myfork (url)
```

Then you need to push your work up to it. It's easiest to push the remote branch you're working on up to your repository, rather than merging into your master branch and pushing that up. The reason is that if the work isn't accepted or is cherry picked, you don't have to rewind your master branch. If the maintainers merge, rebase, or cherry-pick your work, you'll eventually get it back via pulling from their repository anyhow:

```
$ git push -u myfork featureA
```

When your work has been pushed up to your fork, you need to notify the maintainer. This is often called a pull request, and you can either generate it via the website—GitHub has it's own Pull Request mechanism that we'll go over in Chapter 6—or you can run the `git request-pull` command and e-mail the output to the project maintainer manually.

The `request-pull` command takes the base branch into which you want your topic branch pulled and the Git repository URL you want them to pull from, and outputs a summary of all the changes you're asking to be pulled in. For instance, if Jessica wants to send John a pull request, and she's done two commits on the topic branch she just pushed up, she can run this:

```
$ git request-pull origin/master myfork
The following changes since commit 1edee6b1d61823a2de3b09c160d7080b8d1b3a40:
  John Smith (1):
        added a new function
```

are available in the git repository at:

```
  git://githost/simplegit.git featureA
```

```
Jessica Smith (2):
      add limit to log function
      change log output to 30 from 25
```

```
  lib/simplegit.rb |   10 +++++++++-
  1 files changed, 9 insertions(+), 1 deletions(-)
```

The output can be sent to the maintainer—it tells them where the work was branched from, summarizes the commits, and tells where to pull this work from.

On a project for which you're not the maintainer, it's generally easier to have a branch like master always track origin/master and to do your work in topic branches that you can easily discard if they're rejected. Having work themes isolated into topic branches also makes it easier for you to rebase your work if the tip of the main repository has moved in the meantime and your commits no longer apply cleanly. For example, if you want to submit a second topic of work to the project, don't continue working on the topic branch you just pushed up—start over from the main repository's master branch:

```
$ git checkout -b featureB origin/master
# (work)
$ git commit
$ git push myfork featureB
# (email maintainer)
$ git fetch origin
```

Now, each of your topics is contained within a silo—similar to a patch queue—that you can rewrite, rebase, and modify without the topics interfering or interdepending on each other, like so:

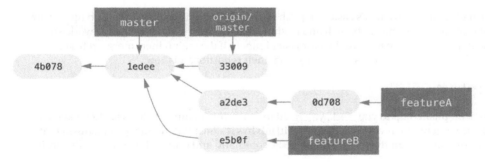

Figure 5-16. *Initial commit history with featureB work*

Let's say the project maintainer has pulled in a bunch of other patches and tried your first branch, but it no longer cleanly merges. In this case, you can try to rebase that branch on top of origin/master, resolve the conflicts for the maintainer, and then resubmit your changes:

```
$ git checkout featureA
$ git rebase origin/master
$ git push -f myfork featureA
```

This rewrites your history to now look like Commit history after featureA work.

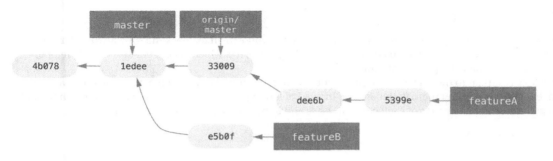

Figure 5-17. *Commit history after featureA work*

Because you rebased the branch, you have to specify the -f to your push command in order to be able to replace the featureA branch on the server with a commit that isn't a descendant of it. An alternative would be to push this new work to a different branch on the server (perhaps called featureAv2).

Let's look at one more possible scenario: the maintainer has looked at work in your second branch and likes the concept but would like you to change an implementation detail. You'll also take this opportunity to move the work to be based off the project's current master branch. You start a new branch based off the current origin/master branch, squash the featureB changes there, resolve any conflicts, make the implementation change, and then push that up as a new branch:

```
$ git checkout -b featureBv2 origin/master^{}
$ git merge --no-commit --squash featureB
# (change implementation)
$ git commit
$ git push myfork featureBv2
```

The --squash option takes all the work on the merged branch and squashes it into one non-merge commit on top of the branch you're on. The --no-commit option tells Git not to automatically record a commit. This allows you to introduce all the changes from another branch and then make more changes before recording the new commit.

Now you can send the maintainer a message that you've made the requested changes and they can find those changes in your featureBv2 branch.

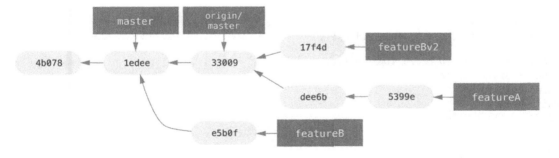

Figure 5-18. *Commit history after featureBv2 work*

Public Project, E-Mail

Many projects have established procedures for accepting patches—you'll need to check the specific rules for each project, because they will differ. Since there are several older, larger projects which accept patches via a developer mailing list, we'll go over an example of that now.

The workflow is similar to the previous use case—you create topic branches for each patch series you work on. The difference is how you submit them to the project. Instead of forking the project and pushing to your own writable version, you generate e-mail versions of each commit series and e-mail them to the developer mailing list:

```
$ git checkout -b topicA
# (work)
$ git commit
# (work)
$ git commit
```

Now you have two commits that you want to send to the mailing list. You use git format-patch to generate the mbox-formatted files that you can e-mail to the list—it turns each commit into an e-mail message with the first line of the commit message as the subject and the rest of the message plus the patch that the commit introduces as the body. The nice thing about this is that applying a patch from an e-mail generated with format-patch preserves all the commit information properly.

```
$ git format-patch -M origin/master
0001-add-limit-to-log-function.patch
0002-changed-log-output-to-30-from-25.patch
```

The format-patch command prints out the names of the patch files it creates. The -M switch tells Git to look for renames. The files end up looking like this:

```
$ cat 0001-add-limit-to-log-function.patch
From 330090432754092d704da8e76ca5c05c198e71a8 Mon Sep 17 00:00:00 2001
From: Jessica Smith <jessica@example.com>
Date: Sun, 6 Apr 2008 10:17:23 -0700
Subject: [PATCH 1/2] add limit to log function

Limit log functionality to the first 20

---
 lib/simplegit.rb |    2 +-
 1 files changed, 1 insertions(+), 1 deletions(-)

diff --git a/lib/simplegit.rb b/lib/simplegit.rb
index 76f47bc..f9815f1 100644
--- a/lib/simplegit.rb
+++ b/lib/simplegit.rb
@@ -14,7 +14,7 @@ class SimpleGit
   end

   def log(treeish = 'master')
-  command("git log #{treeish}")
+  command("git log -n 20 #{treeish}")
   end

   def ls_tree(treeish = 'master')
--
2.1.0
```

You can also edit these patch files to add more information for the e-mail list that you don't want to show up in the commit message. If you add text between the --- line and the beginning of the patch (the diff --git line), then developers can read it; but applying the patch excludes it.

To e-mail this to a mailing list, you can either paste the file into your e-mail program or send it via a command-line program. Pasting the text often causes formatting issues, especially with "smarter" clients that don't preserve newlines and other whitespace appropriately. Luckily, Git provides a tool to help you send properly formatted patches via IMAP, which may be easier for you. We'll demonstrate how to send a patch via Gmail, which happens to be the e-mail agent we know best; you can read detailed instructions for a number of mail programs at the end of the aforementioned Documentation/SubmittingPatches file in the Git source code.

First, you need to set up the imap section in your ~/.gitconfig file. You can set each value separately with a series of git config commands, or you can add them manually, but in the end your config file should look something like this:

```
[imap]
  folder = "[Gmail]/Drafts"
  host = imaps://imap.gmail.com
  user = user@gmail.com
  pass = p4ssw0rd
  port = 993
  sslverify = false
```

If your IMAP server doesn't use SSL, the last two lines probably aren't necessary, and the host value will be imap:// instead of imaps://. When that is set up, you can use git send-email to place the patch series in the Drafts folder of the specified IMAP server:

```
$ git send-email *.patch
0001-added-limit-to-log-function.patch
0002-changed-log-output-to-30-from-25.patch
Who should the emails appear to be from? [Jessica Smith <jessica@example.com>]
Emails will be sent from: Jessica Smith <jessica@example.com>
Who should the emails be sent to? jessica@example.com
Message-ID to be used as In-Reply-To for the first email? y
```

Then, Git spits out a bunch of log information looking something like this for each patch you're sending:

```
(mbox) Adding cc: Jessica Smith <jessica@example.com> from
  \line 'From: Jessica Smith <jessica@example.com>'
OK. Log says:
Sendmail: /usr/sbin/sendmail -i jessica@example.com
From: Jessica Smith <jessica@example.com>
To: jessica@example.com
Subject: [PATCH 1/2] added limit to log function
Date: Sat, 30 May 2009 13:29:15 -0700
Message-Id: <1243715356-61726-1-git-send-email-jessica@example.com>
X-Mailer: git-send-email 1.6.2.rc1.20.g8c5b.dirty
In-Reply-To: <y>
References: <y>

Result: OK
```

At this point, you should be able to go to your Drafts folder, change the To field to the mailing list you're sending the patch to, possibly CC the maintainer or person responsible for that section, and send it off.

Summary

This section has covered a number of common workflows for dealing with several very different types of Git projects you're likely to encounter, and introduced a couple of new tools to help you manage this process. Next, you'll see how to work the other side of the coin: maintaining a Git project. You'll learn how to be a benevolent dictator or integration manager.

Maintaining a Project

In addition to knowing how to effectively contribute to a project, you'll likely need to know how to maintain one. This can consist of accepting and applying patches generated via format-patch and e-mailed to you, or integrating changes in remote branches for repositories you've added as remotes to your project. Whether you maintain a canonical repository or want to help by verifying or approving patches, you need to know how to accept work in a way that is clearest for other contributors and sustainable by you over the long run.

Working in Topic Branches

When you're thinking of integrating new work, it's generally a good idea to try it out in a topic branch—a temporary branch specifically made to try out that new work. This way, it's easy to tweak a patch individually and leave it if it's not working until you have time to come back to it. If you create a simple branch name based on the theme of the work you're going to try, such as ruby_client or something similarly descriptive, you can easily remember it if you have to abandon it for a while and come back later. The maintainer of the Git project tends to namespace these branches as well—such as sc/ruby_client, where sc is short for the person who contributed the work. As you'll remember, you can create the branch based off your master branch like this:

```
$ git branch sc/ruby_client master
```

Or, if you want to also switch to it immediately, you can use the checkout -b option:

```
$ git checkout -b sc/ruby_client master
```

Now you're ready to add your contributed work into this topic branch and determine if you want to merge it into your longer-term branches.

Applying Patches from E-mail

If you receive a patch over e-mail that you need to integrate into your project, you need to apply the patch in your topic branch to evaluate it. There are two ways to apply an e-mailed patch: with git apply or with git am.

Applying a Patch with apply

If you received the patch from someone who generated it with the git diff or a Unix diff command (which is not recommended; see the next section), you can apply it with the git apply command. Assuming you saved the patch at /tmp/patch-ruby-client.patch, you can apply the patch like this:

```
$ git apply /tmp/patch-ruby-client.patch
```

This modifies the files in your working directory. It's almost identical to running a patch -p1 command to apply the patch, although it's more paranoid and accepts fewer fuzzy matches than patch. It also handles file adds, deletes, and renames if they're described in the git diff format, which patch won't do. Finally, git apply is an "apply all or abort all" model where either everything is applied or nothing is, whereas patch can partially apply patchfiles, leaving your working directory in a weird state. git apply is overall much more conservative than patch. It won't create a commit for you—after running it, you must stage and commit the changes introduced manually.

You can also use git apply to see if a patch applies cleanly before you try actually applying it—you can run git apply --check with the patch:

```
$ git apply --check 0001-seeing-if-this-helps-the-gem.patch
error: patch failed: ticgit.gemspec:1
error: ticgit.gemspec: patch does not apply
```

If there is no output, then the patch should apply cleanly. This command also exits with a non-zero status if the check fails, so you can use it in scripts if you want.

Applying a Patch with am

If the contributor is a Git user and was good enough to use the format-patch command to generate their patch, then your job is easier because the patch contains author information and a commit message for you. If you can, encourage your contributors to use format-patch instead of diff to generate patches for you. You should only have to use git apply for legacy patches and things like that.

To apply a patch generated by format-patch, you use git am. Technically, git am is built to read an mbox file, which is a simple, plain-text format for storing one or more e-mail messages in one text file. It looks something like this:

```
From 330090432754092d704da8e76ca5c05c198e71a8 Mon Sep 17 00:00:00 2001
From: Jessica Smith <jessica@example.com>
Date: Sun, 6 Apr 2008 10:17:23 -0700
Subject: [PATCH 1/2] add limit to log function

Limit log functionality to the first 20
```

This is the beginning of the output of the format-patch command that you saw in the previous section. This is also a valid mbox e-mail format. If someone has e-mailed you the patch properly using git send-email, and you download that into an mbox format, then you can point git am to that mbox file, and it will start applying all the patches it sees. If you run a mail client that can save several e-mails out in mbox format, you can save entire patch series into a file and then use git am to apply them one at a time.

However, if someone uploaded a patch file generated via format-patch to a ticketing system or something similar, you can save the file locally and then pass that file saved on your disk to git am to apply it:

```
$ git am 0001-limit-log-function.patch
Applying: add limit to log function
```

You can see that it applied cleanly and automatically created the new commit for you. The author information is taken from the e-mail's From and Date headers, and the message of the commit is taken from the Subject and body (before the patch) of the e-mail. For example, if this patch was applied from the mbox example above, the commit generated would look something like this:

```
$ git log --pretty=fuller -1
commit 6c5e70b984a60b3cecd395edd5b48a7575bf58e0
```

```
Author:     Jessica Smith <jessica@example.com>
AuthorDate: Sun Apr 6 10:17:23 2008 -0700
Commit:     Scott Chacon <schacon@gmail.com>
CommitDate: Thu Apr 9 09:19:06 2009 -0700

    add limit to log function

    Limit log functionality to the first 20
```

The Commit information indicates the person who applied the patch and the time it was applied. The Author information is the individual who originally created the patch and when it was originally created.

But it's possible that the patch won't apply cleanly. Perhaps your main branch has diverged too far from the branch the patch was built from, or the patch depends on another patch you haven't applied yet. In that case, the git am process will fail and ask you what you want to do:

```
$ git am 0001-seeing-if-this-helps-the-gem.patch
Applying: seeing if this helps the gem
error: patch failed: ticgit.gemspec:1
error: ticgit.gemspec: patch does not apply
Patch failed at 0001.
When you have resolved this problem run "git am --resolved".
If you would prefer to skip this patch, instead run "git am --skip".
To restore the original branch and stop patching run "git am --abort".
```

This command puts conflict markers in any files it has issues with, much like a conflicted merge or rebase operation. You solve this issue much the same way—edit the file to resolve the conflict, stage the new file, and then run git am --resolved to continue to the next patch:

```
$ (fix the file)
$ git add ticgit.gemspec
$ git am --resolved
Applying: seeing if this helps the gem
```

If you want Git to try a bit more intelligently to resolve the conflict, you can pass a -3 option to it, which makes Git attempt a three-way merge. This option isn't on by default because it doesn't work if the commit the patch says it was based on isn't in your repository. If you do have that commit—if the patch was based on a public commit—then the -3 option is generally much smarter about applying a conflicting patch:

```
$ git am -3 0001-seeing-if-this-helps-the-gem.patch
Applying: seeing if this helps the gem
error: patch failed: ticgit.gemspec:1
error: ticgit.gemspec: patch does not apply
Using index info to reconstruct a base tree...
Falling back to patching base and 3-way merge...
No changes -- Patch already applied.
```

In this case, this patch had already been applied. Without the -3 option, it looks like a conflict.

If you're applying a number of patches from an mbox, you can also run the am command in interactive mode, which stops at each patch it finds and asks if you want to apply it:

```
$ git am -3 -i mbox
```

```
Commit Body is:
--------------------------
seeing if this helps the gem
--------------------------
Apply? [y]es/[n]o/[e]dit/[v]iew patch/[a]ccept all
```

This is nice if you have a number of patches saved, because you can view the patch first if you don't remember what it is, or not apply the patch if you've already done so.

When all the patches for your topic are applied and committed into your branch, you can choose whether and how to integrate them into a longer-running branch.

Checking Out Remote Branches

If your contribution came from a Git user who set up their own repository, pushed a number of changes into it, and then sent you the URL to the repository and the name of the remote branch the changes are in, you can add them as a remote and do merges locally.

For instance, if Jessica sends you an e-mail saying that she has a great new feature in the ruby-client branch of her repository, you can test it by adding the remote and checking out that branch locally:

```
$ git remote add jessica git://github.com/jessica/myproject.git
$ git fetch jessica
$ git checkout -b rubyclient jessica/ruby-client
```

If she e-mails you again later with another branch containing another great feature, you can fetch and check out because you already have the remote setup.

This is most useful if you're working with a person consistently. If someone only has a single patch to contribute once in a while, then accepting it over e-mail may be less time consuming than requiring everyone to run their own server and having to continually add and remove remotes to get a few patches. You're also unlikely to want to have hundreds of remotes, each for someone who contributes only a patch or two. However, scripts and hosted services may make this easier—it depends largely on how you develop and how your contributors develop.

The other advantage of this approach is that you get the history of the commits as well. Although you may have legitimate merge issues, you know where in your history their work is based; a proper three-way merge is the default rather than having to supply a -3 and hope the patch was generated off a public commit to which you have access.

If you aren't working with a person consistently but still want to pull from them in this way, you can provide the URL of the remote repository to the git pull command. This does a one-time pull and doesn't save the URL as a remote reference:

```
$ git pull https://github.com/onetimeguy/project
From https://github.com/onetimeguy/project
 * branch HEAD -> FETCH_HEAD
Merge made by recursive.
```

Determining What Is Introduced

Now you have a topic branch that contains contributed work. At this point, you can determine what you'd like to do with it. This section revisits a couple of commands so you can see how you can use them to review exactly what you'll be introducing if you merge this into your main branch.

It's often helpful to get a review of all the commits that are in this branch but that aren't in your master branch. You can exclude commits in the master branch by adding the --not option before the branch name. This does the same thing as the master..contrib format that we used earlier. For example, if your contributor sends you two patches and you create a branch called contrib and applied those patches there, you can run this:

```
$ git log contrib --not master
commit 5b6235bd297351589efc4d73316f0a68d484f118
Author: Scott Chacon <schacon@gmail.com>
Date:    Fri Oct 24 09:53:59 2008 -0700

    seeing if this helps the gem

commit 7482e0d16d04bea79d0dba8988cc78df655f16a0
Author: Scott Chacon <schacon@gmail.com>
Date:    Mon Oct 22 19:38:36 2008 -0700

    updated the gemspec to hopefully work better
```

To see what changes each commit introduces, remember that you can pass the -p option to git log and it will append the diff introduced to each commit.

To see a full diff of what would happen if you were to merge this topic branch with another branch, you may have to use a weird trick to get the correct results. You may think to run this:

```
$ git diff master
```

This command gives you a diff, but it may be misleading. If your master branch has moved forward since you created the topic branch from it, then you'll get seemingly strange results. This happens because Git directly compares the snapshots of the last commit of the topic branch you're on and the snapshot of the last commit on the master branch. For example, if you've added a line in a file on the master branch, a direct comparison of the snapshots will look like the topic branch is going to remove that line.

If master is a direct ancestor of your topic branch, this isn't a problem; but if the two histories have diverged, the diff will look like you're adding all the new stuff in your topic branch and removing everything unique to the master branch.

What you really want to see are the changes added to the topic branch—the work you'll introduce if you merge this branch with master. You do that by having Git compare the last commit on your topic branch with the first common ancestor it has with the master branch.

Technically, you can do that by explicitly figuring out the common ancestor and then running your diff on it:

```
$ git merge-base contrib master
36c7dba2c95e6bbb78dfa822519ecfec6e1ca649
$ git diff 36c7db
```

However, that isn't convenient, so Git provides another shorthand for doing the same thing: the triple-dot syntax. In the context of the —command, you can put three periods after another branch to do a —between the last commit of the branch you're on and its common ancestor with another branch:

```
$ git diff master...contrib
```

This command shows you only the work your current topic branch has introduced since its common ancestor with master. That is a very useful syntax to remember.

Integrating Contributed Work

When all the work in your topic branch is ready to be integrated into a more mainline branch, the question is how to do it. Furthermore, what overall workflow do you want to use to maintain your project? You have a number of choices, so we'll cover a few of them.

Merging Workflows

One simple workflow merges your work into your `master` branch. In this scenario, you have a `master` branch that contains basically stable code. When you have work in a topic branch that you've done or that someone has contributed and you've verified, you merge it into your `master` branch, delete the `topic` branch, and then continue the process. If we have a repository with work in two branches named `ruby_client` and `php_client` that looks like History with several topic branches. and merge `ruby_client` first and then `php_client` next, then your history will end up looking like after a topic branch merge.

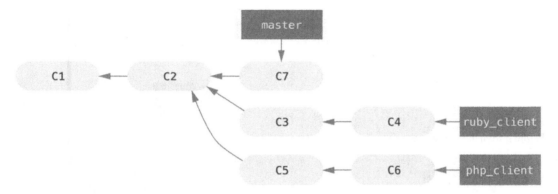

Figure 5-19. *History with several topic branches*

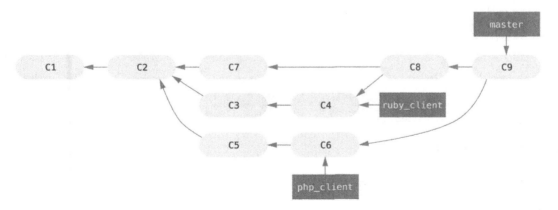

Figure 5-20. *After a topic branch merge*

That is probably the simplest workflow, but it can possibly be problematic if you're dealing with larger or more stable projects where you want to be really careful about what you introduce.

If you have a more important project, you might want to use a two-phase merge cycle. In this scenario, you have two long-running branches, master and develop, in which you determine that master is updated only when a very stable release is cut and all new code is integrated into the develop branch. You regularly push both of these branches to the public repository. Each time you have a new topic branch to merge in (before a topic branch merge), you merge it into develop (after a topic branch merge); then, when you tag a release, you fast-forward master to wherever the now-stable develop branch is (after a project release).

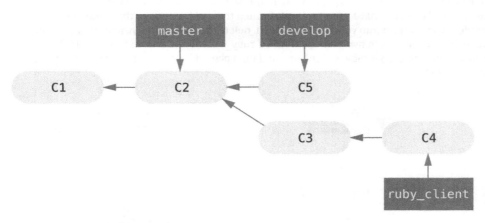

Figure 5-21. *Before a topic branch merge*

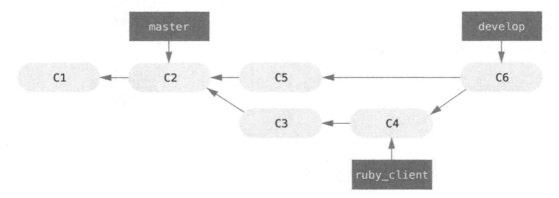

Figure 5-22. *After a topic branch merge*

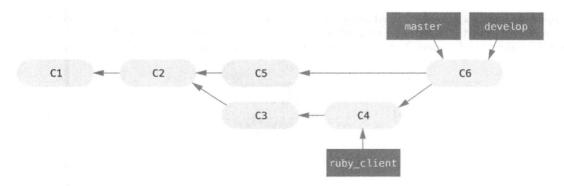

Figure 5-23. *After a project release*

This way, when people clone your project's repository, they can either check out master to build the latest stable version and keep up to date on that easily, or they can check out develop, which is the more cutting-edge stuff. You can also continue this concept, having an integrate branch where all the work is merged together. Then, when the codebase on that branch is stable and passes tests, you merge it into a develop branch; and when that has proven itself stable for a while, you fast-forward your master branch.

Large-Merging Workflows

The Git project has four long-running branches: master, next, and pu (proposed updates) for new work, and maint for maintenance backports. When new work is introduced by contributors, it's collected into topic branches in the maintainer's repository in a manner similar to what we've described. At this point, the topics are evaluated to determine whether they're safe and ready for consumption or whether they need more work. If they're safe, they're merged into next, and that branch is pushed up so everyone can try the topics integrated together.

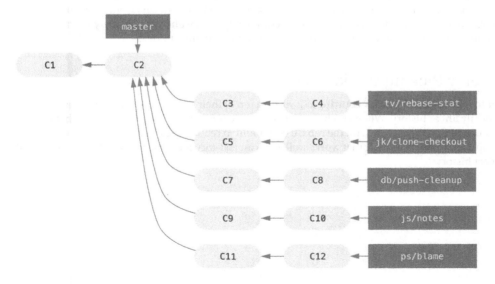

Figure 5-24. *Managing a complex series of parallel contributed topic branches*

If the topics still need work, they're merged into pu instead. When it's determined that they're totally stable, the topics are re-merged into master and are then rebuilt from the topics that were in next but didn't yet graduate to master. This means master almost always moves forward, next is rebased occasionally, and pu is rebased even more often:

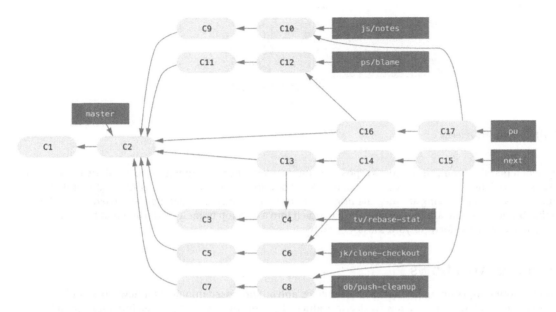

Figure 5-25. *Merging contributed topic branches into long-term integration branches*

When a topic branch has finally been merged into master, it's removed from the repository. The Git project also has a maint branch that is forked off from the last release to provide backported patches in case a maintenance release is required. Thus, when you clone the Git repository, you have four branches that you can check out to evaluate the project in different stages of development, depending on how cutting edge you want to be or how you want to contribute; and the maintainer has a structured workflow to help them vet new contributions.

Rebasing and Cherry Picking Workflows

Other maintainers prefer to rebase or cherry-pick contributed work on top of their master branch, rather than merging it in, to keep a mostly linear history. When you have work in a topic branch and have determined that you want to integrate it, you move to that branch and run the rebase command to rebuild the changes on top of your current master (or develop, and so on) branch. If that works well, you can fast-forward your master branch, and you'll end up with a linear project history.

The other way to move introduced work from one branch to another is to cherry-pick it. A cherry-pick in Git is like a rebase for a single commit. It takes the patch that was introduced in a commit and tries to reapply it on the branch you're currently on. This is useful if you have a number of commits on a topic branch and you want to integrate only one of them, or if you only have one commit on a topic branch and you'd prefer to cherry-pick it rather than run rebase. For example, suppose you have a project that looks like this:

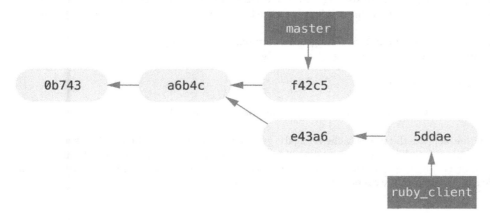

Figure 5-26. *Example history before a cherry-pick*

If you want to pull commit e43a6 into your master branch, you can run

```
$ git cherry-pick e43a6fd3e94888d76779ad79fb568ed180e5fcdf
Finished one cherry-pick.
[master]: created a0a41a9: "More friendly message when locking the index fails."
 3 files changed, 17 insertions(+), 3 deletions(-)
```

This pulls the same change introduced in e43a6, but you get a new commit SHA-1 value, because the date applied is different. Now your history looks like this:

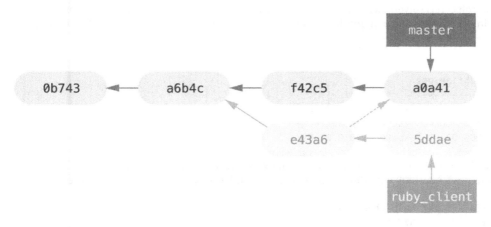

Figure 5-27. *History after cherry-picking a commit on a topic branch*

Now you can remove your topic branch and drop the commits you didn't want to pull in.

Rerere

If you're doing lots of merging and rebasing, or you're maintaining a long-lived topic branch, Git has a feature called "rerere" that can help.

Rerere stands for "reuse recorded resolution" and it's a way of shortcutting manual conflict resolution. When rerere is enabled, Git will keep a set of pre- and post-images from successful merges, and if it notices that there's a conflict that looks exactly like one you've already fixed, it'll just use the fix from last time, without bothering you with it.

This feature comes in two parts: a configuration setting and a command. The configuration setting is `rerere.enabled`, and it's handy enough to put in your `global config`:

```
$ git config --global rerere.enabled true
```

Now, whenever you do a merge that resolves conflicts, the resolution will be recorded in the cache in case you need it in the future. If you need to, you can interact with the rerere cache using the `git rerere` command. When it's invoked alone, Git checks its database of resolutions and tries to find a match with any current merge conflicts and resolve them (although this is done automatically if `rerere.enabled` is set to true). There are also subcommands to see what will be recorded, to erase specific resolution from the cache, and to clear the entire cache.

Tagging Your Releases

When you've decided to cut a release, you'll probably want to drop a tag so you can re-create that release at any point going forward. You can create a new tag. If you decide to sign the tag as the maintainer, the tagging may look something like this:

```
$ git tag -s v1.5 -m 'my signed 1.5 tag'
You need a passphrase to unlock the secret key for
user: "Scott Chacon <schacon@gmail.com>"
1024-bit DSA key, ID F721C45A, created 2009-02-09
```

If you do sign your tags, you may have the problem of distributing the public PGP key used to sign your tags. The maintainer of the Git project has solved this issue by including their public key as a blob in the repository and then adding a tag that points directly to that content. To do this, you can figure out which key you want by running `gpg --list-keys`:

```
$ gpg --list-keys
/Users/schacon/.gnupg/pubring.gpg
---------------------------------
pub   1024D/F721C45A 2009-02-09 [expires: 2010-02-09]
uid                  Scott Chacon <schacon@gmail.com>
sub   2048g/45D02282 2009-02-09 [expires: 2010-02-09]
```

Then, you can directly import the key into the Git database by exporting it and piping that through `git hash-object`, which writes a new blob with those contents into Git and gives you back the SHA-1 of the blob:

```
$ gpg -a --export F721C45A | git hash-object -w --stdin
659ef797d181633c87ec71ac3f9ba29fe5775b92
```

Now that you have the contents of your key in Git, you can create a tag that points directly to it by specifying the new SHA-1 value that the hash-object command gave you:

```
$ git tag -a maintainer-pgp-pub 659ef797d181633c87ec71ac3f9ba29fe5775b92
```

If you run git push --tags, the maintainer-pgp-pub tag will be shared with everyone. If anyone wants to verify a tag, they can directly import your PGP key by pulling the blob directly out of the database and importing it into GPG:

```
$ git show maintainer-pgp-pub | gpg --import
```

They can use that key to verify all your signed tags. Also, if you include instructions in the tag message, running git show <tag> will let you give the end user more specific instructions about tag verification.

Generating a Build Number

Because Git doesn't have monotonically increasing numbers like v123 or the equivalent to go with each commit, if you want to have a human-readable name to go with a commit, you can run git describe on that commit. Git gives you the name of the nearest tag with the number of commits on top of that tag and a partial SHA-1 value of the commit you're describing:

```
$ git describe master
v1.6.2-rc1-20-g8c5b85c
```

This way, you can export a snapshot or build and name it something understandable to people. In fact, if you build Git from source code cloned from the Git repository, git --version gives you something that looks like this. If you're describing a commit that you have directly tagged, it gives you the tag name.

The git describe command favors annotated tags (tags created with the -a or -s flag), so release tags should be created this way if you're using git describe, to ensure the commit is named properly when described. You can also use this string as the target of a checkout or show command, although it relies on the abbreviated SHA-1 value at the end, so it may not be valid forever. For instance, the Linux kernel recently jumped from 8 to 10 characters to ensure SHA-1 object uniqueness, so older git describe output names were invalidated.

Preparing a Release

Now you want to release a build. One of the things you'll want to do is create an archive of the latest snapshot of your code for those poor souls who don't use Git. The command to do this is git archive:

```
$ git archive master --prefix='project/' | gzip > `git describe master`.tar.gz
$ ls *.tar.gz
v1.6.2-rc1-20-g8c5b85c.tar.gz
```

If someone opens that tarball, they get the latest snapshot of your project under a project directory. You can also create a zip archive in much the same way, but by passing the --format=zip option to git archive:

```
$ git archive master --prefix='project/' --format=zip > `git describe master`.zip
```

You now have a nice tarball and a zip archive of your project release that you can upload to your website or e-mail to people.

The Shortlog

It's time to e-mail your mailing list of people who want to know what's happening in your project. A nice way of quickly getting a sort of changelog of what has been added to your project since your last release or e-mail is to use the git shortlog command. It summarizes all the commits in the range you give it; for example, the following gives you a summary of all the commits since your last release, if your last release was named v1.0.1:

```
$ git shortlog --no-merges master --not v1.0.1
Chris Wanstrath (8):
      Add support for annotated tags to Grit::Tag
      Add packed-refs annotated tag support.
      Add Grit::Commit#to_patch
      Update version and History.txt
      Remove stray `puts`
      Make ls_tree ignore nils

Tom Preston-Werner (4):
      fix dates in history
      dynamic version method
      Version bump to 1.0.2
      Regenerated gemspec for version 1.0.2
```

You get a clean summary of all the commits since v1.0.1, grouped by author, that you can e-mail to your list.

Summary

You should feel fairly comfortable contributing to a project in Git as well as maintaining your own project or integrating other users' contributions. Congratulations on being an effective Git developer! In the next chapter, you'll learn about how to use the largest and most popular Git hosting service, GitHub.

## CHAPTER 6

Github

GitHub is the single largest host for Git repositories, and is the central point of collaboration for millions of developers and projects. A large percentage of all Git repositories are hosted on GitHub, and many open-source projects use it for Git hosting, issue tracking, code review, and other things. So while it's not a direct part of the Git open source project, there's a good chance that you'll want or need to interact with GitHub at some point while using Git professionally.

This chapter is about using GitHub effectively. We'll cover signing up for and managing an account, creating and using Git repositories, common workflows to contribute to projects and to accept contributions to yours, GitHub's programmatic interface and lots of little tips to make your life easier in general.

If you are not interested in using GitHub to host your own projects or to collaborate with other projects that are hosted on GitHub, you can safely skip to Chapter 7.

INTERFACES CHANGE

It's important to note that like many active websites, the UI elements in these screenshots are bound to change over time. Hopefully the general idea of what we're trying to accomplish here will still be there, but if you want more up-to-date versions of these screens, the online versions of this book may have newer screenshots.

Account Setup and Configuration

The first thing you need to do is set up a free user account. Simply visit https://github.com, choose a user name that isn't already taken, provide an email address and a password, and click the big green Sign up for GitHub button.

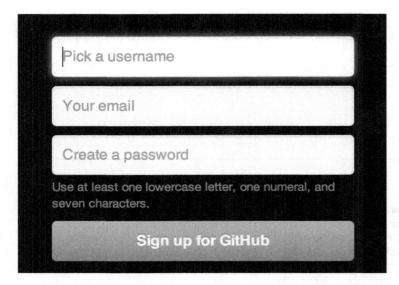

Figure 6-1. *The GitHub sign-up form*

The next thing you'll see is the pricing page for upgraded plans, but it's safe to ignore this for now. GitHub will send you an email to verify the address you provided. Go ahead and do this, it's pretty important (as we'll see later).

■ **Note**   GitHub provides all its functionality with free accounts, with the limitation that all your projects are fully public (everyone has read access). GitHub's paid plans include a set number of private projects, but we won't be covering those in this book.

Clicking the Octocat logo at the top-left of the screen will take you to your dashboard page. You're now ready to use GitHub.

SSH Access

As of right now, you can connect with Git repositories using the https:// protocol, authenticating with the username and password you just set up. However, to simply clone public projects, you don't even need to sign up—the account we just created comes into play when we fork projects and push to our forks a bit later.

If you'd like to use SSH remotes, you'll need to configure a public key. (If you don't already have one, see "Generating Your SSH Public Key" in Chapter 4.) Open up your account settings using the link at the top-right of the window:

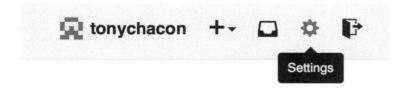

Figure 6-2. *The Account settings link*

Then select the SSH keys section along the left-hand side.

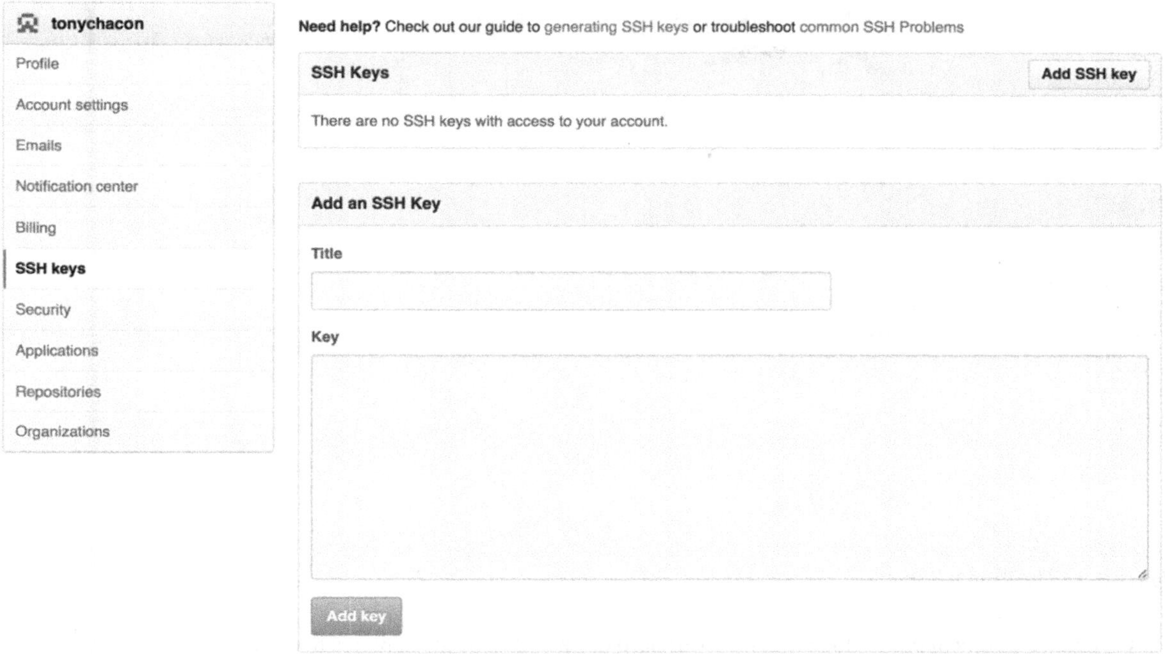

Figure 6-3. *The SSH keys link*

From there, click the Add an SSH key button, give your key a name, paste the contents of your `~/.ssh/id_rsa.pub` (or whatever you named it) public-key file into the text area, and click Add key.

■ **Note** Be sure to name your SSH key something you can remember. You can name each of your keys (for example, "My Laptop" or "Work Account") so that if you need to revoke a key later, you can easily tell which one you're looking for.

Your Avatar

Next, if you wish, you can replace the avatar that is generated for you with an image of your choosing. Go to the Profile tab (above the SSH Keys tab) and click Upload new picture.

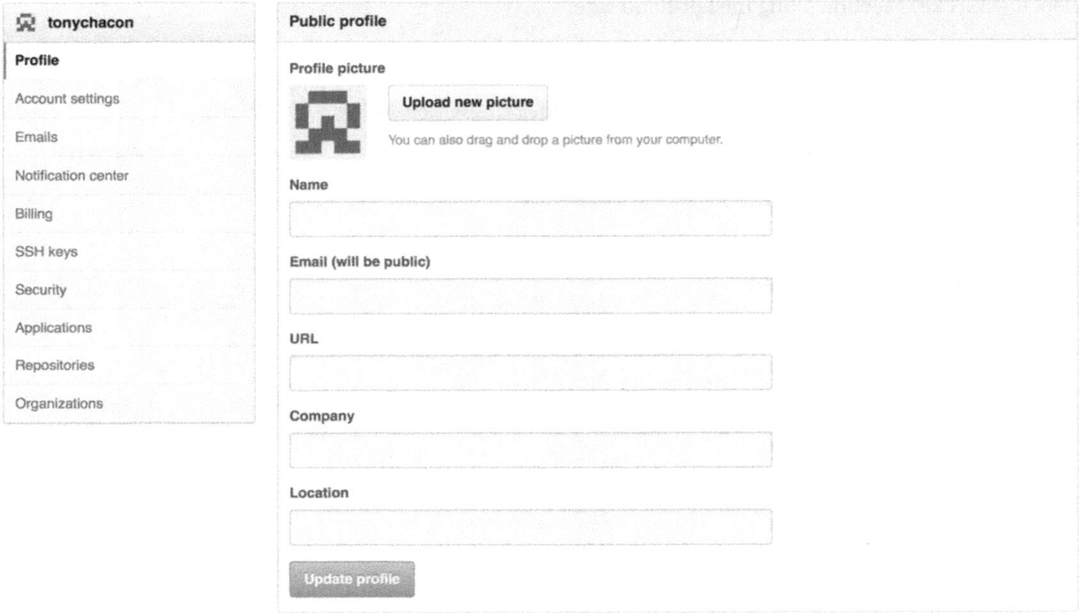

Figure 6-4. *The Profile link*

We choose a copy of the Git logo that is on our hard drive and then get a chance to crop it.

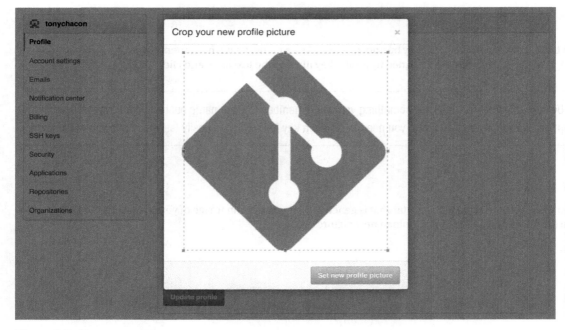

Figure 6-5. *Crop your avatar*

Now anywhere you interact on the site, people will see your avatar next to your username.

If you happen to have uploaded an avatar to the popular Gravatar service (often used for WordPress accounts), that avatar will be used by default and you don't need to do this step.

Your Email Addresses

GitHub maps your Git commits to your user by email address. If you use multiple email addresses in your commits and you want GitHub to link them up properly, you need to add all the email addresses you have used to the Emails section of the admin section.

In Figure 6-6 we can see some of the different states that are possible. The top address is verified and set as the primary address, meaning that is where you'll get any notifications and receipts. The second address is verified and so can be set as the primary if you want to switch them. The final address is unverified, meaning that you can't make it your primary address. If GitHub sees any of these in commit messages in any repository on the site, it will be linked to your user.

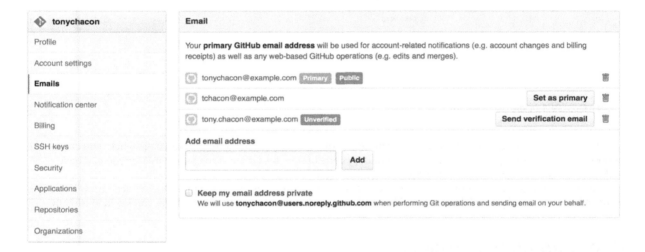

Figure 6-6. *Add email addresses*

Two-Factor Authentication

Finally, for extra security, you should definitely set up Two-factor Authentication or 2FA. Two-factor Authentication is an authentication mechanism that is recently becoming more and more popular to mitigate the risk of your account being compromised if your password is stolen somehow. Turning it on makes GitHub ask you for two different methods of authentication, so that if one of them is compromised, an attacker cannot access your account.

You can find the Two-factor Authentication setup under the Security tab of your Account settings.

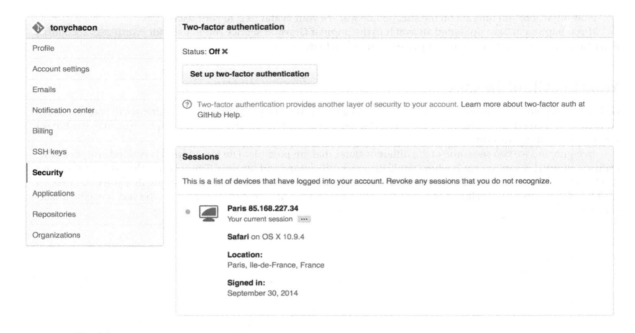

Figure 6-7. *2FA in the Security Tab*

If you click the Set up two-factor authentication button, it takes you to a configuration page where you can choose to use a phone app to generate your secondary code (a time based one-time password), or you can have GitHub send you a code via SMS each time you need to log in.

After you choose which method you prefer and follow the instructions for setting up 2FA, your account will then be a little more secure and you will have to provide a code in addition to your password whenever you log in to GitHub.

Contributing to a Project

Now that our account is setup, let's walk through some details that could be useful in helping you contribute to an existing project.

Forking Projects

If you want to contribute to an existing project to which you don't have push access, you can "fork" the project. What this means is that GitHub makes a copy of the project that is entirely yours; it lives in your user's namespace, and you can push to it.

■ **Note**   Historically, the term "fork" has been somewhat negative in context, meaning that someone took an open source project in a different direction, sometimes creating a competing project and splitting the contributors. In GitHub, a "fork" is simply the same project in your own namespace, allowing you to make changes to a project publicly as a way to contribute in a more open manner.

This way, projects don't have to worry about adding users as collaborators to give them push access. People can fork a project, push to it, and contribute their changes back to the original repository by creating what's called a Pull Request, which we'll cover next. This opens up a discussion thread with code review, and the owner and the contributor can then communicate about the change until the owner is happy with it, at which point the owner can merge it in.

To fork a project, visit the project page and click the Fork button at the top-right of the page.

Figure 6-8. *The Fork button*

After a few seconds, you'll be taken to your new project page, with your own writeable copy of the code.

The GitHub Flow

GitHub is designed around a particular collaboration workflow, centered on Pull Requests. This flow works whether you're collaborating with a tightly knit team in a single shared repository, or a globally distributed company or network of strangers contributing to a project through dozens of forks. It is centered on the topic branch workflow covered in Chapter 3.

Here's how it generally works:

1. Create a topic branch from master.

2. Make some commits to improve the project.

3. Push this branch to your GitHub project.

4. Open a Pull Request on GitHub.

5. Discuss, and optionally continue committing.

6. The project owner merges or closes the Pull Request.

This is basically the Integration Manager workflow covered in Chapter 5, but instead of using email to communicate and review changes, teams use GitHub's web-based tools.

Let's walk through an example of proposing a change to an open source project hosted on GitHub using this flow.

Creating a Pull Request

Tony is looking for code to run on his Arduino programmable microcontroller and has found a great program file on GitHub at https://github.com/schacon/blink.

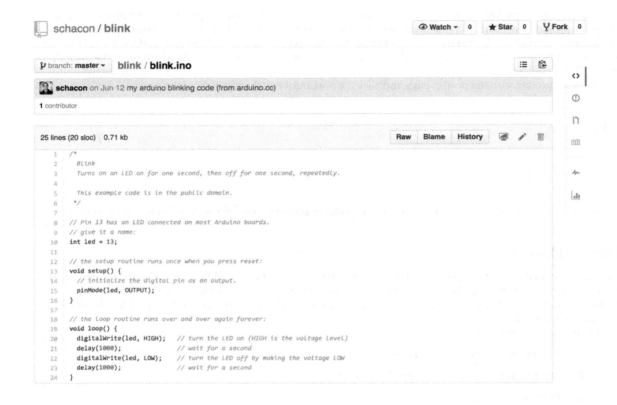

Figure 6-9. *The project we want to contribute to*

The only problem is that the blinking rate is too fast, we think it's much nicer to wait 3 seconds instead of 1 in between each state change. So let's improve the program and submit it back to the project as a proposed change.

First, we click the Fork button as mentioned earlier to get our own copy of the project. Our user name here is tonychacon so our copy of this project is at `https://github.com/tonychacon/blink` and that's where we can edit it. We will clone it locally, create a topic branch, make the code change, and finally push that change back up to GitHub.

```
$ git clone https://github.com/tonychacon/blink (1)
Cloning into 'blink'...

$ cd blink
$ git checkout -b slow-blink (2)
Switched to a new branch 'slow-blink'

$ sed -i '' 's/1000/3000/' blink.ino (3)

$ git diff --word-diff (4)
diff --git a/blink.ino b/blink.ino
index 15b9911..a6cc5a5 100644
--- a/blink.ino
+++ b/blink.ino
@@ -18,7 +18,7 @@ void setup() {
```

```
// the loop routine runs over and over again forever:
void loop() {
  digitalWrite(led, HIGH);   // turn the LED on (HIGH is the voltage level)
  [-delay(1000);-]{+delay(3000);+}              // wait for a second
  digitalWrite(led, LOW);    // turn the LED off by making the voltage LOW
  [-delay(1000);-]{+delay(3000);+}              // wait for a second
}

$ git commit -a -m 'three seconds is better' (5)
[master 5ca509d] three seconds is better
 1 file changed, 2 insertions(+), 2 deletions(-)

$ git push origin slow-blink (6)
Username for 'https://github.com': tonychacon
Password for 'https://tonychacon@github.com':
Counting objects: 5, done.
Delta compression using up to 8 threads.
Compressing objects: 100% (3/3), done.
Writing objects: 100% (3/3), 340 bytes | 0 bytes/s, done.
Total 3 (delta 1), reused 0 (delta 0)
To https://github.com/tonychacon/blink
 * [new branch]      slow-blink -> slow-blink
```

1. Clone our fork of the project locally.

2. Create a descriptive topic branch.

3. Make our change to the code.

4. Check that the change is good.

5. Commit our change to the topic branch.

6. Push our new topic branch back up to our GitHub fork.

Now if we go back to our fork on GitHub, we can see that GitHub noticed that we pushed a new topic branch up and present us with a big green button to check out our changes and open a Pull Request to the original project.

You can alternatively go to the Branches page at https://github.com/<user>/<project>/branches to locate your branch and open a new Pull Request from there.

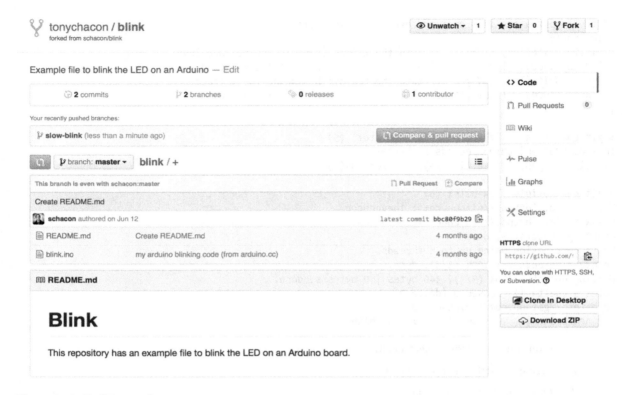

Figure 6-10. *Pull Request button*

If we click that green button, we'll see a screen that allows us to create a title and description for the change we would like to request so the project owner has a good reason to consider it. It is generally a good idea to spend some effort making this description as useful as possible so the author knows why this is being suggested and why it would be a valuable change for them to accept.

We also see a list of the commits in our topic branch that are "ahead" of the master branch (in this case, just the one) and a unified diff of all the changes that will be made should this branch get merged by the project owner.

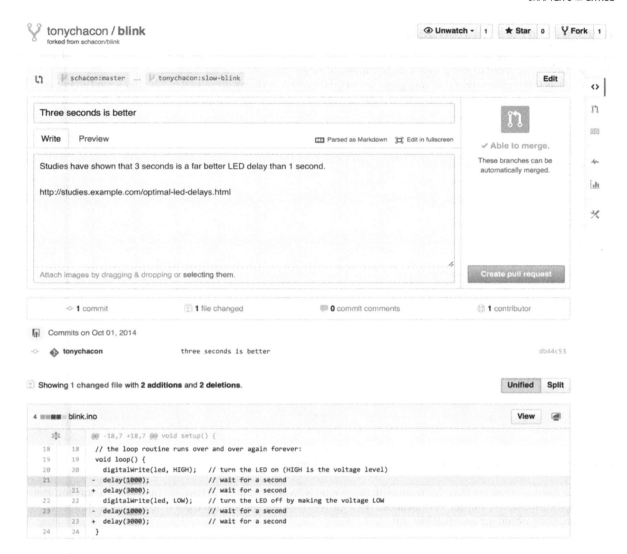

Figure 6-11. *Pull Request creation page*

When you click the Create Pull Request button on this screen, the owner of the project you forked will get a notification that someone is suggesting a change and will link to a page that has all of this information on it.

▪ **Note**   Although Pull Requests are used commonly for public projects like this when the contributor has a complete change ready to be made, they are also often used in internal projects *at the beginning* of the development cycle. Because you can keep pushing to the topic branch even *after* the Pull Request is opened, it's often opened early and used as a way to iterate on work as a team within a context, rather than opened at the very end of the process.

Iterating on a Pull Request

At this point, the project owner can look at the suggested change and merge it, reject it, or comment on it. Let's say that he likes the idea, but would prefer a slightly longer time for the light to be off than on.

Whereas this conversation may take place over email in the workflows presented in Chapter 5, on GitHub this happens online. The project owner can review the unified diff and leave a comment by clicking on any of the lines.

Figure 6-12. *Comment on a specific line of code in a Pull Request*

Once the maintainer makes this comment, the person who opened the Pull Request (and indeed, anyone else watching the repository) will get a notification. We'll go over customizing this later, but if he had email notifications turned on, Tony would get an email like this:

Figure 6-13. *Comments sent as email notifications*

Anyone can also leave general comments on the Pull Request. In Figure 6-14 we can see an example of the project owner both commenting on a line of code and then leaving a general comment in the discussion section. You can see that the code comments are brought into the conversation as well.

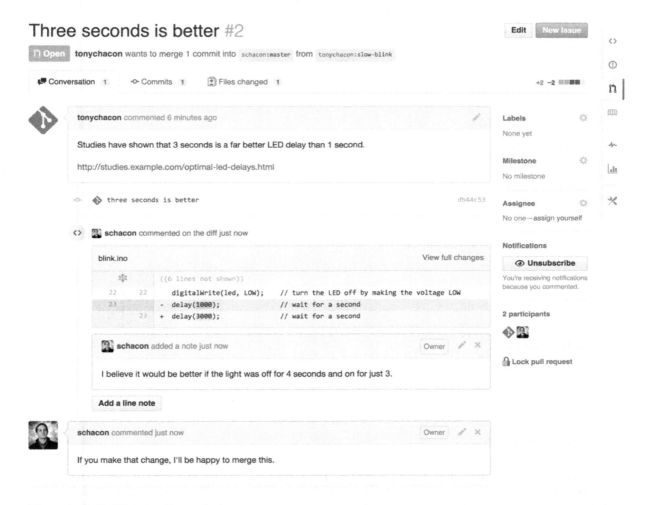

Figure 6-14. *Pull Request discusson page*

Now the contributor can see what they need to do in order to get their change accepted. Luckily, this is also a very simple thing to do. Where over email you may have to re-roll your series and resubmit it to the mailing list, with GitHub you simply commit to the topic branch again and push.

If the contributor does that, then the project owner will get notified again and when they visit the page they will see that it's been addressed. In fact, because a line of code changed that had a comment on it; GitHub notices that and collapses the outdated diff.

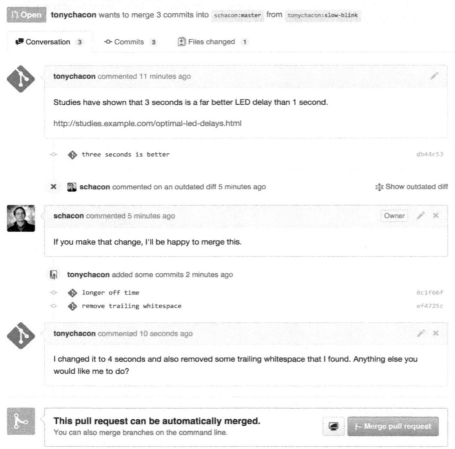

Figure 6-15. *Pull Request final*

An interesting thing to notice is that if you click on the Files Changed tab on this Pull Request, you'll get the unified diff — that is, the total aggregate difference that would be introduced to your main branch if this topic branch was merged in. In `git diff` terms, it basically automatically shows you `git diff master...<branch>` for the branch this Pull Request is based on. See "Determining What Is Introduced" in Chapter 5 for more about this type of diff.

The other thing you'll notice is that GitHub checks to see whether the Pull Request merges cleanly and provides a button to do the merge for you on the server. This button only shows up if you have write access to the repository and a trivial merge is possible. If you click it, GitHub will perform a "non-fast-forward" merge, meaning that even if the merge *could* be a fast-forward, it will still create a merge commit.

If you would prefer, you can simply pull down the branch and merge it locally. If you merge this branch into the `master` branch and push it to GitHub, the Pull Request will automatically be closed.

This is the basic workflow that most GitHub projects use. Topic branches are created, Pull Requests are opened on them, a discussion ensues, possibly more work is done on the branch, and eventually the request is either closed or merged.

NOT ONLY FORKS

It's important to note that you can also open a Pull Request between two branches in the same repository. If you're working on a feature with someone and you both have write access to the project, you can push a topic branch to the repository and open a Pull Request on it to the `master` branch of that same project to initiate the code review and discussion process. No forking necessary

---

Advanced Pull Requests

Now that we've covered the basics of contributing to a project on GitHub, let's cover a few interesting tips and tricks about Pull Requests so you can be more effective in using them.

Pull Requests as Patches

It's important to understand that many projects don't really think of Pull Requests as queues of perfect patches that should apply cleanly in order, as most mailing list-based projects think of patch series contributions. Most GitHub projects think about Pull Request branches as iterative conversations around a proposed change, culminating in a unified diff that is applied by merging.

This is an important distinction, because generally the change is suggested before the code is thought to be perfect, which is far rarer with mailing list–based patch series contributions. This enables an earlier conversation with the maintainers so that arriving at the proper solution is more of a community effort. When code is proposed with a Pull Request and the maintainers or community suggest a change, the patch series is generally not re-rolled, but instead the difference is pushed as a new commit to the branch, moving the conversation forward with the context of the previous work intact.

For instance, if you go back and look again at Figure 6-15, you'll notice that the contributor did not rebase his commit and send another Pull Request. Instead they added new commits and pushed them to the existing branch. This way if you go back and look at this Pull Request in the future, you can easily find all the context of why decisions were made. Pushing the Merge button on the site purposefully creates a merge commit that references the Pull Request so that it's easy to go back and research the original conversation if necessary.

Keeping up with Upstream

If your Pull Request becomes out of date or otherwise doesn't merge cleanly, you will want to fix it so the maintainer can easily merge it. GitHub tests this for you and lets you know at the bottom of every Pull Request whether the merge is trivial.

If you see something like Figure 6-16, you'll want to fix your branch so that it turns green and the maintainer doesn't have to do extra work.

This pull request contains merge conflicts that must be resolved.
Only those with write access to this repository can merge pull requests.

Figure 6-16. *Pull Request does not merge cleanly*

You have two main options to do this. You can either rebase your branch on top of whatever the target branch is (normally the master branch of the repository you forked), or you can merge the target branch into your branch.

Most developers on GitHub will choose to do the latter, for the same reasons we just went over in the previous section. What matters is the history and the final merge, so rebasing isn't getting you much other than a slightly cleaner history and in return is *far* more difficult and error prone.

If you want to merge in the target branch to make your Pull Request mergeable, you would add the original repository as a new remote, fetch from it, merge the main branch of that repository into your topic branch, fix any issues, and finally push it back up to the same branch you opened the Pull Request on.

For example, let's say that in the "tonychacon" example we were using before, the original author made a change that would create a conflict in the Pull Request. Let's go through those steps.

```
$ git remote add upstream https://github.com/schacon/blink (1)

$ git fetch upstream (2)
remote: Counting objects: 3, done.
remote: Compressing objects: 100% (3/3), done.
Unpacking objects: 100% (3/3), done.
remote: Total 3 (delta 0), reused 0 (delta 0)
From https://github.com/schacon/blink
 * [new branch]      master      -> upstream/master

$ git merge upstream/master (3)
Auto-merging blink.ino
CONFLICT (content): Merge conflict in blink.ino
Automatic merge failed; fix conflicts and then commit the result.

$ vim blink.ino (4)
$ git add blink.ino
$ git commit
[slow-blink 3c8d735] Merge remote-tracking branch 'upstream/master' \
    into slower-blink

$ git push origin slow-blink (5)
Counting objects: 6, done.
Delta compression using up to 8 threads.
Compressing objects: 100% (6/6), done.
Writing objects: 100% (6/6), 682 bytes | 0 bytes/s, done.
Total 6 (delta 2), reused 0 (delta 0)
To https://github.com/tonychacon/blink
   ef4725c..3c8d735  slower-blink -> slow-blink
```

1. Add the original repository as a remote named "upstream."

2. Fetch the newest work from that remote.

3. Merge the main branch into your topic branch.

4. Fix the conflict that occurred.

5. Push back up to the same topic branch.

Once you do that, the Pull Request will be automatically updated and re-checked to see whether it merges cleanly.

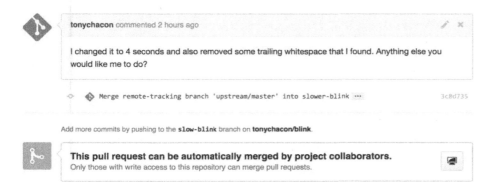

Figure 6-17. *Pull Request now merges cleanly*

One of the great things about Git is that you can do that continuously. If you have a very long-running project, you can easily merge from the target branch over and over again and only have to deal with conflicts that have arisen since the last time that you merged, making the process very manageable.

If you absolutely want to rebase the branch to clean it up, you can certainly do so, but it is highly encouraged to not force push over the branch that the Pull Request is already opened on. If other people have pulled it down and done more work on it, you run into all of the issues outlined in "The Perils of Rebasing" (Chapter 3). Instead, push the rebased branch to a new branch on GitHub and open a brand new Pull Request referencing the old one, then close the original.

References

Your next question may be "How do I reference the old Pull Request?" It turns out there are many ways to reference other things almost anywhere you can write in GitHub.

Let's start with how to cross-reference another Pull Request or an Issue. All Pull Requests and Issues are assigned numbers and they are unique within the project. For example, you can't have Pull Request #3 *and* Issue #3. If you want to reference any Pull Request or Issue from any other one, you can simply put #<num> in any comment or description. You can also be more specific if the Issue or Pull request lives somewhere else; write username#<num> if you're referring to an Issue or Pull Request in a fork of the repository you're in, or username/repo#<num> to reference something in another repository.

Let's look at an example. Say we rebased the branch in the previous example, created a new pull request for it, and now we want to reference the old pull request from the new one. We also want to reference an issue in the fork of the repository and an issue in a completely different project. We can fill out the description just like Figure 6-18.

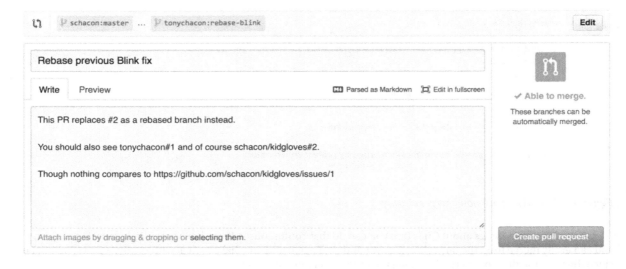

Figure 6-18. *Cross references in a Pull Request*

When we submit this Pull Request, we'll see all of that rendered like Figure 6-19.

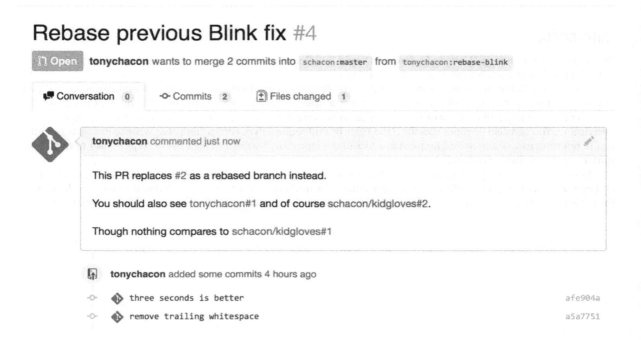

Figure 6-19. *Cross references rendered in a Pull Request*

Notice that the full GitHub URL we put in there was shortened to just the information needed.

Now if Tony goes back and closes out the original Pull Request, we can see that by mentioning it in the new one, GitHub has automatically created a trackback event in the Pull Request timeline. This means that anyone who visits this Pull Request and sees that it is closed can easily link back to the one that superseded it. The link looks something like Figure 6-20.

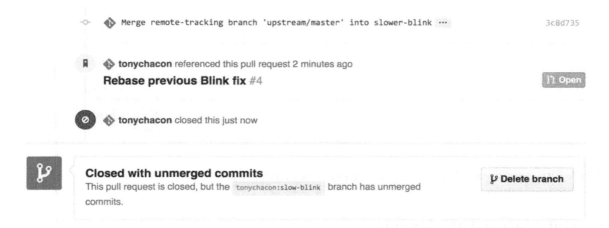

Figure 6-20. *Cross references rendered in a Pull Request*

In addition to issue numbers, you can also reference a specific commit by SHA. You have to specify a full 40 character SHA, but if GitHub sees that in a comment, it will link directly to the commit. Again, you can reference commits in forks or other repositories in the same way you did with issues.

Markdown

Linking to other Issues is just the beginning of interesting things you can do with almost any text box on GitHub. In Issue and Pull Request descriptions, comments, code comments, and more, you can use what is called GitHub Flavored Markdown. Markdown is like writing in plain text but which is rendered richly.

See Figure 6-21 shows an example of how comments or text can be written and then rendered using Markdown.

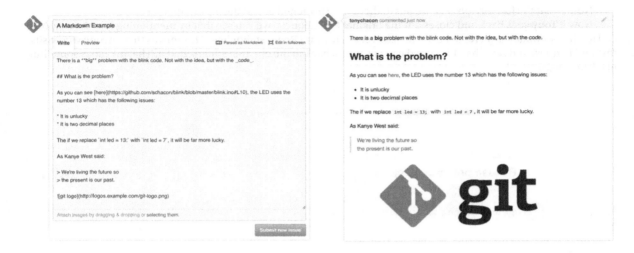

Figure 6-21. *An example of Markdown as written and as rendered*

GitHub Flavored Markdown

The GitHub flavor of Markdown adds more things you can do beyond the basic Markdown syntax. These can all be really useful when creating useful Pull Request or Issue comments or descriptions.

Task Lists

The first really useful GitHub specific Markdown feature, especially for use in Pull Requests, is the task list. A task list is a list of checkboxes of things you want to get done. Putting them into an Issue or Pull Request normally indicates things that you want to get done before you consider the item complete.

You can create a task list like this:

```
- [X] Write the code
- [ ] Write all the tests
- [ ] Document the code
```

If we include this in the description of our Pull Request or Issue, we'll see it rendered like Figure 6-22.

Figure 6-22. *Task lists rendered in a Markdown comment*

This is often used in Pull Requests to indicate what you would like to get done on the branch before the Pull Request will be ready to merge. The really cool part is that you can simply click the checkboxes to update the comment — you don't have to edit the Markdown directly to check off tasks.

What's more, GitHub looks for task lists in your Issues and Pull Requests and shows them as metadata on the pages that list them out. For example, if you have a Pull Request with tasks and you look at the overview page of all Pull Requests, you can see how far done it is. This helps people break down Pull Requests into subtasks and helps other people track the progress of the branch. You can see an example of this in Figure 6-23.

Figure 6-23. *Task list summary in the Pull Request list*

These are incredibly useful when you open a Pull Request early and use it to track your progress through the implementation of the feature.

Code Snippets

You can also add code snippets to comments. This is especially useful if you want to present something that you *could* try to do before actually implementing it as a commit on your branch. This is also often used to add example code of what is not working or what this Pull Request could implement.

To add a snippet of code you have to "fence" it in backticks.

```java
for(int i=0 ; i < 5 ; i++)
{
    System.out.println("i is : " + i);
}
```

If you add a language name like we did there with `java`, GitHub will also try to syntax highlight the snippet. In the case of the preceding example, it would end up rendering like Figure 6-24.

Figure 6-24. *Rendered fenced code example*

Quoting

If you're responding to a small part of a long comment, you can selectively quote out of the other comment by preceding the lines with the > character. In fact, this is so common and so useful that there is a keyboard shortcut for it. If you highlight text in a comment that you want to directly reply to and click the r key, it will quote that text in the comment box for you.

The quotes look something like this:

```
> Whether 'tis Nobler in the mind to suffer
> The Slings and Arrows of outrageous Fortune,

How big are these slings and in particular, these arrows?
```

Once rendered, the comment will look like Figure 6-25.

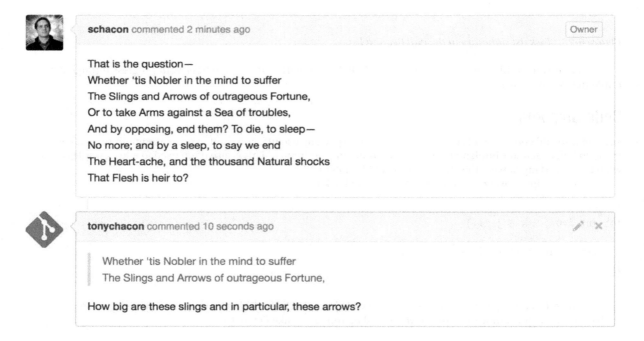

Figure 6-25. *Rendered quoting example*

Emoji

Finally, you can also use emojis in your comments. This is actually used quite extensively in comments you see on many GitHub Issues and Pull Requests. There is even an emoji helper in GitHub. If you are typing a comment and you start with a : character, an autocompleter will help you find what you're looking for.

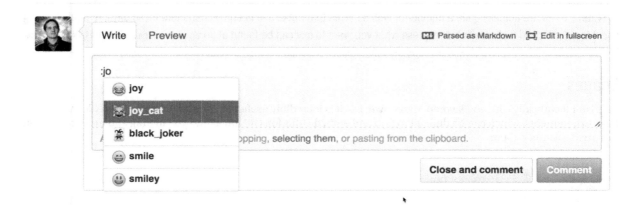

Figure 6-26. *Emoji autocompleter in action*

Emojis take the form of :<name>: anywhere in the comment. For instance, you could write something like this:

I :eyes: that :bug: and I :cold_sweat:.

:trophy: for :microscope: it.

:+1: and :sparkles: on this :ship:, it's :fire::poop:!

:clap::tada::panda_face:

When rendered, it would look something like Figure 6-27.

Figure 6-27. *Heavy emoji commenting*

Not that this is incredibly useful, but it does add an element of fun and emotion to a medium in which it is otherwise hard to convey emotion.

■ **Note**　There are actually quite a number of web services that make use of emoji characters these days. A great cheat sheet to reference to find emojis that express what you want to say can be found at: `http://www.emoji-cheat-sheet.com`.

Images

This isn't technically GitHub Flavored Markdown, but it is incredibly useful. In addition to adding Markdown image links to comments, which can be difficult to find and embed URLs for, GitHub allows you to drag and drop images into text areas to embed them.

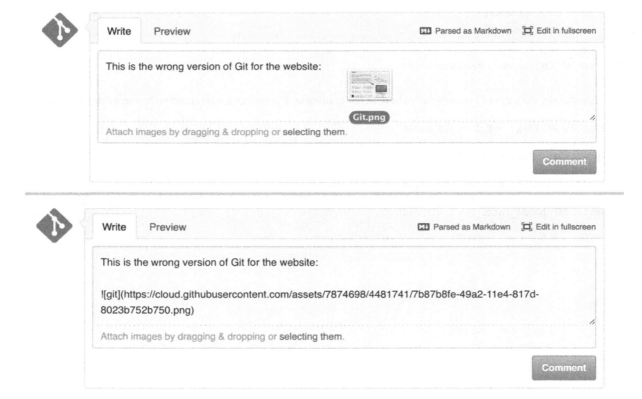

Figure 6-28.　*Drag and drop images to upload them and auto-embed them*

If you look back at Figure 6-18, you can see a small Parsed as Markdown hint above the text area. Clicking on that gives you a full cheat sheet of everything you can do with Markdown on GitHub.

Maintaining a Project

Now that you're comfortable contributing to a project, let's look at the other side: creating, maintaining, and administering your own project.

Creating a New Repository

Let's create a new repository to share our project code with. Start by clicking the New repository button on the right- side of the dashboard, or from the + button in the top toolbar next to your username as seen in Figure 6-30.

Figure 6-29. *The Your repositories area*

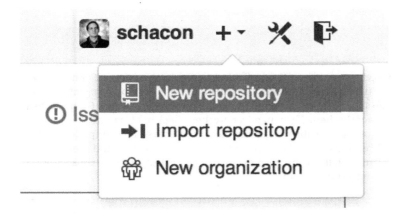

Figure 6-30. *The New repository dropdown*

This takes you to the new repository form:

Owner   **Repository name**

PUBLIC   ben ▾   /   iOSApp   ✓

Great repository names are short and memorable. Need inspiration? How about **drunken-dubstep**.

Description (optional)

iOS project for our mobile group

◉ **Public**
Anyone can see this repository. You choose who can commit.

○ **Private**
You choose who can see and commit to this repository.

☐ **Initialize this repository with a README**
This will allow you to git clone the repository immediately. Skip this step if you have already run git init locally.

Add .gitignore: **None** ▾   Add a license: **None** ▾   ⓘ

Create repository

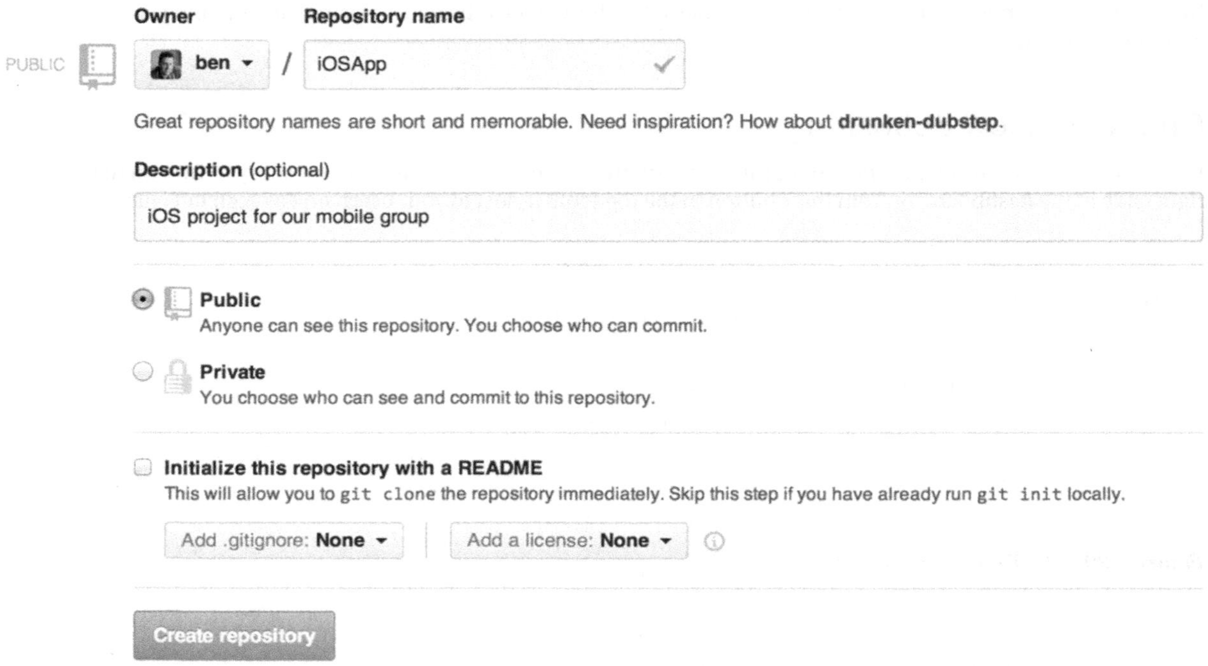

Figure 6-31. *The new repository form*

All you really have to do here is provide a project name; the rest of the fields are completely optional. For now, just click the Create Repository button, and boom—you have a new repository on GitHub, named <user>/<project_name>.

Because you have no code there yet, GitHub shows you instructions for how to create a brand-new Git repository, or connect an existing Git project. We won't belabor this here; if you need a refresher, check out Chapter 2.

Now that your project is hosted on GitHub, you can give the URL to anyone you want to share your project with. Every project on GitHub is accessible over HTTP as https://github.com/<user>/<project_name>, and over SSH as git@github.com:<user>/<project_name>. Git can fetch from and push to both of these URLs, but they are access-controlled based on the credentials of the user connecting to them.

■ **Note** It is often preferable to share the HTTP-based URL for a public project, since the user does not have to have a GitHub account to access it for cloning. Users will have to have an account and an uploaded SSH key to access your project if you give them the SSH URL. The HTTP one is also exactly the same URL they would paste into a browser to view the project there.

Adding Collaborators

If you're working with other people who you want to give commit access to, you need to add them as collaborators. If Ben, Jeff, and Louise all sign up for accounts on GitHub, and you want to give them push access to your repository, you can add them to your project. Doing so will give them push access, which means they have both read and write access to the project and Git repository.

Click the Settings link at the bottom of the right-hand sidebar.

Figure 6-32. *The repository settings link*

Then select Collaborators from the menu on the left-hand side. Then, just type a username into the box, and click Add collaborator. You can repeat this as many times as you like to grant access to everyone you like. If you need to revoke access, just click the X on the right-hand side of their row.

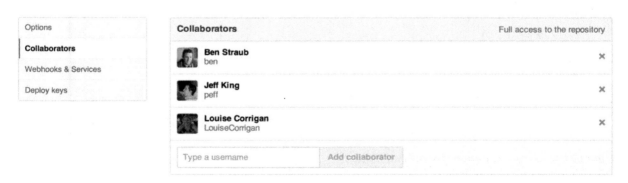

Figure 6-33. *Repository collaborators*

Managing Pull Requests

Now that you have a project with some code in it and maybe even a few collaborators who also have push access, let's go over what to do when you get a Pull Request yourself.

Pull Requests can either come from a branch in a fork of your repository or they can come from another branch in the same repository. The only difference is that the ones in a fork are often from people where you can't push to their branch and they can't push to yours, whereas with internal Pull Requests generally both parties can access the branch.

For these examples, let's assume you are "tonychacon" and you've created a new Arduino code project named "fade."

Email Notifications

Someone comes along and makes a change to your code and sends you a Pull Request. You should get an email notifying you about the new Pull Request and it should look something like Figure 6-34.

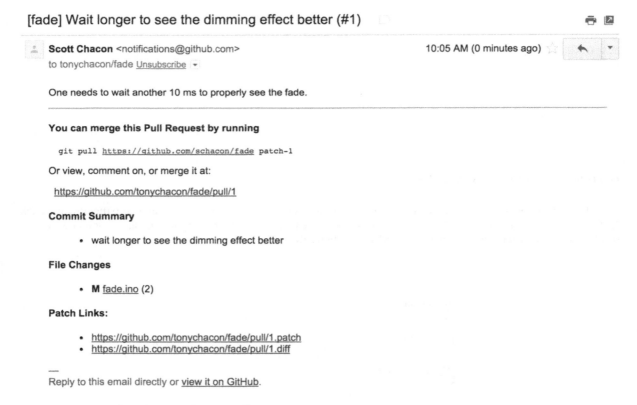

Figure 6-34. *Email notification of a new Pull Request*

There are a few things to notice about this email. It will give you a small diffstat — a list of files that have changed in the Pull Request and by how much. It gives you a link to the Pull Request on GitHub. It also gives you a few URLs that you can use from the command line.

If you notice the line that says `git pull <url> patch-1`, this is a simple way to merge in a remote branch without having to add a remote. We went over this quickly in "Checking Out Remote Branches" in Chapter 5. If you wish, you can create and switch to a topic branch and then run this command to merge in the Pull Request changes.

The other interesting URLs are the `.diff` and `.patch` URLs, which as you may guess, provide unified diff and patch versions of the Pull Request. You could technically merge in the Pull Request work with something like this:

```
$ curl http://github.com/tonychacon/fade/pull/1.patch | git am
```

Collaborating on the Pull Request

As we covered in section "The GitHub Flow," you can now have a conversation with the person who opened the Pull Request. You can comment on specific lines of code, comment on whole commits, or comment on the entire Pull Request itself, using GitHub Flavored Markdown everywhere.

Every time someone else comments on the Pull Request you will continue to get email notifications so you know there is activity happening. They will each have a link to the Pull Request where the activity is happening and you can also directly respond to the email to comment on the Pull Request thread.

Figure 6-35. *Responses to emails are included in the thread*

Once the code is in a place you like and want to merge it in, you can either pull the code down and merge it locally, either with the `git pull <url> <branch>` syntax we saw earlier, or by adding the fork as a remote and fetching and merging.

If the merge is trivial, you can also just click the Merge button on the GitHub site. This does a "non-fast-forward" merge, creating a merge commit even if a fast-forward merge was possible. This means that no matter what, every time you click the Merge button, a merge commit is created. As you can see in Figure 6-36, GitHub gives you all this information if you click the hint link.

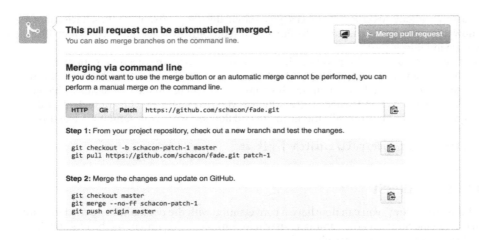

Figure 6-36. *Merge button and instructions for merging a Pull Request manually*

If you decide you don't want to merge it, you can also just close the Pull Request and the person who opened it will be notified.

Pull Request Refs

If you're dealing with a lot of Pull Requests and don't want to add a bunch of remotes or do one time pulls every time, there is a neat trick that GitHub allows you to do. This is a bit of an advanced trick and we'll go over the details of this later, but it can be pretty useful.

GitHub actually advertises the Pull Request branches for a repository as sort of pseudo-branches on the server. By default you don't get them when you clone, but they are there in an obscured way and you can access them pretty easily.

To demonstrate this, we're going to use a low-level command (often referred to as a "plumbing" command, which we'll read about more in Chapter 10) called `ls-remote`. This command is generally not used in day-to-day Git operations but it's useful to show us what references are present on the server.

If we run this command against the `blink` repository we were using earlier, we will get a list of all the branches and tags and other references in the repository.

```
$ git ls-remote https://github.com/schacon/blink
10d539600d86723087810ec636870a504f4fee4d        HEAD
10d539600d86723087810ec636870a504f4fee4d        refs/heads/master
6a83107c62950be9453aac297bb0193fd743cd6e        refs/pull/1/head
afe83c2d1a70674c9505cc1d8b7d380d5e076ed3        refs/pull/1/merge
3c8d735ee16296c242be7a9742ebfbc2665adec1        refs/pull/2/head
15c9f4f80973a2758462ab2066b6ad9fe8dcf03d        refs/pull/2/merge
a5a7751a33b7e86c5e9bb07b26001bb17d775d1a        refs/pull/4/head
31a45fc257e8433c8d8804e3e848cf61c9d3166c        refs/pull/4/merge
```

Of course, if you're in your repository and you run `git ls-remote origin` or whatever remote you want to check, it will show you something similar to this.

If the repository is on GitHub and you have any Pull Requests that have been opened, you'll get these references that are prefixed with refs/pull/. These are basically branches, but since they're not under refs/heads/ you don't get them normally when you clone or fetch from the server — the process of fetching ignores them normally.

There are two references per Pull Request—the one that ends in /head points to exactly the same commit as the last commit in the Pull Request branch. So if someone opens a Pull Request in our repository and their branch is named bug-fix and it points to commit a5a775, then in our repository we will not have a bug-fix branch (because that's in their fork), but we will have pull/<pr#>/head that points to a5a775. This means that we can pretty easily pull down every Pull Request branch in one go without having to add a bunch of remotes.

Now, you could do something like fetching the reference directly.

```
$ git fetch origin refs/pull/958/head
From https://github.com/libgit2/libgit2
 * branch                refs/pull/958/head -> FETCH_HEAD
```

This tells Git, "Connect to the origin remote, and download the ref named refs/pull/958/head." Git happily obeys, and downloads everything you need to construct that ref, and puts a pointer to the commit you want under .git/FETCH_HEAD. You can follow that up with git merge FETCH_HEAD into a branch you want to test it in, but that merge commit message looks a bit weird. Also, if you're reviewing a lot of pull requests, this gets tedious.

There's also a way to fetch all the pull requests, and keep them up to date whenever you connect to the remote. Open up .git/config in your favorite editor, and look for the origin remote. It should look a bit like this:

```
[remote "origin"]
    url = https://github.com/libgit2/libgit2
    fetch = +refs/heads/*:refs/remotes/origin/*
```

That line that begins with fetch = is a "refspec." It's a way of mapping names on the remote with names in your local .git directory. This particular one tells Git, "the things on the remote that are under refs/heads should go in my local repository under refs/remotes/origin." You can modify this section to add another refspec:

```
[remote "origin"]
    url = https://github.com/libgit2/libgit2.git
    fetch = +refs/heads/*:refs/remotes/origin/*
    fetch = +refs/pull/*/head:refs/remotes/origin/pr/*
```

That last line tells Git, "All the refs that look like refs/pull/123/head should be stored locally like refs/remotes/origin/pr/123." Now, if you save that file, and do a git fetch:

```
$ git fetch
# ...
 * [new ref]             refs/pull/1/head -> origin/pr/1
 * [new ref]             refs/pull/2/head -> origin/pr/2
 * [new ref]             refs/pull/4/head -> origin/pr/4
# ...
```

Now all the remote pull requests are represented locally with refs that act much like tracking branches; they're read-only, and they update when you do a fetch. This makes it super easy to try the code from a pull request locally:

```
$ git checkout pr/2
Checking out files: 100% (3769/3769), done.
Branch pr/2 set up to track remote branch pr/2 from origin.
Switched to a new branch 'pr/2'
```

The eagle-eyed among you would note the head on the end of the remote portion of the refspec. There's also a `refs/pull/#/merge` ref on the GitHub side, which represents the commit that would result if you push the Merge button on the site. This can allow you to test the merge before even hitting the button.

Pull Requests on Pull Requests

Not only can you open Pull Requests that target the main or master branch, you can actually open a Pull Request targeting any branch in the network. In fact, you can even target another Pull Request.

If you see a Pull Request that is moving in the right direction and you have an idea for a change that depends on it or you're not sure is a good idea, or you just don't have push access to the target branch, you can open a Pull Request directly to it.

When you go to open a Pull Request, there is a box at the top of the page that specifies which branch you're requesting to pull to and which you're requesting to pull from. If you click the Edit button at the right of that box you can change not only the branches but also which fork.

Figure 6-37. *Manually change the Pull Request target fork and branch*

Here you can fairly easily specify to merge your new branch into another Pull Request or another fork of the project.

Mentions and Notifications

GitHub also has a pretty nice notifications system built in that can come in handy when you have questions or need feedback from specific individuals or teams.

In any comment you can start typing a @ character and it will begin to autocomplete with the names and usernames of people who are collaborators or contributors in the project.

Figure 6-38. Start typing @ to mention someone

You can also mention a user who is not in that dropdown, but often the autocompleter can make it faster.

Once you post a comment with a user mention, that user will be notified. This means that this can be a really effective way of pulling people into conversations rather than making them poll. Very often in Pull Requests on GitHub people will pull in other people on their teams or in their company to review an Issue or Pull Request.

If someone gets mentioned on a Pull Request or Issue, they will be subscribed to it and will continue getting notifications any time some activity occurs on it. You will also be subscribed to something if you opened it, if you're watching the repository, or if you comment on something. If you no longer want to receive notifications, there is an Unsubscribe button on the page you can click to stop receiving updates on it.

Notifications

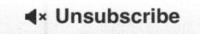

You're receiving notifications because you commented.

Figure 6-39. Unsubscribe from an Issue or Pull Request

The Notifications Page

When we mention "notifications" here with respect to GitHub, we mean a specific way that GitHub tries to get in touch with you when events happen and there are a few different ways you can configure them. If you go to the Notification center tab from the settings page, you can see some of the options you have.

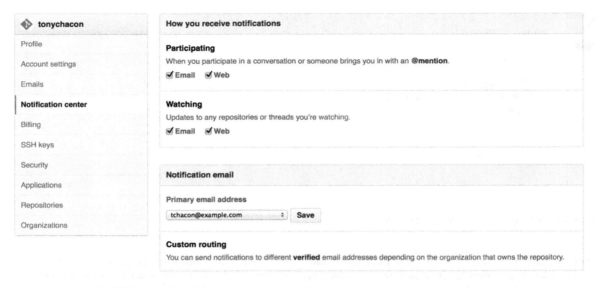

Figure 6-40. *Notification center options*

The two choices are to get notifications via Email and over Web and you can choose either, neither, or both for when you actively participate in things and for activity on repositories you are watching.

Web Notifications

Web notifications only exist on GitHub and you can only check them on GitHub. If you have this option selected in your preferences and a notification is triggered for you, you will see a small blue dot over your notifications icon at the top of your screen as seen in Figure 6-41.

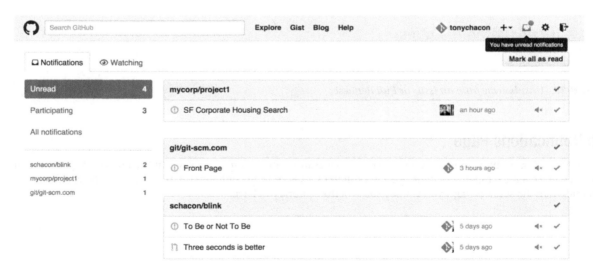

Figure 6-41. *Notification center*

If you click on that, you will see a list of all the items you have been notified about, grouped by project. You can filter to the notifications of a specific project by clicking on its name in the left-hand sidebar. You can also acknowledge the notification by clicking the checkmark icon next to any notification, or acknowledge all the notifications in a project by clicking the checkmark at the top of the group. There is also a mute button next to each checkmark that you can click to not receive any further notifications on that item.

All these tools are very useful for handling large numbers of notifications. Many GitHub power users will simply turn off email notifications entirely and manage all their notifications through this screen.

Email Notifications

Email notifications are the other way you can handle notifications through GitHub. If you have this turned on you will get emails for each notification. We saw examples of this in Figure 6-13 and Figure 6-34. The emails are threaded properly, which is nice if you're using a threading email client.

There is also a fair amount of metadata embedded in the headers of the emails that GitHub sends you, which can be really helpful for setting up custom filters and rules.

For instance, if we look at the actual email headers sent to Tony in the email shown in Figure 6-34, we will see the following among the information sent:

```
To: tonychacon/fade <fade@noreply.github.com>
Message-ID: <tonychacon/fade/pull/1@github.com>
Subject: [fade] Wait longer to see the dimming effect better (#1)
X-GitHub-Recipient: tonychacon
List-ID: tonychacon/fade <fade.tonychacon.github.com>
List-Archive: https://github.com/tonychacon/fade
List-Post: <mailto:reply+i-4XXX@reply.github.com>
List-Unsubscribe: <mailto:unsub+i-XXX@reply.github.com>,...
X-GitHub-Recipient-Address: tchacon@example.com
```

There are a couple of interesting things here. If you want to highlight or re-route emails to this particular project or even Pull Request, the information in Message-ID gives you all the data in <user>/<project>/<type>/<id> format. If this were an issue, for example, the <type> field would have been "issues" rather than "pull."

The List-Post and List-Unsubscribe fields mean that if you have a mail client that understands those, you can easily post to the list or unsubscribe from the thread. That would be essentially the same as clicking the mute button on the web version of the notification or Unsubscribe on the Issue or Pull Request page itself.

It's also worth noting that if you have both email and web notifications enabled and you read the email version of the notification, the web version will be marked as read as well if you have images allowed in your mail client.

Special Files

There are a couple of special files that GitHub will notice if they are present in your repository.

README

The first is the README file, which can be of nearly any format that GitHub recognizes as prose. For example, it could be README, README.md, README.asciidoc, etc. If GitHub sees a README file in your source, it will render it on the landing page of the project.

Many teams use this file to hold all the relevant project information for someone who might be new to the repository or project. This generally includes things such as:

- What the project is for

- How to configure and install it

- An example of how to use it or get it running

- The license that the project is offered under

- How to contribute to it

Because GitHub renders this file, you can embed images or links in it for added ease of understanding.

CONTRIBUTING

The other special file that GitHub recognizes is the CONTRIBUTING file. If you have a file named CONTRIBUTING with any file extension, GitHub will show what you can see in Figure 6-42 when anyone starts opening a Pull Request.

Figure 6-42. *Opening a Pull Request when a CONTRIBUTING file exists*

The idea here is that you can specify specific things you want or don't want in a Pull Request sent to your project. This way people may actually read the guidelines before opening the Pull Request.

Project Administration

Generally there are not a lot of administrative things you can do with a single project, but there are a couple of items that might be of interest.

Changing the Default Branch

If you are using a branch other than "master" as your default branch that you want people to open Pull Requests on or see by default, you can change that in your repository's settings page under the Options tab.

Figure 6-43. *Change the default branch for a project*

Simply change the default branch in the dropdown and that will be the default for all major operations from then on, including which branch is checked out by default when someone clones the repository.

Transferring a Project

If you would like to transfer a project to another user or an organization in GitHub, there is a Transfer ownership option at the bottom of the same Options tab of your repository settings page that allows you to do this.

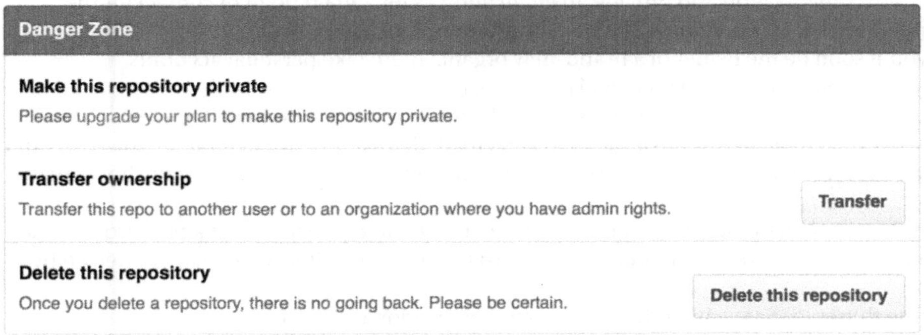

Danger Zone

Make this repository private
Please upgrade your plan to make this repository private.

Transfer ownership
Transfer this repo to another user or to an organization where you have admin rights.   Transfer

Delete this repository
Once you delete a repository, there is no going back. Please be certain.   Delete this repository

Figure 6-44. *Transfer a project to anther GitHub user or organization*

This is helpful if you are abandoning a project and someone wants to take it over, or if your project is getting bigger and you want to move it into an organization.

Not only does this move the repository along with all its watchers and stars to another place, it also sets up a redirect from your URL to the new place. It will also redirect clones and fetches from Git, not just web requests.

Managing an Organization

In addition to single-user accounts, GitHub has what are called organizations. Like personal accounts, organizational accounts have a namespace where all their projects exist, but many other things are different. These accounts represent a group of people with shared ownership of projects, and there are many tools to manage subgroups of those people. Normally these accounts are used for Open Source groups (such as "perl" or "rails") or companies (such as "google" or "twitter").

Organization Basics

An organization is pretty easy to create; just click the + icon at the top-right of any GitHub page, and select New organization from the menu.

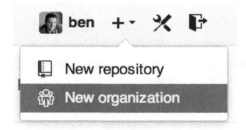

Figure 6-45. *The New organization menu item*

First you'll need to name your organization and provide an email address for a main point of contact for the group. Then you can invite other users to be co-owners of the account if you want to.

Follow these steps and you'll soon be the owner of a brand-new organization. Like personal accounts, organizations are free if everything you plan to store there will be open source.

As an owner in an organization, when you fork a repository, you'll have the choice of forking it to your organization's namespace. When you create new repositories you can create them either under your personal account or under any of the organizations that you are an owner in. You also automatically "watch" any new repository created under these organizations.

Just like your personal avatar, you can upload an avatar for your organization to personalize it a bit. Also just like personal accounts, you have a landing page for the organization that lists all your repositories and can be viewed by other people.

Now let's cover some of the things that are a bit different with an organizational account.

Teams

Organizations are associated with individual people by way of teams, which are simply a grouping of individual user accounts and repositories within the organization and what kind of access those people have in those repositories.

For example, say your company has three repositories: frontend, backend, and deployscripts. You'd want your HTML/CSS/Javascript developers to have access to frontend and maybe backend, and your Operations people to have access to backend and deployscripts. Teams make this easy, without having to manage the collaborators for every individual repository.

The Organization page shows you a simple dashboard of all the repositories, users, and teams that are under this organization.

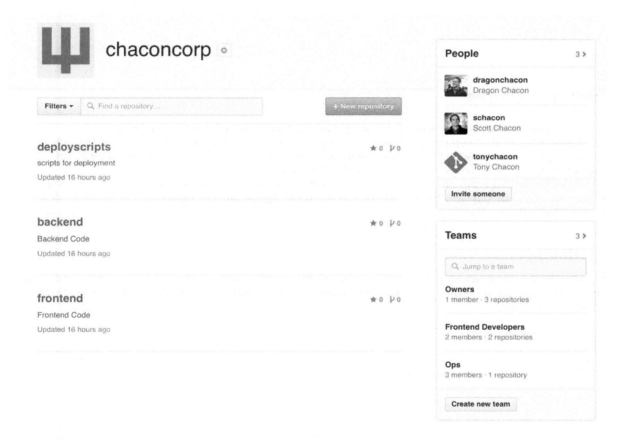

Figure 6-46. *The Organization page*

To manage your teams, you can click on the Teams sidebar on the right-hand side of the page in Figure 6-46. This brings you to a page you can use to add members to the team, add repositories to the team, or manage the settings and access control levels for the team. Each team can have read only, read/write, or administrative access to the repositories. You can change that level by clicking the Settings button in Figure 6-47.

Figure 6-47. *The Team page*

When you invite someone to a team, they will get an email letting them know they've been invited.

Additionally, team @mentions (such as @acmecorp/frontend) work much the same as they do with individual users, except that all members of the team are then subscribed to the thread. This is useful if you want the attention from someone on a team, but you don't know exactly who to ask.

A user can belong to any number of teams, so don't limit yourself to only access-control teams. Special-interest teams such as ux, css, or refactoring are useful for certain kinds of questions, and others such as legal and colorblind for an entirely different kind.

Audit Log

Organizations also give owners access to all the information about what went on under the organization. You can go to the Audit Log tab and see what events have happened at an organization level, who did them, and where in the world they were done.

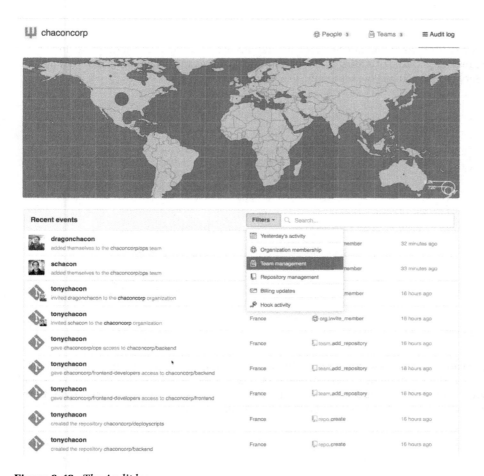

Figure 6-48. *The Audit log*

You can also filter down to specific types of events, specific places, or specific people.

Scripting GitHub

So now we've covered all the major features and workflows of GitHub, but any large group or project will have customizations they may want to make or external services they may want to integrate.

Luckily for us, GitHub is really quite hackable in many ways. In this section we'll cover how to use the GitHub hooks system and its API to make GitHub work how we want it to.

Hooks

The Hooks and Services section of GitHub repository administration is the easiest way to have GitHub interact with external systems.

Services

First we'll take a look at Services. Both the Hooks and Services integrations can be found in the Settings section of your repository, where we previously looked at adding Collaborators and changing the default branch of your project. Under the Webhooks and Services tab you will see something like Figure 6-49.

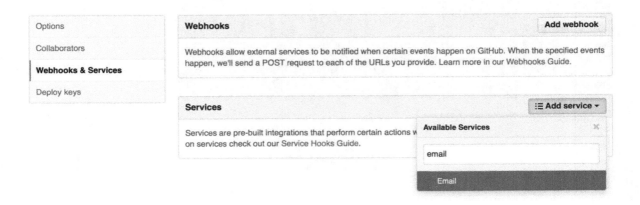

Figure 6-49. *Services and Hooks configuration section*

There are dozens of services you can choose from, most of them integrations into other commercial and open source systems. Most of them are for Continuous Integration services, bug and issue trackers, chat room systems, and documentation systems. We'll walk through setting up a very simple one, the Email hook. If you choose "email" from the Add Service dropdown, you'll get a configuration screen like Figure 6-50.

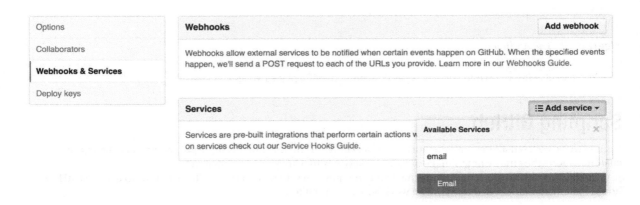

Figure 6-50. *Email service configuration*

In this case, if we click the Add service button, the email address we specified will get an email every time someone pushes to the repository. Services can listen for lots of different types of events, but most only listen for push events and then do something with that data.

If there is a system you are using that you would like to integrate with GitHub, you should check here to see if there is an existing service integration available. For example, if you're using Jenkins to run tests on your codebase, you can enable the Jenkins built-in service integration to kick off a test run every time someone pushes to your repository.

Hooks

If you need something more specific or you want to integrate with a service or site that is not included in this list, you can instead use the more generic hooks system. GitHub repository hooks are pretty simple. You specify a URL and GitHub will post an HTTP payload to that URL on any event you want.

Generally the way this works is you can setup a small web service to listen for a GitHub hook payload and then do something with the data when it is received.

To enable a hook, you click the Add webhook button in Figure 6-49. This brings you to a page that looks like Figure 6-51.

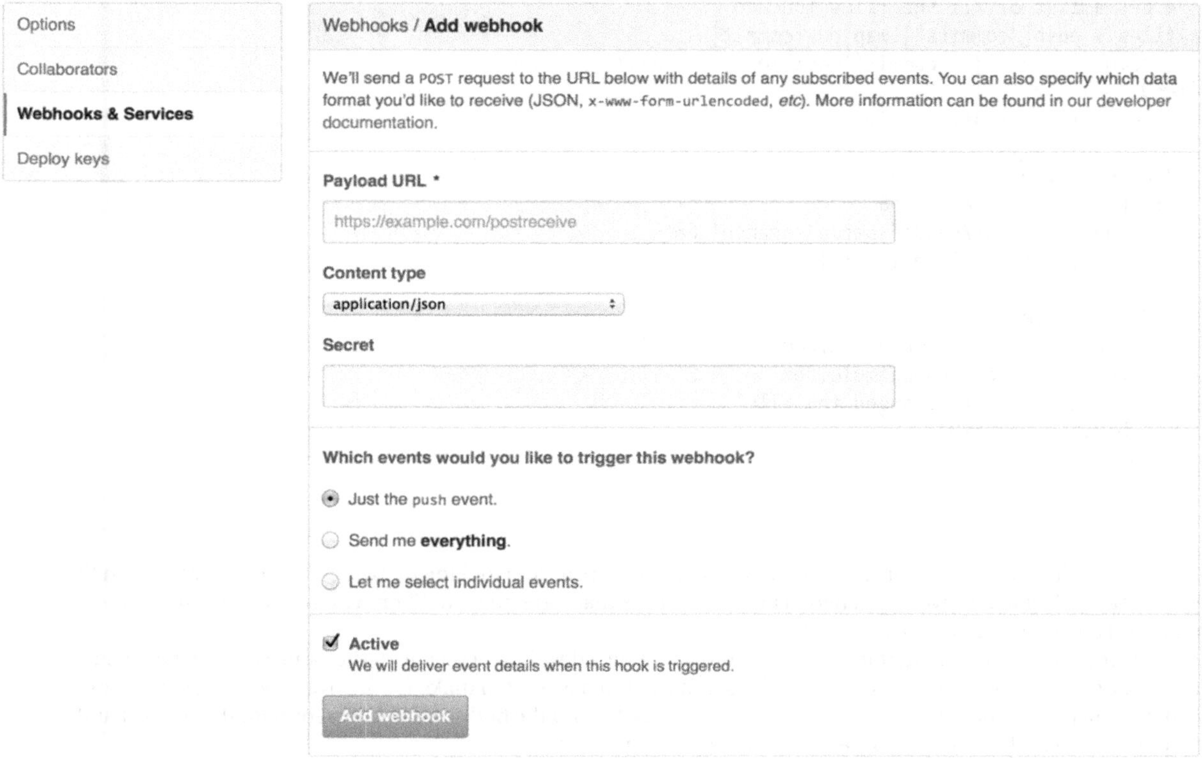

Figure 6-51. *Webhook configuration*

The configuration for a webhook is pretty simple. In most cases you simply enter a URL and a secret key and click Add webhook. There are a few options for which events you want GitHub to send you a payload for — the default is to only get a payload for the push event, when someone pushes new code to any branch of your repository.

Here is a small example of a web service you may set up to handle a webhook. We'll use the Ruby web framework Sinatra because it's fairly concise and you should be able to easily see what we're doing.

Let's say we want to get an email if a specific person pushes to a specific branch of our project modifying a specific file. We could fairly easily do that with code like this:

```ruby
require 'sinatra'
require 'json'
require 'mail'

post '/payload' do
  push = JSON.parse(request.body.read) # parse the JSON

  # gather the data we're looking for
  pusher = push["pusher"]["name"]
  branch = push["ref"]

  # get a list of all the files touched
  files = push["commits"].map do |commit|
    commit['added'] + commit['modified'] + commit['removed']
  end
  files = files.flatten.uniq

  # check for our criteria
  if pusher == 'schacon' &&
     branch == 'ref/heads/special-branch' &&
     files.include?('special-file.txt')

    Mail.deliver do
      from    'tchacon@example.com'
      to      'tchacon@example.com'
      subject 'Scott Changed the File'
      body    "ALARM"
    end
  end
end
```

Here we're taking the JSON payload that GitHub delivers us and looking up who pushed it, what branch they pushed to and what files were touched in all the commits that were pushed. Then we check that against our criteria and send an email if it matches.

To develop and test something like this, you have a nice developer console in the same screen where you set up the hook. You can see the last few deliveries that GitHub has tried to make for that webhook. For each hook you can dig down into when it was delivered, if it was successful and the body and headers for both the request and the response. This makes it incredibly easy to test and debug your hooks.

Figure 6-52. *Webhook debugging information*

The other great feature of this is that you can redeliver any of the payloads to test your service easily.

For more information on how to write webhooks and all the different event types you can listen for, go to the GitHub Developer documentation at: `https://developer.github.com/webhooks/`.

The GitHub API

Services and hooks give you a way to receive push notifications about events that happen on your repositories, but what if you need more information about these events? What if you need to automate something such as adding collaborators or labeling issues?

This is where the GitHub API comes in handy. GitHub has tons of API endpoints for doing nearly anything you can do on the website in an automated fashion. In this section we'll learn how to authenticate and connect to the API, how to comment on an issue, and how to change the status of a Pull Request through the API.

Basic Usage

The most basic thing you can do is a simple GET request on an endpoint that doesn't require authentication. This could be a user or read-only information on an open source project. For example, if we want to know more about a user named schacon, we can run something like this:

```
$ curl https://api.github.com/users/schacon
{
  "login": "schacon",
  "id": 70,
  "avatar_url": "https://avatars.githubusercontent.com/u/70",
# ...
  "name": "Scott Chacon",
  "company": "GitHub",
  "following": 19,
  "created_at": "2008-01-27T17:19:28Z",
  "updated_at": "2014-06-10T02:37:23Z"
}
```

There are tons of endpoints like this to get information about organizations, projects, issues, commits — just about anything you can publicly see on GitHub. You can even use the API to render arbitrary Markdown or find a .gitignore template.

```
$ curl https://api.github.com/gitignore/templates/Java
{
  "name": "Java",
  "source": "*.class

# Mobile Tools for Java (J2ME)
.mtj.tmp/

# Package Files #
*.jar
*.war
*.ear

# virtual machine crash logs, see http://www.java.com/en/download/help/error_hotspot.xml
hs_err_pid*
"
}
```

Commenting on an Issue

However, if you want to do an action on the website such as comment on an Issue or Pull Request or if you want to view or interact with private content, you'll need to authenticate.

There are several ways to authenticate. You can use basic authentication with just your username and password, but generally it's a better idea to use a personal access token. You can generate this from the Applications tab of your settings page.

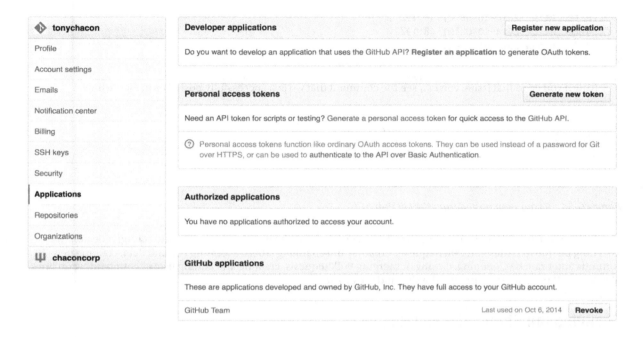

Figure 6-53. *Generate your access token from the Applications tab of your settings page*

It will ask you which scopes you want for this token and a description. Make sure to use a good description so you feel comfortable removing the token when your script or application is no longer used.

GitHub will only show you the token once, so be sure to copy it. You can now use this to authenticate in your script instead of using a username and password. This is nice because you can limit the scope of what you want to do and the token is revocable.

This also has the added advantage of increasing your rate limit. Without authenticating, you will be limited to 60 requests per hour. If you authenticate you can make up to 5,000 requests per hour.

So let's use it to make a comment on one of our issues. Let's say we want to leave a comment on a specific issue, Issue #6. To do so we have to do an HTTP POST request to repos/<user>/<repo>/issues/<num>/comments with the token we just generated as an Authorization header.

```
$ curl -H "Content-Type: application/json" \
       -H "Authorization: token TOKEN" \
       --data '{"body":"A new comment, :+1:"}' \
       https://api.github.com/repos/schacon/blink/issues/6/comments
{
  "id": 58322100,
  "html_url": "https://github.com/schacon/blink/issues/6#issuecomment-58322100",
  ...
  "user": {
    "login": "tonychacon",
    "id": 7874698,
    "avatar_url": "https://avatars.githubusercontent.com/u/7874698?v=2",
    "type": "User",
  },
```

```
  "created_at": "2014-10-08T07:48:19Z",
  "updated_at": "2014-10-08T07:48:19Z",
  "body": "A new comment, :+1:"
}
```

Now if you go to that issue, you can see the comment that we just successfully posted as in Figure 6-54.

Figure 6-54. *A comment posted from the GitHub API*

You can use the API to do just about anything you can do on the website — creating and setting milestones, assigning people to Issues and Pull Requests, creating and changing labels, accessing commit data, creating new commits and branches, opening, closing or merging Pull Requests, creating and editing teams, commenting on lines of code in a Pull Request, searching the site, and on and on.

Changing the Status of a Pull Request

One final example we'll look at since it's really useful if you're working with Pull Requests. Each commit can have one or more statuses associated with it and there is an API to add and query that status.

Most of the Continuous Integration and testing services make use of this API to react to pushes by testing the code that was pushed, and then report back if that commit has passed all the tests. You could also use this to check whether the commit message is properly formatted, if the submitter followed all your contribution guidelines, if the commit was validly signed — any number of things.

Let's say you set up a webhook on your repository that hits a small web service that checks for a Signed-off-by string in the commit message.

```
require 'httparty'
require 'sinatra'
require 'json'

post '/payload' do
  push = JSON.parse(request.body.read) # parse the JSON
  repo_name = push['repository']['full_name']

  # look through each commit message
  push["commits"].each do |commit|

    # look for a Signed-off-by string
    if /Signed-off-by/.match commit['message']
      state = 'success'
      description = 'Successfully signed off!'
    else
      state = 'failure'
      description = 'No signoff found.'
    end
```

```
  # post status to GitHub
  sha = commit["id"]
  status_url = "https://api.github.com/repos/#{repo_name}/statuses/#{sha}"

  status = {
    "state"       => state,
    "description" => description,
    "target_url"  => "http://example.com/how-to-signoff",
    "context"     => "validate/signoff"
  }
  HTTParty.post(status_url,
    :body => status.to_json,
    :headers => {
      'Content-Type'  => 'application/json',
      'User-Agent'    => 'tonychacon/signoff',
      'Authorization' => "token #{ENV['TOKEN']}" }
  )
  end
end
```

Hopefully this is fairly simple to follow. In this webhook handler we look through each commit that was just pushed, we look for the string Signed-off-by in the commit message and finally we POST via HTTP to the /repos/<user>/<repo>/statuses/<commit_sha> API endpoint with the status.

In this case you can send a state (success, failure, error), a description of what happened, a target URL the user can go to for more information and a context in case there are multiple statuses for a single commit. For example, a testing service may provide a status and a validation service like this may also provide a status — the context field is how they're differentiated.

If someone opens a new Pull Request on GitHub and this hook is setup, you may see something like Figure 6-55.

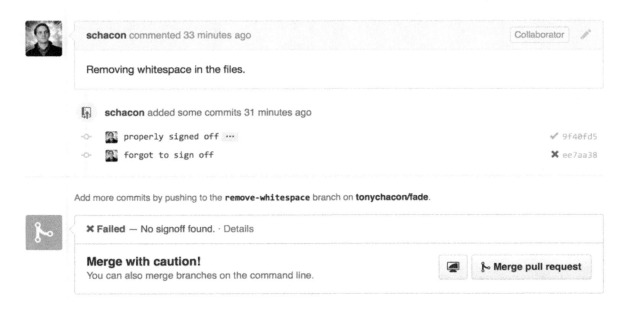

Figure 6-55. Commit status via the API

You can now see a little green checkmark next to the commit that has a "Signed-off-by" string in the message and a red cross through the one where the author forgot to sign off. You can also see that the Pull Request takes the status of the last commit on the branch and warns you if it is a failure. This is really useful if you're using this API for test results so you don't accidentally merge something where the last commit is failing tests.

Octokit

Though we've been doing nearly everything through curl and simple HTTP requests in these examples, several open-source libraries exist that make this API available in a more idiomatic way. At the time of this writing, the supported languages include Go, Objective-C, Ruby, and .NET. Check out `http://github.com/octokit` for more information on these, as they handle much of the HTTP for you.

Hopefully these tools can help you customize and modify GitHub to work better for your specific workflows. For complete documentation on the entire API as well as guides for common tasks, check out `https://developer.github.com`.

Summary

Now you're a GitHub user. You know how to create an account, manage an organization, create and push to repositories, contribute to other people's projects, and accept contributions from others. In the next chapter, you'll learn about more powerful tools and tips for dealing with complex situations, which will truly make you a Git master.

CHAPTER 7

Git Tools

By now, you've learned most of the day-to-day commands and workflows that you need to manage or maintain a Git repository for your source code control. You've accomplished the basic tasks of tracking and committing files, and you've harnessed the power of the staging area and lightweight topic branching and merging.

Now you'll explore a number of very powerful things that Git can do that you may not necessarily use on a day-to-day basis but that you may need at some point.

Revision Selection

Git allows you to specify specific commits or a range of commits in several ways. They aren't necessarily obvious but are helpful to know.

Single Revisions

You can obviously refer to a commit by the SHA-1 hash that it's given, but there are more human-friendly ways to refer to commits as well. This section outlines the various ways you can refer to a single commit.

Short SHA

Git is smart enough to figure out what commit you meant to type if you provide the first few characters, as long as your partial SHA-1 is at least four characters long and unambiguous—that is, only one object in the current repository begins with that partial SHA-1.

For example, to see a specific commit, suppose you run a `git log` command and identify the commit where you added certain functionality:

```
$ git log
commit 734713bc047d87bf7eac9674765ae793478c50d3
Author: Scott Chacon <schacon@gmail.com>
Date:   Fri Jan 2 18:32:33 2009 -0800

    fixed refs handling, added gc auto, updated tests

commit d921970aadf03b3cf0e71becdaab3147ba71cdef
Merge: 1c002dd... 35cfb2b...
Author: Scott Chacon <schacon@gmail.com>
Date:   Thu Dec 11 15:08:43 2008 -0800

    Merge commit 'phedders/rdocs'
```

```
commit 1c002dd4b536e7479fe34593e72e6c6c1819e53b
Author: Scott Chacon <schacon@gmail.com>
Date:   Thu Dec 11 14:58:32 2008 -0800

    added some blame and merge stuff
```

In this case, choose 1c002dd.... If you git show that commit, the following commands are equivalent (assuming the shorter versions are unambiguous):

```
$ git show 1c002dd4b536e7479fe34593e72e6c6c1819e53b
$ git show 1c002dd4b536e7479f
$ git show 1c002d
```

Git can figure out a short, unique abbreviation for your SHA-1 values. If you pass --abbrev-commit to the git log command, the output will use shorter values but keep them unique; it defaults to using seven characters but makes them longer if necessary to keep the SHA-1 unambiguous:

```
$ git log --abbrev-commit --pretty=oneline
ca82a6d changed the version number
085bb3b removed unnecessary test code
a11bef0 first commit
```

Generally, eight to ten characters are more than enough to be unique within a project.

As an example, the Linux kernel, which is a pretty large project with over 450k commits and 3.6 million objects, has no two objects whose SHAs overlap more than the first 11 characters.

A SHORT NOTE ABOUT SHA-1

A lot of people become concerned at some point that they will, by random happenstance, have two objects in their repository that hash to the same SHA-1 value. What then?

If you do happen to commit an object that hashes to the same SHA-1 value as a previous object in your repository, Git will see the previous object already in your Git database and assume it was already written. If you try to check out that object again at some point, you'll always get the data of the first object.

However, you should be aware of how ridiculously unlikely this scenario is. The SHA-1 digest is 20 bytes or 160 bits. The number of randomly hashed objects needed to ensure a 50% probability of a single collision is about 2^{80} (the formula for determining collision probability is $p = (n(n-1)/2) * (1/2^{160})$). 280 is 1.2×10^{24} or 1 million billion billion. That's 1,200 times the number of grains of sand on the earth.

Here's an example to give you an idea of what it would take to get a SHA-1 collision. If all 6.5 billion humans on Earth were programming, and every second, each one was producing code that was the equivalent of the entire Linux kernel history (3.6 million Git objects) and pushing it into one enormous Git repository, it would take roughly 2 years until that repository contained enough objects to have a 50% probability of a single SHA-1 object collision. A higher probability exists that every member of your programming team will be attacked and killed by wolves in unrelated incidents on the same night.

Branch References

The most straightforward way to specify a commit requires that it have a branch reference pointed at it. Then, you can use a branch name in any Git command that expects a commit object or SHA-1 value. For instance, if you want to show the last commit object on a branch, the following commands are equivalent, assuming that the topic1 branch points to ca82a6d:

```
$ git show ca82a6dff817ec66f44342007202690a93763949
$ git show topic1
```

If you want to see which specific SHA a branch points to, or if you want to see what any of these examples boils down to in terms of SHAs, you can use a Git plumbing tool called rev-parse. You can see Chapter 11 for more information about plumbing tools; basically, rev-parse exists for lower-level operations and isn't designed to be used in day-to-day operations. However, it can be helpful sometimes when you need to see what's really going on. Here you can run rev-parse on your branch.

```
$ git rev-parse topic1
ca82a6dff817ec66f44342007202690a93763949
```

RefLog Shortnames

One of the things Git does in the background while you're working away is keep a "reflog"—a log of where your HEAD and branch references have been for the last few months.

You can see your reflog by using git reflog:

```
$ git reflog
734713b... HEAD@{0}: commit: fixed refs handling, added gc auto, updated
d921970... HEAD@{1}: merge phedders/rdocs: Merge made by recursive.
1c002dd... HEAD@{2}: commit: added some blame and merge stuff
1c36188... HEAD@{3}: rebase -i (squash): updating HEAD
95df984... HEAD@{4}: commit: # This is a combination of two commits.
1c36188... HEAD@{5}: rebase -i (squash): updating HEAD
7e05da5... HEAD@{6}: rebase -i (pick): updating HEAD
```

Every time your branch tip is updated for any reason, Git stores that information for you in this temporary history. And you can specify older commits with this data, as well. If you want to see the fifth prior value of the HEAD of your repository, you can use the @{n} reference that you see in the reflog output:

```
$ git show HEAD@{5}
```

You can also use this syntax to see where a branch was some specific amount of time ago. For instance, to see where your master branch was yesterday, you can type

```
$ git show master@{yesterday}
```

That shows you where the branch tip was yesterday. This technique only works for data that's still in your reflog, so you can't use it to look for commits older than a few months.

To see reflog information formatted like the git log output, you can run git log -g:

```
$ git log -g master
commit 734713bc047d87bf7eac9674765ae793478c50d3
Reflog: master@{0} (Scott Chacon <schacon@gmail.com>)
Reflog message: commit: fixed refs handling, added gc auto, updated
Author: Scott Chacon <schacon@gmail.com>
Date:   Fri Jan 2 18:32:33 2009 -0800

    fixed refs handling, added gc auto, updated tests

commit d921970aadf03b3cf0e71becdaab3147ba71cdef
Reflog: master@{1} (Scott Chacon <schacon@gmail.com>)
Reflog message: merge phedders/rdocs: Merge made by recursive.
Author: Scott Chacon <schacon@gmail.com>
Date:   Thu Dec 11 15:08:43 2008 -0800

    Merge commit 'phedders/rdocs'
```

It's important to note that the reflog information is strictly local—it's a log of what you've done in your repository. The references won't be the same on someone else's copy of the repository; and right after you initially clone a repository, you'll have an empty reflog, as no activity has occurred yet in your repository. Running git show HEAD@{2.months.ago} will work only if you cloned the project at least two months ago—if you cloned it five minutes ago, you'll get no results.

Ancestry References

The other main way to specify a commit is via its ancestry. If you place a ^ at the end of a reference, Git resolves it to mean the parent of that commit. Suppose you look at the history of your project:

```
$ git log --pretty=format:'%h %s' --graph
* 734713b fixed refs handling, added gc auto, updated tests
*   d921970 Merge commit 'phedders/rdocs'
|\
| * 35cfb2b Some rdoc changes
* | 1c002dd added some blame and merge stuff
|/
* 1c36188 ignore *.gem
* 9b29157 add open3_detach to gemspec file list
```

Then, you can see the previous commit by specifying HEAD^, which means "the parent of HEAD."

```
$ git show HEAD^
commit d921970aadf03b3cf0e71becdaab3147ba71cdef
Merge: 1c002dd... 35cfb2b...
Author: Scott Chacon <schacon@gmail.com>
Date:   Thu Dec 11 15:08:43 2008 -0800

    Merge commit 'phedders/rdocs'
```

You can also specify a number after the ^—for example, d921970^2 means "the second parent of d921970." This syntax is only useful for merge commits, which have more than one parent. The first parent is the branch you were on when you merged, and the second is the commit on the branch that you merged in:

```
$ git show d921970^
commit 1c002dd4b536e7479fe34593e72e6c6c1819e53b
Author: Scott Chacon <schacon@gmail.com>
Date:   Thu Dec 11 14:58:32 2008 -0800

    added some blame and merge stuff

$ git show d921970^2
commit 35cfb2b795a55793d7cc56a6cc2060b4bb732548
Author: Paul Hedderly <paul+git@mjr.org>
Date:   Wed Dec 10 22:22:03 2008 +0000

    Some rdoc changes
```

The other main ancestry specification is the ~. This also refers to the first parent, so HEAD~ and HEAD^ are equivalent. The difference becomes apparent when you specify a number. HEAD~2 means "the first parent of the first parent," or "the grandparent"—it traverses the first parents the number of times you specify. For example, in the history listed earlier, HEAD~3 would be

```
$ git show HEAD~3
commit 1c3618887afb5fbcbea25b7c013f4e2114448b8d
Author: Tom Preston-Werner <tom@mojombo.com>
Date:   Fri Nov 7 13:47:59 2008 -0500

    ignore *.gem
```

This can also be written HEAD^^^, which again is the first parent of the first parent of the first parent:

```
$ git show HEAD^^^
commit 1c3618887afb5fbcbea25b7c013f4e2114448b8d
Author: Tom Preston-Werner <tom@mojombo.com>
Date:   Fri Nov 7 13:47:59 2008 -0500

    ignore *.gem
```

You can also combine these syntaxes—you can get the second parent of the previous reference (assuming it was a merge commit) by using HEAD~3^2, and so on.

Commit Ranges

Now that you can specify individual commits, let's see how to specify ranges of commits. This is particularly useful for managing your branches—if you have a lot of branches, you can use range specifications to answer questions such as, "What work is on this branch that I haven't yet merged into my main branch?"

Double Dot

The most common range specification is the double-dot syntax. This basically asks Git to resolve a range of commits that are reachable from one commit but aren't reachable from another. For example, say you have a commit history that looks like Figure 7-1.

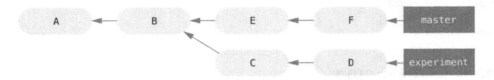

Figure 7-1. *Example history for range selection*

You want to see what is in your experiment branch that hasn't yet been merged into your master branch. You can ask Git to show you a log of just those commits with `master..experiment`—that means "all commits reachable by experiment that aren't reachable by master." For the sake of brevity and clarity in these examples, I'll use the letters of the commit objects from the diagram in place of the actual log output in the order that they would display:

```
$ git log master..experiment
D
C
```

If, on the other hand, you want to see the opposite—all commits in `master` that aren't in `experiment`—you can reverse the branch names. `experiment..master` shows you everything in master not reachable from experiment:

```
$ git log experiment..master
F
E
```

This is useful if you want to keep the `experiment` branch up to date and preview what you're about to merge in. Another very frequent use of this syntax is to see what you're about to push to a remote:

```
$ git log origin/master..HEAD
```

This command shows you any commits in your current branch that aren't in the `master` branch on your `origin` remote. If you run a `git push` and your current branch is tracking `origin/master`, the commits listed by `git log origin/master..HEAD` are the commits that will be transferred to the server. You can also leave off one side of the syntax to have Git assume HEAD. For example, you can get the same results as in the previous example by typing `git log origin/master..` – Git substitutes HEAD if one side is missing.

Multiple Points

The double-dot syntax is useful as shorthand; but perhaps you want to specify more than two branches to indicate your revision, such as seeing what commits are in any of several branches that aren't in the branch you're currently on. Git allows you to do this by using either the ^ character or --not before any reference from which you don't want to see reachable commits. Thus these three commands are equivalent:

```
$ git log refA..refB
$ git log ^refA refB
$ git log refB --not refA
```

This is nice because with this syntax you can specify more than two references in your query, which you cannot do with the double-dot syntax. For instance, if you want to see all commits that are reachable from refA or refB but not from refC, you can type one of these:

```
$ git log refA refB ^refC
$ git log refA refB --not refC
```

This makes for a very powerful revision query system that should help you figure out what is in your branches.

Triple Dot

The last major range-selection syntax is the triple-dot syntax, which specifies all the commits that are reachable by either of two references but not by both of them. Look back at the example commit history in Example history for range selection. If you want to see what is in master or experiment but not any common references, you can run

```
$ git log master...experiment
F
E
D
C
```

Again, this gives you normal log output but shows you only the commit information for those four commits, appearing in the traditional commit date ordering.

A common switch to use with the log command in this case is --left-right, which shows you which side of the range each commit is in. This helps make the data more useful:

```
$ git log --left-right master...experiment
< F
< E
> D
> C
```

With these tools, you can much more easily let Git know what commit or commits you want to inspect.

Interactive Staging

Git comes with a couple of scripts that make some command-line tasks easier. Here, you'll look at a few interactive commands that can help you easily craft your commits to include only certain combinations and parts of files. These tools are very helpful if you modify a bunch of files and then decide that you want those changes to be in several focused commits rather than one big messy commit. This way, you can make sure your commits are logically separate changesets and can be easily reviewed by the developers working with you. If you run `git add` with the `-i` or `--interactive` option, Git goes into an interactive shell mode, displaying something like this:

```
$ git add -i
          staged     unstaged path
  1:    unchanged     +0/-1 TODO
  2:    unchanged     +1/-1 index.html
  3:    unchanged     +5/-1 lib/simplegit.rb

*** Commands ***
  1: status     2: update     3: revert     4: add untracked
  5: patch      6: diff       7: quit       8: help
What now>
```

You can see that this command shows you a much different view of your staging area—basically the same information you get with `git status` but a bit more succinct and informative. It lists the changes you've staged on the left and unstaged changes on the right.

After this comes a Commands section. Here you can do a number of things, including staging files, unstaging files, staging parts of files, adding untracked files, and seeing diffs of what has been staged.

Staging and Unstaging Files

If you type 2 or u at the `What now>` prompt, the script prompts you for which files you want to stage:

```
What now> 2
          staged     unstaged path
  1:    unchanged     +0/-1 TODO
  2:    unchanged     +1/-1 index.html
  3:    unchanged     +5/-1 lib/simplegit.rb
Update>>
```

To stage the `TODO` and `index.html` files, you can type the numbers:

```
Update>> 1,2
          staged     unstaged path
* 1:    unchanged     +0/-1 TODO
* 2:    unchanged     +1/-1 index.html
  3:    unchanged     +5/-1 lib/simplegit.rb
Update>>
```

The * next to each file means the file is selected to be staged. If you press Enter after typing nothing at the Update>> prompt, Git takes anything selected and stages it for you:

```
Update>>
updated 2 paths

*** Commands ***
  1: status     2: update     3: revert     4: add untracked
  5: patch      6: diff       7: quit       8: help
What now> 1
           staged     unstaged path
  1:       +0/-1      nothing TODO
  2:       +1/-1      nothing index.html
  3:     unchanged     +5/-1 lib/simplegit.rb
```

Now you can see that the TODO and index.html files are staged and the simplegit.rb file is still unstaged. If you want to unstage the TODO file at this point, you use the 3 or r (for revert) option:

```
*** Commands ***
  1: status     2: update     3: revert     4: add untracked
  5: patch      6: diff       7: quit       8: help
What now> 3
           staged     unstaged path
  1:       +0/-1      nothing TODO
  2:       +1/-1      nothing index.html
  3:     unchanged     +5/-1 lib/simplegit.rb
Revert>> 1
           staged     unstaged path
* 1:       +0/-1      nothing TODO
  2:       +1/-1      nothing index.html
  3:     unchanged     +5/-1 lib/simplegit.rb
Revert>> [enter]
reverted one path
```

Looking at your Git status again, you can see that you've unstaged the TODO file:

```
*** Commands ***
  1: status     2: update     3: revert     4: add untracked
  5: patch      6: diff       7: quit       8: help
What now> 1
           staged     unstaged path
  1:     unchanged     +0/-1 TODO
  2:       +1/-1      nothing index.html
  3:     unchanged     +5/-1 lib/simplegit.rb
```

To see the diff of what you've staged, you can use the 6 or d (for diff) command. It shows you a list of your staged files, and you can select the ones for which you would like to see the staged diff. This is much like specifying git diff --cached on the command line:

```
*** Commands ***
  1: status     2: update     3: revert     4: add untracked
  5: patch      6: diff       7: quit       8: help
What now> 6
           staged       unstaged path
  1:        +1/-1         nothing index.html
Review diff>> 1
diff --git a/index.html b/index.html
index 4d07108..4335f49 100644
--- a/index.html
+++ b/index.html
@@ -16,7 +16,7 @@ Date Finder

 <p id="out">...</p>

-<div id="footer">contact : support@github.com</div>
+<div id="footer">contact : email.support@github.com</div>

 <script type="text/javascript">
```

With these basic commands, you can use the interactive add mode to deal with your staging area a little more easily.

Staging Patches

It's also possible for Git to stage certain parts of files and not the rest. For example, if you make two changes to your simplegit.rb file and want to stage one of them and not the other, doing so is very easy in Git. From the interactive prompt, type 5 or p (for patch). Git will ask you which files you would like to partially stage; then, for each section of the selected files, it will display hunks of the file diff and ask if you would like to stage them, one by one:

```
diff --git a/lib/simplegit.rb b/lib/simplegit.rb
index dd5ecc4..57399e0 100644
--- a/lib/simplegit.rb
+++ b/lib/simplegit.rb
@@ -22,7 +22,7 @@ class SimpleGit
    end

    def log(treeish = 'master')
-     command("git log -n 25 #{treeish}")
+     command("git log -n 30 #{treeish}")
    end

    def blame(path)
Stage this hunk [y,n,a,d,/,j,J,g,e,?]?
```

You have a lot of options at this point. Typing ? shows a list of what you can do:

```
Stage this hunk [y,n,a,d,/,j,J,g,e,?]? ?
y - stage this hunk
n - do not stage this hunk
a - stage this and all the remaining hunks in the file
d - do not stage this hunk nor any of the remaining hunks in the file
g - select a hunk to go to
/ - search for a hunk matching the given regex
j - leave this hunk undecided, see next undecided hunk
J - leave this hunk undecided, see next hunk
k - leave this hunk undecided, see previous undecided hunk
K - leave this hunk undecided, see previous hunk
s - split the current hunk into smaller hunks
e - manually edit the current hunk
? - print help
```

Generally, you'll type y or n if you want to stage each hunk, but staging all of them in certain files or skipping a hunk decision until later can be helpful too. If you stage one part of the file and leave another part unstaged, your status output will look like this:

```
What now> 1
           staged     unstaged path
  1:    unchanged        +0/-1 TODO
  2:        +1/-1      nothing index.html
  3:        +1/-1        +4/-0 lib/simplegit.rb
```

The status of the `simplegit.rb` file is interesting. It shows you that a couple of lines are staged and a couple are unstaged. You've partially staged this file. At this point, you can exit the interactive adding script and run `git commit` to commit the partially staged files.

You also don't need to be in interactive add mode to do the partial-file staging—you can start the same script by using `git add -p` or `git add --patch` on the command line.

Furthermore, you can use patch mode for partially resetting files with the reset `--patch` command, for checking out parts of files with the checkout `--patch` command and for stashing parts of files with the `stash save --patch` command. We'll go into more details on each of these as we get to more advanced usages of these commands.

Stashing and Cleaning

Often, when you've been working on part of your project, things are in a messy state and you want to switch branches for a bit to work on something else. The problem is, you don't want to do a commit of half-done work just so you can get back to this point later. The answer to this issue is the `git stash` command.

Stashing takes the dirty state of your working directory—that is, your modified tracked files and staged changes—and saves it on a stack of unfinished changes that you can reapply at any time.

Stashing Your Work

To demonstrate, you'll go into your project and start working on a couple of files and possibly stage one of the changes. If you run git status, you can see your dirty state:

```
$ git status
Changes to be committed:
  (use "git reset HEAD <file>..." to unstage)

      modified: index.html

Changes not staged for commit:
  (use "git add <file>..." to update what will be committed)
  (use "git checkout -- <file>..." to discard changes in working directory)

      modified: lib/simplegit.rb
```

Now you want to switch branches, but you don't want to commit what you've been working on yet; so you'll stash the changes. To push a new stash onto your stack, run git stash or git stash save:

```
$ git stash
Saved working directory and index state \
  "WIP on master: 049d078 added the index file"
HEAD is now at 049d078 added the index file
(To restore them type "git stash apply")
```

Your working directory is clean:

```
$ git status
# On branch master
nothing to commit (working directory clean)
```

At this point, you can easily switch branches and do work elsewhere; your changes are stored on your stack. To see which stashes you've stored, you can use git stash list:

```
$ git stash list
stash@{0}: WIP on master: 049d078 added the index file
stash@{1}: WIP on master: c264051... Revert "added file_size"
stash@{2}: WIP on master: 21d80a5... added number to log
```

In this case, two stashes were done previously, so you have access to three different stashed works. You can reapply the one you just stashed by using the command shown in the help output of the original stash command: git stash apply. If you want to apply one of the older stashes, you can specify it by naming it, like this: git stash apply stash@{2}. If you don't specify a stash, Git assumes the most recent stash and tries to apply it:

```
$ git stash apply
# On branch master
# Changed but not updated:
#   (use "git add <file>..." to update what will be committed)
#
```

```
#        modified: index.html
#        modified: lib/simplegit.rb
#
```

You can see that Git remodifies the files you reverted when you saved the stash. In this case, you had a clean working directory when you tried to apply the stash, and you tried to apply it on the same branch you saved it from; but having a clean working directory and applying it on the same branch aren't necessary to successfully apply a stash. You can save a stash on one branch, switch to another branch later, and try to reapply the changes. You can also have modified and uncommitted files in your working directory when you apply a stash—Git gives you merge conflicts if anything no longer applies cleanly.

The changes to your files were reapplied, but the file you staged before wasn't restaged. To do that, you must run the git stash apply command with a --index option to tell the command to try to reapply the staged changes. If you had run that instead, you'd have gotten back to your original position:

```
$ git stash apply --index
# On branch master
# Changes to be committed:
#   (use "git reset HEAD <file>..." to unstage)
#
#       modified: index.html
#
# Changed but not updated:
#   (use "git add <file>..." to update what will be committed)
#
#       modified: lib/simplegit.rb
#
```

The apply option only tries to apply the stashed work—you continue to have it on your stack. To remove it, you can run git stash drop with the name of the stash to remove:

```
$ git stash list
stash@{0}: WIP on master: 049d078 added the index file
stash@{1}: WIP on master: c264051... Revert "added file_size"
stash@{2}: WIP on master: 21d80a5... added number to log
$ git stash drop stash@{0}
Dropped stash@{0} (364e91f3f268f0900bc3ee613f9f733e82aaed43)
```

You can also run git stash pop to apply the stash and then immediately drop it from your stack.

Creative Stashing

There are a few stash variants that may also be helpful. The first option that is quite popular is the --keep-index option to the stash save command. This tells Git to not stash anything that you've already staged with the git add command.

This can be really helpful if you've made a number of changes but want to only commit some of them and then come back to the rest of the changes at a later time.

```
$ git status -s
M  index.html
 M lib/simplegit.rb

$ git stash --keep-index
Saved working directory and index state WIP on master: 1b65b17 added the index file
HEAD is now at 1b65b17 added the index file

$ git status -s
M  index.html
```

Another common thing you may want to do with stash is to stash the untracked files as well as the tracked ones. By default, git stash will only store files that are already in the index. If you specify --include-untracked or -u, Git will also stash any untracked files you have created.

```
$ git status -s
M  index.html
 M lib/simplegit.rb
?? new-file.txt

$ git stash -u
Saved working directory and index state WIP on master: 1b65b17 added the index file
HEAD is now at 1b65b17 added the index file

$ git status -s
$
```

Finally, if you specify the --patch flag, Git will not stash everything that is modified but will instead prompt you interactively which of the changes you would like to stash and which you would like to keep in your working directory.

```
$ git stash --patch
diff --git a/lib/simplegit.rb b/lib/simplegit.rb
index 66d332e..8bb5674 100644
--- a/lib/simplegit.rb
+++ b/lib/simplegit.rb
@@ -16,6 +16,10 @@ class SimpleGit
        return `#{git_cmd} 2>&1`.chomp
      end
    end
+
+    def show(treeish = 'master')
+      command("git show #{treeish}")
+    end

  end
  test
Stash this hunk [y,n,q,a,d,/,e,?]? y

Saved working directory and index state WIP on master: 1b65b17 added the index file
```

Unapplying a Stash

In some use case scenarios you might want to apply stashed changes, do some work, but then unapply those changes that originally came from the stash. Git does not provide such a `stash` unapply command, but it is possible to achieve the effect by simply retrieving the patch associated with a stash and applying it in reverse:

```
$ git stash show -p stash@{0} | git apply -R
```

Again, if you don't specify a stash, Git assumes the most recent stash:

```
$ git stash show -p | git apply -R
```

You may want to create an alias and effectively add a `stash-unapply` command to your git. For example:

```
$ git config --global alias.stash-unapply '!git stash show -p | git apply -R'
$ git stash
$ #... work work work
$ git stash-unapply
```

Creating a Branch from a Stash

If you stash some work, leave it there for a while, and continue on the branch from which you stashed the work, you may have a problem reapplying the work. If the apply tries to modify a file that you've since modified, you'll get a merge conflict and will have to try to resolve it. If you want an easier way to test the stashed changes again, you can run `git stash branch`, which creates a new branch for you, checks out the commit you were on when you stashed your work, reapplies your work there, and then drops the stash if it applies successfully:

```
$ git stash branch testchanges
Switched to a new branch "testchanges"
# On branch testchanges
# Changes to be committed:
#   (use "git reset HEAD <file>..." to unstage)
#
#       modified: index.html
#
# Changed but not updated:
#   (use "git add <file>..." to update what will be committed)
#
#       modified: lib/simplegit.rb
#
Dropped refs/stash@{0} (f0dfc4d5dc332d1cee34a634182e168c4efc3359)
```

This is a nice shortcut to recover stashed work easily and work on it in a new branch.

Cleaning Your Working Directory

Finally, you may not want to stash some work or files in your working directory, but simply get rid of them. The `git clean` command will do this for you.

Some common reasons for this might be to remove cruft that has been generated by merges or external tools or to remove build artifacts in order to run a clean build.

You'll want to be pretty careful with this command, because it's designed to remove files from your working directory that are not tracked. If you change your mind, there is often no retrieving the content of those files. A safer option is to run git stash --all to remove everything but save it in a stash.

Assuming you do want to remove cruft files or clean your working directory, you can do so with git clean. To remove all the untracked files in your working directory, you can run git clean -f -d, which removes any files and also any subdirectories that become empty as a result. The -f means force or "really do this."

If you ever want to see what it would do, you can run the command with the -n option, which means "do a dry run and tell me what you would have removed."

```
$ git clean -d -n
Would remove test.o
Would remove tmp/
```

By default, the git clean command will only remove untracked files that are not ignored. Any file that matches a pattern in your .gitignore or other ignore files will not be removed. If you want to remove those files too, such as to remove all .o files generated from a build so you can do a fully clean build, you can add a -x to the clean command.

```
$ git status -s
 M lib/simplegit.rb
?? build.TMP
?? tmp/

$ git clean -n -d
Would remove build.TMP
Would remove tmp/

$ git clean -n -d -x
Would remove build.TMP
Would remove test.o
Would remove tmp/
```

If you don't know what the git clean command is going to do, always run it with a -n first to double check before changing the -n to a -f and doing it for real. The other way you can be careful about the process is to run it with the -i or "interactive" flag.

This runs the clean command in an interactive mode.

```
$ git clean -x -i
Would remove the following items:
  build.TMP  test.o
*** Commands ***
    1: clean 2: filter by pattern 3: select by numbers 4: ask each 5: quit
    6: help
What now>
```

This way you can step through each file individually or specify patterns for deletion interactively.

Signing Your Work

Git is cryptographically secure, but it's not foolproof. If you're taking work from others on the Internet and want to verify that commits are actually from a trusted source, Git has a few ways to sign and verify work using GPG.

GPG Introduction

First of all, if you want to sign anything, you need to get GPG configured and your personal key installed.

```
$ gpg --list-keys
/Users/schacon/.gnupg/pubring.gpg
---------------------------------
pub   2048R/0A46826A 2014-06-04
uid                  Scott Chacon (Git signing key) <schacon@gmail.com>
sub   2048R/874529A9 2014-06-04
```

If you don't have a key installed, you can generate one with gpg --gen-key.

```
gpg --gen-key
```

Once you have a private key to sign with, you can configure Git to use it for signing things by setting the user.signingkey config setting:

```
git config --global user.signingkey 0A46826A
```

Now Git uses your key by default to sign tags and commits if you want.

Signing Tags

If you have a GPG private key setup, you can now use it to sign new tags. All you have to do is use -s instead of -a:

```
$ git tag -s v1.5 -m 'my signed 1.5 tag'
```

You need a passphrase to unlock the secret key for

```
user: "Ben Straub <ben@straub.cc>"
2048-bit RSA key, ID 800430EB, created 2014-05-04
```

If you run git show on that tag, you can see your GPG signature attached to it:

```
$ git show v1.5
tag v1.5
Tagger: Ben Straub <ben@straub.cc>
Date:   Sat May 3 20:29:41 2014 -0700

my signed 1.5 tag
-----BEGIN PGP SIGNATURE-----
Version: GnuPG v1

iQEcBAABAgAGBQJTZbQlAAoJEFO+sviABDDrZbQH/O9PfE51KPVPlanr6q1v4/Ut
LQxfojUWiLQdg2ESJItkcuweYg+kc3HCyFejeDIBw9dpXtOOrY26pO5qrpnG+85b
hM1/PswpPLuBSr+oCIDj5GMC2r2iEKsfv2fJbNW8iWAXVLoWZRF8BOMfqX/YTMbm
ecorc4iXzQu7tupRihslbNkfvfciMnSDeSvzCpWAHl7h8Wj6hhqePmLm9lAYqnKp
8S5B/1SSQuEAjRZgI4IexpZoeKGVDptPHxLLS38fozsyiOQyDyzEgJxcJQVMXxVi
RUysgqjcpT8+iQM1PblGfHR4XAhuOqN5FxO6PSaFZhqvWFezJ28/CLyX5q+oIVk=
=EFTF
-----END PGP SIGNATURE-----
```

```
commit ca82a6dff817ec66f44342007202690a93763949
Author: Scott Chacon <schacon@gee-mail.com>
Date:   Mon Mar 17 21:52:11 2008 -0700

    changed the verison number
```

Verifying Tags

To verify a signed tag, you use git tag -v [tag-name]. This command uses GPG to verify the signature. You need the signer's public key in your keyring for this to work properly:

```
$ git tag -v v1.4.2.1
object 883653babd8ee7ea23e6a5c392bb739348b1eb61
type commit
tag v1.4.2.1
tagger Junio C Hamano <junkio@cox.net> 1158138501 -0700

GIT 1.4.2.1

Minor fixes since 1.4.2, including git-mv and git-http with alternates.
gpg: Signature made Wed Sep 13 02:08:25 2006 PDT using DSA key ID F3119B9A
gpg: Good signature from "Junio C Hamano <junkio@cox.net>"
gpg:                 aka "[jpeg image of size 1513]"
Primary key fingerprint: 3565 2A26 2040 E066 C9A7  4A7D C0C6 D9A4 F311 9B9A
If you don't have the signer's public key, you get something like this instead:

gpg: Signature made Wed Sep 13 02:08:25 2006 PDT using DSA key ID F3119B9A
gpg: Can't check signature: public key not found
error: could not verify the tag 'v1.4.2.1'
```

Signing Commits

In more recent versions of Git (v1.7.9 and above), you can now also sign individual commits. If you're interested in signing commits directly instead of just the tags, all you need to do is add a -S to your git commit command.

```
$ git commit -a -S -m 'signed commit'

You need a passphrase to unlock the secret key for
user: "Scott Chacon (Git signing key) <schacon@gmail.com>"
2048-bit RSA key, ID 0A46826A, created 2014-06-04

[master 5c3386c] signed commit
 4 files changed, 4 insertions(+), 24 deletions(-)
 rewrite Rakefile (100%)
 create mode 100644 lib/git.rb
```

To see and verify these signatures, there is also a --show-signature option to git log.

```
$ git log --show-signature -1
commit 5c3386cf54bba0a33a32da706aa52bc0155503c2
gpg: Signature made Wed Jun  4 19:49:17 2014 PDT using RSA key ID 0A46826A
gpg: Good signature from "Scott Chacon (Git signing key) <schacon@gmail.com>"
Author: Scott Chacon <schacon@gmail.com>
Date:   Wed Jun 4 19:49:17 2014 -0700

    signed commit
```

Additionally, you can configure git log to check any signatures it finds and list them in its output with the %G? format.

```
$ git log --pretty="format:%h %G? %aN  %s"

5c3386c G Scott Chacon  signed commit
ca82a6d N Scott Chacon  changed the verison number
085bb3b N Scott Chacon  removed unnecessary test code
a11bef0 N Scott Chacon  first commit
```

Here we can see that only the latest commit is signed and valid and the previous commits are not.

In Git 1.8.3 and later, git merge and git pull can be told to inspect and reject when merging a commit that does not carry a trusted GPG signature with the --verify-signatures command.

If you use this option when merging a branch and it contains commits that are not signed and valid, the merge will not work.

```
$ git merge --verify-signatures non-verify
fatal: Commit ab06180 does not have a GPG signature.
```

If the merge contains only valid signed commits, the merge command will show you all the signatures it has checked and then move forward with the merge.

```
$ git merge --verify-signatures signed-branch
Commit 13ad65e has a good GPG signature by Scott Chacon (Git signing key) <schacon@gmail.com>
Updating 5c3386c..13ad65e
Fast-forward
 README | 2 ++
 1 file changed, 2 insertions(+)
```

You can also use the -S option with the git merge command itself to sign the resulting merge commit. The following example both verifies that every commit in the branch to be merged is signed and furthermore signs the resulting merge commit.

```
$ git merge --verify-signatures -S  signed-branch
Commit 13ad65e has a good GPG signature by Scott Chacon (Git signing key) <schacon@gmail.com>

You need a passphrase to unlock the secret key for
user: "Scott Chacon (Git signing key) <schacon@gmail.com>"
2048-bit RSA key, ID 0A46826A, created 2014-06-04

Merge made by the 'recursive' strategy.
 README | 2 ++
 1 file changed, 2 insertions(+)
```

Everyone Must Sign

Signing tags and commits is great, but if you decide to use this in your normal workflow, you'll have to make sure that everyone on your team understands how to do so. If you don't, you'll end up spending a lot of time helping people figure out how to rewrite their commits with signed versions. Make sure you understand GPG and the benefits of signing things before adopting this as part of your standard workflow.

Searching

With just about any size codebase, you'll often need to find where a function is called or defined, or find the history of a method. Git provides a couple of useful tools for looking through the code and commits stored in its database quickly and easily. We'll go through a few of them.

Git Grep

Git ships with a command called grep that allows you to easily search through any committed tree or the working directory for a string or regular expression. For these examples, we'll look through the Git source code itself.

By default, grep looks through the files in your working directory. You can pass -n to print out the line numbers where Git has found matches.

```
$ git grep -n gmtime_r
compat/gmtime.c:3:#undef gmtime_r
compat/gmtime.c:8:        return git_gmtime_r(timep, &result);
compat/gmtime.c:11:struct tm *git_gmtime_r(const time_t *timep, struct tm *result)
compat/gmtime.c:16:        ret = gmtime_r(timep, result);
compat/mingw.c:606:struct tm *gmtime_r(const time_t *timep, struct tm *result)
compat/mingw.h:162:struct tm *gmtime_r(const time_t *timep, struct tm *result);
date.c:429:            if (gmtime_r(&now, &now_tm))
date.c:492:            if (gmtime_r(&time, tm)) {
git-compat-util.h:721:struct tm *git_gmtime_r(const time_t *, struct tm *);
git-compat-util.h:723:#define gmtime_r git_gmtime_r
```

There are a number of interesting options you can provide for the grep command.

For instance, instead of the previous call, you can have Git summarize the output by just showing you which files matched and how many matches there were in each file with the --count option:

```
$ git grep --count gmtime_r
compat/gmtime.c:4
compat/mingw.c:1
compat/mingw.h:1
date.c:2
git-compat-util.h:2
```

If you want to see what method or function it thinks it has found a match in, you can pass -p:

```
$ git grep -p gmtime_r *.c
date.c=static int match_multi_number(unsigned long num, char c, const char *date, char *end, struct tm *tm)
date.c:          if (gmtime_r(&now, &now_tm))
date.c=static int match_digit(const char *date, struct tm *tm, int *offset, int *tm_gmt)
date.c:          if (gmtime_r(&time, tm)) {
```

So here we can see that gmtime_r is called in the match_multi_number and match_digit functions in the date.c file.

You can also look for complex combinations of strings with the --and flag, which makes sure that multiple matches are in the same line. For instance, let's look for any lines that define a constant with either the strings LINK or BUF_MAX in them in the Git codebase in an older 1.8.0 version.

Here we'll also use the --break and --heading options that help split up the output into a more readable format.

```
$ git grep --break --heading \
    -n -e '#define' --and \( -e LINK -e BUF_MAX \) v1.8.0
v1.8.0:builtin/index-pack.c
62:#define FLAG_LINK (1u<<20)

v1.8.0:cache.h
73:#define S_IFGITLINK   0160000
74:#define S_ISGITLINK(m) (((m) & S_IFMT) == S_IFGITLINK)

v1.8.0:environment.c
54:#define OBJECT_CREATION_MODE OBJECT_CREATION_USES_HARDLINKS

v1.8.0:strbuf.c
326:#define STRBUF_MAXLINK (2*PATH_MAX)

v1.8.0:symlinks.c
53:#define FL_SYMLINK (1 << 2)

v1.8.0:zlib.c
30:/* #define ZLIB_BUF_MAX ((uInt)-1) */
31:#define ZLIB_BUF_MAX ((uInt) 1024 * 1024 * 1024) /* 1GB */
```

The git grep command has a few advantages over normal searching commands such as grep and ack. The first is that it's really fast, and the second is that you can search through any tree in Git, not just the working directory. As we saw in the previous example, we looked for terms in an older version of the Git source code, not the version that was currently checked out.

Git Log Searching

Perhaps you're looking not for where a term exists, but when it existed or was introduced. The git log command has a number of powerful tools for finding specific commits by the content of their messages or even the content of the diff they introduce.

If we want to find out for example when the ZLIB_BUF_MAX constant was originally introduced, we can tell Git to only show us the commits that either added or removed that string with the -S option.

```
$ git log -SZLIB_BUF_MAX --oneline
e01503b zlib: allow feeding more than 4GB in one go
ef49a7a zlib: zlib can only process 4GB at a time
```

If we look at the diff of those commits we can see that in ef49a7a the constant was introduced and in e01503b it was modified.

If you need to be more specific, you can provide a regular expression to search for with the -G option.

Line Log Search

Another fairly advanced log search that is insanely useful is the line history search. This is a fairly recent addition and not very well known, but it can be really helpful. It is called with the -L option to git log and shows you the history of a function or line of code in your codebase.

For example, if we wanted to see every change made to the function git_deflate_bound in the zlib.c file, we could run git log -L :git_deflate_bound:zlib.c. This tries to figure out what the bounds of that function are and then looks through the history and shows every change that was made to the function as a series of patches back to when the function was first created.

```
$ git log -L :git_deflate_bound:zlib.c
commit ef49a7a0126d64359c974b4b3b71d7ad42ee3bca
Author: Junio C Hamano <gitster@pobox.com>
Date:   Fri Jun 10 11:52:15 2011 -0700

    zlib: zlib can only process 4GB at a time

diff --git a/zlib.c b/zlib.c
--- a/zlib.c
+++ b/zlib.c
@@ -85,5 +130,5 @@
-unsigned long git_deflate_bound(z_streamp strm, unsigned long size)
+unsigned long git_deflate_bound(git_zstream *strm, unsigned long size)
 {
-       return deflateBound(strm, size);
+       return deflateBound(&strm->z, size);
 }


commit 225a6f1068f71723a910e8565db4e252b3ca21fa
Author: Junio C Hamano <gitster@pobox.com>
Date:   Fri Jun 10 11:18:17 2011 -0700

    zlib: wrap deflateBound() too

diff --git a/zlib.c b/zlib.c
--- a/zlib.c
+++ b/zlib.c
@@ -81,0 +85,5 @@
+unsigned long git_deflate_bound(z_streamp strm, unsigned long size)
+{
+       return deflateBound(strm, size);
+}
+
```

If Git can't figure out how to match a function or method in your programming language, you can also provide it a regex. For example, this would have done the same thing: git log -L '/unsigned long git_deflate_bound/',/^}/:zlib.c. You could also give it a range of lines or a single line number and you'll get the same sort of output.

Rewriting History

Many times, when working with Git, you may want to revise your commit history for some reason. One of the great things about Git is that it allows you to make decisions at the last possible moment. You can decide what files go into which commits right before you commit with the staging area, you can decide that you didn't mean to be working on something yet with the `stash` command, and you can rewrite commits that already happened so they look like they happened in a different way. This can involve changing the order of the commits, changing messages or modifying files in a commit, squashing together or splitting apart commits, or removing commits entirely—all before you share your work with others.

In this section, you'll cover how to accomplish these very useful tasks so that you can make your commit history look the way you want before you share it with others.

Changing the Last Commit

Changing your last commit is probably the most common rewriting of history that you'll do. You'll often want to do two basic things to your last commit: change the commit message, or change the snapshot you just recorded by adding, changing, and removing files.

If you only want to modify your last commit message, it's very simple:

```
$ git commit --amend
```

That drops you into your text editor, which has your last commit message in it, ready for you to modify the message. When you save and close the editor, the editor writes a new commit containing that message and makes it your new last commit.

If you've committed and then you want to change the snapshot you committed by adding or changing files, possibly because you forgot to add a newly created file when you originally committed, the process works basically the same way. You stage the changes you want by editing a file and running `git add` on it or `git rm` to a tracked file, and the subsequent `git commit --amend` takes your current staging area and makes it the snapshot for the new commit.

You need to be careful with this technique because amending changes the SHA-1 of the commit. It's like a very small rebase—don't amend your last commit if you've already pushed it.

Changing Multiple Commit Messages

To modify a commit that is farther back in your history, you must move to more complex tools. Git doesn't have a modify-history tool, but you can use the rebase tool to rebase a series of commits onto the HEAD they were originally based on instead of moving them to another one. With the interactive rebase tool, you can then stop after each commit you want to modify and change the message, add files, or do whatever you wish. You can run rebase interactively by adding the `-i` option to `git rebase`. You must indicate how far back you want to rewrite commits by telling the command which commit to rebase onto.

For example, if you want to change the last three commit messages, or any of the commit messages in that group, you supply as an argument to `git rebase -i` the parent of the last commit you want to edit, which is `HEAD~2^` or `HEAD~3`. It may be easier to remember the `~3` because you're trying to edit the last three commits; but keep in mind that you're actually designating four commits ago, the parent of the last commit you want to edit:

```
$ git rebase -i HEAD~3
```

Remember again that this is a rebasing command—every commit included in the range `HEAD~3..HEAD` will be rewritten, whether or not you change the message. Don't include any commit you've already pushed to a central server—doing so will confuse other developers by providing an alternate version of the same change.

Running this command gives you a list of commits in your text editor that looks something like this:

```
pick f7f3f6d changed my name a bit
pick 310154e updated README formatting and added blame
pick a5f4a0d added cat-file

# Rebase 710f0f8..a5f4a0d onto 710f0f8
#
# Commands:
#  p, pick = use commit
#  r, reword = use commit, but edit the commit message
#  e, edit = use commit, but stop for amending
#  s, squash = use commit, but meld into previous commit
#  f, fixup = like "squash", but discard this commit's log message
#  x, exec = run command (the rest of the line) using shell
#
# These lines can be re-ordered; they are executed from top to bottom.
#
# If you remove a line here THAT COMMIT WILL BE LOST.
#
# However, if you remove everything, the rebase will be aborted.
#
# Note that empty commits are commented out
```

It's important to note that these commits are listed in the opposite order than you normally see them using the log command. If you run a log, you see something like this:

```
$ git log --pretty=format:"%h %s" HEAD~3..HEAD
a5f4a0d added cat-file
310154e updated README formatting and added blame
f7f3f6d changed my name a bit
```

Notice the reverse order. The interactive rebase gives you a script that it's going to run. It will start at the commit you specify on the command line (HEAD~3) and replay the changes introduced in each of these commits from top to bottom. It lists the oldest at the top, rather than the newest, because that's the first one it will replay.

You need to edit the script so that it stops at the commit you want to edit. To do so, change the word pick to the word edit for each of the commits you want the script to stop after. For example, to modify only the third commit message, you change the file to look like this:

```
edit f7f3f6d changed my name a bit
pick 310154e updated README formatting and added blame
pick a5f4a0d added cat-file
```

When you save and exit the editor, Git rewinds to the last commit in that list and drops you on the command line with the following message:

```
$ git rebase -i HEAD~3
Stopped at 7482e0d... updated the gemspec to hopefully work better
```

You can amend the commit now, with

```
    git commit –amend
```

Once you're satisfied with your changes, run

```
git rebase --continue
```

These instructions tell you exactly what to do. Type

```
$ git commit --amend
```

Change the commit message, and exit the editor. Then, run

```
$ git rebase --continue
```

This command applies the other two commits automatically, and then you're done. If you change `pick` to `edit` on more lines, you can repeat these steps for each commit you change to edit. Each time, Git will stop, let you amend the commit, and continue when you're finished.

Reordering Commits

You can also use interactive rebases to reorder or remove commits entirely. If you want to remove the `added cat-file` commit and change the order in which the other two commits are introduced, you can change the rebase script from this

```
pick f7f3f6d changed my name a bit
pick 310154e updated README formatting and added blame
pick a5f4a0d added cat-file
```

to this:

```
pick 310154e updated README formatting and added blame
pick f7f3f6d changed my name a bit
```

When you save and exit the editor, Git rewinds your branch to the parent of these commits, applies `310154e` and then `f7f3f6d`, and then stops. You effectively change the order of those commits and remove the `added cat-file` commit completely.

Squashing a Commit

It's also possible to take a series of commits and squash them down into a single commit with the interactive rebasing tool. The script puts helpful instructions in the rebase message:

```
#
# Commands:
#  p, pick = use commit
#  e, edit = use commit, but stop for amending
#  s, squash = use commit, but meld into previous commit
#
# If you remove a line here THAT COMMIT WILL BE LOST.
# However, if you remove everything, the rebase will be aborted.
#
```

If, instead of "pick" or "edit," you specify "squash," Git applies both that change and the change directly before it and makes you merge the commit messages. So, if you want to make a single commit from these three commits, you make the script look like this:

```
pick f7f3f6d changed my name a bit
squash 310154e updated README formatting and added blame
squash a5f4a0d added cat-file
```

When you save and exit the editor, Git applies all three changes and then puts you back into the editor to merge the three commit messages:

```
# This is a combination of 3 commits.
# The first commit's message is:
changed my name a bit

# This is the 2nd commit message:

updated README formatting and added blame

# This is the 3rd commit message:

added cat-file
```

When you save that, you have a single commit that introduces the changes of all three previous commits.

Splitting a Commit

Splitting a commit undoes a commit and then partially stages and commits as many times as commits you want to end up with. For example, suppose you want to split the middle commit of your three commits. Instead of "updated README formatting and added blame," you want to split it into two commits: "updated README formatting" for the first, and "added blame" for the second. You can do that in the rebase -i script by changing the instruction on the commit you want to split to "edit."

```
pick f7f3f6d changed my name a bit
edit 310154e updated README formatting and added blame
pick a5f4a0d added cat-file
```

Then, when the script drops you to the command line, you reset that commit, take the changes that have been reset, and create multiple commits out of them. When you save and exit the editor, Git rewinds to the parent of the first commit in your list, applies the first commit (f7f3f6d), applies the second (310154e), and drops you to the console. There, you can do a mixed reset of that commit with git reset HEAD^, which effectively undoes that commit and leaves the modified files unstaged. Now you can stage and commit files until you have several commits, and run git rebase --continue when you're done:

```
$ git reset HEAD^
$ git add README
$ git commit -m 'updated README formatting'
$ git add lib/simplegit.rb
$ git commit -m 'added blame'
$ git rebase --continue
```

Git applies the last commit (a5f4a0d) in the script, and your history looks like this:

```
$ git log -4 --pretty=format:"%h %s"
1c002dd added cat-file
9b29157 added blame
35cfb2b updated README formatting
f3cc40e changed my name a bit
```

Once again, this changes the SHAs of all the commits in your list, so make sure no commit shows up in that list that you've already pushed to a shared repository.

The Nuclear Option: filter-branch

There is another history-rewriting option that you can use if you need to rewrite a larger number of commits in some scriptable way—for instance, changing your e-mail address globally or removing a file from every commit. The command is filter-branch, and it can rewrite huge swaths of your history, so you probably shouldn't use it unless your project isn't yet public and other people haven't based work off the commits you're about to rewrite. However, it can be very useful. You'll learn a few of the common uses so you can get an idea of some of the things it's capable of.

Removing a File from Every Commit

This occurs fairly commonly. Someone accidentally commits a huge binary file with a thoughtless git add, and you want to remove it everywhere. Perhaps you accidentally committed a file that contained a password, and you want to make your project open source. filter-branch is the tool you probably want to use to scrub your entire history. To remove a file named passwords.txt from your entire history, you can use the --tree-filter option to filter-branch:

```
$ git filter-branch --tree-filter 'rm -f passwords.txt' HEAD
Rewrite 6b9b3cf04e7c5686a9cb838c3f36a8cb6a0fc2bd (21/21)
Ref 'refs/heads/master' was rewritten
```

The --tree-filter option runs the specified command after each checkout of the project and then recommits the results. In this case, you remove a file called passwords.txt from every snapshot, whether or not it exists. If you want to remove all accidentally committed editor backup files, you can run something like git filter-branch --tree-filter 'rm -f *~' HEAD.

You'll be able to watch Git rewriting trees and commits and then move the branch pointer at the end. It's generally a good idea to do this in a testing branch and then hard-reset your master branch after you've determined the outcome is what you really want. To run filter-branch on all your branches, you can pass --all to the command.

Making a Subdirectory the New Root

Suppose you've done an import from another source control system and have subdirectories that make no sense (trunk, tags, and so on). If you want to make the trunk subdirectory be the new project root for every commit, filter-branch can help you do that, too:

```
$ git filter-branch --subdirectory-filter trunk HEAD
Rewrite 856f0bf61e41a27326cdae8f09fe708d679f596f (12/12)
Ref 'refs/heads/master' was rewritten
```

Now your new project root is what was in the `trunk` subdirectory each time. Git will also automatically remove commits that did not affect the subdirectory.

Changing E-Mail Addresses Globally

Another common case is that you forgot to run `git config` to set your name and e-mail address before you started working, or perhaps you want to open-source a project at work and change all your work e-mail addresses to your personal address. In any case, you can change e-mail addresses in multiple commits in a batch with `filter-branch` as well. You need to be careful to change only the e-mail addresses that are yours, so you use `--commit-filter`:

```
$ git filter-branch --commit-filter '
        if [ "$GIT_AUTHOR_EMAIL" = "schacon@localhost" ];
        then
                GIT_AUTHOR_NAME="Scott Chacon";
                GIT_AUTHOR_EMAIL="schacon@example.com";
                git commit-tree "$@";
        else
                git commit-tree "$@";
        fi' HEAD
```

This goes through and rewrites every commit to have your new address. Because commits contain the SHA-1 values of their parents, this command changes every commit SHA in your history, not just those that have the matching e-mail address.

Reset Demystified

Before moving on to more specialized tools, let's talk about `reset` and `checkout`. These commands are two of the most confusing parts of Git when you first encounter them. They do so many things, that it seems hopeless to actually understand them and employ them properly. For this, we recommend a simple metaphor.

The Three Trees

An easier way to think about `reset` and `checkout` is through the mental frame of Git being a content manager of three different trees. By "tree" here we really mean "collection of files," not specifically the data structure. (There are a few cases where the index doesn't exactly act like a tree, but for our purposes it is easier to think about it this way for now.)

Git as a system manages and manipulates three trees in its normal operation:

Tree	Role
HEAD	Last commit snapshot, next parent
Index	Proposed next commit snapshot
Working Directory	Sandbox

The HEAD

HEAD is the pointer to the current branch reference, which is in turn a pointer to the last commit made on that branch. That means HEAD will be the parent of the next commit that is created. It's generally simplest to think of HEAD as the snapshot of your last commit.

In fact, it's pretty easy to see what that snapshot looks like. Here is an example of getting the actual directory listing and SHA checksums for each file in the HEAD snapshot:

```
$ git cat-file -p HEAD
tree cfda3bf379e4f8dba8717dee55aab78aef7f4daf
author Scott Chacon  1301511835 -0700
committer Scott Chacon  1301511835 -0700

initial commit

$ git ls-tree -r HEAD
100644 blob a906cb2a4a904a152...    README
100644 blob 8f94139338f9404f2...    Rakefile
040000 tree 99f1a6d12cb4b6f19...    lib
```

The cat-file and ls-tree commands are "plumbing" commands that are used for lower-level things and not really used in day-to-day work, but they help us see what's going on here.

The Index

The Index is your *proposed next commit*. We've also been referring to this concept as Git's "Staging Area" as this is what Git looks at when you run git commit.

Git populates this index with a list of all the file contents that were last checked out into your Working Directory and what they looked like when they were originally checked out. You then replace some of those files with new versions of them, and git commit converts that into the tree for a new commit.

```
$ git ls-files -s
100644 a906cb2a4a904a152e80877d4088654daad0c859 0    README
100644 8f94139338f9404f26296befa88755fc2598c289 0    Rakefile
100644 47c6340d6459e05787f644c2447d2595f5d3a54b 0    lib/simplegit.rb
```

Again, here we're using ls-files, which is more of a behind-the-scenes command that shows you what your index currently looks like.

The Index is not technically a tree structure—it's actually implemented as a flattened manifest—but for our purposes it's close enough.

The Working Directory

Finally, you have your Working Directory. The other two trees store their content in an efficient but inconvenient manner, inside the .git folder. The Working Directory unpacks them into actual files, which makes it much easier for you to edit them. Think of the Working Directory as a sandbox, where you can try changes out before committing them to your staging area (Index) and then to history.

```
$ tree
.
├── README
├── Rakefile
└── lib
    └── simplegit.rb

1 directory, 3 files
```

The Workflow

Git's main purpose is to record snapshots of your project in successively better states, by manipulating these three trees.

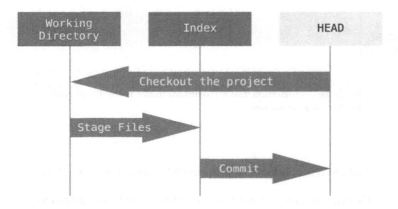

Figure 7-2.

Let's say you go into a new directory with a single file in it. We'll call this v1 of the file, and we'll indicate it in blue. Now we run git init, which creates a Git repository with a HEAD reference that points to an unborn branch (master doesn't exist yet).

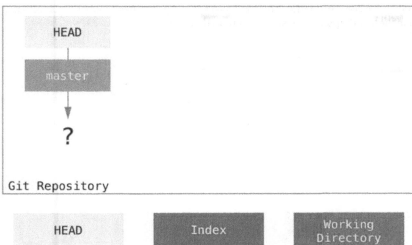

Figure 7-3.

At this point, only the Working Directory tree has any content.

Now we want to commit this file, so we use git add to take content in the Working Directory and copy it to the Index.

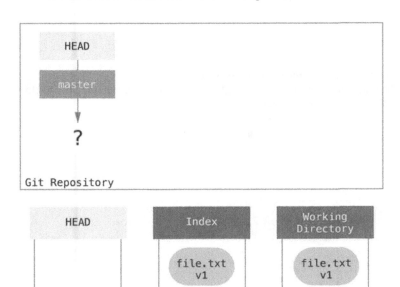

Figure 7-4.

Then we run git commit, which takes the contents of the Index and saves it as a permanent snapshot, creates a commit object which points to that snapshot, and updates master to point to that commit.

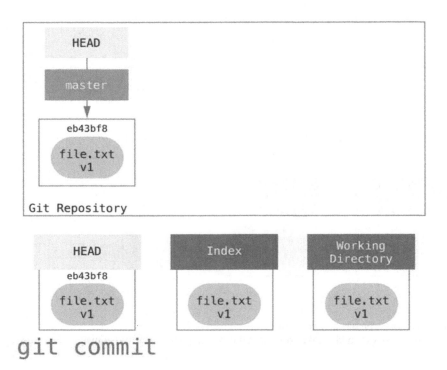

Figure 7-5.

If we run git status, we'll see no changes, because all three trees are the same.

Now we want to make a change to that file and commit it. We'll go through the same process, changing the file in our Working Directory. Let's call this v2 of the file, and indicate it in red.

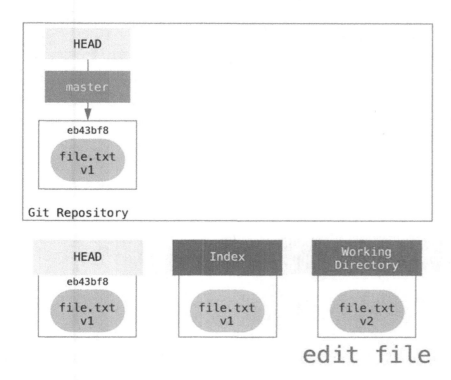

Figure 7-6.

If we run git status right now, we'll see the file in red as "Changes not staged for commit," because that entry differs between the Index and the Working Directory. Next we run git add on it to stage it into our Index.

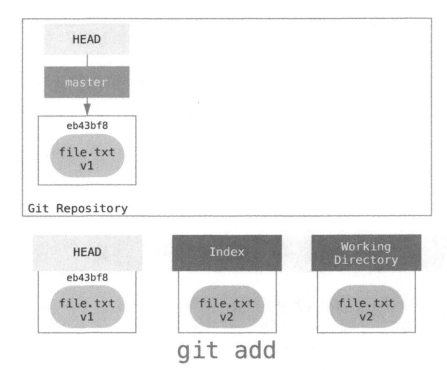

Figure 7-7.

At this point if we run `git status` we will see the file in green under "Changes to be committed" because the Index and HEAD differ – that is, our proposed next commit is now different from our last commit. Finally, we run `git commit` to finalize the commit.

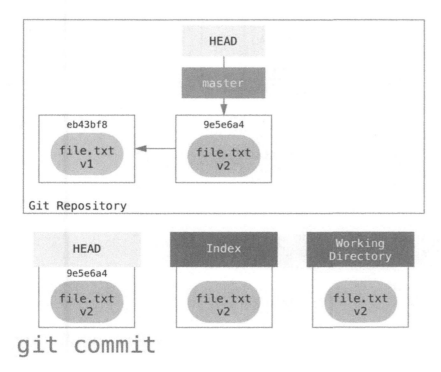

Figure 7-8.

Now git status will give us no output, because all three trees are the same again.

Switching branches or cloning goes through a similar process. When you checkout a branch, it changes HEAD to point to the new branch ref, populates your Index with the snapshot of that commit, then copies the contents of the Index into your Working Directory.

The Role of Reset

The reset command makes more sense when viewed in this context.

For the purposes of these examples, let's say that we've modified file.txt again and committed it a third time. So now our history looks like this:

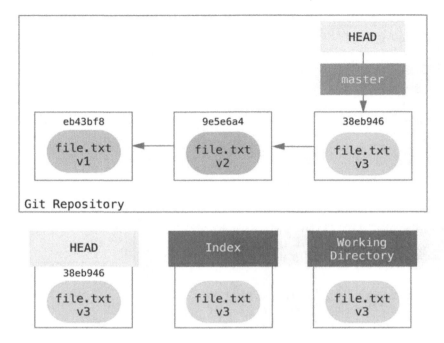

Figure 7-9.

Let's now walk through exactly what reset does when you call it. It directly manipulates these three trees in a simple and predictable way. It does up to three basic operations.

Step 1: Move HEAD

The first thing reset will do is move what HEAD points to. This isn't the same as changing HEAD itself (which is what checkout does); reset moves the branch that HEAD is pointing to. This means if HEAD is set to the master branch (i.e., you're currently on the master branch), running git reset 9e5e64a will start by making master point to 9e5e64a.

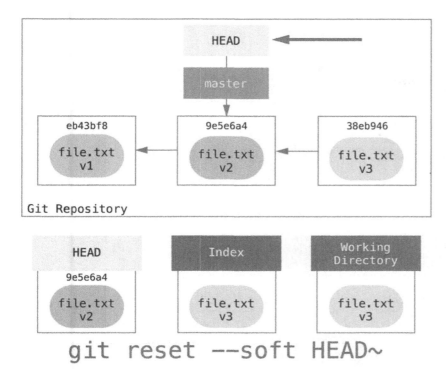

Figure 7-10.

No matter what form of reset with a commit you invoke, this is the first thing it will always try to do. With reset --soft, it will simply stop there.

Now take a second to look at that diagram and realize what happened—it essentially undid the last git commit command. When you run git commit, Git creates a new commit and moves the branch that HEAD points to up to it. When you reset to HEAD~ (the parent of HEAD), you are moving the branch back to where it was, without changing the Index or Working Directory. You could now update the Index and run git commit again to accomplish what git commit --amend would have done.

Step 2: Updating the Index (--mixed)

Note that if you run git status now you'll see in green the difference between the Index and what the new HEAD is.

The next thing reset will do is to update the Index with the contents of whatever snapshot HEAD now points to.

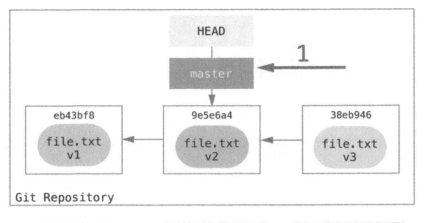

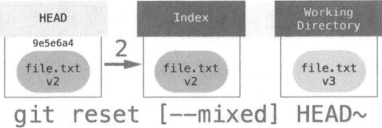

Figure 7-11.

If you specify the --mixed option, reset will stop at this point. This is also the default, so if you specify no option at all (just git reset HEAD~ in this case), this is where the command will stop.

Now take another second to look at that diagram and realize what happened: it still undid your last commit, but also unstaged everything. You rolled back to before you ran all your git add and git commit commands.

Step 3: Updating the Working Directory (--hard)

The third thing that reset does is makes the Working Directory look like the Index. If you use the --hard option, it will continue to this stage.

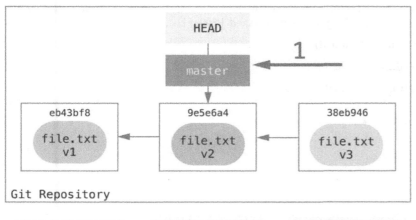

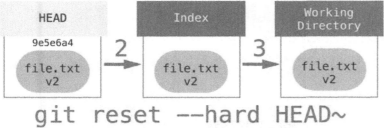

Figure 7-12.

So let's think about what just happened. You undid your last commit, the `git add` and `git commit` commands, and all the work you did in your Working Directory.

It's important to note that this flag (`--hard`) is the only way to make the `reset` command dangerous, and one of the very few cases where Git will actually destroy data. Any other invocation of `reset` can be pretty easily undone, but the `--hard` option cannot, since it forcibly overwrites files in the Working Directory. In this particular case, we still have the v3 version of our file in a commit in our Git DB, and we could get it back by looking at our reflog, but if we had not committed it, Git still would have overwritten the file and it would be unrecoverable.

Recap

The reset command overwrites these three trees in a specific order, stopping when you tell it to:

1. Move the branch HEAD points to (stop here if `--soft`)
2. Make the Index look like HEAD (stop here unless `--hard`)
3. Make the Working Directory look like the Index

Reset with a Path

That covers the behavior of `reset` in its basic form, but you can also provide it with a path to act upon. If you specify a path, reset will skip step 1, and limit the remainder of its actions to a specific file or set of files. This actually sort of makes sense—HEAD is just a pointer, and you can't point to part of one commit and part of another. But the Index and Working Directory can be partially updated, so reset proceeds with steps 2 and 3.

So, assume we run git reset file.txt. This form (because you did not specify a commit SHA or branch, and you didn't specify --soft or --hard) is shorthand for git reset --mixed HEAD file.txt, which:

1. Moves the branch HEAD points to (skipped)

2. Makes the Index look like HEAD (stop here)

So it essentially just copies file.txt from HEAD to the Index.

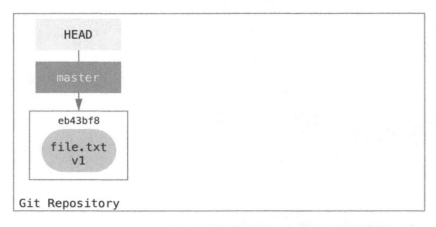

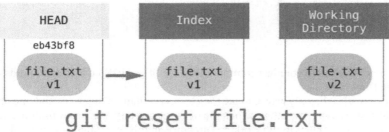

Figure 7-13.

This has the practical effect of unstaging the file. If we look at the diagram for that command and think about what git add does, they are exact opposites.

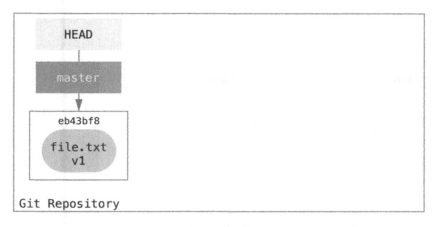

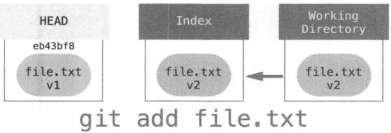

Figure 7-14.

This is why the output of the git status command suggests that you run this to unstage a file.

We could just as easily not let Git assume we meant "pull the data from HEAD" by specifying a specific commit to pull that file version from. We would just run something like git reset eb43bf file.txt.

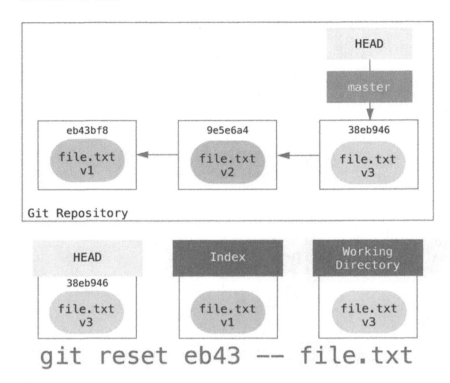

Figure 7-15.

This effectively does the same thing as if we had reverted the content of the file to v1 in the Working Directory, ran `git add` on it, then reverted to v3 again (without actually going through all those steps). If we run `git commit` now, it will record a change that reverts that file to v1, even though we never actually had it in our Working Directory again.

It's also interesting to note that like `git add`, the `reset` command will accept a `--patch` option to unstage content on a hunk-by-hunk basis. So you can selectively unstage or revert content.

Squashing

Let's look at how to do something interesting with this newfound power—squashing commits.

Say you have a series of commits with messages like "oops", "WIP," and "forgot this file." You can use `reset` to quickly and easily squash them into a single commit that makes you look really smart.

Let's say you have a project where the first commit has one file, the second commit added a new file and changed the first, and the third commit changed the first file again. The second commit was a work in progress and you want to squash it down.

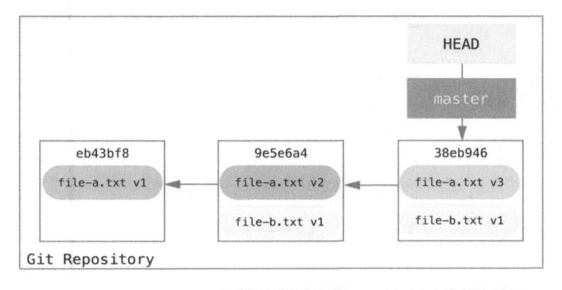

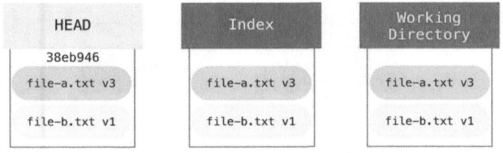

Figure 7-16.

You can run `git reset --soft HEAD~2` to move the HEAD branch back to an older commit (the first commit you want to keep):

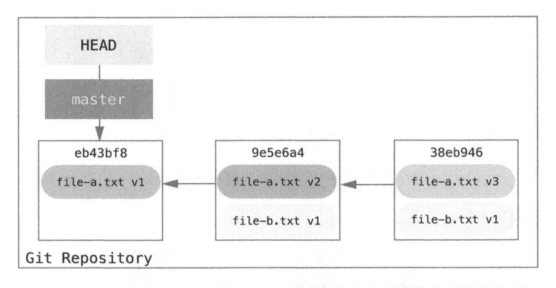

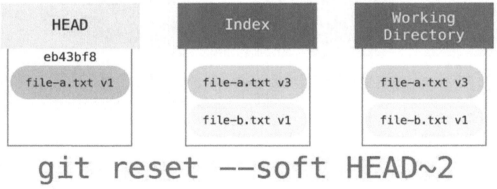

Figure 7-17.

And then simply run git commit again:

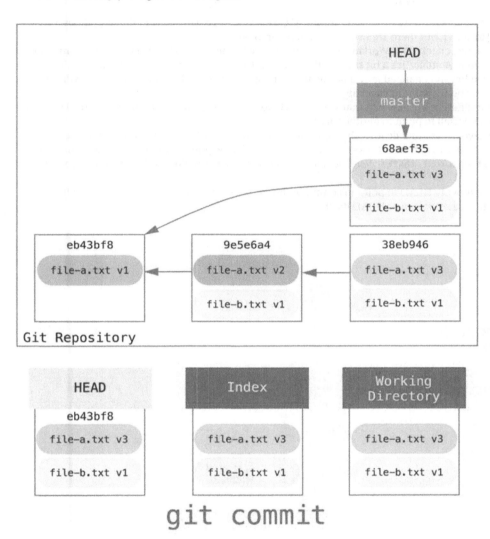

Figure 7-18.

Now you can see that your reachable history, the history you would push, now looks like you had one commit with file-a.txt v1, then a second that both modified file-a.txt to v3 and added file-b.txt. The commit with the v2 version of the file is no longer in the history.

Check It Out

Finally, you may wonder what the difference between checkout and reset is. Like reset, checkout manipulates the three trees, and it is a bit different depending on whether or not you give the command a file path.

Without Paths

Running git checkout [branch] is pretty similar to running git reset --hard [branch] in that it updates all three trees for you to look like [branch], but there are two important differences.

First, unlike reset --hard, checkout is Working-Directory safe; it will check to make sure it's not blowing away files that have changes to them. Actually, it's a bit smarter than that—it tries to do a trivial merge in the Working Directory, so all the files you haven't changed in will be updated. reset --hard, and on the other hand, will simply replace everything across the board without checking.

The second important difference is how it updates HEAD. Where reset will move the branch that HEAD points to, checkout will move HEAD itself to point to another branch.

For instance, say we have master and develop branches that point at different commits, and we're currently on hat (so HEAD points to it). If we run git reset master, develop itself will now point to the same commit that master does. If we instead run git checkout master, develop does not move, HEAD itself does. HEAD will now point to master.

So, in both cases we're moving HEAD to point to commit A, but how we do so is very different. reset will move the branch HEAD points to, checkout moves HEAD itself.

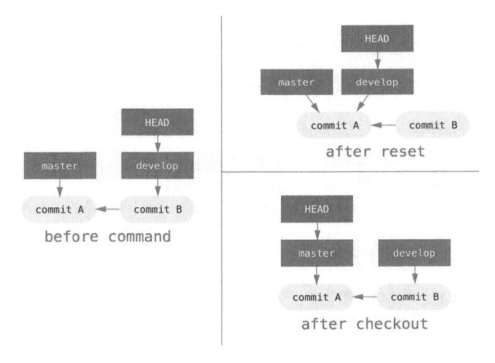

Figure 7-19.

With Paths

The other way to run checkout is with a file path, which, like reset, does not move HEAD. It is just like git reset [branch] file in that it updates the index with that file at that commit, but it also overwrites the file in the working directory. It would be exactly like git reset --hard [branch] file (if reset would let you run that)—it's not Working-Directory safe, and it does not move HEAD.

Also, like git reset and git add, checkout will accept a --patch option to allow you to selectively revert file contents on a hunk-by-hunk basis.

Summary

Hopefully now you understand and feel more comfortable with the `reset` command, but are probably still a little confused about how exactly it differs from `checkout` and could not possibly remember all the rules of the different invocations.

Here's a cheat-sheet for which commands affect which trees. The "HEAD" column reads "REF" if that command moves the reference (branch) that HEAD points to, and "HEAD" if it moves HEAD itself. Pay especial attention to the WD Safe? column—if it says NO, take a second to think before running that command.

	HEAD	Index	Workdir	WD Safe?
Commit Level				
`reset --soft [commit]`	REF	NO	NO	YES
`reset [commit]`	REF	YES	NO	YES
`reset --hard [commit]`	REF	YES	YES	**NO**
`checkout [commit]`	HEAD	YES	YES	YES
File Level				
`reset (commit) [file]`	NO	YES	NO	YES
`checkout (commit) [file]`	NO	YES	YES	**NO**

Advanced Merging

Merging in Git is typically fairly easy. Because Git makes it easy to merge another branch multiple times, it means that you can have a very long-lived branch but you can keep it up to date as you go, solving small conflicts often, rather than be surprised by one enormous conflict at the end of the series.

However, sometimes tricky conflicts do occur. Unlike some other version control systems, Git does not try to be overly clever about merge conflict resolution. Git's philosophy is to be smart about determining when a merge resolution is unambiguous, but if there is a conflict, it does not try to be clever about automatically resolving it. Therefore, if you wait too long to merge two branches that diverge quickly, you can run into some issues.

In this section, we'll go over what some of those issues might be and what tools Git gives you to help handle these more tricky situations. We'll also cover some of the different, non-standard types of merges you can do, as well as see how to back out of merges that you've done.

Merge Conflicts

While we covered some basics on resolving merge conflicts earlier, for more complex conflicts, Git provides a few tools to help you figure out what's going on and how to better deal with the conflict.

First of all, if at all possible, try to make sure your working directory is clean before doing a merge that may have conflicts. If you have work in progress, either commit it to a temporary branch or stash it. This makes it so that you can undo anything you try here. If you have unsaved changes in your working directory when you try a merge, some of these tips may help you lose that work.

Let's walk through a very simple example. We have a super simple Ruby file that prints hello world.

```
#! /usr/bin/env ruby

def hello
  puts 'hello world'
end

hello()
```

In our repository, we create a new branch named whitespace and proceed to change all the Unix line endings to DOS line endings, essentially changing every line of the file, but just with whitespace. Then we change the line "hello world" to "hello mundo."

```
$ git checkout -b whitespace
Switched to a new branch 'whitespace'

$ unix2dos hello.rb
unix2dos: converting file hello.rb to DOS format ...
$ git commit -am 'converted hello.rb to DOS'
[whitespace 3270f76] converted hello.rb to DOS
 1 file changed, 7 insertions(+), 7 deletions(-)

$ vim hello.rb
$ git diff -w
diff --git a/hello.rb b/hello.rb
index ac51efd..e85207e 100755
--- a/hello.rb
+++ b/hello.rb
@@ -1,7 +1,7 @@
 #! /usr/bin/env ruby

 def hello
-  puts 'hello world'
+  puts 'hello mundo'^M
 end

 hello()

$ git commit -am 'hello mundo change'
[whitespace 6d338d2] hello mundo change
 1 file changed, 1 insertion(+), 1 deletion(-)
```

Now we switch back to our master branch and add some documentation for the function.

```
$ git checkout master
Switched to branch 'master'

$ vim hello.rb
$ git diff
diff --git a/hello.rb b/hello.rb
index ac51efd..36c06c8 100755
--- a/hello.rb
+++ b/hello.rb
@@ -1,5 +1,6 @@
 #! /usr/bin/env ruby
```

```
+# prints out a greeting
 def hello
   puts 'hello world'
 end

$ git commit -am 'document the function'
[master bec6336] document the function
 1 file changed, 1 insertion(+)
```

Now we try to merge in our whitespace branch and we'll get conflicts because of the whitespace changes.

```
$ git merge whitespace
Auto-merging hello.rb
CONFLICT (content): Merge conflict in hello.rb
Automatic merge failed; fix conflicts and then commit the result.
```

Aborting a Merge

We now have a few options. First, let's cover how to get out of this situation. If you perhaps weren't expecting conflicts and don't want to quite deal with the situation yet, you can simply back out of the merge with git merge --abort.

```
$ git status -sb
## master
UU hello.rb

$ git merge --abort

$ git status -sb
## master
```

The git merge --abort option tries to revert to your state before you ran the merge. The only cases where it may not be able to do this perfectly would be if you had unstashed, uncommitted changes in your working directory when you ran it, otherwise it should work fine.

If for some reason you find yourself in a horrible state and just want to start over, you can also run git reset --hard HEAD or wherever you want to get back to. Remember again that this will blow away your working directory, so make sure you don't want any changes there.

Ignoring Whitespace

In this specific case, the conflicts are whitespace related. We know this because the case is simple, but it's also pretty easy to tell in real cases when looking at the conflict because every line is removed on one side and added again on the other. By default, Git sees all these lines as being changed, so it can't merge the files.

The default merge strategy can take arguments though, and a few of them are about properly ignoring whitespace changes. If you see that you have a lot of whitespace issues in a merge, you can simply abort it and do it again, this time with -Xignore-all-space or -Xignore-space-change. The first option ignores changes in any amount of existing whitespace, the second ignores all whitespace changes altogether.

```
$ git merge -Xignore-all-space whitespace
Auto-merging hello.rb
Merge made by the 'recursive' strategy.
 hello.rb | 2 +-
 1 file changed, 1 insertion(+), 1 deletion(-)
```

Since in this case, the actual file changes were not conflicting, once we ignore the whitespace changes, everything merges just fine.

This is a lifesaver if you have someone on your team who likes to occasionally reformat everything from spaces to tabs or vice versa.

Manual File Re-merging

Although Git handles whitespace pre-processing pretty well, there are other types of changes that perhaps Git can't handle automatically, but are scriptable fixes. As an example, let's pretend that Git could not handle the whitespace change and we needed to do it by hand.

What we really need to do is run the file we're trying to merge in through a dos2unix program before trying the actual file merge. So how would we do that?

First, we get into the merge conflict state. Then we want to get copies of my version of the file, their version (from the branch we're merging in), and the common version (from where both sides branched off). Then we want to fix up either their side or our side and re-try the merge again for just this single file.

Getting the three file versions is actually pretty easy. Git stores all these versions in the index under "stages," which each have numbers associated with them. Stage 1 is the common ancestor, stage 2 is your version, and stage 3 is from the MERGE_HEAD, the version you're merging in ("theirs").

You can extract a copy of each of these versions of the conflicted file with the `git show` command and a special syntax.

```
$ git show :1:hello.rb > hello.common.rb
$ git show :2:hello.rb > hello.ours.rb
$ git show :3:hello.rb > hello.theirs.rb
```

If you want to get a little more hard core, you can also use the `ls-files -u` plumbing command to get the actual SHAs of the Git blobs for each of these files.

```
$ git ls-files -u
100755 ac51efdc3df4f4fd328d1a02ad05331d8e2c9111 1    hello.rb
100755 36c06c8752c78d2aff89571132f3bf7841a7b5c3 2    hello.rb
100755 e85207e04dfdd5eb0a1e9febbc67fd837c44a1cd 3    hello.rb
```

The `:1:hello.rb` is just shorthand for looking up that blob SHA.

Now that we have the content of all three stages in our working directory, we can manually fix up theirs to fix the whitespace issue and re-merge the file with the little-known `git merge-file` command, which does just that.

```
$ dos2unix hello.theirs.rb
dos2unix: converting file hello.theirs.rb to Unix format ...

$ git merge-file -p \
    hello.ours.rb hello.common.rb hello.theirs.rb > hello.rb

$ git diff -w
diff --cc hello.rb
index 36c06c8,e85207e..0000000
--- a/hello.rb
+++ b/hello.rb
@@ -1,8 -1,7 +1,8 @@
  #! /usr/bin/env ruby
```

```
+# prints out a greeting
 def hello
-    puts 'hello world'
+    puts 'hello mundo'
 end

 hello()
```

At this point we have nicely merged the file. In fact, this works better than the `ignore-all-space` option because this actually fixes the whitespace changes before merge instead of simply ignoring them. In the `ignore-all-space` merge, we ended up with a few lines with DOS line endings, making things mixed.

If you want to get an idea before finalizing this commit about what was actually changed between one side or the other, you can ask `git diff` to compare what is in your working directory that you're about to commit as the result of the merge to any of these stages. Let's go through them all.

To compare your result to what you had in your branch before the merge, in other words, to see what the merge introduced, you can run `git diff --ours`:

```
$ git diff --ours
* Unmerged path hello.rb
diff --git a/hello.rb b/hello.rb
index 36c06c8..44d0a25 100755
--- a/hello.rb
+++ b/hello.rb
@@ -2,7 +2,7 @@

 # prints out a greeting
 def hello
-    puts 'hello world'
+    puts 'hello mundo'
 end

 hello()
```

So here we can easily see that what happened in our branch, what we're actually introducing to this file with this merge, is changing that single line.

If we want to see how the result of the merge differed from what was on their side, you can run `git diff --theirs`. In this and the following example, we have to use `-w` to strip out the whitespace because we're comparing it to what is in Git, not our cleaned up `hello.theirs.rb` file.

```
$ git diff --theirs -w
* Unmerged path hello.rb
diff --git a/hello.rb b/hello.rb
index e85207e..44d0a25 100755
--- a/hello.rb
+++ b/hello.rb
@@ -1,5 +1,6 @@
 #! /usr/bin/env ruby

+# prints out a greeting
 def hello
   puts 'hello mundo'
 end
```

Finally, you can see how the file has changed from both sides with git diff --base.

```
$ git diff --base -w
* Unmerged path hello.rb
diff --git a/hello.rb b/hello.rb
index ac51efd..44d0a25 100755
--- a/hello.rb
+++ b/hello.rb
@@ -1,7 +1,8 @@
 #! /usr/bin/env ruby

+# prints out a greeting
 def hello
-  puts 'hello world'
+  puts 'hello mundo'
 end

 hello()
```

At this point we can use the git clean command to clear out the extra files we created to do the manual merge but no longer need.

```
$ git clean -f
Removing hello.common.rb
Removing hello.ours.rb
Removing hello.theirs.rb
```

Checking Out Conflicts

Perhaps we're not happy with the resolution at this point for some reason, or maybe manually editing one or both sides still didn't work well and we need more context.

Let's change up the example a little. For this example, we have two longer lived branches that each have a few commits in them but create a legitimate content conflict when merged.

```
$ git log --graph --oneline --decorate --all
* f1270f7 (HEAD, master) update README
* 9af9d3b add a README
* 694971d update phrase to hola world
| * e3eb223 (mundo) add more tests
| * 7cff591 add testing script
| * c3ffff1 changed text to hello mundo
|/
* b7dcc89 initial hello world code
```

We now have three unique commits that live only on the master branch and three others that live on the mundo branch. If we try to merge the mundo branch in, we get a conflict.

```
$ git merge mundo
Auto-merging hello.rb
CONFLICT (content): Merge conflict in hello.rb
Automatic merge failed; fix conflicts and then commit the result.
```

We would like to see what the merge conflict is. If we open up the file, we'll see something like this:

```
#! /usr/bin/env ruby

def hello
<<<<<<< HEAD
  puts 'hola world'
=======
  puts 'hello mundo'
>>>>>>> mundo
end

hello()
```

Both sides of the merge added content to this file, but some of the commits modified the file in the same place that caused this conflict.

Let's explore a couple of tools that you now have at your disposal to determine how this conflict came to be. Perhaps it's not obvious how exactly you should fix this conflict. You need more context.

One helpful tool is git checkout with the --conflict option. This re-checkouts the file and replaces the merge conflict markers. This can be useful if you want to reset the markers and try to resolve them again.

You can pass --conflict either diff3 or merge (which is the default). If you pass it diff3, Git will use a slightly different version of conflict markers, not only giving you the "ours" and "theirs" versions, but also the "base" version inline to give you more context.

```
$ git checkout --conflict=diff3 hello.rb
```
Once we run that, the file will look like this instead:

```
#! /usr/bin/env ruby

def hello
<<<<<<< ours
  puts 'hola world'
||||||| base
  puts 'hello world'
=======
  puts 'hello mundo'
>>>>>>> theirs
end

hello()
```

If you like this format, you can set it as the default for future merge conflicts by setting the merge.conflictstyle setting to diff3.

```
$ git config --global merge.conflictstyle diff3
```

The git checkout command can also take --ours and --theirs options, which can be a really fast way of just choosing either one side or the other without merging things at all.

This can be particularly useful for conflicts of binary files where you can simply choose one side, or where you only want to merge certain files in from another branch—you can do the merge and then checkout certain files from one side or the other before committing.

Merge Log

Another useful tool when resolving merge conflicts is git log. This can help you get context on what may have contributed to the conflicts. Reviewing a little bit of history to remember why two lines of development were touching the same area of code can be really helpful sometimes.

To get a full list of all the unique commits that were included in either branch involved in this merge, we can use the "triple dot" syntax.

```
$ git log --oneline --left-right HEAD...MERGE_HEAD
< f1270f7 update README
< 9af9d3b add a README
< 694971d update phrase to hola world
> e3eb223 add more tests
> 7cff591 add testing script
> c3ffff1 changed text to hello mundo
```

That's a nice list of the six total commits involved, as well as which line of development each commit was on.

We can further simplify this though to give us much more specific context. If we add the --merge option to git log, it will only show the commits in either side of the merge that touch a file that's currently conflicted.

```
$ git log --oneline --left-right --merge
< 694971d update phrase to hola world
> c3ffff1 changed text to hello mundo
```

If you run that with the -p option instead, you get just the diffs to the file that ended up in conflict. This can be really helpful in quickly giving you the context you need to help understand why something conflicts and how to more intelligently resolve it.

Combined Diff Format

Because Git stages any merge results that are successful, when you run git diff while in a conflicted merge state, you only get what is currently still in conflict. This can be helpful to see what you still have to resolve.

When you run git diff directly after a merge conflict, it will give you information in a rather unique diff output format.

```
$ git diff
diff --cc hello.rb
index 0399cd5,59727f0..0000000
--- a/hello.rb
+++ b/hello.rb
@@@ -1,7 -1,7 +1,11 @@@
  #! /usr/bin/env ruby

  def hello
++<<<<<<< HEAD
 +  puts 'hola world'
++=======
+   puts 'hello mundo'
++>>>>>>> mundo
  end

  hello()
```

The format is called "Combined Diff" and gives you two columns of data next to each line. The first column shows you if that line is different (added or removed) between the "ours" branch and the file in your working directory and the second column does the same between the "theirs" branch and your working directory copy.

So in that example you can see that the <<<<<<< and >>>>>>> lines are in the working copy but were not in either side of the merge. This makes sense because the merge tool stuck them in there for our context, but we're expected to remove them.

If we resolve the conflict and run git diff again, we'll see the same thing, but it's a little more useful.

```
$ vim hello.rb
$ git diff
diff --cc hello.rb
index 0399cd5,59727f0..0000000
--- a/hello.rb
+++ b/hello.rb
@@@ -1,7 -1,7 +1,7 @@@
  #! /usr/bin/env ruby

  def hello
-    puts 'hola world'
 -   puts 'hello mundo'
++   puts 'hola mundo'
  end

  hello()
```

This shows us that "hola world" was in our side but not in the working copy, that "hello mundo" was in their side but not in the working copy and finally that "hola mundo" was not in either side but is now in the working copy. This can be useful to review before committing the resolution.

You can also get this from the git log for any merge after the fact to see how something was resolved after the fact. Git will output this format if you run git show on a merge commit, or if you add a --cc option to a git log -p (which by default only shows patches for non-merge commits).

```
$ git log --cc -p -1
commit 14f41939956d80b9e17bb8721354c33f8d5b5a79
Merge: f1270f7 e3eb223
Author: Scott Chacon <schacon@gmail.com>
Date:   Fri Sep 19 18:14:49 2014 +0200

    Merge branch 'mundo'

    Conflicts:
        hello.rb

diff --cc hello.rb
index 0399cd5,59727f0..e1d0799
--- a/hello.rb
+++ b/hello.rb
@@@ -1,7 -1,7 +1,7 @@@
  #! /usr/bin/env ruby
```

```
  def hello
-    puts 'hola world'
 -   puts 'hello mundo'
++   puts 'hola mundo'
  end

  hello()
```

Undoing Merges

Now that you know how to create a merge commit, you'll probably make some by mistake. One of the great things about working with Git is that it's okay to make mistakes, because it's possible (and in many cases easy) to fix them.

Merge commits are no different. Let's say you started work on a topic branch, accidentally merged it into master, and now your commit history looks like this:

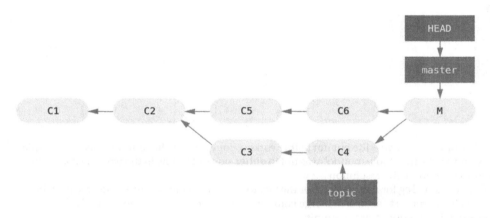

Figure 7-20. *Accidental merge commit*

There are two ways to approach this problem, depending on what your desired outcome is.

Fix the References

If the unwanted merge commit only exists on your local repository, the easiest and best solution is to move the branches so that they point where you want them to. In most cases, if you follow the errant `git merge` with `git reset --hard HEAD~`, this will reset the branch pointers so they look like this:

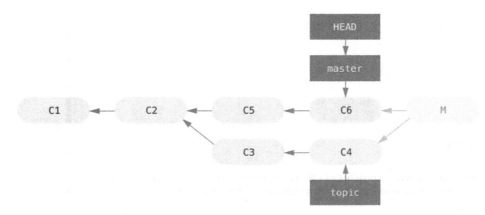

Figure 7-21. *History after git reset --hard HEAD~*

We covered reset earlier, so it shouldn't be too hard to figure out what's going on here. Here's a quick refresher: `reset --hard` usually goes through three steps:

1. Move the branch HEAD points to. In this case, we want to move master to where it was before the merge commit (C6).

2. Make the Index look like HEAD.

3. Make the Working Directory look like the index.

The downside of this approach is that it's rewriting history, which can be problematic with a shared repository. If other people have the commits you're rewriting, you should probably avoid reset. This approach also won't work if any other commits have been created since the merge; moving the refs would effectively lose those changes.

Reverse the Commit

If moving the branch pointers around isn't going to work for you, Git gives you the option of making a new commit that undoes all the changes from an existing one. Git calls this operation a "revert," and in this particular scenario, you'd invoke it like this:

```
$ git revert -m 1 HEAD
[master b1d8379] Revert "Merge branch 'topic'"
```

The `-m 1` flag indicates which parent is the "mainline" and should be kept. When you invoke a merge into HEAD (`git merge topic`), the new commit has two parents: the first one is HEAD (C6), and the second is the tip of the branch being merged in (C4). In this case, we want to undo all the changes introduced by merging in parent #2 (C4), while keeping all the content from parent #1 (C6).

The history with the revert commit looks like this:

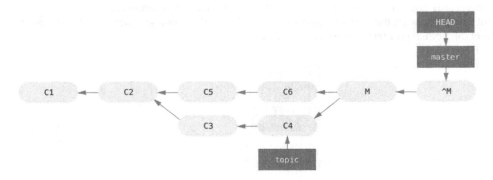

Figure 7-22. *History after git revert -m 1*

The new commit ^M has exactly the same contents as C6, so starting from here it's as if the merge never happened, except that the now-unmerged commits are still in HEAD's history. Git will get confused if you try to merge topic into master again:

```
$ git merge topic
Already up-to-date.
```

There's nothing in topic that isn't already reachable from master. What's worse, if you add work to topic and merge again, Git will only bring in the changes since the reverted merge:

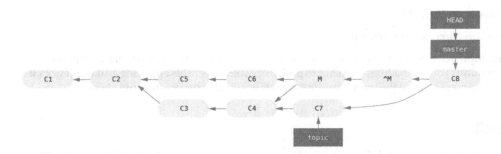

Figure 7-23. *History with a bad merge*

The best way around this is to un-revert the original merge, because now you want to bring in the changes that were reverted out, then create a new merge commit:

```
$ git revert ^M
[master 09f0126] Revert "Revert "Merge branch 'topic'""
$ git merge topic
```

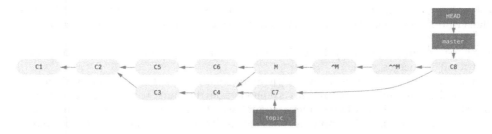

Figure 7-24. *History after re-merging a reverted merge*

In this example, M and ^M cancel out. ^^M effectively merges in the changes from C3 and C4, and C8 merges in the changes from C7, so now topic is fully merged.

Other Types of Merges

So far we've covered the normal merge of two branches, normally handled with what is called the "recursive" strategy of merging. There are other ways to merge branches however. Let's cover a few of them quickly.

Our or Theirs Preference

First of all, there is another useful thing we can do with the normal "recursive" mode of merging. We've already seen the ignore-all-space and ignore-space-change options that are passed with a -X but we can also tell Git to favor one side or the other when it sees a conflict.

By default, when Git sees a conflict between two branches being merged, it will add merge conflict markers into your code and mark the file as conflicted and let you resolve it. If you would prefer for Git to simply choose a specific side and ignore the other side instead of letting you manually merge the conflict, you can pass the merge command either a -Xours or -Xtheirs.

If Git sees this, it will not add conflict markers. Any differences that are mergeable, it will merge. Any differences that conflict, it will simply choose the side you specify in whole, including binary files.

If we go back to the "hello world" example we were using before, we can see that merging in our branch causes conflicts.

```
$ git merge mundo
Auto-merging hello.rb
CONFLICT (content): Merge conflict in hello.rb
Resolved 'hello.rb' using previous resolution.
Automatic merge failed; fix conflicts and then commit the result.
However if we run it with -Xours or -Xtheirs it does not.

$ git merge -Xours mundo
Auto-merging hello.rb
Merge made by the 'recursive' strategy.
 hello.rb | 2 +-
 test.sh  | 2 ++
 2 files changed, 3 insertions(+), 1 deletion(-)
 create mode 100644 test.sh
```

In that case, instead of getting conflict markers in the file with "hello mundo" on one side and "hola world" on the other, it will simply pick "hola world." However, all the other non-conflicting changes on that branch are merged in successfully.

This option can also be passed to the git merge-file command we saw earlier by running something like git merge-file --ours for individual file merges.

If you want to do something like this but not have Git even try to merge changes from the other side in, there is a more draconian option, which is the "ours" merge strategy. This is different from the "ours" recursive merge option.

This will basically do a fake merge. It will record a new merge commit with both branches as parents, but it will not even look at the branch you're merging in. It will simply record as the result of the merge the exact code in your current branch.

```
$ git merge -s ours mundo
Merge made by the 'ours' strategy.
$ git diff HEAD HEAD~
$
```

You can see that there is no difference between the branch we were on and the result of the merge.

This can often be useful to basically trick Git into thinking that a branch is already merged when doing a merge later on. For example, say you branched off a "release" branch and have done some work on it that you will want to merge back into your "master" branch at some point. In the meantime some bugfix on "master" needs to be backported into your release branch. You can merge the bugfix branch into the release branch and also merge -s ours the same branch into your master branch (even though the fix is already there) so when you later merge the release branch again, there are no conflicts from the bugfix.

Subtree Merging

The idea of the subtree merge is that you have two projects, and one of the projects maps to a subdirectory of the other one and vice versa. When you specify a subtree merge, Git is often smart enough to figure out that one is a subtree of the other and merge appropriately.

We'll go through an example of adding a separate project into an existing project and then merging the code of the second into a subdirectory of the first.

First, we'll add the Rack application to our project. We'll add the Rack project as a remote reference in our own project and then check it out into its own branch:

```
$ git remote add rack_remote https://github.com/rack/rack
$ git fetch rack_remote
warning: no common commits
remote: Counting objects: 3184, done.
remote: Compressing objects: 100% (1465/1465), done.
remote: Total 3184 (delta 1952), reused 2770 (delta 1675)
Receiving objects: 100% (3184/3184), 677.42 KiB | 4 KiB/s, done.
Resolving deltas: 100% (1952/1952), done.
From https://github.com/rack/rack
 * [new branch]      build      -> rack_remote/build
 * [new branch]      master     -> rack_remote/master
 * [new branch]      rack-0.4   -> rack_remote/rack-0.4
 * [new branch]      rack-0.9   -> rack_remote/rack-0.9
$ git checkout -b rack_branch rack_remote/master
Branch rack_branch set up to track remote branch refs/remotes/rack_remote/master.
Switched to a new branch "rack_branch"
```

Now we have the root of the Rack project in our `rack_branch` branch and our own project in the `master` branch. If you check out one and then the other, you can see that they have different project roots:

```
$ ls
AUTHORS         KNOWN-ISSUES   Rakefile    contrib     lib
COPYING         README         bin         example     test
$ git checkout master
Switched to branch "master"
$ ls
README
```

This is sort of a strange concept. Not all the branches in your repository actually have to be branches of the same project. It's not common, because it's rarely helpful, but it's fairly easy to have branches contain completely different histories.

In this case, we want to pull the Rack project into our master project as a subdirectory. We can do that in Git with `git read-tree`. You'll learn more about `read-tree` and its friends later, but for now know that it reads the root tree of one branch into your current staging area and working directory. We just switched back to your `master` branch, and we pull the rack branch into the `rack` subdirectory of our `master` branch of our main project:

```
$ git read-tree --prefix=rack/ -u rack_branch
```

When we commit, it looks like we have all the Rack files under that subdirectory—as though we copied them in from a tarball. What gets interesting is that we can fairly easily merge changes from one of the branches to the other. So, if the Rack project updates, we can pull in upstream changes by switching to that branch and pulling:

```
$ git checkout rack_branch
$ git pull
```

Then, we can merge those changes back into our `master` branch. We can use `git merge -s subtree` and it will work fine; but Git will also merge the histories, which we probably don't want. To pull in the changes and prepopulate the commit message, use the `--squash` and `--no-commit` options as well as the `-s subtree` strategy option:

```
$ git checkout master
$ git merge --squash -s subtree --no-commit rack_branch
Squash commit -- not updating HEAD
Automatic merge went well; stopped before committing as requested
```

All the changes from the Rack project are merged in and ready to be committed locally. You can also do the opposite—make changes in the rack subdirectory of your `master` branch and then merge them into your `rack_branch` branch later to submit them to the maintainers or push them upstream.

This gives us a way to have a workflow somewhat similar to the submodule workflow without using submodules. We can keep branches with other related projects in our repository and subtree merge them into our project occasionally. It is nice in some ways, for example all the code is committed to a single place. However, it has other drawbacks in that it's a bit more complex and easier to make mistakes in reintegrating changes or accidentally pushing a branch into an unrelated repository.

Another slightly weird thing is that to get a diff between what you have in your `rack` subdirectory and the code in your `rack_branch` branch—to see if you need to merge them—you can't use the normal `diff` command. Instead, you must run `git diff-tree` with the branch you want to compare to:

```
$ git diff-tree -p rack_branch
```

Or, to compare what is in your `rack` subdirectory with what the `master` branch on the server was the last time you fetched, you can run

```
$ git diff-tree -p rack_remote/master
```

Rerere

The `git rerere` functionality is a bit of a hidden feature. The name stands for "reuse recorded resolution" and as the name implies, it allows you to ask Git to remember how you've resolved a hunk conflict so that the next time it sees the same conflict, Git can automatically resolve it for you.

There are a number of scenarios in which this functionality might be really handy. One of the examples that is mentioned in the documentation is if you want to make sure a long lived topic branch will merge cleanly but don't want to have a bunch of intermediate merge commits. With `rerere` turned on you can merge occasionally, resolve the conflicts, and then back out the merge. If you do this continuously, then the final merge should be easy because rerere can just do everything for you automatically.

This same tactic can be used if you want to keep a branch rebased so you don't have to deal with the same rebasing conflicts each time you do it. Or if you want to take a branch that you merged and fixed a bunch of conflicts and then decide to rebase it instead—you likely won't have to do all the same conflicts again.

Another situation is where you merge a bunch of evolving topic branches into a testable head occasionally, as the Git project itself often does. If the tests fail, you can rewind the merges and re-do them without the topic branch that made the tests fail without having to re-resolve the conflicts again.

To enable the `rerere` functionality, you simply have to run this config setting:

```
$ git config --global rerere.enabled true
```

You can also turn it on by creating the `.git/rr-cache` directory in a specific repository, but the config setting is clearer and it can be done globally.

Now let's see a simple example, similar to our previous one. Let's say we have a file that looks like this:

```
#! /usr/bin/env ruby

def hello
  puts 'hello world'
end
```

In one branch we change the word "hello" to "hola", then in another branch we change the "world" to "mundo," just like before.

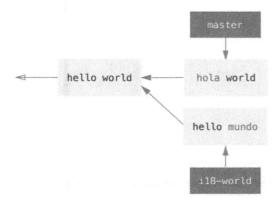

When we merge the two branches, we'll get a merge conflict:

```
$ git merge i18n-world
Auto-merging hello.rb
CONFLICT (content): Merge conflict in hello.rb
Recorded preimage for 'hello.rb'
Automatic merge failed; fix conflicts and then commit the result.
```

You should notice the new line Recorded preimage for FILE in there. Otherwise it should look exactly like a normal merge conflict. At this point, rerere can tell us a few things. Normally, you might run git status at this point to see what all conflicted:

```
$ git status
# On branch master
# Unmerged paths:
#   (use "git reset HEAD <file>..." to unstage)
#   (use "git add <file>..." to mark resolution)
#
#       both modified: hello.rb
#
```

However, git rerere will also tell you what it has recorded the pre-merge state for with git rerere status:

```
$ git rerere status
hello.rb
```

And git rerere diff will show the current state of the resolution—what you started with to resolve and what you've resolved it to.

```
$ git rerere diff
--- a/hello.rb
+++ b/hello.rb
@@ -1,11 +1,11 @@
 #! /usr/bin/env ruby
```

```
 def hello
-<<<<<<<
- puts 'hello mundo'
-=======
+<<<<<<< HEAD
   puts 'hola world'
->>>>>>>
+=======
+ puts 'hello mundo'
+>>>>>>> i18n-world
 end
```

Also (and this isn't really related to rerere), you can use ls-files -u to see the conflicted files and the before, left, and right versions:

```
$ git ls-files -u
100644 39804c942a9c1f2c03dc7c5ebcd7f3e3a6b97519 1    hello.rb
100644 a440db6e8d1fd76ad438a49025a9ad9ce746f581 2    hello.rb
100644 54336ba847c3758ab604876419607e9443848474 3    hello.rb
```

Now you can resolve it to just be puts 'hola mundo' and you can run the rerere diff command again to see what rerere will remember:

```
$ git rerere diff
--- a/hello.rb
+++ b/hello.rb
@@ -1,11 +1,7 @@
 #! /usr/bin/env ruby

 def hello
-<<<<<<<
- puts 'hello mundo'
-=======
- puts 'hola world'
->>>>>>>
+ puts 'hola mundo'
 end
```

So that basically says, when Git sees a hunk conflict in a hello.rb file that has "hello mundo" on one side and "hola world" on the other, it will resolve it to "hola mundo".

Now we can mark it as resolved and commit it:

```
$ git add hello.rb
$ git commit
Recorded resolution for 'hello.rb'.
[master 68e16e5] Merge branch 'i18n'
```

You can see that it "Recorded resolution for FILE".

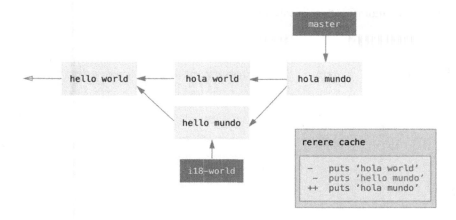

Now, let's undo that merge and then rebase it on top of our master branch instead. We can move our branch back by using reset.

```
$ git reset --hard HEAD^
HEAD is now at ad63f15 i18n the hello
```

Our merge is undone. Now let's rebase the topic branch.

```
$ git checkout i18n-world
Switched to branch 'i18n-world'
```

```
$ git rebase master
First, rewinding head to replay your work on top of it...
Applying: i18n one word
Using index info to reconstruct a base tree...
Falling back to patching base and 3-way merge...
Auto-merging hello.rb
CONFLICT (content): Merge conflict in hello.rb
Resolved 'hello.rb' using previous resolution.
Failed to merge in the changes.
Patch failed at 0001 i18n one word
```

Now, we have the same merge conflict we expected, but take a look at the Resolved FILE using previous resolution line. If we look at the file, we'll see that it's already been resolved, there are no merge conflict markers in it.

```
$ cat hello.rb
#! /usr/bin/env ruby

def hello
  puts 'hola mundo'
end
```

Also, `git diff` will show you how it was automatically re-resolved:

```
$ git diff
diff --cc hello.rb
index a440db6,54336ba..0000000
--- a/hello.rb
+++ b/hello.rb
@@@ -1,7 -1,7 +1,7 @@@
  #! /usr/bin/env ruby

  def hello
-   puts 'hola world'
 -  puts 'hello mundo'
++  puts 'hola mundo'
  end
rerere3
```

You can also re-create the conflicted file state with the `checkout` command:

```
$ git checkout --conflict=merge hello.rb
$ cat hello.rb
#! /usr/bin/env ruby

def hello
<<<<<<< ours
  puts 'hola world'
=======
  puts 'hello mundo'
>>>>>>> theirs
end
```

Let's re-resolve it by just running rerere again:

```
$ git rerere
Resolved 'hello.rb' using previous resolution.
$ cat hello.rb
#! /usr/bin/env ruby

def hello
  puts 'hola mundo'
end
```

We have re-resolved the file automatically using the rerere cached resolution. You can now add and continue the rebase to complete it.

```
$ git add hello.rb
$ git rebase --continue
Applying: i18n one word
```

So, if you do a lot of re-merges, or want to keep a topic branch up to date with your master branch without a ton of merges, or you rebase often, you can turn on rerere to help your life out a bit.

Debugging with Git

Git also provides a couple of tools to help you debug issues in your projects. Because Git is designed to work with nearly any type of project, these tools are pretty generic, but they can often help you hunt for a bug or culprit when things go wrong.

File Annotation

If you track down a bug in your code and want to know when it was introduced and why, file annotation is often your best tool. It shows you what commit was the last to modify each line of any file. So, if you see that a method in your code is buggy, you can annotate the file with git blame to see when each line of the method was last edited and by whom. This example uses the -L option to limit the output to lines 12 through 22:

```
$ git blame -L 12,22 simplegit.rb
^4832fe2 (Scott Chacon  2008-03-15 10:31:28 -0700 12)  def show(tree = 'master')
^4832fe2 (Scott Chacon  2008-03-15 10:31:28 -0700 13)   command("git show #{tree}")
^4832fe2 (Scott Chacon  2008-03-15 10:31:28 -0700 14)  end
^4832fe2 (Scott Chacon  2008-03-15 10:31:28 -0700 15)
9f6560e4 (Scott Chacon  2008-03-17 21:52:20 -0700 16)  def log(tree = 'master')
79eaf55d (Scott Chacon  2008-04-06 10:15:08 -0700 17)   command("git log #{tree}")
9f6560e4 (Scott Chacon  2008-03-17 21:52:20 -0700 18)  end
9f6560e4 (Scott Chacon  2008-03-17 21:52:20 -0700 19)
42cf2861 (Magnus Chacon 2008-04-13 10:45:01 -0700 20)  def blame(path)
42cf2861 (Magnus Chacon 2008-04-13 10:45:01 -0700 21)   command("git blame #{path}")
42cf2861 (Magnus Chacon 2008-04-13 10:45:01 -0700 22)  end
```

Notice that the first field is the partial SHA-1 of the commit that last modified that line. The next two fields are values extracted from that commit—the author name and the authored date of that commit—so you can easily see who modified that line and when. After that come the line number and the content of the file. Also note the ^4832fe2 commit lines, which designate that those lines were in this file's original commit. That commit is when this file was first added to this project, and those lines have been unchanged since. This is a tad confusing, because now you've seen at least three different ways that Git uses the ^ to modify a commit SHA, but that is what it means here.

Another cool thing about Git is that it doesn't track file renames explicitly. It records the snapshots and then tries to figure out what was renamed implicitly, after the fact. One of the interesting features of this is that you can ask it to figure out all sorts of code movement as well. If you pass -C to git blame, Git analyzes the file you're annotating and tries to figure out where snippets of code within it originally came from if they were copied from elsewhere. For example, say you are refactoring a file named GITServerHandler.m into multiple files, one of which is GITPackUpload.m. By blaming GITPackUpload.m with the -C option, you can see where sections of the code originally came from:

```
$ git blame -C -L 141,153 GITPackUpload.m
f344f58d GITServerHandler.m (Scott 2009-01-04 141)
f344f58d GITServerHandler.m (Scott 2009-01-04 142) - (void) gatherObjectShasFromC
f344f58d GITServerHandler.m (Scott 2009-01-04 143) {
70befddd GITServerHandler.m (Scott 2009-03-22 144)      //NSLog(@"GATHER COMMI
ad11ac80 GITPackUpload.m    (Scott 2009-03-24 145)
ad11ac80 GITPackUpload.m    (Scott 2009-03-24 146)      NSString *parentSha;
ad11ac80 GITPackUpload.m    (Scott 2009-03-24 147)      GITCommit *commit = [g
ad11ac80 GITPackUpload.m    (Scott 2009-03-24 148)
ad11ac80 GITPackUpload.m    (Scott 2009-03-24 149)      //NSLog(@"GATHER COMMI
ad11ac80 GITPackUpload.m    (Scott 2009-03-24 150)
```

```
56ef2caf GITServerHandler.m (Scott 2009-01-05 151)          if(commit) {
56ef2caf GITServerHandler.m (Scott 2009-01-05 152)              [refDict setOb
56ef2caf GITServerHandler.m (Scott 2009-01-05 153)
```

This is really useful. Normally, you get as the original commit the commit where you copied the code over, because that is the first time you touched those lines in this file. Git tells you the original commit where you wrote those lines, even if it was in another file.

Binary Search

Annotating a file helps if you know where the issue is to begin with. If you don't know what is breaking, and there have been dozens or hundreds of commits since the last state where you know the code worked, you'll likely turn to `git bisect` for help. The `bisect` command does a binary search through your commit history to help you identify as quickly as possible which commit introduced an issue.

Let's say you just pushed out a release of your code to a production environment, you're getting bug reports about something that wasn't happening in your development environment, and you can't imagine why the code is doing that. You go back to your code, and it turns out you can reproduce the issue, but you can't figure out what is going wrong. You can bisect the code to find out. First you run `git bisect` start to get things going, and then you use `git bisect bad` to tell the system that the current commit you're on is broken. Then, you must tell bisect when the last known good state was, using `git bisect good [good_commit]`:

```
$ git bisect start
$ git bisect bad
$ git bisect good v1.0
Bisecting: 6 revisions left to test after this
[ecb6e1bc347ccecc5f9350d878ce677feb13d3b2] error handling on repo
```

Git figured out that about 12 commits came between the commit you marked as the last good commit (v1.0) and the current bad version, and it checked out the middle one for you. At this point, you can run your test to see whether the issue exists as of this commit. If it does, then it was introduced sometime before this middle commit; if it doesn't, then the problem was introduced sometime after the middle commit. It turns out there is no issue here, and you tell Git that by typing `git bisect good` and continue your journey:

```
$ git bisect good
Bisecting: 3 revisions left to test after this
[b047b02ea83310a70fd603dc8cd7a6cd13d15c04] secure this thing
```

Now you're on another commit, halfway between the one you just tested and your bad commit. You run your test again and find that this commit is broken, so you tell Git that with `git bisect bad`:

```
$ git bisect bad
Bisecting: 1 revisions left to test after this
[f71ce38690acf49c1f3c9bea38e09d82a5ce6014] drop exceptions table
```

This commit is fine, and now Git has all the information it needs to determine where the issue was introduced. It tells you the SHA-1 of the first bad commit and shows some of the commit information and which files were modified in that commit so you can figure out what happened that may have introduced this bug:

```
$ git bisect good
b047b02ea83310a70fd603dc8cd7a6cd13d15c04 is first bad commit
commit b047b02ea83310a70fd603dc8cd7a6cd13d15c04
```

```
Author: PJ Hyett <pjhyett@example.com>
Date:   Tue Jan 27 14:48:32 2009 -0800

    secure this thing

:040000 040000 40ee3e7821b895e52c1695092db9bdc4c61d1730
f24d3c6ebcfc639b1a3814550e62d60b8e68a8e4 M  config
```

When you're finished, you should run git bisect reset to reset your HEAD to where you were before you started, or you'll end up in a weird state:

```
$ git bisect reset
```

This is a powerful tool that can help you check hundreds of commits for an introduced bug in minutes. In fact, if you have a script that will exit 0 if the project is good or non-0 if the project is bad, you can fully automate git bisect. First, you again tell it the scope of the bisect by providing the known bad and good commits. You can do this by listing them with the bisect start command if you want, listing the known bad commit first and the known good commit second:

```
$ git bisect start HEAD v1.0
$ git bisect run test-error.sh
```

Doing so automatically runs test-error.sh on each checked-out commit until Git finds the first broken commit. You can also run something such as make or make tests or whatever you have that runs automated tests for you.

Submodules

It often happens that while working on one project, you need to use another project from within it. Perhaps it's a library that a third party developed or that you're developing separately and using in multiple parent projects. A common issue arises in these scenarios: you want to be able to treat the two projects as separate yet still be able to use one from within the other.

Here's an example. Suppose you're developing a web site and creating Atom feeds. Instead of writing your own Atom-generating code, you decide to use a library. You're likely to have to either include this code from a shared library like a CPAN install or Ruby gem, or copy the source code into your own project tree. The issue with including the library is that it's difficult to customize the library in any way and often more difficult to deploy it, because you need to make sure every client has that library available. The issue with vendoring the code into your own project is that any custom changes you make are difficult to merge when upstream changes become available.

Git addresses this issue using submodules. Submodules allow you to keep a Git repository as a subdirectory of another Git repository. This lets you clone another repository into your project and keep your commits separate.

Starting with Submodules

We'll walk through developing a simple project that has been split up into a main project and a few subprojects.

Let's start by adding an existing Git repository as a submodule of the repository that we're working on. To add a new submodule you use the git submodule add command with the URL of the project you would like to start tracking. In this example, we'll add a library called DbConnector.

```
$ git submodule add https://github.com/chaconinc/DbConnector
Cloning into 'DbConnector'...
remote: Counting objects: 11, done.
```

```
remote: Compressing objects: 100% (10/10), done.
remote: Total 11 (delta 0), reused 11 (delta 0)
Unpacking objects: 100% (11/11), done.
Checking connectivity... done.
```

By default, submodules will add the subproject into a directory named the same as the repository, in this case DbConnector. You can add a different path at the end of the command if you want it to go elsewhere.

If you run git status at this point, you'll notice a few things.

```
$ git status
On branch master
Your branch is up-to-date with 'origin/master'.

Changes to be committed:
  (use "git reset HEAD <file>..." to unstage)

        new file:   .gitmodules
        new file:   DbConnector
```

First you should notice the new .gitmodules file. This is a configuration file that stores the mapping between the project's URL and the local subdirectory you've pulled it into:

```
$ cat .gitmodules
[submodule "DbConnector"]
        path = DbConnector
        url = https://github.com/chaconinc/DbConnector
```

If you have multiple submodules, you'll have multiple entries in this file. It's important to note that this file is version-controlled with your other files, like your .gitignore file. It's pushed and pulled with the rest of your project. This is how other people who clone this project know where to get the submodule projects from.

■ **Note** Since the URL in the .gitmodules file is what other people will first try to clone/fetch from, make sure to use a URL that they can access if possible. For example, if you use a different URL to push to than others would to pull from, use the one that others have access to. You can overwrite this value locally with git config submodule.DbConnector.url PRIVATE_URL for your own use.

The other listing in the git status output is the project folder entry. If you run git diff on that, you see something interesting:

```
$ git diff --cached DbConnector
diff --git a/DbConnector b/DbConnector
new file mode 160000
index 0000000..c3f01dc
--- /dev/null
+++ b/DbConnector
@@ -0,0 +1 @@
+Subproject commit c3f01dc8862123d317dd46284b05b6892c7b29bc
```

Although DbConnector is a subdirectory in your working directory, Git sees it as a submodule and doesn't track its contents when you're not in that directory. Instead, Git sees it as a particular commit from that repository.

If you want a little nicer diff output, you can pass the --submodule option to git diff.

```
$ git diff --cached --submodule
diff --git a/.gitmodules b/.gitmodules
new file mode 100644
index 0000000..71fc376
--- /dev/null
+++ b/.gitmodules
@@ -0,0 +1,3 @@
+[submodule "DbConnector"]
+       path = DbConnector
+       url = https://github.com/chaconinc/DbConnector
Submodule DbConnector 0000000...c3f01dc (new submodule)
```

When you commit, you see something like this:

```
$ git commit -am 'added DbConnector module'
[master fb9093c] added DbConnector module
 2 files changed, 4 insertions(+)
 create mode 100644 .gitmodules
 create mode 160000 DbConnector
```

Notice the 160000 mode for the rack entry. That is a special mode in Git that basically means you're recording a commit as a directory entry rather than a subdirectory or a file.

Cloning a Project with Submodules

Here we'll clone a project with a submodule in it. When you clone such a project, by default you get the directories that contain submodules, but none of the files within them yet:

```
$ git clone https://github.com/chaconinc/MainProject
Cloning into 'MainProject'...
remote: Counting objects: 14, done.
remote: Compressing objects: 100% (13/13), done.
remote: Total 14 (delta 1), reused 13 (delta 0)
Unpacking objects: 100% (14/14), done.
Checking connectivity... done.
$ cd MainProject
$ ls -la
total 16
drwxr-xr-x    9 schacon  staff  306 Sep 17 15:21 .
drwxr-xr-x    7 schacon  staff  238 Sep 17 15:21 ..
drwxr-xr-x   13 schacon  staff  442 Sep 17 15:21 .git
-rw-r--r--    1 schacon  staff   92 Sep 17 15:21 .gitmodules
drwxr-xr-x    2 schacon  staff   68 Sep 17 15:21 DbConnector
-rw-r--r--    1 schacon  staff  756 Sep 17 15:21 Makefile
drwxr-xr-x    3 schacon  staff  102 Sep 17 15:21 includes
```

```
drwxr-xr-x    4 schacon   staff   136 Sep 17 15:21 scripts
drwxr-xr-x    4 schacon   staff   136 Sep 17 15:21 src
$ cd DbConnector/
$ ls
$
```

The DbConnector directory is there, but empty. You must run two commands: git submodule init to initialize your local configuration file, and git submodule update to fetch all the data from that project and check out the appropriate commit listed in your superproject:

```
$ git submodule init
Submodule 'DbConnector' (https://github.com/chaconinc/DbConnector) registered for path 'DbConnector'
$ git submodule update
Cloning into 'DbConnector'...
remote: Counting objects: 11, done.
remote: Compressing objects: 100% (10/10), done.
remote: Total 11 (delta 0), reused 11 (delta 0)
Unpacking objects: 100% (11/11), done.
Checking connectivity... done.
Submodule path 'DbConnector': checked out 'c3f01dc8862123d317dd46284b05b6892c7b29bc'
```

Now your DbConnector subdirectory is at the exact state it was in when you committed earlier.

There is another way to do this which is a little simpler, however. If you pass --recursive to the git clone command, it will automatically initialize and update each submodule in the repository.

```
$ git clone --recursive https://github.com/chaconinc/MainProject
Cloning into 'MainProject'...
remote: Counting objects: 14, done.
remote: Compressing objects: 100% (13/13), done.
remote: Total 14 (delta 1), reused 13 (delta 0)
Unpacking objects: 100% (14/14), done.
Checking connectivity... done.
Submodule 'DbConnector' (https://github.com/chaconinc/DbConnector) registered for path 'DbConnector'
Cloning into 'DbConnector'...
remote: Counting objects: 11, done.
remote: Compressing objects: 100% (10/10), done.
remote: Total 11 (delta 0), reused 11 (delta 0)
Unpacking objects: 100% (11/11), done.
Checking connectivity... done.
Submodule path 'DbConnector': checked out 'c3f01dc8862123d317dd46284b05b6892c7b29bc'
```

Working on a Project with Submodules

Now we have a copy of a project with submodules in it and will collaborate with our teammates on both the main project and the submodule project.

Pulling in Upstream Changes

The simplest model of using submodules in a project would be if you were simply consuming a subproject and wanted to get updates from it from time to time but were not actually modifying anything in your checkout. Let's walk through a simple example there.

If you want to check for new work in a submodule, you can go into the directory and run git fetch and git merge the upstream branch to update the local code.

```
$ git fetch
From https://github.com/chaconinc/DbConnector
   c3f01dc..d0354fc  master      -> origin/master
Scotts-MacBook-Pro-3:DbConnector schacon$ git merge origin/master
Updating c3f01dc..d0354fc
Fast-forward
 scripts/connect.sh | 1 +
 src/db.c           | 1 +
 2 files changed, 2 insertions(+)
```

Now if you go back into the main project and run git diff --submodule you can see that the submodule was updated and get a list of commits that were added to it. If you don't want to type --submodule every time you run git diff, you can set it as the default format by setting the diff.submodule config value to log.

```
$ git config --global diff.submodule log
$ git diff
Submodule DbConnector c3f01dc..d0354fc:
  > more efficient db routine
  > better connection routine
```

If you commit at this point, then you will lock the submodule into having the new code when other people update.

There is an easier way to do this as well, if you prefer to not manually fetch and merge in the subdirectory. If you run git submodule update --remote, Git will go into your submodules and fetch and update for you.

```
$ git submodule update --remote DbConnector
remote: Counting objects: 4, done.
remote: Compressing objects: 100% (2/2), done.
remote: Total 4 (delta 2), reused 4 (delta 2)
Unpacking objects: 100% (4/4), done.
From https://github.com/chaconinc/DbConnector
   3f19983..d0354fc  master      -> origin/master
Submodule path 'DbConnector': checked out 'd0354fc054692d3906c85c3af05ddce39a1c0644'
```

This command by default assumes that you want to update the checkout to the master branch of the submodule repository. You can, however, set this to something different if you want. For example, if you want to have the DbConnector submodule track that repository's "stable" branch, you can set it in either your .gitmodules file (so everyone else also tracks it), or just in your local .git/config file. Let's set it in the .gitmodules file:

```
$ git config -f .gitmodules submodule.DbConnector.branch stable
```

```
$ git submodule update --remote
remote: Counting objects: 4, done.
remote: Compressing objects: 100% (2/2), done.
remote: Total 4 (delta 2), reused 4 (delta 2)
Unpacking objects: 100% (4/4), done.
From https://github.com/chaconinc/DbConnector
   27cf5d3..c87d55d  stable -> origin/stable
Submodule path 'DbConnector': checked out 'c87d55d4c6d4b05ee34fbc8cb6f7bf4585ae6687'
```

If you leave off the -f .gitmodules it will only make the change for you, but it probably makes more sense to track that information with the repository so everyone else does as well.

When we run git status at this point, Git will show us that we have new commits on the submodule.

```
$ git status
On branch master
Your branch is up-to-date with 'origin/master'.

Changes not staged for commit:
  (use "git add <file>..." to update what will be committed)
  (use "git checkout -- <file>..." to discard changes in working directory)

  modified: .gitmodules
  modified: DbConnector (new commits)

no changes added to commit (use "git add" and/or "git commit -a")
```

If you set the configuration setting status.submodulesummary, Git will also show you a short summary of changes to your submodules:

```
$ git config status.submodulesummary 1

$ git status
On branch master
Your branch is up-to-date with 'origin/master'.

Changes not staged for commit:
  (use "git add <file>..." to update what will be committed)
  (use "git checkout -- <file>..." to discard changes in working directory)

    modified: .gitmodules
    modified: DbConnector (new commits)

Submodules changed but not updated:

* DbConnector c3f01dc...c87d55d (4):
  > catch non-null terminated lines
```

At this point if you run git diff we can see both that we have modified our .gitmodules file and also that there are a number of commits that we've pulled down and are ready to commit to our submodule project.

```
$ git diff
diff --git a/.gitmodules b/.gitmodules
index 6fc0b3d..fd1cc29 100644
--- a/.gitmodules
+++ b/.gitmodules
@@ -1,3 +1,4 @@
 [submodule "DbConnector"]
        path = DbConnector
        url = https://github.com/chaconinc/DbConnector
+       branch = stable
```

```
Submodule DbConnector c3f01dc..c87d55d:
  > catch non-null terminated lines
  > more robust error handling
  > more efficient db routine
  > better connection routine
```

This is pretty cool as we can actually see the log of commits that we're about to commit to in our submodule. Once committed, you can see this information after the fact as well when you run git log -p.

```
$ git log -p --submodule
commit 0a24cfc121a8a3c118e0105ae4ae4c00281cf7ae
Author: Scott Chacon <schacon@gmail.com>
Date:   Wed Sep 17 16:37:02 2014 +0200

    updating DbConnector for bug fixes

diff --git a/.gitmodules b/.gitmodules
index 6fc0b3d..fd1cc29 100644
--- a/.gitmodules
+++ b/.gitmodules
@@ -1,3 +1,4 @@
 [submodule "DbConnector"]
        path = DbConnector
        url = https://github.com/chaconinc/DbConnector
+       branch = stable
Submodule DbConnector c3f01dc..c87d55d:
  > catch non-null terminated lines
  > more robust error handling
  > more efficient db routine
  > better connection routine
```

Git will by default try to update all your submodules when you run git submodule update --remote so if you have a lot of them, you may want to pass the name of just the submodule you want to try to update.

Working on a Submodule

It's quite likely that if you're using submodules, you're doing so because you really want to work on the code in the submodule at the same time as you're working on the code in the main project (or across several submodules). Otherwise you would probably instead be using a simpler dependency management system (such as Maven or Rubygems).

So now let's go through an example of making changes to the submodule at the same time as the main project and committing and publishing those changes at the same time.

So far, when we've run the git submodule update command to fetch changes from the submodule repositories, Git would get the changes and update the files in the subdirectory but will leave the subrepository in what's called a "detached HEAD" state. This means that there is no local working branch (like master, for example) tracking changes. So any changes you make aren't being tracked well.

In order to set up your submodule to be easier to go in and hack on, you need do two things. You need to go into each submodule and check out a branch to work on. Then you need to tell Git what to do if you have made changes and then git submodule update --remote pulls in new work from upstream. The options are that you can merge them into your local work, or you can try to rebase your local work on top of the new changes.

First of all, let's go into our submodule directory and check out a branch.

```
$ git checkout stable
Switched to branch 'stable'
```

Let's try it with the "merge" option. To specify it manually, we can just add the --merge option to our update call. Here we'll see that there was a change on the server for this submodule and it gets merged in.

```
$ git submodule update --remote --merge
remote: Counting objects: 4, done.
remote: Compressing objects: 100% (2/2), done.
remote: Total 4 (delta 2), reused 4 (delta 2)
Unpacking objects: 100% (4/4), done.
From https://github.com/chaconinc/DbConnector
   c87d55d..92c7337  stable      -> origin/stable
Updating c87d55d..92c7337
Fast-forward
 src/main.c | 1 +
 1 file changed, 1 insertion(+)
Submodule path 'DbConnector': merged in '92c7337b30ef9e0893e758dac2459d07362ab5ea'
```

If we go into the DbConnector directory, we have the new changes already merged into our local stable branch. Now let's see what happens when we make our own local change to the library and someone else pushes another change upstream at the same time.

```
$ cd DbConnector/
$ vim src/db.c
$ git commit -am 'unicode support'
[stable f906e16] unicode support
 1 file changed, 1 insertion(+)
```

Now if we update our submodule we can see what happens when we have made a local change and upstream also has a change we need to incorporate.

```
$ git submodule update --remote --rebase
First, rewinding head to replay your work on top of it...
Applying: unicode support
Submodule path 'DbConnector': rebased into '5d60ef9bbebf5a0c1c1050f242ceeb54ad58da94'
```

If you forget the --rebase or --merge, Git will just update the submodule to whatever is on the server and reset your project to a detached HEAD state.

```
$ git submodule update --remote
Submodule path 'DbConnector': checked out '5d60ef9bbebf5a0c1c1050f242ceeb54ad58da94'
```

If this happens, don't worry, you can simply go back into the directory and check out your branch again (which will still contain your work) and merge or rebase origin/stable (or whatever remote branch you want) manually.

If you haven't committed your changes in your submodule and you run a submodule update that would cause issues, Git will fetch the changes but not overwrite unsaved work in your submodule directory.

```
$ git submodule update --remote
remote: Counting objects: 4, done.
remote: Compressing objects: 100% (3/3), done.
remote: Total 4 (delta 0), reused 4 (delta 0)
```

```
Unpacking objects: 100% (4/4), done.
From https://github.com/chaconinc/DbConnector
   5d60ef9..c75e92a  stable        -> origin/stable
error: Your local changes to the following files would be overwritten by checkout:
        scripts/setup.sh
Please, commit your changes or stash them before you can switch branches.
Aborting
Unable to checkout 'c75e92a2b3855c9e5b66f915308390d9db204aca' in submodule path 'DbConnector'
```

If you made changes that conflict with something changed upstream, Git will let you know when you run the update.

```
$ git submodule update --remote --merge
Auto-merging scripts/setup.sh
CONFLICT (content): Merge conflict in scripts/setup.sh
Recorded preimage for 'scripts/setup.sh'
Automatic merge failed; fix conflicts and then commit the result.
Unable to merge 'c75e92a2b3855c9e5b66f915308390d9db204aca' in submodule path 'DbConnector'
```

You can go into the submodule directory and fix the conflict just as you normally would.

Publishing Submodule Changes

Now we have some changes in our submodule directory. Some of these were brought in from upstream by our updates and others were made locally and aren't available to anyone else yet as we haven't pushed them yet.

```
$ git diff
Submodule DbConnector c87d55d..82d2ad3:
  > Merge from origin/stable
  > updated setup script
  > unicode support
  > remove unnessesary method
  > add new option for conn pooling
```

If we commit in the main project and push it up without pushing the submodule changes up as well, other people who try to check out our changes are going to be in trouble since they will have no way to get the submodule changes that are depended on. Those changes will only exist on our local copy.

In order to make sure this doesn't happen, you can ask Git to check that all your submodules have been pushed properly before pushing the main project. The git push command takes the --recurse-submodules argument which can be set to either check or on-demand. The check option will make push simply fail if any of the committed submodule changes haven't been pushed.

```
$ git push --recurse-submodules=check
The following submodule paths contain changes that can
not be found on any remote:
  DbConnector

Please try

        git push --recurse-submodules=on-demand
```

or cd to the path and use

      git push

to push them to a remote.

As you can see, it also gives us some helpful advice on what we might want to do next. The simple option is to go into each submodule and manually push to the remotes to make sure they're externally available and then try this push again.

The other option is to use the on-demand value, which will try to do this for you.

```
$ git push --recurse-submodules=on-demand
Pushing submodule 'DbConnector'
Counting objects: 9, done.
Delta compression using up to 8 threads.
Compressing objects: 100% (8/8), done.
Writing objects: 100% (9/9), 917 bytes | 0 bytes/s, done.
Total 9 (delta 3), reused 0 (delta 0)
To https://github.com/chaconinc/DbConnector
   c75e92a..82d2ad3  stable -> stable
Counting objects: 2, done.
Delta compression using up to 8 threads.
Compressing objects: 100% (2/2), done.
Writing objects: 100% (2/2), 266 bytes | 0 bytes/s, done.
Total 2 (delta 1), reused 0 (delta 0)
To https://github.com/chaconinc/MainProject
   3d6d338..9a377d1  master -> master
```

As you can see there, Git went into the DbConnector module and pushed it before pushing the main project. If that submodule push fails for some reason, the main project push will also fail.

Merging Submodule Changes

If you change a submodule reference at the same time as someone else, you may run into some problems. That is, if the submodule histories have diverged and are committed to diverging branches in a superproject, it may take a bit of work for you to fix.

If one of the commits is a direct ancestor of the other (a fast-forward merge), then Git will simply choose the latter for the merge, so that works fine.

Git will not attempt even a trivial merge for you, however. If the submodule commits diverge and need to be merged, you will get something that looks like this:

```
$ git pull
remote: Counting objects: 2, done.
remote: Compressing objects: 100% (1/1), done.
remote: Total 2 (delta 1), reused 2 (delta 1)
Unpacking objects: 100% (2/2), done.
From https://github.com/chaconinc/MainProject
   9a377d1..eb974f8  master      -> origin/master
Fetching submodule DbConnector
warning: Failed to merge submodule DbConnector (merge following commits not found)
Auto-merging DbConnector
```

```
CONFLICT (submodule): Merge conflict in DbConnector
Automatic merge failed; fix conflicts and then commit the result.
```

So basically what has happened here is that Git has figured out that the two branches record points in the submodule's history that are divergent and need to be merged. It explains it as merge following commits not found, which is confusing but we'll explain why that is in a bit.

To solve the problem, you need to figure out what state the submodule should be in. Strangely, Git doesn't really give you much information to help out here, not even the SHAs of the commits of both sides of the history. Fortunately, it's simple to figure out. If you run git diff you can get the SHAs of the commits recorded in both branches you were trying to merge.

```
$ git diff
diff --cc DbConnector
index eb41d76,c771610..0000000
--- a/DbConnector
+++ b/DbConnector
```

So, in this case, eb41d76 is the commit in our submodule that we had and c771610 is the commit that upstream had. If we go into our submodule directory, it should already be on eb41d76 as the merge would not have touched it. If for whatever reason it's not, you can simply create and checkout a branch pointing to it.

What is important is the SHA of the commit from the other side. This is what you'll have to merge in and resolve. You can either just try the merge with the SHA directly, or you can create a branch for it and then try to merge that in. We would suggest the latter, even if only to make a nicer merge commit message.

So, we will go into our submodule directory, create a branch based on that second SHA from git diff and manually merge.

```
$ cd DbConnector

$ git rev-parse HEAD
eb41d764bccf88be77aced643c13a7fa86714135

$ git branch try-merge c771610
(DbConnector) $ git merge try-merge
Auto-merging src/main.c
CONFLICT (content): Merge conflict in src/main.c
Recorded preimage for 'src/main.c'
Automatic merge failed; fix conflicts and then commit the result.
```

We got an actual merge conflict here, so if we resolve that and commit it, then we can simply update the main project with the result.

```
$ vim src/main.c (1)
$ git add src/main.c
$ git commit -am 'merged our changes'
Recorded resolution for 'src/main.c'.
[master 9fd905e] merged our changes

$ cd .. (2)
$ git diff (3)
diff --cc DbConnector
index eb41d76,c771610..0000000
```

```
--- a/DbConnector
+++ b/DbConnector
@@ -1,1 -1,1 +1,1 @@
- Subproject commit eb41d764bccf88be77aced643c13a7fa86714135
 -Subproject commit c77161012afbbe1f58b5053316ead08f4b7e6d1d
++Subproject commit 9fd905e5d7f45a0d4cbc43d1ee550f16a30e825a
$ git add DbConnector (4)

$ git commit -m "Merge Tom's Changes" (5)
[master 10d2c60] Merge Tom's Changes
```

1. First we resolve the conflict

2. Then we go back to the main project directory

3. We can check the SHAs again

4. Resolve the conflicted submodule entry

5. Commit our merge

It can be a bit confusing, but it's really not very hard.

Interestingly, there is another case that Git handles. If a merge commit exists in the submodule directory that contains both commits in its history, Git will suggest it to you as a possible solution. It sees that at some point in the submodule project, someone merged branches containing these two commits, so maybe you'll want that one.

This is why the error message from before was merge following commits not found, because it could not do this. It's confusing because who would expect it to try to do this?

If it does find a single acceptable merge commit, you'll see something like this:

```
$ git merge origin/master
warning: Failed to merge submodule DbConnector (not fast-forward)
Found a possible merge resolution for the submodule:
 9fd905e5d7f45a0d4cbc43d1ee550f16a30e825a: > merged our changes
If this is correct simply add it to the index for example
by using:

  git update-index --cacheinfo 160000 9fd905e5d7f45a0d4cbc43d1ee550f16a30e825a "DbConnector"

which will accept this suggestion.
Auto-merging DbConnector
CONFLICT (submodule): Merge conflict in DbConnector
Automatic merge failed; fix conflicts and then commit the result.
```

What it's suggesting that you do is to update the index like you had run git add, which clears the conflict, then commit. You probably shouldn't do this though. You can just as easily go into the submodule directory, see what the difference is, fast-forward to this commit, test it properly, and then commit it.

```
$ cd DbConnector/
$ git merge 9fd905e
Updating eb41d76..9fd905e
Fast-forward
```

```
$ cd ..
$ git add DbConnector
$ git commit -am 'Fast forwarded to a common submodule child'
```

This accomplishes the same thing, but at least this way you can verify that it works and you have the code in your submodule directory when you're done.

Submodule Tips

There are a few things you can do to make working with submodules a little easier.

Submodule Foreach

There is a foreach submodule command to run some arbitrary command in each submodule. This can be really helpful if you have a number of submodules in the same project.

For example, let's say we want to start a new feature or do a bugfix and we have work going on in several submodules. We can easily stash all the work in all our submodules.

```
$ git submodule foreach 'git stash'
Entering 'CryptoLibrary'
No local changes to save
Entering 'DbConnector'
Saved working directory and index state WIP on stable: 82d2ad3 Merge from origin/stable
HEAD is now at 82d2ad3 Merge from origin/stable
```

Then we can create a new branch and switch to it in all our submodules.

```
$ git submodule foreach 'git checkout -b featureA'
Entering 'CryptoLibrary'
Switched to a new branch 'featureA'
Entering 'DbConnector'
Switched to a new branch 'featureA'
```

You get the idea. One really useful thing you can do is produce a nice unified diff of what is changed in your main project and all your subprojects as well.

```
$ git diff; git submodule foreach 'git diff'
Submodule DbConnector contains modified content
diff --git a/src/main.c b/src/main.c
index 210f1ae..1f0acdc 100644
--- a/src/main.c
+++ b/src/main.c
@@ -245,6 +245,8 @@ static int handle_alias(int *argcp, const char ***argv)

        commit_pager_choice();

+       url = url_decode(url_orig);
+
        /* build alias_argv */
        alias_argv = xmalloc(sizeof(*alias_argv) * (argc + 1));
```

```
        alias_argv[0] = alias_string + 1;
Entering 'DbConnector'
diff --git a/src/db.c b/src/db.c
index 1aaefb6..5297645 100644
--- a/src/db.c
+++ b/src/db.c
@@ -93,6 +93,11 @@ char *url_decode_mem(const char *url, int len)
        return url_decode_internal(&url, len, NULL, &out, 0);
 }

+char *url_decode(const char *url)
+{
+       return url_decode_mem(url, strlen(url));
+}
+
 char *url_decode_parameter_name(const char **query)
 {
        struct strbuf out = STRBUF_INIT;
```

Here we can see that we're defining a function in a submodule and calling it in the main project. This is obviously a simplified example, but hopefully it gives you an idea of how this may be useful.

Useful Aliases

You may want to set up some aliases for some of these commands as they can be quite long and you can't set configuration options for most of them to make them defaults. We covered setting up Git aliases earlier, but here is an example of what you may want to set up if you plan on working with submodules in Git a lot.

```
$ git config alias.sdiff '!'"git diff && git submodule foreach 'git diff'"
$ git config alias.spush 'push --recurse-submodules=on-demand'
$ git config alias.supdate 'submodule update --remote --merge'
```

This way you can simply run git supdate when you want to update your submodules, or git spush to push with submodule dependency checking.

Issues with Submodules

Using submodules isn't without hiccups, however.

For instance switching branches with submodules in them can also be tricky. If you create a new branch, add a submodule there, and then switch back to a branch without that submodule, you still have the submodule directory as an untracked directory:

```
$ git checkout -b add-crypto
Switched to a new branch 'add-crypto'

$ git submodule add https://github.com/chaconinc/CryptoLibrary
Cloning into 'CryptoLibrary'...
...
```

```
$ git commit -am 'adding crypto library'
[add-crypto 4445836] adding crypto library
 2 files changed, 4 insertions(+)
 create mode 160000 CryptoLibrary

$ git checkout master
warning: unable to rmdir CryptoLibrary: Directory not empty
Switched to branch 'master'
Your branch is up-to-date with 'origin/master'.

$ git status
On branch master
Your branch is up-to-date with 'origin/master'.

Untracked files:
  (use "git add <file>..." to include in what will be committed)

        CryptoLibrary/

nothing added to commit but untracked files present (use "git add" to track)
```

Removing the directory isn't difficult, but it can be a bit confusing to have that in there. If you do remove it and then switch back to the branch that has that submodule, you will need to run submodule update --init to repopulate it.

```
$ git clean -ffdx
Removing CryptoLibrary/

$ git checkout add-crypto
Switched to branch 'add-crypto'

$ ls CryptoLibrary/

$ git submodule update --init
Submodule path 'CryptoLibrary': checked out 'b8dda6aa182ea4464f3f3264b11e0268545172af'

$ ls CryptoLibrary/
Makefile        includes        scripts                 src
```

Again, not really very difficult, but it can be a little confusing.

The other main caveat that many people run into involves switching from subdirectories to submodules. If you've been tracking files in your project and you want to move them out into a submodule, you must be careful or Git will get angry at you. Assume that you have files in a subdirectory of your project, and you want to switch it to a submodule. If you delete the subdirectory and then run submodule add, Git yells at you:

```
$ rm -Rf CryptoLibrary/
$ git submodule add https://github.com/chaconinc/CryptoLibrary
'CryptoLibrary' already exists in the index
```

You have to unstage the CryptoLibrary directory first. Then you can add the submodule:

```
$ git rm -r CryptoLibrary
$ git submodule add https://github.com/chaconinc/CryptoLibrary
Cloning into 'CryptoLibrary'...
remote: Counting objects: 11, done.
remote: Compressing objects: 100% (10/10), done.
remote: Total 11 (delta 0), reused 11 (delta 0)
Unpacking objects: 100% (11/11), done.
Checking connectivity... done.
```

Now suppose you did that in a branch. If you try to switch back to a branch where those files are still in the actual tree rather than a submodule—you get this error:

```
$ git checkout master
error: The following untracked working tree files would be overwritten by checkout:
  CryptoLibrary/Makefile
  CryptoLibrary/includes/crypto.h
  ...
Please move or remove them before you can switch branches.
```

Aborting

You can force it to switch with checkout -f, but be careful that you don't have unsaved changes in there as they could be overwritten with that command.

```
$ git checkout -f master
warning: unable to rmdir CryptoLibrary: Directory not empty
Switched to branch 'master'
```

Then, when you switch back, you get an empty CryptoLibrary directory for some reason and git submodule update may not fix it either. You may need to go into your submodule directory and run a git checkout to get all your files back. You could run this in a submodule foreach script to run it for multiple submodules.

It's important to note that submodules these days keep all their Git data in the top project's .git directory, so unlike much older versions of Git, destroying a submodule directory won't lose any commits or branches that you had.

With these tools, submodules can be a fairly simple and effective method for developing on several related but still separate projects simultaneously.

Bundling

Though we've covered the common ways to transfer Git data over a network (HTTP, SSH, etc.), there is actually one more way to do so that is not commonly used but can actually be quite useful.

Git is capable of "bundling" its data into a single file. This can be useful in various scenarios. Maybe your network is down and you want to send changes to your co-workers. Perhaps you're working somewhere offsite and don't have access to the local network for security reasons. Maybe your wireless/ethernet card just broke. Maybe you don't have access to a shared server for the moment, you want to e-mail someone updates and you don't want to transfer 40 commits via format-patch.

This is where the git bundle command can be helpful. The bundle command will package up everything that would normally be pushed over the wire with a git push command into a binary file that you can e-mail to someone or put on a flash drive, then unbundle into another repository.

Let's see a simple example. Let's say you have a repository with two commits:

```
$ git log
commit 9a466c572fe88b195efd356c3f2bbeccdb504102
Author: Scott Chacon <schacon@gmail.com>
Date:   Wed Mar 10 07:34:10 2010 -0800

    second commit

commit b1ec3248f39900d2a406049d762aa68e9641be25
Author: Scott Chacon <schacon@gmail.com>
Date:   Wed Mar 10 07:34:01 2010 -0800

    first commit
```

If you want to send that repository to someone and you don't have access to a repository to push to, or simply don't want to set one up, you can bundle it with git bundle create.

```
$ git bundle create repo.bundle HEAD master
Counting objects: 6, done.
Delta compression using up to 2 threads.
Compressing objects: 100% (2/2), done.
Writing objects: 100% (6/6), 441 bytes, done.
Total 6 (delta 0), reused 0 (delta 0)
```

Now you have a file named repo.bundle that has all the data needed to re-create the repository's master branch. With the bundle command you need to list out every reference or specific range of commits that you want to be included. If you intend for this to be cloned somewhere else, you should add HEAD as a reference as well as we've done here.

You can e-mail this repo.bundle file to someone else, or put it on a USB drive and walk it over.

On the other side, say you are sent this - file and want to work on the project. You can clone from the binary file into a directory, much like you would from a URL.

```
$ git clone repo.bundle repo
Initialized empty Git repository in /private/tmp/bundle/repo/.git/
$ cd repo
$ git log --oneline
9a466c5 second commit
b1ec324 first commit
```

If you don't include HEAD in the references, you have to also specify -b master or whatever branch is included because otherwise it won't know what branch to check out.

Now let's say you do three commits on it and want to send the new commits back via a bundle on a USB stick or e-mail.

```
$ git log --oneline
71b84da last commit - second repo
c99cf5b fourth commit - second repo
7011d3d third commit - second repo
9a466c5 second commit
b1ec324 first commit
```

First we need to determine the range of commits we want to include in the bundle. Unlike the network protocols which figure out the minimum set of data to transfer over the network for us, we'll have to figure this out manually. Now, you could just do the same thing and bundle the entire repository, which will work, but it's better to just bundle up the difference—just the three commits we just made locally.

In order to do that, you'll have to calculate the difference. As we described earlier, you can specify a range of commits in a number of ways. To get the three commits that we have in our master branch that weren't in the branch we originally cloned, we can use something like origin/master..master or master ^origin/master. You can test that with the log command.

```
$ git log --oneline master ^origin/master
71b84da last commit - second repo
c99cf5b fourth commit - second repo
7011d3d third commit - second repo
```

So now that we have the list of commits we want to include in the bundle, let's bundle them up. We do that with the git bundle create command, giving it a filename we want our bundle to be and the range of commits we want to go into it.

```
$ git bundle create commits.bundle master ^9a466c5
Counting objects: 11, done.
Delta compression using up to 2 threads.
Compressing objects: 100% (3/3), done.
Writing objects: 100% (9/9), 775 bytes, done.
Total 9 (delta 0), reused 0 (delta 0)
```

Now we have a commits.bundle file in our directory. If we take that and send it to our partner, she can then import it into the original repository, even if more work has been done there in the meantime.

When she gets the bundle, she can inspect it to see what it contains before she imports it into her repository. The first command is the bundle verify command that will make sure the file is actually a valid Git bundle and that you have all the necessary ancestors to reconstitute it properly.

```
$ git bundle verify ../commits.bundle
The bundle contains 1 ref
71b84daaf49abed142a373b6e5c59a22dc6560dc refs/heads/master
The bundle requires these 1 ref
9a466c572fe88b195efd356c3f2bbeccdb504102 second commit
../commits.bundle is okay
```

If the bundler had created a bundle of just the last two commits they had done, rather than all three, the original repository would not be able to import it, because it is missing requisite history. The verify command would have looked like this instead:

```
$ git bundle verify ../commits-bad.bundle
error: Repository lacks these prerequisite commits:
error: 7011d3d8fc200abe0ad561c011c3852a4b7bbe95 third commit - second repo
```

However, our first bundle is valid, so we can fetch in commits from it. If you want to see what branches are in the bundle that can be imported, there is also a command to just list the heads:

```
$ git bundle list-heads ../commits.bundle
71b84daaf49abed142a373b6e5c59a22dc6560dc refs/heads/master
```

The verify sub-command will tell you the heads as well. The point is to see what can be pulled in, so you can use the fetch or pull command to import commits from this bundle. Here we'll fetch the master branch of the bundle to a branch named other-master in our repository:

```
$ git fetch ../commits.bundle master:other-master
From ../commits.bundle
 * [new branch]      master     -> other-master
```

Now we can see that we have the imported commits on the other-master branch as well as any commits we've done in the meantime in our own master branch.

```
$ git log --oneline --decorate --graph --all
* 8255d41 (HEAD, master) third commit - first repo
| * 71b84da (other-master) last commit - second repo
| * c99cf5b fourth commit - second repo
| * 7011d3d third commit - second repo
|/
* 9a466c5 second commit
* b1ec324 first commit
```

So, git bundle can be really useful for sharing or doing network-type operations when you don't have the proper network or shared repository to do so.

Replace

Git's objects are unchangeable, but it does provide an interesting way to pretend to replace objects in its database with other objects.

The replace command lets you specify an object in Git and say "every time you see this, pretend it's this other thing." This is useful for replacing one commit in your history with another one.

For example, let's say you have a huge code history and want to split your repository into one short history for new developers and one much longer and larger history for people interested in data mining. You can graft one history onto the other by replacing the earliest commit in the new line with the latest commit on the older one. This is nice because it means that you don't actually have to rewrite every commit in the new history, as you would normally have to do to join them together (because the parentage effects the SHAs).

Let's try this out. Let's take an existing repository, split it into two repositories, one recent and one historical, and then we'll see how we can recombine them without modifying the recent repositories SHA values via replace.

We'll use a simple repository with five simple commits:

```
$ git log --oneline
ef989d8 fifth commit
c6e1e95 fourth commit
9c68fdc third commit
945704c second commit
c1822cf first commit
```

We want to break this up into two lines of history. One line goes from commit one to commit four—that will be the historical one. The second line will just be commits four and five—that will be the recent history.

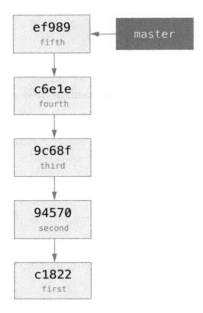

Well, creating the historical history is easy, we can just put a branch in the history and then push that branch to the master branch of a new remote repository.

```
$ git branch history c6e1e95
$ git log --oneline --decorate
ef989d8 (HEAD, master) fifth commit
c6e1e95 (history) fourth commit
9c68fdc third commit
945704c second commit
c1822cf first commit
```

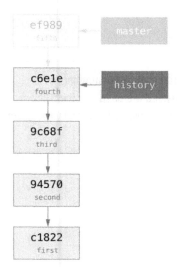

Now we can push the new history branch to the master branch of our new repository:

```
$ git remote add project-history https://github.com/schacon/project-history
$ git push project-history history:master
Counting objects: 12, done.
Delta compression using up to 2 threads.
Compressing objects: 100% (4/4), done.
Writing objects: 100% (12/12), 907 bytes, done.
Total 12 (delta 0), reused 0 (delta 0)
Unpacking objects: 100% (12/12), done.
To git@github.com:schacon/project-history.git
 * [new branch]      history -> master
```

Okay, so our history is published. Now the harder part is truncating our recent history so it's smaller. We need an overlap so we can replace a commit in one with an equivalent commit in the other, so we're going to truncate this to just commits four and five (so commit four overlaps).

```
$ git log --oneline --decorate
ef989d8 (HEAD, master) fifth commit
c6e1e95 (history) fourth commit
9c68fdc third commit
945704c second commit
c1822cf first commit
```

It's useful in this case to create a base commit that has instructions on how to expand the history, so other developers know what to do if they hit the first commit in the truncated history and need more. So, what we're going to do is create an initial commit object as our base point with instructions, then rebase the remaining commits (four and five) on top of it.

To do that, we need to choose a point to split at, which for us is the third commit, which is 9c68fdc in SHA-speak. So, our base commit will be based off of that tree. We can create our base commit using the commit-tree command, which just takes a tree and will give us a brand new, parentless commit object SHA back.

```
$ echo 'get history from blah blah blah' | git commit-tree 9c68fdc^{tree}
622e88e9cbfbacfb75b5279245b9fb38dfea10cf
```

■ **Note** The `commit-tree` command is one of a set of commands that are commonly referred to as plumbing commands. These are commands that are not generally meant to be used directly, but instead are used by other Git commands to do smaller jobs. On occasions when we're doing weirder things like this, they allow us to do really low-level things but are not meant for daily use.

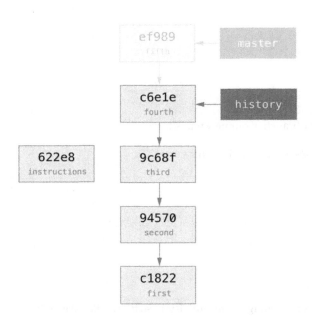

Okay, so now that we have a base commit, we can rebase the rest of our history on top of that with git rebase --onto. The --onto argument will be the SHA we just got back from commit-tree and the rebase point will be the third commit (the parent of the first commit we want to keep, 9c68fdc):

```
$ git rebase --onto 622e88 9c68fdc
First, rewinding head to replay your work on top of it...
Applying: fourth commit
Applying: fifth commit
```

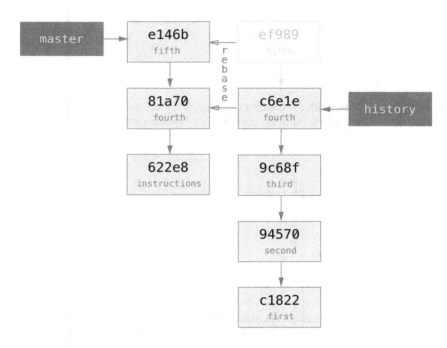

So now we've rewritten our recent history on top of a throw away base commit that now has instructions in it on how to reconstitute the entire history if we wanted to. We can push that new history to a new project and now when people clone that repository, they will only see the most recent two commits and then a base commit with instructions.

Let's now switch roles to someone cloning the project for the first time who wants the entire history. To get the history data after cloning this truncated repository, one would have to add a second remote for the historical repository and fetch:

```
$ git clone https://github.com/schacon/project
$ cd project

$ git log --oneline master
e146b5f fifth commit
81a708d fourth commit
622e88e get history from blah blah blah

$ git remote add project-history https://github.com/schacon/project-history
$ git fetch project-history
From https://github.com/schacon/project-history
 * [new branch]      master     -> project-history/master
```

Now the collaborator would have their recent commits in the master branch and the historical commits in the project-history/master branch.

```
$ git log --oneline master
e146b5f fifth commit
81a708d fourth commit
622e88e get history from blah blah blah
```

```
$ git log --oneline project-history/master
c6e1e95 fourth commit
9c68fdc third commit
945704c second commit
c1822cf first commit
```

To combine them, you can simply call git replace with the commit you want to replace and then the commit you want to replace it with. So we want to replace the "fourth" commit in the master branch with the "fourth" commit in the project-history/master branch:

```
$ git replace 81a708d c6e1e95
```

Now, if you look at the history of the master branch, it appears to look like this:

```
$ git log --oneline master
e146b5f fifth commit
81a708d fourth commit
9c68fdc third commit
945704c second commit
c1822cf first commit
```

Cool, right? Without having to change all the SHAs upstream, we were able to replace one commit in our history with an entirely different commit and all the normal tools (bisect, blame, etc.) will work how we would expect them to.

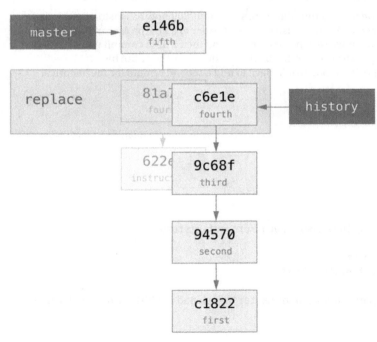

Interestingly, it still shows 81a708d as the SHA, even though it's actually using the c6e1e95 commit data that we replaced it with. Even if you run a command like cat-file, it will show you the replaced data:

```
$ git cat-file -p 81a708d
tree 7bc544cf438903b65ca9104a1e30345eee6c083d
parent 9c68fdceee073230f19ebb8b5e7fc71b479c0252
author Scott Chacon <schacon@gmail.com> 1268712581 -0700
committer Scott Chacon <schacon@gmail.com> 1268712581 -0700

fourth commit
```

Remember that the actual parent of 81a708d was our placeholder commit (622e88e), not 9c68fdce as it states here. Another interesting thing is that this data is kept in our references:

```
$ git for-each-ref
e146b5f14e79d4935160c0e83fb9ebe526b8da0d commit refs/heads/master
c6e1e95051d41771a649f3145423f8809d1a74d4 commit refs/remotes/history/master
e146b5f14e79d4935160c0e83fb9ebe526b8da0d commit refs/remotes/origin/HEAD
e146b5f14e79d4935160c0e83fb9ebe526b8da0d commit refs/remotes/origin/master
c6e1e95051d41771a649f3145423f8809d1a74d4 commit refs/replace/81a708dd0e167a3f691541c7a6463343b
c457040
```

This means that it's easy to share our replacement with others, because we can push this to our server and other people can easily download it. This is not that helpful in the history grafting scenario we've gone over here (because everyone would be downloading both histories anyhow, so why separate them?) but it can be useful in other circumstances.

Credential Storage

If you use the SSH transport for connecting to remotes, it's possible for you to have a key without a passphrase, which allows you to securely transfer data without typing in your username and password. However, this isn't possible with the HTTP protocols—every connection needs a username and password. This gets even harder for systems with two-factor authentication, where the token you use for a password is randomly generated and unpronounceable.

Fortunately, Git has a credentials system that can help with this. Git has a few options provided in the box:

- The default is not to cache at all. Every connection will prompt you for your username and password.

- The "cache" mode keeps credentials in memory for a certain period of time. None of the passwords are ever stored on disk, and they are purged from the cache after 15 minutes.

- The "store" mode saves the credentials to a plain-text file on disk, and they never expire. This means that until you change your password for the Git host, you won't ever have to type in your credentials again. The downside of this approach is that your passwords are stored in cleartext in a plain file in your home directory.

- If you're using a Mac, Git comes with an "osxkeychain" mode, which caches credentials in the secure keychain that's attached to your system account. This method stores the credentials on disk, and they never expire, but they're encrypted with the same system that stores HTTPS certificates and Safari auto-fills.

- If you're using Windows, you can install a helper called "winstore." This is similar to the "osxkeychain" helper described above, but uses the Windows Credential Store to control sensitive information. It can be found at https://gitcredentialstore.codeplex.com.

You can choose one of these methods by setting a Git configuration value:

```
$ git config --global credential.helper cache
```

Some of these helpers have options. The store helper can take a --file <path> argument, which customizes where the plaintext file is saved (the default is ~/.git-credentials). The cache helper accepts the --timeout <seconds> option, which changes the amount of time its daemon is kept running (the default is "900", or 15 minutes). Here's an example of how you'd configure the store helper with a custom file name:

```
$ git config --global credential.helper store --file ~/.my-credentials
```

Git even allows you to configure several helpers. When looking for credentials for a particular host, Git queries them in order, and stops after the first answer is provided. When saving credentials, Git sends the username and password to all the helpers in the list, and they can choose what to do with them. Here's what a .gitconfig would look like if you had a credentials file on a thumb drive, but wanted to use the in-memory cache to save some typing if the drive isn't plugged in:

```
[credential]
    helper = store --file /mnt/thumbdrive/.git-credentials
    helper = cache --timeout 30000
```

Under the Hood

How does this all work? Git's root command for the credential-helper system is git credential, which takes a command as an argument, and then more input through stdin.

This might be easier to understand with an example. Let's say that a credential helper has been configured, and the helper has stored credentials for mygithost. Here's a session that uses the fill command, which is invoked when Git is trying to find credentials for a host:

```
$ git credential fill (1)
protocol=https (2)
host=mygithost
(3)
protocol=https (4)
host=mygithost
username=bob
password=s3cre7
$ git credential fill (5)
protocol=https
host=unknownhost

Username for 'https://unknownhost': bob
Password for 'https://bob@unknownhost':
protocol=https
host=unknownhost
username=bob
password=s3cre7
```

1. This is the command line that initiates the interaction.

2. Git-credential is then waiting for input on stdin. We provide it with the things we know: the protocol and hostname.

3. A blank line indicates that the input is complete, and the credential system should answer with what it knows.

4. Git-credential then takes over, and writes to stdout with the bits of information it found.

5. If credentials are not found, Git asks the user for the username and password, and provides them back to the invoking stdout (here they're attached to the same console).

The credential system is actually invoking a program that's separate from Git itself; which one and how depends on the credential.helper configuration value. There are several forms it can take:

Configuration Value	Behavior
foo	Runs git-credential-foo
foo -a --opt=bcd	Runs git-credential-foo -a --opt=bcd
/absolute/path/foo -xyz	Runs /absolute/path/foo -xyz
!f() { echo "password=s3cre7"; }; f	Code after ! evaluated in shell

So the helpers described here are actually named git-credential-cache, git-credential-store, and so on, and we can configure them to take command-line arguments. The general form for this is git-credential-foo [args] <action>. The stdin/stdout protocol is the same as git-credential, but they use a slightly different set of actions:

- get is a request for a username/password pair.

- store is a request to save a set of credentials in this helper's memory.

- erase purges the credentials for the given properties from this helper's memory.

For the store and erase actions, no response is required (Git ignores it anyway). For the get action, however, Git is very interested in what the helper has to say. If the helper doesn't know anything useful, it can simply exit with no output, but if it does know, it should augment the provided information with the information it has stored. The output is treated like a series of assignment statements; anything provided will replace what Git already knows.

Here's the same example from above, but skipping git-credential and going straight for git-credential-store:

```
$ git credential-store --file ~/git.store store (1)
protocol=https
host=mygithost
username=bob
password=s3cre7
$ git credential-store --file ~/git.store get (2)
protocol=https
host=mygithost

username=bob (3)
password=s3cre7
```

1. Here we tell `git-credential-store` to save some credentials: the username `bob` and the password `s3cre7` are to be used when `https://mygithost` is `accessed`.

2. Now we'll retrieve those credentials. We provide the parts of the connection we already know (`https://mygithost`), and an empty line.

3. `git-credential-store` replies with the username and password we stored above.

Here's what the `~/git.store` file looks like:

```
https://bob:s3cre7@mygithost
```

It's just a series of lines, each of which contains a credential-decorated URL. The osxkeychain and winstore helpers use the native format of their backing stores, while cache uses its own in-memory format (which no other process can read).

A Custom Credential Cache

Given that `git-credential-store` and friends are separate programs from Git, it's not much of a leap to realize that any program can be a Git credential helper. The helpers provided by Git cover many common use cases, but not all. For example, let's say your team has some credentials that are shared with the entire team, perhaps for deployment. These are stored in a shared directory, but you don't want to copy them to your own credential store, because they change often. None of the existing helpers cover this case; let's see what it would take to write our own. There are several key features this program needs to have:

1. The only action we need to pay attention to is `get`; `store` and `erase` are write operations, so we'll just exit cleanly when they're received.

2. The file format of the `shared-credential` file is the same as that used by `git-credential-store`.

3. The location of that file is fairly standard, but we should allow the user to pass a custom path just in case.

Once again, we'll write this extension in Ruby, but any language will work so long as Git can execute the finished product. Here's the full source code of our new credential helper:

```
link:../git-credential-read-only[]
```

1. Here we parse the command-line options, allowing the user to specify the input file. The default is `~/.git-credentials`.

2. This program only responds if the action is get and the backing-store file exists.

3. This loop reads from `stdin` until the first blank line is reached. The inputs are stored in the known hash for later reference.

4. This loop reads the contents of the storage file, looking for matches. If the protocol and host from known match this line, the program prints the results to `stdout` and exits.

We'll save our helper as `git-credential-read-only`, put it somewhere in our PATH and mark it executable. Here's what an interactive session looks like:

```
$ git credential-read-only --file=/mnt/shared/creds get
protocol=https
host=mygithost

protocol=https
host=mygithost
username=bob
password=s3cre7
```

Because its name starts with `git-`, we can use the simple syntax for the configuration value:

```
$ git config --global credential.helper read-only --file /mnt/shared/creds
```

As you can see, extending this system is pretty straightforward, and can solve some common problems for you and your team.

Summary

You've seen a number of advanced tools that allow you to manipulate your commits and staging area more precisely. When you notice issues, you should be able to easily figure out what commit introduced them, when, and by whom. If you want to use subprojects in your project, you've learned how to accommodate those needs. At this point, you should be able to do most of the things in Git that you'll need on the command line day to day and feel comfortable doing so.

## CHAPTER 8

Customizing Git

So far, we've covered the basics of how Git works and how to use it, and we've introduced a number of tools that Git provides to help you use it easily and efficiently. In this chapter, we'll see how you can make Git operate in a more customized fashion, by introducing several important configuration settings and the hooks system. With these tools, it's easy to get Git to work exactly the way you, your company, or your group needs it to.

Git Configuration

As you briefly saw in Chapter 1, you can specify Git configuration settings with the `git config` command. One of the first things you did was set up your name and e-mail address:

```
$ git config --global user.name "John Doe"
$ git config --global user.email johndoe@example.com
```

Now you'll learn a few of the more interesting options that you can set in this manner to customize your Git usage.

First, a quick review: Git uses a series of configuration files to determine non-default behavior that you may want. The first place Git looks for these values is in an `/etc/gitconfig` file, which contains values for every user on the system and all their repositories. If you pass the option `--system` to `git config`, it reads and writes from this file specifically.

The next place Git looks is the `~/.gitconfig` (or `~/.config/git/config`) file, which is specific to each user. You can make Git read and write to this file by passing the `--global` option.

Finally, Git looks for configuration values in the configuration file in the Git directory (`.git/config`) of whatever repository you're currently using. These values are specific to that single repository.

Each of these "levels" (system, global, local) overwrites values in the previous level, so values in `.git/config` trump those in `/etc/gitconfig`, for instance.

■ **Note**   Git's configuration files are plain-text, so you can also set these values by manually editing the file and inserting the correct syntax. It's generally easier to run the `git config` command, though.

Basic Client Configuration

The configuration options recognized by Git fall into two categories: client-side and server-side. The majority of the options are client-side—configuring your personal working preferences. Many, many configuration options are supported, but a large fraction of them are only useful in certain edge cases. We'll only be covering the most common and most useful here. If you want to see a list of all the options your version of Git recognizes, you can run

```
$ man git-config
```

This command lists all the available options in quite a bit of detail. You can also find this reference material at http://git-scm.com/docs/git-config.html.

core.editor

By default, Git uses whatever you've set as your default text editor ($VISUAL or $EDITOR) or else falls back to the vi editor to create and edit your commit and tag messages. To change that default to something else, you can use the core.editor setting:

```
$ git config --global core.editor emacs
```

Now, no matter what is set as your default shell editor, Git will fire up Emacs to edit messages.

commit.template

If you set this to the path of a file on your system, Git will use that file as the default message when you commit. For instance, suppose you create a template file at ~/.gitmessage.txt that looks like this:

```
subject line

what happened

[ticket: X]
```

To tell Git to use it as the default message that appears in your editor when you run git commit, set the commit.template configuration value:

```
$ git config --global commit.template ~/.gitmessage.txt
$ git commit
```

Then, your editor will open to something like this for your placeholder commit message when you commit:

```
subject line

what happened

[ticket: X]
# Please enter the commit message for your changes. Lines starting
# with '#' will be ignored, and an empty message aborts the commit.
# On branch master
# Changes to be committed:
#    (use "git reset HEAD <file>..." to unstage)
#
# modified:    lib/test.rb
#
~
~
".git/COMMIT_EDITMSG" 14L, 297C
```

If your team has a commit-message policy, then putting a template for that policy on your system and configuring Git to use it by default can help increase the chance of that policy being followed regularly.

core.pager

This setting determines which pager is used when Git pages output such as log and diff. You can set it to more or to your favorite pager (by default, it's less), or you can turn it off by setting it to a blank string:

```
$ git config --global core.pager ''
```

If you run that, Git will page the entire output of all commands, no matter how long they are.

user.signingkey

If you're making signed annotated tags, setting your GPG signing key as a configuration setting makes things easier. Set your key ID like so:

```
$ git config --global user.signingkey <gpg-key-id>
```

Now, you can sign tags without having to specify your key every time with the git tag command:

```
$ git tag -s <tag-name>
```

core.excludesfile

You can put patterns in your project's .gitignore file to have Git not see them as untracked files or try to stage them when you run git add on them.

But sometimes you want to ignore certain files for all repositories that you work with. If your computer is running Mac OS X, you're probably familiar with .DS_Store files. If your preferred editor is Emacs or Vim, you know about files that end with a ~.

This setting lets you write a kind of global `.gitignore` file. If you create a `~/.gitignore_global` file with these contents:

```
*~
.DS_Store
```

...and you run `git config --global core.excludesfile ~/.gitignore_global`, Git will never again bother you about those files.

help.autocorrect

If you mistype a command, it shows you something like this:

```
$ git chekcout master
git: 'chekcout' is not a git command. See 'git --help'.

Did you mean this?
    checkout
```

Git helpfully tries to figure out what you meant, but it still refuses to do it. If you set `help.autocorrect` to 1, Git will actually run this command for you:

```
$ git chekcout master
WARNING: You called a Git command named 'chekcout', which does not exist.
Continuing under the assumption that you meant 'checkout'
in 0.1 seconds automatically...
```

Note that "0.1 seconds" business. `help.autocorrect` is actually an integer which represents tenths of a second. So if you set it to 50, Git will give you 5 seconds to change your mind before executing the autocorrected command.

Colors in Git

Git fully supports colored terminal output, which greatly aids in visually parsing command output quickly and easily. A number of options can help you set the coloring to your preference.

color.ui

Git automatically colors most of its output, but there's a master switch if you don't like this behavior. To turn off all Git's colored terminal output, do this:

```
$ git config --global color.ui false
```

The default setting is `auto`, which colors output when it's going straight to a terminal, but omits the color-control codes when the output is redirected to a pipe or a file.

You can also set it to `always` to ignore the difference between terminals and pipes. You'll rarely want this; in most scenarios, if you want color codes in your redirected output, you can instead pass a `--color` flag to the Git command to force it to use color codes. The default setting is almost always what you'll want.

color.*

If you want to be more specific about which commands are colored and how, Git provides verb-specific coloring settings. Each of these can be set to true, false, or always:

```
color.branch
color.diff
color.interactive
color.status
```

In addition, each of these has subsettings you can use to set specific colors for parts of the output, if you want to override each color. For example, to set the meta information in your diff output to blue foreground, black background, and bold text, you can run

```
$ git config --global color.diff.meta "blue black bold"
```

You can set the color to any of the following values: normal, black, red, green, yellow, blue, magenta, cyan, or white. If you want an attribute like bold in the previous example, you can choose from bold, dim, ul (underline), blink, and reverse (swap foreground and background).

External Merge and Diff Tools

Although Git has an internal implementation of diff, which is what we've been showing in this book, you can set up an external tool instead. You can also set up a graphical merge-conflict-resolution tool instead of having to resolve conflicts manually. We'll demonstrate setting up the Perforce Visual Merge Tool (P4Merge) to do your diffs and merge resolutions, because it's a nice graphical tool and it's free.

If you want to try this out, P4Merge works on all major platforms, so you should be able to do so. I'll use path names in the examples that work on Mac and Linux systems; for Windows, you'll have to change /usr/local/bin to an executable path in your environment.

To begin, download P4Merge from http://www.perforce.com/downloads/Perforce/. Next, you'll set up external wrapper scripts to run your commands. I'll use the Mac path for the executable; in other systems, it will be where your p4merge binary is installed. Set up a merge wrapper script named extMerge that calls your binary with all the arguments provided:

```
$ cat /usr/local/bin/extMerge
#!/bin/sh
/Applications/p4merge.app/Contents/MacOS/p4merge $*
```

The diff wrapper checks to make sure seven arguments are provided and passes two of them to your merge script. By default, Git passes the following arguments to the diff program:

```
path old-file old-hex old-mode new-file new-hex new-mode
```

Because you only want the old-file and new-file arguments, you use the wrapper script to pass the ones you need.

```
$ cat /usr/local/bin/extDiff
#!/bin/sh
[ $# -eq 7 ] && /usr/local/bin/extMerge "$2" "$5"
```

You also need to make sure these tools are executable:

```
$ sudo chmod +x /usr/local/bin/extMerge
$ sudo chmod +x /usr/local/bin/extDiff
```

Now you can set up your config file to use your custom merge resolution and diff tools. This takes a number of custom settings: merge.tool to tell Git what strategy to use, mergetool.*.cmd to specify how to run the command, mergetool.trustExitCode to tell Git if the exit code of that program indicates a successful merge resolution or not, and diff.external to tell Git what command to run for diffs. So, you can either run four config commands

```
$ git config --global merge.tool extMerge
$ git config --global mergetool.extMerge.cmd \
  'extMerge "$BASE" "$LOCAL" "$REMOTE" "$MERGED"'
$ git config --global mergetool.trustExitCode false
$ git config --global diff.external extDiff
```

or you can edit your ~/.gitconfig file to add these lines:

```
[merge]
  tool = extMerge
[mergetool "extMerge"]
  cmd = extMerge "$BASE" "$LOCAL" "$REMOTE" "$MERGED"
  trustExitCode = false
[diff]
  external = extDiff
```

After all this is set, if you run diff commands such as this:

```
$ git diff 32d1776b1^ 32d1776b1
```

Instead of getting the diff output on the command line, Git fires up P4Merge, which looks something like this:

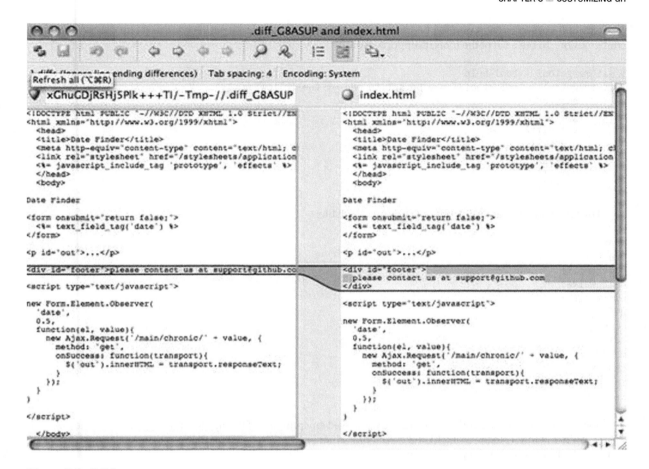

Figure 8-1. *P4Merge*

If you try to merge two branches and subsequently have merge conflicts, you can run the command git mergetool; it starts P4Merge to let you resolve the conflicts through that GUI tool.

The nice thing about this wrapper setup is that you can change your diff and merge tools easily. For example, to change your extDiff and extMerge tools to run the KDiff3 tool instead, all you have to do is edit your extMerge file:

```
$ cat /usr/local/bin/extMerge
#!/bin/sh
/Applications/kdiff3.app/Contents/MacOS/kdiff3 $*
```

Now, Git will use the KDiff3 tool for diff viewing and merge conflict resolution.

Git comes preset to use a number of other merge-resolution tools without your having to set up the cmd configuration. To see a list of the tools it supports, try this:

```
$ git mergetool --tool-help
'git mergetool --tool=<tool>' may be set to one of the following:
        emerge
        gvimdiff
        gvimdiff2
        opendiff
        p4merge
        vimdiff
        vimdiff2
```

The following tools are valid, but not currently available:

```
araxis
bc3
codecompare
deltawalker
diffmerge
diffuse
ecmerge
kdiff3
meld
tkdiff
tortoisemerge
xxdiff
```

Some of the tools listed above only work in a windowed environment. If run in a terminal-only session, they will fail.

If you're not interested in using KDiff3 for diff but rather want to use it just for merge resolution, and the kdiff3 command is in your path, then you can run

```
$ git config --global merge.tool kdiff3
```

If you run this instead of setting up the extMerge and extDiff files, Git will use KDiff3 for merge resolution and the normal Git diff tool for diffs.

Formatting and Whitespace

Formatting and whitespace issues are some of the more frustrating and subtle problems that many developers encounter when collaborating, especially cross-platform. It's very easy for patches or other collaborated work to introduce subtle whitespace changes because editors silently introduce them, and if your files ever touch a Windows system, their line endings might be replaced. Git has a few configuration options to help with these issues.

core.autocrlf

If you're programming on Windows and working with people who are not (or vice versa), you'll probably run into line-ending issues at some point. This is because Windows uses both a carriage-return character and a linefeed character for newlines in its files, whereas Mac and Linux systems use only the linefeed character. This is a subtle but incredibly annoying fact of cross-platform work; many editors on Windows silently replace existing LF-style line endings with CRLF, or insert both line-ending characters when the user hits the enter key.

Git can handle this by auto-converting CRLF line endings into LF when you add a file to the index, and vice versa when it checks out code onto your filesystem. You can turn on this functionality with the `core.autocrlf` setting. If you're on a Windows machine, set it to `true`—this converts LF endings into CRLF when you check out code:

```
$ git config --global core.autocrlf true
```

If you're on a Linux or Mac system that uses LF line endings, then you don't want Git to automatically convert them when you check out files; however, if a file with CRLF endings accidentally gets introduced, then you may want Git to fix it. You can tell Git to convert CRLF to LF on commit but not the other way around by setting `core.autocrlf` to input:

```
$ git config --global core.autocrlf input
```

This setup should leave you with CRLF endings in Windows checkouts, but LF endings on Mac and Linux systems and in the repository.

If you're a Windows programmer doing a Windows-only project, then you can turn off this functionality, recording the carriage returns in the repository by setting the config value to `false`:

```
$ git config --global core.autocrlf false
```

core.whitespace

Git comes preset to detect and fix some whitespace issues. It can look for six primary whitespace issues—three are enabled by default and can be turned off, and three are disabled by default but can be activated.

The ones that are turned on by default are blank-at-eol, which looks for spaces at the end of a line; blank-at-eof, which notices blank lines at the end of a file; and space-before-tab, which looks for spaces before tabs at the beginning of a line.

The three that are disabled by default but can be turned on are indent-with-non-tab, which looks for lines that begin with spaces instead of tabs (and is controlled by the tabwidth option); tab-in-indent, which watches for tabs in the indentation portion of a line; and cr-at-eol, which tells Git that carriage returns at the end of lines are OK.

You can tell Git which of these you want enabled by setting core.whitespace to the values you want on or off, separated by commas. You can disable settings by either leaving them out of the setting string or prepending a - in front of the value. For example, if you want all but `cr-at-eol` to be set, you can do this:

```
$ git config --global core.whitespace \
    trailing-space,space-before-tab,indent-with-non-tab
```

Git will detect these issues when you run a `git diff` command and try to color them so you can possibly fix them before you commit. It will also use these values to help you when you apply patches with `git apply`. When you're applying patches, you can ask Git to warn you if it's applying patches with the specified whitespace issues:

```
$ git apply --whitespace=warn <patch>
```

Or you can have Git try to automatically fix the issue before applying the patch:

```
$ git apply --whitespace=fix <patch>
```

These options apply to the git rebase command as well. If you've committed whitespace issues but haven't yet pushed upstream, you can run `git rebase --whitespace=fix` to have Git automatically fix whitespace issues as it's rewriting the patches.

Server Configuration

Not nearly as many configuration options are available for the server side of Git, but there are a few interesting ones you may want to take note of.

receive.fsckObjects

Git is capable of making sure every object received during a push still matches its SHA-1 checksum and points to valid objects. However, it doesn't do this by default; it's a fairly expensive operation, and might slow down the operation, especially on large repositories or pushes. If you want Git to check object consistency on every push, you can force it to do so by setting receive.fsckObjects to true:

```
$ git config --system receive.fsckObjects true
```

Now, Git will check the integrity of your repository before each push is accepted to make sure faulty (or malicious) clients aren't introducing corrupt data.

receive.denyNonFastForwards

If you rebase commits that you've already pushed and then try to push again, or otherwise try to push a commit to a remote branch that doesn't contain the commit that the remote branch currently points to, you'll be denied. This is generally good policy; but in the case of the rebase, you may determine that you know what you're doing and can force-update the remote branch with a -f flag to your push command.

To tell Git to refuse force-pushes, set receive.denyNonFastForwards:

```
$ git config --system receive.denyNonFastForwards true
```

The other way you can do this is via server-side receive hooks, which we'll cover in a bit. That approach lets you do more complex things like deny non-fast-forwards to a certain subset of users.

receive.denyDeletes

One of the workarounds to the denyNonFastForwards policy is for the user to delete the branch and then push it back up with the new reference. To avoid this, set receive.denyDeletes to true:

```
$ git config --system receive.denyDeletes true
```

This denies any deletion of branches or tags – no user can do it. To remove remote branches, you must remove the ref files from the server manually. There are also more interesting ways to do this on a per-user basis via ACLs, as you'll learn later.

Git Attributes

Some of these settings can also be specified for a path, so that Git applies those settings only for a subdirectory or subset of files. These path-specific settings are called Git attributes and are set either in a .gitattributes file in one of your directories (normally the root of your project) or in the .git/info/attributes file if you don't want the attributes file committed with your project.

Using attributes, you can do things like specify separate merge strategies for individual files or directories in your project, tell Git how to diff non-text files, or have Git filter content before you check it into or out of Git. In this section, you'll learn about some of the attributes you can set on your paths in your Git project and see a few examples of using this feature in practice.

Binary Files

One cool trick for which you can use Git attributes is telling Git which files are binary (in cases it otherwise may not be able to figure out) and giving Git special instructions about how to handle those files. For instance, some text files may be machine generated and not diffable, whereas some binary files can be diffed. You'll see how to tell Git which is which.

Identifying Binary Files

Some files look like text files but for all intents and purposes are to be treated as binary data. For instance, Xcode projects on the Mac contain a file that ends in .pbxproj, which is basically a JSON (plain-text Javascript data format) dataset written out to disk by the IDE, which records your build settings, and so on. Although it's technically a text file (because it's all UTF-8), you don't want to treat it as such because it's really a lightweight database—you can't merge the contents if two people change it, and diffs generally aren't helpful. The file is meant to be consumed by a machine. In essence, you want to treat it like a binary file.

To tell Git to treat all .pbxproj files as binary data, add the following line to your .gitattributes file:

```
*.pbxproj binary
```

Now, Git won't try to convert or fix CRLF issues; nor will it try to compute or print a diff for changes in this file when you run git show or git diff on your project.

Diffing Binary Files

You can also use the Git attributes functionality to effectively diff binary files. You do this by telling Git how to convert your binary data to a text format that can be compared via the normal diff.

Because this is a pretty cool and not widely known feature, we'll go over a few examples. First, you'll use this technique to solve one of the most annoying problems known to humanity: version-controlling Microsoft Word documents. Everyone knows that Word is the most horrific editor around, but oddly, everyone still uses it. If you want to version-control Word documents, you can stick them in a Git repository and commit every once in a while; but what good does that do? If you run git diff normally, you only see something like this:

```
$ git diff
diff --git a/chapter1.docx b/chapter1.docx
index 88839c4..4afcb7c 100644
Binary files a/chapter1.docx and b/chapter1.docx differ
```

You can't directly compare two versions unless you check them out and scan them manually, right? It turns out you can do this fairly well using Git attributes. Put the following line in your .gitattributes file:

```
*.docx diff=word
```

This tells Git that any file that matches this pattern (.docx) should use the "word" filter when you try to view a diff that contains changes. What is the "word" filter? You have to set it up. Here you'll configure Git to use the docx2txt program to convert Word documents into readable text files, which it will then diff properly.

First, you'll need to install docx2txt; you can download it from http://docx2txt.sourceforge.net. Follow the instructions in the INSTALL file to put it somewhere your shell can find it. Next, you'll write a wrapper script to convert output to the format Git expects. Create a file that's somewhere in your path called docx2txt, and add these contents:

```
#!/bin/bash
docx2txt.pl $1 -
```

Don't forget to chmod a+x that file. Finally, you can configure Git to use this script:

```
$ git config diff.word.textconv docx2txt
```

Now Git knows that if it tries to do a diff between two snapshots, and any of the files end in .docx, it should run those files through the "word" filter, which is defined as the docx2txt program. This effectively makes nice text-based versions of your Word files before attempting to diff them.

Here's an example: Chapter 1 of this book was converted to Word format and committed in a Git repository. Then a new paragraph was added. Here's what git diff shows:

```
$ git diff
diff --git a/chapter1.docx b/chapter1.docx
index 0b013ca..ba25db5 100644
--- a/chapter1.docx
+++ b/chapter1.docx
@@ -2,6 +2,7 @@
```

This chapter will be about getting started with Git. We will begin at the beginning by explaining some background on version control tools, then move on to how to get Git running on your system and finally how to get it setup to start working with. At the end of this chapter you should understand why Git is around, why you should use it and you should be all setup to do so.

1.1. About Version Control

What is "version control", and why should you care? Version control is a system that records changes to a file or set of files over time so that you can recall specific versions later. For the examples in this book you will use software source code as the files being version controlled, though in reality you can do this with nearly any type of file on a computer.

+Testing: 1, 2, 3.

If you are a graphic or web designer and want to keep every version of an image or layout (which you would most certainly want to), a Version Control System (VCS) is a very wise thing to use. It allows you to revert files back to a previous state, revert the entire project back to a previous state, compare changes over time, see who last modified something that might be causing a problem, who introduced an issue and when, and more. Using a VCS also generally means that if you screw things up or lose files, you can easily recover. In addition, you get all this for very little overhead.

1.1.1. Local Version Control Systems

Many people's version-control method of choice is to copy files into another directory (perhaps a time-stamped directory, if they're clever). This approach is very common because it is so simple, but it is also incredibly error prone. It is easy to forget which directory you're in and accidentally write to the wrong file or copy over files you don't mean to.

Git successfully and succinctly tells me that I added the string "Testing: 1, 2, 3.", which is correct. It's not perfect—formatting changes wouldn't show up here—but it certainly works.

Another interesting problem you can solve this way involves diffing image files. One way to do this is to run JPEG files through a filter that extracts their EXIF information—metadata that is recorded with most image formats. If you download and install the exiftool program, you can use it to convert your images into text about the metadata, so at least the diff will show you a textual representation of any changes that happened:

```
$ echo '*.png diff=exif' >> .gitattributes
$ git config diff.exif.textconv exiftool
```

If you replace an image in your project and run git diff, you see something like this:

```
diff --git a/image.png b/image.png
index 88839c4..4afcb7c 100644
--- a/image.png
+++ b/image.png
@@ -1,12 +1,12 @@
 ExifTool Version Number         : 7.74
-File Size                       : 70 kB
-File Modification Date/Time     : 2009:04:21 07:02:45-07:00
+File Size                       : 94 kB
+File Modification Date/Time     : 2009:04:21 07:02:43-07:00
 File Type                       : PNG
 MIME Type                       : image/png
-Image Width                     : 1058
-Image Height                    : 889
+Image Width                     : 1056
+Image Height                    : 827
 Bit Depth                       : 8
 Color Type                      : RGB with Alpha
```

You can easily see that the file size and image dimensions have both changed.

Keyword Expansion

SVN- or CVS-style keyword expansion is often requested by developers used to those systems. The main problem with this in Git is that you can't modify a file with information about the commit after you've committed, because Git checksums the file first. However, you can inject text into a file when it's checked out and remove it again before it's added to a commit. Git attributes offers you two ways to do this.

First, you can inject the SHA-1 checksum of a blob into an Id field in the file automatically. If you set this attribute on a file or set of files, then the next time you check out that branch, Git will replace that field with the SHA-1 of the blob. It's important to notice that it isn't the SHA of the commit, but of the blob itself:

```
$ echo '*.txt ident' >> .gitattributes
$ echo '$Id$' > test.txt
```

The next time you check out this file, Git injects the SHA of the blob:

```
$ rm text.txt
$ git checkout -- text.txt
$ cat test.txt
$Id: 42812b7653c7b88933f8a9d6cad0ca16714b9bb3 $
```

However, that result is of limited use. If you've used keyword substitution in CVS or Subversion, you can include a datestamp—the SHA isn't all that helpful, because it's fairly random and you can't tell if one SHA is older or newer than another just by looking at them.

It turns out that you can write your own filters for doing substitutions in files on commit/checkout. These are called "clean" and "smudge" filters. In the .gitattributes file, you can set a filter for particular paths and then set up scripts that will process files just before they're checked out (the smudge filter is run on checkout) and just before they're staged (the clean filter is run when files are staged). These filters can be set to do all sorts of fun things.

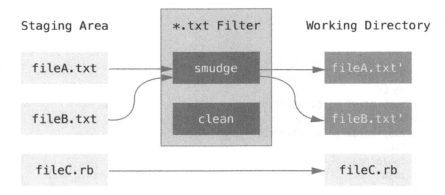

Figure 8-2. *The "smudge" filter is run on checkout*

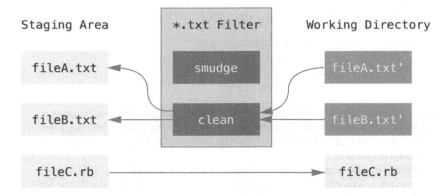

Figure 8-3. *The "clean" filter is run when files are staged*

The original commit message for this feature gives a simple example of running all your C source code through the indent program before committing. You can set it up by setting the filter attribute in your .gitattributes file to filter *.c files with the indent filter:

```
*.c filter=indent
```

Then, tell Git what the indent filter does on smudge and clean:

```
$ git config --global filter.indent.clean indent
$ git config --global filter.indent.smudge cat
```

In this case, when you commit files that match *.c, Git will run them through the indent program before it stages them and then run them through the cat program before it checks them back out onto disk. The cat program does essentially nothing: it spits out the same data that it comes in. This combination effectively filters all C source code files through indent before committing.

Another interesting example gets $Date$ keyword expansion, RCS style. To do this properly, you need a small script that takes a filename, figures out the last commit date for this project, and inserts the date into the file. Here is a small Ruby script that does that:

```
#! /usr/bin/env ruby
data = STDIN.read
last_date = `git log --pretty=format:"%ad" -1`
puts data.gsub('$Date$', '$Date: ' + last_date.to_s + '$')
```

All the script does is get the latest commit date from the git log command, stick that into any $Date$ strings it sees in stdin, and print the results – it should be simple to do in whatever language you're most comfortable in. You can name this file expand_date and put it in your path. Now, you need to set up a filter in Git (call it dater) and tell it to use your expand_date filter to smudge the files on checkout. You'll use a Perl expression to clean that up on commit:

```
$ git config filter.dater.smudge expand_date
$ git config filter.dater.clean 'perl -pe "s/\\\$Date[^\\\$]*\\\$/\\\$Date\\\$/"'
```

This Perl snippet strips out anything it sees in a $Date$ string, to get back to where you started. Now that your filter is ready, you can test it by setting up a file with your $Date$ keyword and then setting up a Git attribute for that file that engages the new filter:

```
$ echo '# $Date$' > date_test.txt
$ echo 'date*.txt filter=dater' >> .gitattributes
```

If you commit those changes and check out the file again, you see the keyword properly substituted:

```
$ git add date_test.txt .gitattributes
$ git commit -m "Testing date expansion in Git"
$ rm date_test.txt
$ git checkout date_test.txt
$ cat date_test.txt
# $Date: Tue Apr 21 07:26:52 2009 -0700$
```

You can see how powerful this technique can be for customized applications. You have to be careful, though, because the .gitattributes file is committed and passed around with the project, but the driver (in this case, dater) isn't, so it won't work everywhere. When you design these filters, they should be able to fail gracefully and have the project still work properly.

Exporting Your Repository

Git attribute data also allows you to do some interesting things when exporting an archive of your project.

export-ignore

You can tell Git not to export certain files or directories when generating an archive. If there is a subdirectory or file that you don't want to include in your archive file but that you do want checked into your project, you can determine those files via the export-ignore attribute.

For example, say you have some test files in a test/ subdirectory, and it doesn't make sense to include them in the tarball export of your project. You can add the following line to your Git attributes file:

```
test/ export-ignore
```

Now, when you run git archive to create a tarball of your project, that directory won't be included in the archive.

export-subst

Another thing you can do for your archives is some simple keyword substitution. Git lets you put the string $Format:$ in any file with any of the --pretty=format formatting shortcodes, many of which you saw in Chapter 2. For instance, if you want to include a file named LAST_COMMIT in your project, and the last commit date was automatically injected into it when git archive ran, you can set up the file like this:

```
$ echo 'Last commit date: $Format:%cd$' > LAST_COMMIT
$ echo "LAST_COMMIT export-subst" >> .gitattributes
$ git add LAST_COMMIT .gitattributes
$ git commit -am 'adding LAST_COMMIT file for archives'
```

When you run git archive, the contents of that file when people open the archive file will look like this:

```
$ cat LAST_COMMIT
Last commit date: $Format:Tue Apr 21 08:38:48 2009 -0700$
```

Merge Strategies

You can also use Git attributes to tell Git to use different merge strategies for specific files in your project. One very useful option is to tell Git to not try to merge specific files when they have conflicts, but rather to use your side of the merge over someone else's.

This is helpful if a branch in your project has diverged or is specialized, but you want to be able to merge changes back in from it, and you want to ignore certain files. Say you have a database settings file called database.xml that is different in two branches, and you want to merge in your other branch without messing up the database file. You can set up an attribute like this:

```
database.xml merge=ours
```

If you merge in the other branch, instead of having merge conflicts with the database.xml file, you see something like this:

```
$ git merge topic
Auto-merging database.xml
Merge made by recursive.
```

In this case, database.xml stays at whatever version you originally had.

Git Hooks

Like many other Version Control Systems, Git has a way to fire off custom scripts when certain important actions occur. There are two groups of these hooks: client-side and server-side. Client-side hooks are triggered by operations such as committing and merging, while server-side hooks run on network operations such as receiving pushed commits. You can use these hooks for all sorts of reasons.

Installing a Hook

The hooks are all stored in the hooks subdirectory of the Git directory. In most projects, that's .git/hooks. When you initialize a new repository with git init, Git populates the hooks directory with a bunch of example scripts, many of which are useful by themselves; but they also document the input values of each script. All the examples are written as shell scripts, with some Perl thrown in, but any properly named executable scripts will work fine—you can write them in Ruby or Python or what have you. If you want to use the bundled hook scripts, you'll have to rename them; their filenames all end with sample.

To enable a hook script, put a file in the hooks subdirectory of your Git directory that is named appropriately and is executable. From that point forward, it should be called. I'll cover most of the major hook filenames here.

Client-Side Hooks

There are a lot of client-side hooks. This section splits them into committing-workflow hooks, e-mail-workflow scripts, and everything else.

■ **Note** It's important to note that client-side hooks are not copied when you clone a repository. If your intent with these scripts is to enforce a policy, you'll probably want to do that on the server side.

Committing-Workflow Hooks

The first four hooks have to do with the committing process.

The pre-commit hook is run first, before you even type in a commit message. It's used to inspect the snapshot that's about to be committed, to see if you've forgotten something, to make sure tests run, or to examine whatever you need to inspect in the code. Exiting non-zero from this hook aborts the commit, although you can bypass it with git commit --no-verify. You can do things like check for code style (run lint or something equivalent), check for trailing whitespace (the default hook does exactly this), or check for appropriate documentation on new methods.

The prepare-commit-msg hook is run before the commit message editor is fired up but after the default message is created. It lets you edit the default message before the commit author sees it. This hook takes a few parameters: the path to the file that holds the commit message so far, the type of commit, and the commit SHA-1 if this is an amended commit. This hook generally isn't useful for normal commits; rather, it's good for commits where the default message is auto-generated, such as templated commit messages, merge commits, squashed commits, and amended commits. You may use it in conjunction with a commit template to programmatically insert information.

The commit-msg hook takes one parameter, which again is the path to a temporary file that contains the commit message written by the developer. If this script exits non-zero, Git aborts the commit process, so you can use it to validate your project state or commit message before allowing a commit to go through. In the last section of this chapter, I'll demonstrate using this hook to check that your commit message is conformant to a required pattern.

After the entire commit process is completed, the post-commit hook runs. It doesn't take any parameters, but you can easily get the last commit by running git log -1 HEAD. Generally, this script is used for notification or something similar.

E-mail Workflow Hooks

You can set up three client-side hooks for an e-mail-based workflow. They're all invoked by the git am command, so if you aren't using that command in your workflow, you can safely skip to the next section. If you're taking patches over e-mail prepared by git format-patch, then some of these may be helpful to you.

The first hook that is run is applypatch-msg. It takes a single argument: the name of the temporary file that contains the proposed commit message. Git aborts the patch if this script exits non-zero. You can use this to make sure a commit message is properly formatted, or to normalize the message by having the script edit it in place.

The next hook to run when applying patches via git am is pre-applypatch. Somewhat confusingly, it is run after the patch is applied but before a commit is made, so you can use it to inspect the snapshot before making the commit. You can run tests or otherwise inspect the working tree with this script. If something is missing or the tests don't pass, exiting non-zero aborts the git am script without committing the patch.

The last hook to run during a git am operation is post-applypatch, which runs after the commit is made. You can use it to notify a group or the author of the patch you pulled in that you've done so. You can't stop the patching process with this script.

Other Client Hooks

The pre-rebase hook runs before you rebase anything and can halt the process by exiting non-zero. You can use this hook to disallow rebasing any commits that have already been pushed. The example pre-rebase hook that Git installs does this, although it makes some assumptions that may not match with your workflow.

The post-rewrite hook is run by commands that replace commits, such as git commit --amend and git rebase (though not by git filter-branch). Its single argument is which command triggered the rewrite, and it receives a list of rewrites on stdin. This hook has many of the same uses as the post-checkout and post-merge hooks.

After you run a successful git checkout, the post-checkout hook runs; you can use it to set up your working directory properly for your project environment. This may mean moving in large binary files that you don't want source controlled, auto-generating documentation, or something along those lines.

The post-merge hook runs after a successful merge command. You can use it to restore data in the working tree that Git can't track, such as permissions data. This hook can likewise validate the presence of files external to Git control that you may want copied in when the working tree changes.

The pre-push hook runs during git push, after the remote refs have been updated but before any objects have been transferred. It receives the name and location of the remote as parameters, and a list of to-be-updated refs through stdin. You can use it to validate a set of ref updates before a push occurs (a non-zero exit code will abort the push).

Git occasionally does garbage collection as part of its normal operation, by invoking git gc --auto. The pre-auto-gc hook is invoked just before the garbage collection takes place, and can be used to notify you that this is happening, or to abort the collection if now isn't a good time.

Server-Side Hooks

In addition to the client-side hooks, you can use a couple of important server-side hooks as a system administrator to enforce nearly any kind of policy for your project. These scripts run before and after pushes to the server. The pre hooks can exit non-zero at any time to reject the push as well as print an error message back to the client; you can set up a push policy that's as complex as you wish.

pre-receive

The first script to run when handling a push from a client is pre-receive. It takes a list of references that are being pushed from stdin; if it exits non-zero, none of them are accepted. You can use this hook to do things like make sure none of the updated references are non-fast-forwards, or to do access control for all the refs and files they're modifying with the push.

update

The update script is very similar to the pre-receive script, except that it's run once for each branch the pusher is trying to update. If the pusher is trying to push to multiple branches, pre-receive runs only once, whereas update runs once per branch they're pushing to. Instead of reading from stdin, this script takes three arguments: the name of the reference (branch), the SHA-1 that reference pointed to before the push, and the SHA-1 the user is trying to push. If the update script exits non-zero, only that reference is rejected; other references can still be updated.

post-receive

The post-receive hook runs after the entire process is completed and can be used to update other services or notify users. It takes the same stdin data as the pre-receive hook. Examples include e-mailing a list, notifying a continuous integration server, or updating a ticket-tracking system—you can even parse the commit messages to see if any tickets need to be opened, modified, or closed. This script can't stop the push process, but the client doesn't disconnect until it has completed, so be careful if you try to do anything that may take a long time.

An Example Git-Enforced Policy

In this section, you'll use what you've learned to establish a Git workflow that checks for a custom commit message format, and allows only certain users to modify certain subdirectories in a project. You'll build client scripts that help the developer know if their push will be rejected and server scripts that actually enforce the policies.

The scripts we'll show are written in Ruby; partly because of our intellectual inertia, but also because Ruby is easy to read, even if you can't necessarily write it. However, any language will work—all the sample hook scripts distributed with Git are in either Perl or Bash, so you can also see plenty of examples of hooks in those languages by looking at the samples.

Server-Side Hook

All the server-side work will go into the update file in your hooks directory. The update hook runs once per branch being pushed and takes three arguments:

- The name of the reference being pushed to
- The old revision where that branch was
- The new revision being pushed

You also have access to the user doing the pushing if the push is being run over SSH. If you've allowed everyone to connect with a single user (like "git") via public-key authentication, you may have to give that user a shell wrapper that determines which user is connecting based on the public key, and set an environment variable accordingly. Here we'll assume the connecting user is in the $USER environment variable, so your update script begins by gathering all the information you need:

```
#!/usr/bin/env ruby

$refname = ARGV[0]
$oldrev  = ARGV[1]
$newrev  = ARGV[2]
$user    = ENV['USER']

puts "Enforcing Policies..."
puts "(#{$refname}) (#{$oldrev[0,6]}) (#{$newrev[0,6]})"
```

Yes, those are global variables. Don't judge—it's easier to demonstrate this way.

Enforcing a Specific Commit-Message Format

Your first challenge is to enforce that each commit message adheres to a particular format. Just to have a target, assume that each message has to include a string that looks like "ref: 1234" because you want each commit to link to a work item in your ticketing system. You must look at each commit being pushed up, see if that string is in the commit message, and, if the string is absent from any of the commits, exit non-zero so the push is rejected.

You can get a list of the SHA-1 values of all the commits that are being pushed by taking the $newrev and $oldrev values and passing them to a Git plumbing command called git rev-list. This is basically the git log command, but by default it prints out only the SHA-1 values and no other information.

So, to get a list of all the commit SHAs introduced between one commit SHA and another, you can run something like this:

```
$ git rev-list 538c33..d14fc7
d14fc7c847ab946ec39590d87783c69b031bdfb7
9f585da4401b0a3999e84113824d15245c13f0be
234071a1be950e2a8d078e6141f5cd20c1e61ad3
dfa04c9ef3d5197182f13fb5b9b1fb7717d2222a
17716ec0f1ff5c77eff40b7fe912f9f6cfd0e475
```

You can take that output, loop through each of those commit SHAs, grab the message for it, and test that message against a regular expression that looks for a pattern.

You have to figure out how to get the commit message from each of these commits to test. To get the raw commit data, you can use another plumbing command called git cat-file. We'll go over all these plumbing commands in detail later; but for now, here's what that command gives you:

```
$ git cat-file commit ca82a6
tree cfda3bf379e4f8dba8717dee55aab78aef7f4daf
parent 085bb3bcb608e1e8451d4b2432f8ecbe6306e7e7
author Scott Chacon <schacon@gmail.com> 1205815931 -0700
committer Scott Chacon <schacon@gmail.com> 1240030591 -0700

changed the version number
```

A simple way to get the commit message from a commit when you have the SHA-1 value is to go to the first blank line and take everything after that. You can do so with the sed command on Unix systems:

```
$ git cat-file commit ca82a6 | sed '1,/^$/d'

changed the version number
```

You can use that incantation to grab the commit message from each commit that is trying to be pushed and exit if you see anything that doesn't match. To exit the script and reject the push, exit non-zero. The whole method looks like this:

```
$regex = /\[ref: (\d+)\]/

# enforced custom commit message format
def check_message_format
  missed_revs = `git rev-list #{$oldrev}..#{$newrev}`.split("\n")
  missed_revs.each do |rev|
    message = `git cat-file commit #{rev} | sed '1,/^$/d'`
    if !$regex.match(message)
      puts "[POLICY] Your message is not formatted correctly"
      exit 1
    end
  end
end
check_message_format
```

Putting that in your update script will reject updates that contain commits that have messages that don't adhere to your rule.

Enforcing a User-Based ACL System

Suppose you want to add a mechanism that uses an access control list (ACL) that specifies which users are allowed to push changes to which parts of your projects. Some people have full access, and others can only push changes to certain subdirectories or specific files. To enforce this, you'll write those rules to a file named acl that lives in your bare Git repository on the server. You'll have the update hook look at those rules, see what files are being introduced for all the commits being pushed, and determine whether the user doing the push has access to update all those files.

The first thing you'll do is write your ACL. Here you'll use a format very much like the CVS ACL mechanism: it uses a series of lines, where the first field is avail or unavail, the next field is a comma-delimited list of the users to which the rule applies, and the last field is the path to which the rule applies (blank meaning open access). All of these fields are delimited by a pipe (|) character.

In this case, you have a couple of administrators, some documentation writers with access to the doc directory, and one developer who only has access to the lib and tests directories, and your ACL file looks like this:

```
avail|nickh,pjhyett,defunkt,tpw
avail|usinclair,cdickens,ebronte|doc
avail|schacon|lib
avail|schacon|tests
```

You begin by reading this data into a structure that you can use. In this case, to keep the example simple, you'll only enforce the avail directives. Here is a method that gives you an associative array where the key is the user name and the value is an array of paths to which the user has write access:

```
def get_acl_access_data(acl_file)
  # read in ACL data
  acl_file = File.read(acl_file).split("\n").reject { |line| line == '' }
  access = {}
  acl_file.each do |line|
    avail, users, path = line.split('|')
    next unless avail == 'avail'
    users.split(',').each do |user|
      access[user] ||= []
      access[user] << path
    end
  end
  access
end
```

On the ACL file you looked at earlier, this get_acl_access_data method returns a data structure that looks like this:

```
{"defunkt"=>[nil],
 "tpw"=>[nil],
 "nickh"=>[nil],
 "pjhyett"=>[nil],
 "schacon"=>["lib", "tests"],
 "cdickens"=>["doc"],
 "usinclair"=>["doc"],
 "ebronte"=>["doc"]}
```

Now that you have the permissions sorted out, you need to determine what paths the commits being pushed have modified, so you can make sure the user who's pushing has access to all of them.

You can pretty easily see what files have been modified in a single commit with the --name-only option to the git log command (mentioned briefly in Chapter 2):

```
$ git log -1 --name-only --pretty=format:'' 9f585d

README
lib/test.rb
```

If you use the ACL structure returned from the get_acl_access_data method and check it against the listed files in each of the commits, you can determine whether the user has access to push all their commits:

```ruby
# only allows certain users to modify certain subdirectories in a project
def check_directory_perms
  access = get_acl_access_data('acl')

  # see if anyone is trying to push something they can't
  new_commits = `git rev-list #{$oldrev}..#{$newrev}`.split("\n")
  new_commits.each do |rev|
    files_modified = `git log -1 --name-only --pretty=format:'' #{rev}`.split("\n")
    files_modified.each do |path|
      next if path.size == 0
      has_file_access = false
      access[$user].each do |access_path|
        if !access_path  # user has access to everything
           || (path.start_with? access_path) # access to this path
          has_file_access = true
        end
      end
      if !has_file_access
        puts "[POLICY] You do not have access to push to #{path}"
        exit 1
      end
    end
  end
end

check_directory_perms
```

You get a list of new commits being pushed to your server with git rev-list. Then, for each of those commits, you find which files are modified and make sure the user who's pushing has access to all the paths being modified.

Now your users can't push any commits with badly formed messages or with modified files outside of their designated paths.

Testing It Out

If you run chmod u+x .git/hooks/ update, which is the file you into which you should have put all this code, and then try to push a commit with a non-compliant message, you get something like this:

```
$ git push -f origin master
Counting objects: 5, done.
Compressing objects: 100% (3/3), done.
Writing objects: 100% (3/3), 323 bytes, done.
Total 3 (delta 1), reused 0 (delta 0)
Unpacking objects: 100% (3/3), done.
Enforcing Policies...
(refs/heads/master) (8338c5) (c5b616)
[POLICY] Your message is not formatted correctly
error: hooks/update exited with error code 1
error: hook declined to update refs/heads/master
To git@gitserver:project.git
 ! [remote rejected] master -> master (hook declined)
error: failed to push some refs to 'git@gitserver:project.git'
```

There are a couple of interesting things here. First, you see this where the hook starts running.

```
Enforcing Policies...
(refs/heads/master) (fb8c72) (c56860)
```

Remember that you printed that out at the very beginning of your update script. Anything your script echoes to stdout will be transferred to the client.

The next thing you'll notice is the error message.

```
[POLICY] Your message is not formatted correctly
error: hooks/update exited with error code 1
error: hook declined to update refs/heads/master
```

The first line was printed out by you, the other two were Git telling you that the update script exited non-zero and that is what is declining your push. Lastly, you have this:

```
To git@gitserver:project.git
 ! [remote rejected] master -> master (hook declined)
error: failed to push some refs to 'git@gitserver:project.git'
```

You'll see a remote rejected message for each reference that your hook declined, and it tells you that it was declined specifically because of a hook failure.

Furthermore, if someone tries to edit a file they don't have access to and push a commit containing it, they will see something similar. For instance, if a documentation author tries to push a commit modifying something in the lib directory, they see

```
[POLICY] You do not have access to push to lib/test.rb
```

From now on, as long as that update script is there and executable, your repository will never have a commit message without your pattern in it, and your users will be sandboxed.

Client-Side Hooks

The downside to this approach is the whining that will inevitably result when your users' commit pushes are rejected. Having their carefully crafted work rejected at the last minute can be extremely frustrating and confusing; and furthermore, they will have to edit their history to correct it, which isn't always for the faint of heart.

The answer to this dilemma is to provide some client-side hooks that users can run to notify them when they're doing something that the server is likely to reject. That way, they can correct any problems before committing and before those issues become more difficult to fix. Because hooks aren't transferred with a clone of a project, you must distribute these scripts some other way and then have your users copy them to their .git/hooks directory and make them executable. You can distribute these hooks within the project or in a separate project, but Git won't set them up automatically.

To begin, you should check your commit message just before each commit is recorded, so you know the server won't reject your changes due to badly formatted commit messages. To do this, you can add the commit-msg hook. If you have it read the message from the file passed as the first argument and compare that to the pattern, you can force Git to abort the commit if there is no match:

```ruby
#!/usr/bin/env ruby
message_file = ARGV[0]
message = File.read(message_file)

$regex = /\[ref: (\d+)\]/

if !$regex.match(message)
  puts "[POLICY] Your message is not formatted correctly"
  exit 1
end
```

If that script is in place (in .git/hooks/commit-msg) and executable, and you commit with a message that isn't properly formatted, you see this:

```
$ git commit -am 'test'
[POLICY] Your message is not formatted correctly
```

No commit was completed in that instance. However, if your message contains the proper pattern, Git allows you to commit:

```
$ git commit -am 'test [ref: 132]'
[master e05c914] test [ref: 132]
 1 file changed, 1 insertions(+), 0 deletions(-)
```

Next, you want to make sure you aren't modifying files that are outside your ACL scope. If your project's .git directory contains a copy of the ACL file you used previously, then the following pre-commit script will enforce those constraints for you:

```ruby
#!/usr/bin/env ruby

$user    = ENV['USER']

# [ insert acl_access_data method from above ]

# only allows certain users to modify certain subdirectories in a project
def check_directory_perms
  access = get_acl_access_data('.git/acl')

  files_modified = `git diff-index --cached --name-only HEAD`.split("\n")
  files_modified.each do |path|
    next if path.size == 0
    has_file_access = false
    access[$user].each do |access_path|
    if !access_path || (path.index(access_path) == 0)
      has_file_access = true
    end
    if !has_file_access
      puts "[POLICY] You do not have access to push to #{path}"
      exit 1
    end
  end
end

check_directory_perms
```

This is roughly the same script as the server-side part, but with two important differences. First, the ACL file is in a different place, because this script runs from your working directory, not from your .git directory. You have to change the path to the ACL file from this

```ruby
access = get_acl_access_data('acl')
```

to this:

```ruby
access = get_acl_access_data('.git/acl')
```

The other important difference is the way you get a listing of the files that have been changed. Because the server-side method looks at the log of commits, and, at this point, the commit hasn't been recorded yet, you must get your file listing from the staging area instead. Instead of

```ruby
files_modified = `git log -1 --name-only --pretty=format:'' #{ref}`
```

you have to use

```ruby
files_modified = `git diff-index --cached --name-only HEAD`
```

But those are the only two differences—otherwise, the script works the same way. One caveat is that it expects you to be running locally as the same user you push as to the remote machine. If that is different, you must set the $user variable manually.

One other thing we can do here is make sure the user doesn't push non-fast-forwarded references. To get a reference that isn't a fast-forward, you either have to rebase past a commit you've already pushed up or try pushing a different local branch up to the same remote branch.

Presumably, the server is already configured with receive.denyDeletes and receive.denyNonFastForwards to enforce this policy, so the only accidental thing you can try to catch is rebasing commits that have already been pushed.

Here is an example pre-rebase script that checks for that. It gets a list of all the commits you're about to rewrite and checks whether they exist in any of your remote references. If it sees one that is reachable from one of your remote references, it aborts the rebase.

```ruby
#!/usr/bin/env ruby

base_branch = ARGV[0]
if ARGV[1]
  topic_branch = ARGV[1]
else
  topic_branch = "HEAD"
end

target_shas = `git rev-list #{base_branch}..#{topic_branch}`.split("\n")
remote_refs = `git branch -r`.split("\n").map { |r| r.strip }

target_shas.each do |sha|
  remote_refs.each do |remote_ref|
    shas_pushed = `git rev-list ^#{sha}^@ refs/remotes/#{remote_ref}`
    if shas_pushed.split("\n").include?(sha)
      puts "[POLICY] Commit #{sha} has already been pushed to #{remote_ref}"
      exit 1
    end
  end
end
```

This script uses a syntax that wasn't covered in the "Revision Selection" section of Chapter 6. You get a list of commits that have already been pushed up by running this:

```
`git rev-list ^#{sha}^@ refs/remotes/#{remote_ref}`
.
```

The SHA^@ syntax resolves to all the parents of that commit. You're looking for any commit that is reachable from the last commit on the remote and that isn't reachable from any parent of any of the SHAs you're trying to push up—meaning it's a fast-forward.

The main drawback to this approach is that it can be very slow and is often unnecessary – if you don't try to force the push with -f, the server will warn you and not accept the push. However, it's an interesting exercise and can in theory help you avoid a rebase that you might later have to go back and fix.

Summary

We've covered most of the major ways that you can customize your Git client and server to best fit your workflow and projects. You've learned about all sorts of configuration settings, file-based attributes, and event hooks, and you've built an example policy-enforcing server. You should now be able to make Git fit nearly any workflow you can dream up.

CHAPTER 9

■ ■ ■

Git and Other Systems

The world isn't perfect. Usually, you can't immediately switch every project you come in contact with to Git. Sometimes you're stuck on a project using another VCS, and wish it was Git. We'll spend the first part of this chapter learning about ways to use Git as a client when the project you're working on is hosted in a different system.

At some point, you may want to convert your existing project to Git. The second part of this chapter covers how to migrate your project into Git from several specific systems, as well as a method that will work if no pre-built import tool exists.

Git as a Client

Git provides such a nice experience for developers that many people have figured out how to use it on their workstation, even if the rest of their team is using an entirely different VCS. There are a number of these adapters, called "bridges," available. Here we'll cover the ones you're most likely to run into in the wild.

Git and Subversion

A large fraction of open source development projects and a good number of corporate projects use Subversion to manage their source code. It's been around for more than a decade, and for most of that time was the de facto VCS choice for open-source projects. It's also very similar in many ways to CVS, which was the big boy of the source-control world before that.

One of Git's great features is a bidirectional bridge to Subversion called git svn. This tool allows you to use Git as a valid client to a Subversion server, so you can use all the local features of Git and then push to a Subversion server as if you were using Subversion locally. This means you can do local branching and merging, use the staging area, use rebasing and cherry-picking, and so on, while your collaborators continue to work in their dark and ancient ways. It's a good way to sneak Git into the corporate environment and help your fellow developers become more efficient while you lobby to get the infrastructure changed to support Git fully. The Subversion bridge is the gateway drug to the DVCS world.

git svn

The base command in Git for all the Subversion bridging commands is git svn. It takes quite a few commands, so we'll show the most common while going through a few simple workflows.

It's important to note that when you're using git svn, you're interacting with Subversion, which is a system that works very differently from Git. Although you can do local branching and merging, it's generally best to keep your history as linear as possible by rebasing your work, and avoiding doing things such as simultaneously interacting with a Git remote repository.

Don't rewrite your history and try to push again, and don't push to a parallel Git repository to collaborate with fellow Git developers at the same time. Subversion can have only a single linear history, and confusing it is very easy. If you're working with a team, and some are using SVN and others are using Git, make sure everyone is using the SVN server to collaborate —doing so will make your life easier.

Setting Up

To demonstrate this functionality, you need a typical SVN repository that you have write access to. If you want to copy these examples, you'll have to make a writeable copy of my test repository. In order to do that easily, you can use a tool called svnsync that comes with Subversion. For these tests, we created a new Subversion repository on Google Code that was a partial copy of the protobuf project, which is a tool that encodes structured data for network transmission.

To follow along, you first need to create a new local Subversion repository:

```
$ mkdir /tmp/test-svn
$ svnadmin create /tmp/test-svn
```

Then, enable all users to change revprops—the easy way is to add a pre-revprop-change script that always exits 0:

```
$ cat /tmp/test-svn/hooks/pre-revprop-change
#!/bin/sh
exit 0;
$ chmod +x /tmp/test-svn/hooks/pre-revprop-change
```

You can now sync this project to your local machine by calling svnsync init with the to and from repositories.

```
$ svnsync init file:///tmp/test-svn http://progit-example.googlecode.com/svn/
```

This sets up the properties to run the sync. You can then clone the code by running

```
$ svnsync sync file:///tmp/test-svn
Committed revision 1.
Copied properties for revision 1.
Transmitting file data .............................[...]
Committed revision 2.
Copied properties for revision 2.
[...]
```

Although this operation may take only a few minutes, if you try to copy the original repository to another remote repository instead of a local one, the process will take nearly an hour, even though there are fewer than 100 commits. Subversion has to clone one revision at a time and then push it back into another repository—it's ridiculously inefficient, but it's the only easy way to do this.

Getting Started

Now that you have a Subversion repository to which you have write access, you can go through a typical workflow. You'll start with the git svn clone command, which imports an entire Subversion repository into a local Git repository. Remember that if you're importing from a real hosted Subversion repository, you should replace the file:///tmp/test-svn here with the URL of your Subversion repository:

```
$ git svn clone file:///tmp/test-svn -T trunk -b branches -t tags
Initialized empty Git repository in /private/tmp/progit/test-svn/.git/
r1 = dcbfb5891860124cc2e8cc616cded42624897125 (refs/remotes/origin/trunk)
    A    m4/acx_pthread.m4
    A    m4/stl_hash.m4
    A    java/src/test/java/com/google/protobuf/UnknownFieldSetTest.java
    A    java/src/test/java/com/google/protobuf/WireFormatTest.java
...
r75 = 556a3e1e7ad1fde0a32823fc7e4d046bcfd86dae (refs/remotes/origin/trunk)
Found possible branch point: file:///tmp/test-svn/trunk => file:///tmp/test-svn/branches/my-calc-branch, 75
Found branch parent: (refs/remotes/origin/my-calc-branch) 556a3e1e7ad1fde0a32823fc7e4d046bcfd86dae
Following parent with do_switch
Successfully followed parent
r76 = 0fb585761df569eaecd8146c71e58d70147460a2 (refs/remotes/origin/my-calc-branch)
Checked out HEAD:
  file:///tmp/test-svn/trunk r75
```

This runs the equivalent of two commands—git svn init followed by git svn fetch—on the URL you provide. This can take a while. The test project has only about 75 commits and the codebase isn't that big, but Git has to check out each version, one at a time, and commit it individually. For a project with hundreds or thousands of commits, this can literally take hours or even days to finish.

The -T trunk -b branches -t tags part tells Git that this Subversion repository follows the basic branching and tagging conventions. If you name your trunk, branches, or tags differently, you can change these options. Because this is so common, you can replace this entire part with -s, which means standard layout and implies all those options. The following command is equivalent:

```
$ git svn clone file:///tmp/test-svn -s
```

At this point, you should have a valid Git repository that has imported your branches and tags:

```
$ git branch -a
* master
  remotes/origin/my-calc-branch
  remotes/origin/tags/2.0.2
  remotes/origin/tags/release-2.0.1
  remotes/origin/tags/release-2.0.2
  remotes/origin/tags/release-2.0.2rc1
  remotes/origin/trunk
```

Note how this tool manages Subversion tags as remote refs. Let's take a closer look with the Git plumbing command show-ref:

```
$ git show-ref
556a3e1e7ad1fde0a32823fc7e4d046bcfd86dae refs/heads/master
0fb585761df569eaecd8146c71e58d70147460a2 refs/remotes/origin/my-calc-branch
bfd2d79303166789fc73af4046651a4b35c12f0b refs/remotes/origin/tags/2.0.2
285c2b2e36e467dd4d91c8e3c0c0e1750b3fe8ca refs/remotes/origin/tags/release-2.0.1
cbda99cb45d9abcb9793db1d4f70ae562a969f1e refs/remotes/origin/tags/release-2.0.2
a9f074aa89e826d6f9d30808ce5ae3ffe711feda refs/remotes/origin/tags/release-2.0.2rc1
556a3e1e7ad1fde0a32823fc7e4d046bcfd86dae refs/remotes/origin/trunk
```

Git doesn't do this when it clones from a Git server; here's what a repository with tags looks like after a fresh clone:

```
$ git show-ref
c3dcbe8488c6240392e8a5d7553bbffcb0f94ef0 refs/remotes/origin/master
32ef1d1c7cc8c603ab78416262cc421b80a8c2df refs/remotes/origin/branch-1
75f703a3580a9b81ead89fe1138e6da858c5ba18 refs/remotes/origin/branch-2
23f8588dde934e8f33c263c6d8359b2ae095f863 refs/tags/v0.1.0
7064938bd5e7ef47bfd79a685a62c1e2649e2ce7 refs/tags/v0.2.0
6dcb09b5b57875f334f61aebed695e2e4193db5e refs/tags/v1.0.0
```

Git fetches the tags directly into refs/tags, rather than treating them remote branches.

Committing Back to Subversion

Now that you have a working repository, you can do some work on the project and push your commits back upstream, using Git effectively as an SVN client. If you edit one of the files and commit it, you have a commit that exists in Git locally that doesn't exist on the Subversion server:

```
$ git commit -am 'Adding git-svn instructions to the README'
[master 4af61fd] Adding git-svn instructions to the README
 1 file changed, 5 insertions(+)
```

Next, you need to push your change upstream. Notice how this changes the way you work with Subversion—you can do several commits offline and then push them all at once to the Subversion server. To push to a Subversion server, you run the git svn dcommit command:

```
$ git svn dcommit
Committing to file:///tmp/test-svn/trunk ...
    M    README.txt
Committed r77
    M    README.txt
r77 = 95e0222ba6399739834380eb10afcd73e0670bc5 (refs/remotes/origin/trunk)
No changes between 4af61fd05045e07598c553167e0f31c84fd6ffe1 and refs/remotes/origin/trunk
Resetting to the latest refs/remotes/origin/trunk
```

This takes all the commits you've made on top of the Subversion server code, does a Subversion commit for each, and then rewrites your local Git commit to include a unique identifier. This is important because it means that all the SHA-1 checksums for your commits change. Partly for this reason, working with Git-based remote versions of your projects concurrently with a Subversion server isn't a good idea. If you look at the last commit, you can see the new git-svn-id that was added:

```
$ git log -1
commit 95e0222ba6399739834380eb10afcd73e0670bc5
Author: ben <ben@0b684db3-b064-4277-89d1-21af03df0a68>
Date:   Thu Jul 24 03:08:36 2014 +0000

    Adding git-svn instructions to the README

    git-svn-id: file:///tmp/test-svn/trunk@77 0b684db3-b064-4277-89d1-21af03df0a68
```

Notice that the SHA checksum that originally started with 4af61fd when you committed now begins with 95e0222. If you want to push to both a Git server and a Subversion server, you have to push (dcommit) to the Subversion server first, because that action changes your commit data.

Pulling in New Changes

If you're working with other developers, then at some point one of you will push, and then the other one will try to push a change that conflicts. That change will be rejected until you merge in their work. In git svn, it looks like this:

```
$ git svn dcommit
Committing to file:///tmp/test-svn/trunk ...

ERROR from SVN:
Transaction is out of date: File '/trunk/README.txt' is out of date
W: d5837c4b461b7c0e018b49d12398769d2bfc240a and refs/remotes/origin/trunk differ, using rebase:
:100644 100644 f414c433af0fd6734428cf9d2a9fd8ba00ada145 c80b6127dd04f5fcda218730ddf3a2da4eb39138
M	README.txt
Current branch master is up to date.
ERROR: Not all changes have been committed into SVN, however the committed
ones (if any) seem to be successfully integrated into the working tree.
Please see the above messages for details.
```

To resolve this situation, you can run git svn rebase, which pulls down any changes on the server that you don't have yet and rebases any work you have on top of what is on the server:

```
$ git svn rebase
Committing to file:///tmp/test-svn/trunk ...

ERROR from SVN:
Transaction is out of date: File '/trunk/README.txt' is out of date
W: eaa029d99f87c5c822c5c29039d19111ff32ef46 and refs/remotes/origin/trunk differ, using rebase:
:100644 100644 65536c6e30d263495c17d781962cfff12422693a b34372b25ccf4945fe5658fa381b075045e7702a
M	README.txt
First, rewinding head to replay your work on top of it...
Applying: update foo
```

```
Using index info to reconstruct a base tree...
M       README.txt
Falling back to patching base and 3-way merge...
Auto-merging README.txt
ERROR: Not all changes have been committed into SVN, however the committed
ones (if any) seem to be successfully integrated into the working tree.
Please see the above messages for details.
```

Now, all your work is on top of what is on the Subversion server, so you can successfully dcommit:

```
$ git svn dcommit
Committing to file:///tmp/test-svn/trunk ...
    M       README.txt
Committed r85
    M       README.txt
r85 = 9c29704cc0bbbed7bd58160cfb66cb9191835cd8 (refs/remotes/origin/trunk)
No changes between 5762f56732a958d6cfda681b661d2a239cc53ef5 and refs/remotes/origin/trunk
Resetting to the latest refs/remotes/origin/trunk
```

Note that unlike Git, which requires you to merge upstream work you don't yet have locally before you can push, git svn makes you do that only if the changes conflict (much like how Subversion works). If someone else pushes a change to one file and then you push a change to another file, your dcommit will work fine:

```
$ git svn dcommit
Committing to file:///tmp/test-svn/trunk ...
    M       configure.ac
Committed r87
    M       autogen.sh
r86 = d8450bab8a77228a644b7dc0e95977ffc61adff7 (refs/remotes/origin/trunk)
    M       configure.ac
r87 = f3653ea40cb4e26b6281cec102e35dcba1fe17c4 (refs/remotes/origin/trunk)
W: a0253d06732169107aa020390d9fefd2b1d92806 and refs/remotes/origin/trunk differ, using rebase:
:100755 100755 efa5a59965fbbb5b2b0a12890f1b351bb5493c18 e757b59a9439312d80d5d43bb65d4a7d0389ed6d
M       autogen.sh
First, rewinding head to replay your work on top of it...
```

This is important to remember, because the outcome is a project state that didn't exist on either of your computers when you pushed. If the changes are incompatible but don't conflict, you may get issues that are difficult to diagnose. This is different than using a Git server—in Git, you can fully test the state on your client system before publishing it, whereas in SVN, you can't ever be certain that the states immediately before commit and after commit are identical.

You should also run this command to pull in changes from the Subversion server, even if you're not ready to commit yourself. You can run git svn fetch to grab the new data, but git svn rebase does the fetch and then updates your local commits.

```
$ git svn rebase
    M       autogen.sh
r88 = c9c5f83c64bd755368784b444bc7a0216cc1e17b (refs/remotes/origin/trunk)
First, rewinding head to replay your work on top of it...
Fast-forwarded master to refs/remotes/origin/trunk.
```

Running git svn rebase every once in a while makes sure your code is always up to date. You need to be sure your working directory is clean when you run this, though. If you have local changes, you must either stash your work or temporarily commit it before running git svn rebase—otherwise, the command will stop if it sees that the rebase will result in a merge conflict.

Git Branching Issues

When you've become comfortable with a Git workflow, you'll likely create topic branches, do work on them, and then merge them in. If you're pushing to a Subversion server via git svn, you may want to rebase your work onto a single branch each time instead of merging branches together. The reason to prefer rebasing is that Subversion has a linear history and doesn't deal with merges like Git does, so git svn follows only the first parent when converting the snapshots into Subversion commits.

Suppose your history looks like the following: you created an experiment branch, did two commits, and then merged them back into master. When you dcommit, you see output like this:

```
$ git svn dcommit
Committing to file:///tmp/test-svn/trunk ...
    M   CHANGES.txt
Committed r89
    M   CHANGES.txt
r89 = 89d492c884ea7c834353563d5d913c6adf933981 (refs/remotes/origin/trunk)
    M   COPYING.txt
    M   INSTALL.txt
Committed r90
    M   INSTALL.txt
    M   COPYING.txt
r90 = cb522197870e61467473391799148f6721bcf9a0 (refs/remotes/origin/trunk)
No changes between 71af502c214ba13123992338569f4669877f55fd and refs/remotes/origin/trunk
Resetting to the latest refs/remotes/origin/trunk
```

Running dcommit on a branch with merged history works fine, except that when you look at your Git project history, it hasn't rewritten either of the commits you made on the experiment branch—instead, all those changes appear in the SVN version of the single merge commit.

When someone else clones that work, all they see is the merge commit with all the work squashed into it, as though you ran git merge --squash; they don't see the commit data about where it came from or when it was committed.

Subversion Branching

Branching in Subversion isn't the same as branching in Git; if you can avoid using it much, that's probably best. However, you can create and commit to branches in Subversion using git svn.

Creating a New SVN Branch

To create a new branch in Subversion, you run git svn branch [branchname]:

```
$ git svn branch opera
Copying file:///tmp/test-svn/trunk at r90 to file:///tmp/test-svn/branches/opera...
Found possible branch point: file:///tmp/test-svn/trunk => file:///tmp/test-svn/branches/opera, 90
Found branch parent: (refs/remotes/origin/opera) cb522197870e614674733391799148f6721bcf9a0
Following parent with do_switch
Successfully followed parent
r91 = f1b64a3855d3c8dd84ee0ef10fa89d27f1584302 (refs/remotes/origin/opera)
```

This does the equivalent of the svn copy trunk branches/opera command in Subversion and operates on the Subversion server. It's important to note that it doesn't check you out into that branch; if you commit at this point, that commit will go to trunk on the server, not opera.

Switching Active Branches

Git figures out what branch your dcommits go to by looking for the tip of any of your Subversion branches in your history—you should have only one, and it should be the last one with a git-svn-id in your current branch history.

If you want to work on more than one branch simultaneously, you can set up local branches to dcommit to specific Subversion branches by starting them at the imported Subversion commit for that branch. If you want an opera branch that you can work on separately, you can run

```
$ git branch opera remotes/origin/opera
```

Now, if you want to merge your opera branch into trunk (your master branch), you can do so with a normal git merge. But you need to provide a descriptive commit message (via -m), or the merge will say "Merge branch opera" instead of something useful.

Remember that although you're using git merge to do this operation, and the merge likely will be much easier than it would be in Subversion (because Git will automatically detect the appropriate merge base for you), this isn't a normal Git merge commit. You have to push this data back to a Subversion server that can't handle a commit that tracks more than one parent; so, after you push it up, it will look like a single commit that squashed in all the work of another branch under a single commit. After you merge one branch into another, you can't easily go back and continue working on that branch, as you normally can in Git. The dcommit command that you run erases any information that says what branch was merged in, so subsequent merge-base calculations will be wrong—the dcommit makes your git merge result look like you ran git merge --squash. Unfortunately, there's no good way to avoid this situation—Subversion can't store this information, so you'll always be crippled by its limitations while you're using it as your server. To avoid issues, you should delete the local branch (in this case, opera) after you merge it into trunk.

Subversion Commands

The git svn toolset provides a number of commands to help ease the transition to Git by providing some functionality that's similar to what you had in Subversion. Here are a few commands that give you what Subversion used to.

SVN Style History

If you're used to Subversion and want to see your history in SVN output style, you can run git svn log to view your commit history in SVN formatting:

```
$ git svn log
------------------------------------------------------------------------
r87 | schacon | 2014-05-02 16:07:37 -0700 (Sat, 02 May 2014) | 2 lines

autogen change

------------------------------------------------------------------------
r86 | schacon | 2014-05-02 16:00:21 -0700 (Sat, 02 May 2014) | 2 lines

Merge branch 'experiment'

------------------------------------------------------------------------
r85 | schacon | 2014-05-02 16:00:09 -0700 (Sat, 02 May 2014) | 2 lines

updated the changelog
```

You should know two important things about git svn log. First, it works offline, unlike the real svn log command, which asks the Subversion server for the data. Second, it only shows you commits that have been committed up to the Subversion server. Local Git commits that you haven't dcommited don't show up; neither do commits that people have made to the Subversion server in the meantime. It's more like the last known state of the commits on the Subversion server.

SVN Annotation

Much as the git svn log command simulates the svn log command offline, you can get the equivalent of svn annotate by running git svn blame [FILE]. The output looks like this:

```
$ git svn blame README.txt
   2    temporal Protocol Buffers - Google's data interchange format
   2    temporal Copyright 2008 Google Inc.
   2    temporal http://code.google.com/apis/protocolbuffers/
   2    temporal
  22    temporal C++ Installation - Unix
  22    temporal =======================
   2    temporal
  79     schacon Committing in git-svn.
  78     schacon
   2    temporal To build and install the C++ Protocol Buffer runtime and the Protocol
   2    temporal Buffer compiler (protoc) execute the following:
   2    temporal
```

Again, it doesn't show commits that you did locally in Git or that have been pushed to Subversion in the meantime.

SVN Server Information

You can also get the same sort of information that svn info gives you by running git svn info:

```
$ git svn info
Path: .
URL: https://schacon-test.googlecode.com/svn/trunk
Repository Root: https://schacon-test.googlecode.com/svn
Repository UUID: 4c93b258-373f-11de-be05-5f7a86268029
Revision: 87
Node Kind: directory
Schedule: normal
Last Changed Author: schacon
Last Changed Rev: 87
Last Changed Date: 2009-05-02 16:07:37 -0700 (Sat, 02 May 2009)
```

This is like blame and log in that it runs offline and is up to date only as of the last time you communicated with the Subversion server.

Ignoring What Subversion Ignores

If you clone a Subversion repository that has svn:ignore properties set anywhere, you'll likely want to set corresponding .gitignore files so you don't accidentally commit files that you shouldn't. git svn has two commands to help with this issue. The first is git svn create-ignore, which automatically creates corresponding .gitignore files for you so your next commit can include them.

The second command is git svn show-ignore, which prints to stdout the lines you need to put in a .gitignore file so you can redirect the output into your project exclude file:

```
$ git svn show-ignore > .git/info/exclude
```

That way, you don't litter the project with .gitignore files. This is a good option if you're the only Git user on a Subversion team, and your teammates don't want .gitignore files in the project.

Git-Svn Summary

The git svn tools are useful if you're stuck with a Subversion server, or are otherwise in a development environment that necessitates running a Subversion server. You should consider it crippled Git, however, or you'll hit issues in translation that may confuse you and your collaborators. To stay out of trouble, try to follow these guidelines:

- Keep a linear Git history that doesn't contain merge commits made by git merge. Rebase any work you do outside of your mainline branch back onto it; don't merge it in.

- Don't set up and collaborate on a separate Git server. Possibly have one to speed up clones for new developers, but don't push anything to it that doesn't have a git-svn-id entry. You may even want to add a pre-receive hook that checks each commit message for a git-svn-id and rejects pushes that contain commits without it.

If you follow those guidelines, working with a Subversion server can be more bearable. However, if it's possible to move to a real Git server, doing so can gain your team a lot more.

Git and Mercurial

The DVCS universe is larger than just Git. In fact, there are many other systems in this space, each with their own angle on how to do distributed version control correctly. Apart from Git, the most popular is Mercurial, and the two are very similar in many respects.

The good news, if you prefer Git's client-side behavior but are working with a project whose source code is controlled with Mercurial, is that there's a way to use Git as a client for a Mercurial-hosted repository. Since the way Git talks to server repositories is through remotes, it should come as no surprise that this bridge is implemented as a remote helper. The project's name is git-remote-hg, and it can be found at https://github.com/felipec/git-remote-hg.

git-remote-hg

First, you need to install git-remote-hg. This basically entails dropping its file somewhere in your path, like so:

```
$ curl -o ~/bin/git-remote-hg \
  https://raw.githubusercontent.com/felipec/git-remote-hg/master/git-remote-hg
$ chmod +x ~/bin/git-remote-hg
```

. . . assuming ~/bin is in your $PATH. Git-remote-hg has one other dependency: the Mercurial library for Python. If you have Python installed, this is as simple as:

```
$ pip install mercurial
```

(If you don't have Python installed, visit https://www.python.org/ and get it first).

The last thing you'll need is the Mercurial client. Go to http://mercurial.selenic.com/ and install it if you haven't already.

Now you're ready to rock. All you need is a Mercurial repository you can push to. Fortunately, every Mercurial repository can act this way, so we'll just use the "hello world" repository everyone uses to learn Mercurial:

```
$ hg clone http://selenic.com/repo/hello /tmp/hello
```

Getting Started

Now that we have a suitable "server-side" repository, we can go through a typical workflow. As you'll see, these two systems are similar enough that there isn't much friction.

As always with Git, first we clone:

```
$ git clone hg::/tmp/hello /tmp/hello-git
$ cd /tmp/hello-git
$ git log --oneline --graph --decorate
* ac7955c (HEAD, origin/master, origin/branches/default, origin/HEAD, refs/hg/origin/branches/
default, refs/hg/origin/bookmarks/master, master) Create a makefile
* 65bb417 Create a standard "hello, world" program
```

You'll notice that working with a Mercurial repository uses the standard git clone command. That's because git-remote-hg is working at a fairly low level, using a similar mechanism to how Git's HTTP/S protocol is implemented (remote helpers). Since Git and Mercurial are both designed for every client to have a full copy of the repository history, this command makes a full clone, including all the project's history, and does it fairly quickly.

The log command shows two commits, the latest of which is pointed to by a whole slew of refs. It turns out some of these aren't actually there. Let's take a look at what's actually in the .git directory:

```
$ tree .git/refs
.git/refs
├── heads
│   └── master
├── hg
│   └── origin
│       ├── bookmarks
│       │   └── master
│       └── branches
│           └── default
├── notes
│   └── hg
├── remotes
│   └── origin
│       └── HEAD
└── tags

9 directories, 5 files
```

Git-remote-hg is trying to make things more idiomatically Git-esque, but under the hood it's managing the conceptual mapping between two slightly different systems. The refs/hg directory is where the actual remote refs are stored. For example, the refs/hg/origin/branches/default is a Git ref file that contains the SHA starting with ac7955c, which is the commit that master points to. So the refs/hg directory is kind of like a fake refs/remotes/origin, but it has the added distinction between bookmarks and branches.

The notes/hg file is the starting point for how git-remote-hg maps Git commit hashes to Mercurial changeset IDs. Let's explore a bit:

```
$ cat notes/hg
d4c10386...

$ git cat-file -p d4c10386...
tree 1781c96...
author remote-hg <> 1408066400 -0800
committer remote-hg <> 1408066400 -0800

Notes for master

$ git ls-tree 1781c96...
100644 blob ac9117f...    65bb417...
100644 blob 485e178...    ac7955c...

$ git cat-file -p ac9117f
0a04b987be5ae354b710cefeba0e2d9de7ad41a9
```

So refs/notes/hg points to a tree, which in the Git object database is a list of other objects with names. git ls-tree outputs the mode, type, object hash, and filename for items inside a tree. Once we dig down to one of the tree items, we find that inside it is a blob named ac9117f (the SHA-1 hash of the commit pointed to by master), with contents 0a04b98 (which is the ID of the Mercurial changeset at the tip of the default branch).

The good news is that we mostly don't have to worry about all of this. The typical workflow won't be very different from working with a Git remote.

There's one more thing we should attend to before we continue: ignores. Mercurial and Git use a very similar mechanism for this, but it's likely you don't want to actually commit a `.gitignore` file into a Mercurial repository. Fortunately, Git has a way to ignore files that's local to an on-disk repository, and the Mercurial format is compatible with Git, so you just have to copy it over:

```
$ cp .hgignore .git/info/exclude
```

The `.git/info/exclude` file acts just like a `.gitignore`, but isn't included in commits.

Workflow

Let's assume we've done some work and made some commits on the `master` branch, and you're ready to push it to the remote repository. Here's what our repository looks like right now:

```
$ git log --oneline --graph --decorate
* ba04a2a (HEAD, master) Update makefile
* d25d16f Goodbye
* ac7955c (origin/master, origin/branches/default, origin/HEAD, refs/hg/origin/branches/default,
refs/hg/origin/bookmarks/master) Create a makefile
* 65bb417 Create a standard "hello, world" program
```

Our `master` branch is two commits ahead of `origin/master`, but those two commits exist only on our local machine. Let's see if anyone else has been doing important work at the same time:

```
$ git fetch
From hg::/tmp/hello
   ac7955c..df85e87  master      -> origin/master
   ac7955c..df85e87  branches/default -> origin/branches/default
$ git log --oneline --graph --decorate --all
* 7b07969 (refs/notes/hg) Notes for default
* d4c1038 Notes for master
* df85e87 (origin/master, origin/branches/default, origin/HEAD, refs/hg/origin/branches/default,
refs/hg/origin/bookmarks/master) Add some documentation
| * ba04a2a (HEAD, master) Update makefile
| * d25d16f Goodbye
|/
* ac7955c Create a makefile
* 65bb417 Create a standard "hello, world" program
```

Since we used the `--all` flag, we see the "notes" refs that are used internally by `git-remote-hg`, but we can ignore them. The rest is what we expected; `origin/master` has advanced by one commit, and our history has now diverged. Unlike the other systems we work with in this chapter, Mercurial is capable of handling merges, so we're not going to do anything fancy.

```
$ git merge origin/master
Auto-merging hello.c
Merge made by the 'recursive' strategy.
 hello.c | 2 +-
 1 file changed, 1 insertion(+), 1 deletion(-)
$ git log --oneline --graph --decorate
*   0c64627 (HEAD, master) Merge remote-tracking branch 'origin/master'
```

```
|\
| * df85e87 (origin/master, origin/branches/default, origin/HEAD, refs/hg/origin/branches/default,
refs/hg/origin/bookmarks/master) Add some documentation
* | ba04a2a Update makefile
* | d25d16f Goodbye
|/
* ac7955c Create a makefile
* 65bb417 Create a standard "hello, world" program
```

Perfect. We run the tests and everything passes, so we're ready to share our work with the rest of the team:

```
$ git push
To hg::/tmp/hello
   df85e87..0c64627  master -> master
```

That's it! If you take a look at the Mercurial repository, you'll see that this did what we'd expect:

```
$ hg log -G --style compact
o    5[tip]:4,2   dc8fa4f932b8   2014-08-14 19:33 -0700   ben
|\     Merge remote-tracking branch 'origin/master'
| |
| o  4   64f27bcefc35    2014-08-14 19:27 -0700    ben
| |    Update makefile
| |
| o  3:1   4256fc29598f    2014-08-14 19:27 -0700   ben
| |    Goodbye
| |
@ |  2   7db0b4848b3c    2014-08-14 19:30 -0700    ben
|/    Add some documentation
|
o  1   82e55d328c8c   2005-08-26 01:21 -0700    mpm
|    Create a makefile
|
o  0   0a04b987be5a   2005-08-26 01:20 -0700    mpm
     Create a standard "hello, world" program
```

The changeset numbered 2 was made by Mercurial, and the changesets numbered 3 and 4 were made by git-remote-hg, by pushing commits made with Git.

Branches and Bookmarks

Git has only one kind of branch: a reference that moves when commits are made. In Mercurial, this kind of a reference is called a "bookmark," and it behaves in much the same way as a Git branch.

Mercurial's concept of a "branch" is more heavyweight. The branch that a changeset is made on is recorded with the changeset, which means it will always be in the repository history. Here's an example of a commit that was made on the develop branch:

```
$ hg log -l 1
changeset:   6:8f65e5e02793
branch:      develop
tag:         tip
```

```
user:       Ben Straub <ben@straub.cc>
date:       Thu Aug 14 20:06:38 2014 -0700
summary:    More documentation
```

Note the line that begins with "branch". Git can't really replicate this (and doesn't need to; both types of branch can be represented as a Git ref), but git-remote-hg needs to understand the difference, because Mercurial cares.

Creating Mercurial bookmarks is as easy as creating Git branches. On the Git side:

```
$ git checkout -b featureA
Switched to a new branch 'featureA'
$ git push origin featureA
To hg::/tmp/hello
 * [new branch]      featureA -> featureA
```

That's all there is to it. On the Mercurial side, it looks like this:

```
$ hg bookmarks
   featureA                  5:bd5ac26f11f9
$ hg log --style compact -G
@  6[tip]  8f65e5e02793   2014-08-14 20:06 -0700    ben
|     More documentation
|
o    5[featureA]:4,2  bd5ac26f11f9   2014-08-14 20:02 -0700     ben
|\     Merge remote-tracking branch 'origin/master'
| |
| o  4    0434aaa6b91f   2014-08-14 20:01 -0700    ben
| |    update makefile
| |
| o  3:1   318914536c86   2014-08-14 20:00 -0700    ben
| |    goodbye
| |
o |  2    f098c7f45c4f   2014-08-14 20:01 -0700    ben
|/     Add some documentation
|
o  1   82e55d328c8c   2005-08-26 01:21 -0700    mpm
|    Create a makefile
|
o  0   0a04b987be5a   2005-08-26 01:20 -0700    mpm
     Create a standard "hello, world" program
```

Note the new [featureA] tag on revision 5. These act exactly like Git branches on the Git side, with one exception: you can't delete a bookmark from the Git side (this is a limitation of remote helpers).

You can work on a "heavyweight" Mercurial branch also: just put a branch in the branches namespace:

```
$ git checkout -b branches/permanent
Switched to a new branch 'branches/permanent'
$ vi Makefile
$ git commit -am 'A permanent change'
$ git push origin branches/permanent
To hg::/tmp/hello
 * [new branch]      branches/permanent -> branches/permanent
```

Here's what that looks like on the Mercurial side:

```
$ hg branches
permanent                   7:a4529d07aad4
develop                     6:8f65e5e02793
default                     5:bd5ac26f11f9 (inactive)
$ hg log -G
o   changeset:   7:a4529d07aad4
|   branch:      permanent
|   tag:         tip
|   parent:      5:bd5ac26f11f9
|   user:        Ben Straub <ben@straub.cc>
|   date:        Thu Aug 14 20:21:09 2014 -0700
|   summary:     A permanent change
|
| @ changeset:   6:8f65e5e02793
|/  branch:      develop
|   user:        Ben Straub <ben@straub.cc>
|   date:        Thu Aug 14 20:06:38 2014 -0700
|   summary:     More documentation
|
o   changeset:   5:bd5ac26f11f9
|\  bookmark:    featureA
| | parent:      4:0434aaa6b91f
| | parent:      2:f098c7f45c4f
| | user:        Ben Straub <ben@straub.cc>
| | date:        Thu Aug 14 20:02:21 2014 -0700
| | summary:     Merge remote-tracking branch 'origin/master'
[...]
```

The branch name "permanent" was recorded with the changeset marked 7.

From the Git side, working with either of these branch styles is the same: just checkout, commit, fetch, merge, pull, and push as you normally would. One thing you should know is that Mercurial doesn't support rewriting history, only adding to it. Here's what our Mercurial repository looks like after an interactive rebase and a force-push:

```
$ hg log --style compact -G
o   10[tip]   99611176cbc9   2014-08-14 20:21 -0700   ben
|     A permanent change
|
o   9    f23e12f939c3   2014-08-14 20:01 -0700   ben
|     Add some documentation
|
o   8:1  c16971d33922   2014-08-14 20:00 -0700   ben
|     goodbye
|
| o   7:5  a4529d07aad4   2014-08-14 20:21 -0700   ben
| |     A permanent change
| |
| | @ 6    8f65e5e02793   2014-08-14 20:06 -0700   ben
| |/     More documentation
| |
| o     5[featureA]:4,2  bd5ac26f11f9   2014-08-14 20:02 -0700   ben
```

```
| |\       Merge remote-tracking branch 'origin/master'
| | |
| | o  4   0434aaa6b91f   2014-08-14 20:01 -0700    ben
| | |     update makefile
| | |
+---o  3:1  318914536c86   2014-08-14 20:00 -0700    ben
| |       goodbye
| |
| o  2   f098c7f45c4f   2014-08-14 20:01 -0700    ben
|/     Add some documentation
|
o  1   82e55d328c8c   2005-08-26 01:21 -0700    mpm
|    Create a makefile
|
o  0   0a04b987be5a   2005-08-26 01:20 -0700    mpm
     Create a standard "hello, world" program
```

Changesets 8, 9, and 10 have been created and belong to the permanent branch, but the old changesets are still there. This can be very confusing for your teammates who are using Mercurial, so try to avoid it.

Mercurial Summary

Git and Mercurial are similar enough that working across the boundary is fairly painless. If you avoid changing history that's left your machine (as is generally recommended), you may not even be aware that the other end is Mercurial.

Git and Perforce

Perforce is a very popular version-control system in corporate environments. It's been around since 1995, which makes it the oldest system covered in this chapter. As such, it's designed with the constraints of its day; it assumes you're always connected to a single central server, and only one version is kept on the local disk. To be sure, its features and constraints are well-suited to several specific problems, but there are lots of projects using Perforce where Git would actually work better.

There are two options if you'd like to mix your use of Perforce and Git. The first one we'll cover is the "Git Fusion" bridge from the makers of Perforce, which lets you expose subtrees of your Perforce depot as read-write Git repositories. The second is git-p4, a client-side bridge that lets you use Git as a Perforce client, without requiring any reconfiguration of the Perforce server.

Git Fusion

Perforce provides a product called Git Fusion (available at http://www.perforce.com/git-fusion), which synchronizes a Perforce server with Git repositories on the server side.

Setting Up

For our examples, we'll be using the easiest installation method for Git Fusion, which is downloading a virtual machine that runs the Perforce daemon and Git Fusion. You can get the virtual machine image from http://www.perforce.com/downloads/Perforce/20-User, and once it's finished downloading, import it into your favorite virtualization software (we'll use VirtualBox).

Upon first starting the machine, it asks you to customize the password for three Linux users (root, perforce, and git), and provide an instance name, which can be used to distinguish this installation from others on the same network. When that has all completed, you'll see this:

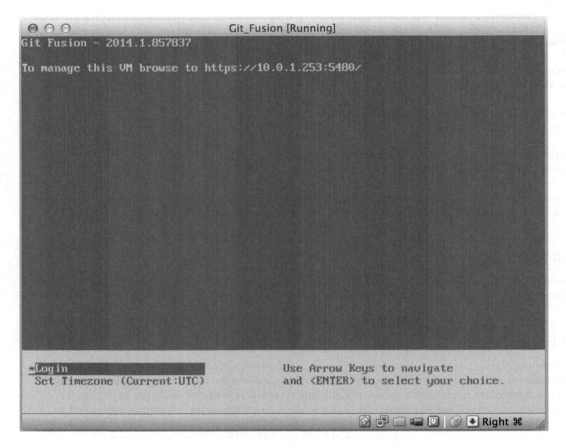

Figure 9-1. *The Git Fusion virtual machine boot screen*

You should take note of the IP address that's shown here, we'll be using it later on. Next, we'll create a Perforce user. Select the "Login" option at the bottom and press enter (or SSH to the machine), and log in as root. Then use these commands to create a user:

```
$ p4 -p localhost:1666 -u super user -f john
$ p4 -p localhost:1666 -u john passwd
$ exit
```

The first one will open a vi editor to customize the user, but you can accept the defaults by typing :wq and hitting enter. The second one will prompt you to enter a password twice. That's all we need to do with a shell prompt, so exit out of the session.

The next thing you'll need to do to follow along is to tell Git not to verify SSL certificates. The Git Fusion image comes with a certificate, but it's for a domain that won't match your virtual machine's IP address, so Git will reject the HTTPS connection. If this is going to be a permanent installation, consult the Perforce Git Fusion manual to install a different certificate; for our example purposes, this will suffice:

```
$ export GIT_SSL_NO_VERIFY=true
```

Now we can test that everything is working.

```
$ git clone https://10.0.1.254/Talkhouse
Cloning into 'Talkhouse'...
Username for 'https://10.0.1.254': john
Password for 'https://john@10.0.1.254':
remote: Counting objects: 630, done.
remote: Compressing objects: 100% (581/581), done.
remote: Total 630 (delta 172), reused 0 (delta 0)
Receiving objects: 100% (630/630), 1.22 MiB | 0 bytes/s, done.
Resolving deltas: 100% (172/172), done.
Checking connectivity... done.
```

The virtual-machine image comes equipped with a sample project that you can clone. Here we're cloning over HTTPS, with the john user that we created above; Git asks for credentials for this connection, but the credential cache will allow us to skip this step for any subsequent requests.

Fusion Configuration

Once you've got Git Fusion installed, you'll want to tweak the configuration. This is actually fairly easy to do using your favorite Perforce client; just map the //.git-fusion directory on the Perforce server into your workspace. The file structure looks like this:

```
$ tree
.
├── objects
│   ├── repos
│   │   └── [...]
│   └── trees
│       └── [...]
│
├── p4gf_config
├── repos
│   └── Talkhouse
│       └── p4gf_config
└── users
    └── p4gf_usermap

498 directories, 287 files
```

The objects directory is used internally by Git Fusion to map Perforce objects to Git and vice versa, you won't have to mess with anything in there. There's a global p4gf_config file in this directory, as well as one for each repository—these are the configuration files that determine how Git Fusion behaves. Let's take a look at the file in the root:

```
[repo-creation]
charset = utf8

[git-to-perforce]
change-owner = author
enable-git-branch-creation = yes
enable-swarm-reviews = yes
enable-git-merge-commits = yes
enable-git-submodules = yes
preflight-commit = none
ignore-author-permissions = no
read-permission-check = none
git-merge-avoidance-after-change-num = 12107

[perforce-to-git]
http-url = none
ssh-url = none

[@features]
imports = False
chunked-push = False
matrix2 = False
parallel-push = False

[authentication]
email-case-sensitivity = no
```

We won't go into the meanings of these flags here, but note that this is just an INI-formatted text file, much like Git uses for configuration. This file specifies the global options, which can then be overridden by repository-specific configuration files, like repos/Talkhouse/p4gf_config. If you open this file, you'll see a [@repo] section with some settings that are different from the global defaults. You'll also see sections that look like this:

```
[Talkhouse-master]
git-branch-name = master
view = //depot/Talkhouse/main-dev/... ...
```

This is a mapping between a Perforce branch and a Git branch. The section can be named whatever you like, so long as the name is unique. git-branch-name lets you convert a depot path that would be cumbersome under Git to a more friendly name. The view setting controls how Perforce files are mapped into the Git repository, using the standard view mapping syntax. More than one mapping can be specified, as in this example:

```
[multi-project-mapping]
git-branch-name = master
view = //depot/project1/main/... project1/...
       //depot/project2/mainline/... project2/...
```

This way, if your normal workspace mapping includes changes in the structure of the directories, you can replicate that with a Git repository.

The last file we'll discuss is users/p4gf_usermap, which maps Perforce users to Git users, and which you may not even need. When converting from a Perforce changeset to a Git commit, Git Fusion's default behavior is to look up the Perforce user, and use the email address and full name stored there for the author/committer field in Git. When converting the other way, the default is to look up the Perforce user with the email address stored in the Git commit's author field, and submit the changeset as that user (with permissions applying). In most cases, this behavior will do just fine, but consider the following mapping file:

```
john john@example.com "John Doe"
john johnny@appleseed.net "John Doe"
bob employeeX@example.com "Anon X. Mouse"
joe employeeY@example.com "Anon Y. Mouse"
```

Each line is of the format <user> <email> "<full name>", and creates a single user mapping. The first two lines map two distinct email addresses to the same Perforce user account. This is useful if you've created Git commits under several different email addresses (or change email addresses), but want them to be mapped to the same Perforce user. When creating a Git commit from a Perforce changeset, the first line matching the Perforce user is used for Git authorship information.

The last two lines mask Bob and Joe's actual names and email addresses from the Git commits that are created. This is nice if you want to open-source an internal project, but don't want to publish your employee directory to the entire world. Note that the email addresses and full names should be unique, unless you want all the Git commits to be attributed to a single fictional author.

Workflow

Perforce Git Fusion is a two-way bridge between Perforce and Git version control. Let's have a look at how it feels to work from the Git side. We'll assume we've mapped in the "Jam" project using a configuration file as shown previously, which we can clone like this:

```
$ git clone https://10.0.1.254/Jam
Cloning into 'Jam'...
Username for 'https://10.0.1.254': john
Password for 'https://ben@10.0.1.254':
remote: Counting objects: 2070, done.
remote: Compressing objects: 100% (1704/1704), done.
Receiving objects: 100% (2070/2070), 1.21 MiB | 0 bytes/s, done.
remote: Total 2070 (delta 1242), reused 0 (delta 0)
Resolving deltas: 100% (1242/1242), done.
Checking connectivity... done.
$ git branch -a
* master
  remotes/origin/HEAD -> origin/master
  remotes/origin/master
  remotes/origin/rel2.1
$ git log --oneline --decorate --graph --all
* 0a38c33 (origin/rel2.1) Create Jam 2.1 release branch.
| * d254865 (HEAD, origin/master, origin/HEAD, master) Upgrade to latest metrowerks on Beos -- the
Intel one.
| * bd2f54a Put in fix for jam's NT handle leak.
| * c0f29e7 Fix URL in a jam doc
| * cc644ac Radstone's lynx port.
[...]
```

The first time you do this, it may take some time. What's happening is that Git Fusion is converting all the applicable changesets in the Perforce history into Git commits. This happens locally on the server, so it's relatively fast, but if you have a lot of history, it can still take some time. Subsequent fetches do incremental conversion, so it'll feel more like Git's native speed.

As you can see, our repository looks exactly like any other Git repository you might work with. There are three branches, and Git has helpfully created a local master branch that tracks origin/master. Let's do a bit of work, and create a couple of new commits:

```
# ...
$ git log --oneline --decorate --graph --all
* cfd46ab (HEAD, master) Add documentation for new feature
* a730d77 Whitespace
* d254865 (origin/master, origin/HEAD) Upgrade to latest metrowerks on Beos -- the Intel one.
* bd2f54a Put in fix for jam's NT handle leak.
[...]
```

We have two new commits. Now let's check if anyone else has been working:

```
$ git fetch
remote: Counting objects: 5, done.
remote: Compressing objects: 100% (3/3), done.
remote: Total 3 (delta 2), reused 0 (delta 0)
Unpacking objects: 100% (3/3), done.
From https://10.0.1.254/Jam
   d254865..6afeb15  master     -> origin/master
$ git log --oneline --decorate --graph --all
* 6afeb15 (origin/master, origin/HEAD) Update copyright
| * cfd46ab (HEAD, master) Add documentation for new feature
| * a730d77 Whitespace
|/
* d254865 Upgrade to latest metrowerks on Beos -- the Intel one.
* bd2f54a Put in fix for jam's NT handle leak.
[...]
```

It looks like someone was! You wouldn't know it from this view, but the 6afeb15 commit was actually created using a Perforce client. It just looks like another commit from Git's point of view, which is exactly the point. Let's see how the Perforce server deals with a merge commit:

```
$ git merge origin/master
Auto-merging README
Merge made by the 'recursive' strategy.
 README | 2 +-
 1 file changed, 1 insertion(+), 1 deletion(-)
$ git push
Counting objects: 9, done.
Delta compression using up to 8 threads.
Compressing objects: 100% (9/9), done.
Writing objects: 100% (9/9), 917 bytes | 0 bytes/s, done.
Total 9 (delta 6), reused 0 (delta 0)
remote: Perforce: 100% (3/3) Loading commit tree into memory...
remote: Perforce: 100% (5/5) Finding child commits...
remote: Perforce: Running git fast-export...
```

```
remote: Perforce: 100% (3/3) Checking commits...
remote: Processing will continue even if connection is closed.
remote: Perforce: 100% (3/3) Copying changelists...
remote: Perforce: Submitting new Git commit objects to Perforce: 4
To https://10.0.1.254/Jam
   6afeb15..89cba2b  master -> master
```

Git thinks it worked. Let's take a look at the history of the README file from Perforce's point of view, using the revision graph feature of p4v:

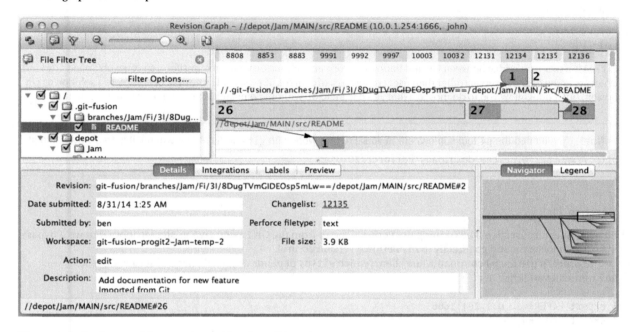

Figure 9-2. *Perforce revision graph resulting from Git push*

If you've never seen this view before, it may seem confusing, but it shows the same concepts as a graphical viewer for Git history. We're looking at the history of the README file, so the directory tree at top left only shows that file as it surfaces in various branches. At top right, we have a visual graph of how different revisions of the file are related, and the big-picture view of this graph is at bottom right. The rest of the view is given to the details view for the selected revision (2 in this case).

One thing to notice is that the graph looks exactly like the one in Git's history. Perforce didn't have a named branch to store the 1 and 2 commits, so it made an "anonymous" branch in the .git-fusion directory to hold it. This will also happen for named Git branches that don't correspond to a named Perforce branch (and you can later map them to a Perforce branch using the configuration file).

Most of this happens behind the scenes, but the end result is that one person on a team can be using Git, another can be using Perforce, and neither of them will know about the other's choice.

Git-Fusion Summary

If you have (or can get) access to your Perforce server, Git Fusion is a great way to make Git and Perforce talk to each other. There's a bit of configuration involved, but the learning curve isn't very steep. This is one of the few sections in this chapter where cautions about using Git's full power will not appear. That's not to say that Perforce will be happy with everything you throw at it—if you try to rewrite history that's already been pushed, Git Fusion will reject it—but Git Fusion tries very hard to feel native. You can even use Git submodules (though they'll look strange to Perforce users), and merge branches (this will be recorded as an integration on the Perforce side).

If you can't convince the administrator of your server to set up Git Fusion, there is still a way to use these tools together.

Git-p4

Git-p4 is a two-way bridge between Git and Perforce. It runs entirely inside your Git repository, so you won't need any kind of access to the Perforce server (other than user credentials, of course). Git-p4 isn't as flexible or complete a solution as Git Fusion, but it does allow you to do most of what you'd want to do without being invasive to the server environment.

■ **Note** You'll need the p4 tool somewhere in your PATH to work with git-p4. As of this writing, it is freely available at http://www.perforce.com/downloads/Perforce/20-User.

Setting Up

For example purposes, we'll be running the Perforce server from the Git Fusion OVA as shown above, but we'll bypass the Git Fusion server and go directly to the Perforce version control.

In order to use the p4 command-line client (which git-p4 depends on), you'll need to set a couple of environment variables:

```
$ export P4PORT=10.0.1.254:1666
$ export P4USER=john
```

Getting Started

As with anything in Git, the first command is to clone:

```
$ git p4 clone //depot/www/live www-shallow
Importing from //depot/www/live into www-shallow
Initialized empty Git repository in /private/tmp/www-shallow/.git/
Doing initial import of //depot/www/live/ from revision #head into refs/remotes/p4/master
```

This creates what in Git terms is a "shallow" clone; only the very latest Perforce revision is imported into Git; remember, Perforce isn't designed to give every revision to every user. This is enough to use Git as a Perforce client, but for other purposes it's not enough.

Once it's finished, we have a fully-functional Git repository:

```
$ cd myproject
$ git log --oneline --all --graph --decorate
* 70eaf78 (HEAD, p4/master, p4/HEAD, master) Initial import of //depot/www/live/ from the state at
revision #head
```

Note how there's a "p4" remote for the Perforce server, but everything else looks like a standard clone. Actually, that's a bit misleading; there isn't actually a remote there.

```
$ git remote -v
```

No remotes exist in this repository at all. Git-p4 has created some refs to represent the state of the server, and they look like remote refs to git log, but they're not managed by Git itself, and you can't push to them.

Workflow

Okay, let's do some work. Let's assume you've made some progress on a very important feature, and you're ready to show it to the rest of your team.

```
$ git log --oneline --all --graph --decorate
* 018467c (HEAD, master) Change page title
* c0fb617 Update link
* 70eaf78 (p4/master, p4/HEAD) Initial import of //depot/www/live/ from the state at revision #head
```

We've made two new commits that we're ready to submit to the Perforce server. Let's check if anyone else was working today:

```
$ git p4 sync
git p4 sync
Performing incremental import into refs/remotes/p4/master git branch
Depot paths: //depot/www/live/
Import destination: refs/remotes/p4/master
Importing revision 12142 (100%)
$ git log --oneline --all --graph --decorate
* 75cd059 (p4/master, p4/HEAD) Update copyright
| * 018467c (HEAD, master) Change page title
| * c0fb617 Update link
|/
* 70eaf78 Initial import of //depot/www/live/ from the state at revision #head
```

Looks like they were, and master and p4/master have diverged. Perforce's branching system is nothing like Git's, so submitting merge commits doesn't make any sense. Git-p4 recommends that you rebase your commits, and even comes with a shortcut to do so:

```
$ git p4 rebase
Performing incremental import into refs/remotes/p4/master git branch
Depot paths: //depot/www/live/
No changes to import!
Rebasing the current branch onto remotes/p4/master
First, rewinding head to replay your work on top of it...
Applying: Update link
Applying: Change page title
 index.html | 2 +-
 1 file changed, 1 insertion(+), 1 deletion(-)
```

You can probably tell from the output, but git p4 rebase is a shortcut for git p4 sync followed by git rebase p4/master. It's a bit smarter than that, especially when working with multiple branches, but this is a good approximation.

Now our history is linear again, and we're ready to contribute our changes back to Perforce. The `git p4 submit` command will try to create a new Perforce revision for every Git commit between p4/master and master. Running it drops us into our favorite editor, and the contents of the file look something like this:

```
# A Perforce Change Specification.
#
# Change:      The change number. 'new' on a new changelist.
# Date:        The date this specification was last modified.
# Client:      The client on which the changelist was created. Read-only.
# User:        The user who created the changelist.
# Status:      Either 'pending' or 'submitted'. Read-only.
# Type:        Either 'public' or 'restricted'. Default is 'public'.
# Description: Comments about the changelist. Required.
# Jobs:        What opened jobs are to be closed by this changelist.
#              You may delete jobs from this list. (New changelists only.)
# Files:       What opened files from the default changelist are to be added
#              to this changelist. You may delete files from this list.
#              (New changelists only.)

Change: new

Client: john_bens-mbp_8487

User: john

Status: new

Description:
    Update link

Files:
    //depot/www/live/index.html    # edit

######## git author ben@straub.cc does not match your p4 account.
######## Use option --preserve-user to modify authorship.
######## Variable git-p4.skipUserNameCheck hides this message.
######## everything below this line is just the diff #######
--- //depot/www/live/index.html  2014-08-31 18:26:05.000000000 0000
+++ /Users/ben/john_bens-mbp_8487/john_bens-mbp_8487/depot/www/live/index.html 2014-08-31
18:26:05.000000000 0000
@@ -60,7 +60,7 @@
 </td>
 <td valign=top>
 Source and documentation for
-<a href="http://www.perforce.com/jam/jam.html">
+<a href="jam.html">
 Jam/MR</a>,
 a software build tool.
 </td>
```

This is mostly the same content you'd see by running p4 submit, except the stuff at the end which git-p4 has helpfully included. Git-p4 tries to honor your Git and Perforce settings individually when it has to provide a name for a commit or changeset, but in some cases you want to override it. For example, if the Git commit you're importing was written by a contributor who doesn't have a Perforce user account, you may still want the resulting changeset to look like they write it (and not you).

Git-p4 has helpfully imported the message from the Git commit as the content for this Perforce changeset, so all we have to do is save and quit, twice (once for each commit). The resulting shell output will look something like this:

```
$ git p4 submit
Perforce checkout for depot path //depot/www/live/ located at /Users/ben/john_bens-mbp_8487/
john_bens-mbp_8487/depot/www/live/
Synchronizing p4 checkout...
... - file(s) up-to-date.
Applying dbac45b Update link
//depot/www/live/index.html#4 - opened for edit
Change 12143 created with 1 open file(s).
Submitting change 12143.
Locking 1 files ...
edit //depot/www/live/index.html#5
Change 12143 submitted.
Applying 905ec6a Change page title
//depot/www/live/index.html#5 - opened for edit
Change 12144 created with 1 open file(s).
Submitting change 12144.
Locking 1 files ...
edit //depot/www/live/index.html#6
Change 12144 submitted.
All commits applied!
Performing incremental import into refs/remotes/p4/master git branch
Depot paths: //depot/www/live/
Import destination: refs/remotes/p4/master
Importing revision 12144 (100%)
Rebasing the current branch onto remotes/p4/master
First, rewinding head to replay your work on top of it...
$ git log --oneline --all --graph --decorate
* 775a46f (HEAD, p4/master, p4/HEAD, master) Change page title
* 05f1ade Update link
* 75cd059 Update copyright
* 70eaf78 Initial import of //depot/www/live/ from the state at revision #head
```

The result is as though we just did a git push, which is the closest analogy to what actually did happen.

Note that during this process every Git commit is turned into a Perforce changeset; if you want to squash them down into a single changeset, you can do that with an interactive rebase before running git p4 submit. Also note that the SHA hashes of all the commits that were submitted as changesets have changed; this is because git-p4 adds a line to the end of each commit it converts:

```
$ git log -1
commit 775a46f630d8b46535fc9983cf3ebe6b9aa53145
Author: John Doe <john@example.com>
Date:   Sun Aug 31 10:31:44 2014 -0800
```

```
    Change page title

    [git-p4: depot-paths = "//depot/www/live/": change = 12144]
```

What happens if you try to submit a merge commit? Let's give it a try. Here's the situation we've gotten ourselves into:

```
$ git log --oneline --all --graph --decorate
* 3be6fd8 (HEAD, master) Correct email address
*   1dcbf21 Merge remote-tracking branch 'p4/master'
|\
| * c4689fc (p4/master, p4/HEAD) Grammar fix
* | cbacd0a Table borders: yes please
* | b4959b6 Trademark
|/
* 775a46f Change page title
* 05f1ade Update link
* 75cd059 Update copyright
* 70eaf78 Initial import of //depot/www/live/ from the state at revision #head
```

The Git and Perforce history diverge after 775a46f. The Git side has two commits, then a merge commit with the Perforce head, then another commit. We're going to try to submit these on top of a single changeset on the Perforce side. Let's see what would happen if we tried to submit now:

```
$ git p4 submit -n
Perforce checkout for depot path //depot/www/live/ located at /Users/ben/john_bens-mbp_8487/
john_bens-mbp_8487/depot/www/live/
Would synchronize p4 checkout in /Users/ben/john_bens-mbp_8487/john_bens-mbp_8487/depot/www/live/
Would apply
  b4959b6 Trademark
  cbacd0a Table borders: yes please
  3be6fd8 Correct email address
```

The -n flag is short for --dry-run, which tries to report what would happen if the submit command were run for real. In this case, it looks like we'd be creating three Perforce changesets, which correspond to the three non-merge commits that don't yet exist on the Perforce server. That sounds like exactly what we want, let's see how it turns out:

```
$ git p4 submit
[...]
$ git log --oneline --all --graph --decorate
* dadbd89 (HEAD, p4/master, p4/HEAD, master) Correct email address
* 1b79a80 Table borders: yes please
* 0097235 Trademark
* c4689fc Grammar fix
* 775a46f Change page title
* 05f1ade Update link
* 75cd059 Update copyright
* 70eaf78 Initial import of //depot/www/live/ from the state at revision #head
```

Our history became linear, just as though we had rebased before submitting (which is in fact exactly what happened). This means you can be free to create, work on, throw away, and merge branches on the Git side without fear that your history will somehow become incompatible with Perforce. If you can rebase it, you can contribute it to a Perforce server.

Branching

If your Perforce project has multiple branches, you're not out of luck; `git-p4` can handle that in a way that makes it feel like Git. Let's say your Perforce depot is laid out like this:

```
//depot
  └── project
        ├── main
        └── dev
```

And let's say you have a dev branch, which has a view spec that looks like this:

```
//depot/project/main/... //depot/project/dev/...
```

Git-p4 can automatically detect that situation and do the right thing:

```
$ git p4 clone --detect-branches //depot/project@all
Importing from //depot/project@all into project
Initialized empty Git repository in /private/tmp/project/.git/
Importing revision 20 (50%)
    Importing new branch project/dev

    Resuming with change 20
Importing revision 22 (100%)
Updated branches: main dev
$ cd project; git log --oneline --all --graph --decorate
* eae77ae (HEAD, p4/master, p4/HEAD, master) main
| * 10d55fb (p4/project/dev) dev
| * a43cfae Populate //depot/project/main/... //depot/project/dev/....
|/
* 2b83451 Project init
```

Note the `@all` specifier in the depot path; that tells `git-p4` to clone not just the latest changeset for that subtree, but all changesets that have ever touched those paths. This is closer to Git's concept of a clone, but if you're working on a project with a long history, it could take a while.

The `--detect-branches` flag tells `git-p4` to use Perforce's branch specs to map the branches to Git refs. If these mappings aren't present on the Perforce server (which is a perfectly valid way to use Perforce), you can tell `git-p4` what the branch mappings are, and you get the same result:

```
$ git init project
Initialized empty Git repository in /tmp/project/.git/
$ cd project
$ git config git-p4.branchList main:dev
$ git clone --detect-branches //depot/project@all.
```

Setting the `git-p4.branchList` configuration variable to `main:dev` tells `git-p4` that "main" and "dev" are both branches, and the second one is a child of the first one.

If we now `git checkout -b dev p4/project/dev` and make some commits, `git-p4` is smart enough to target the right branch when we do `git p4 submit`. Unfortunately, `git-p4` can't mix shallow clones and multiple branches; if you have a huge project and want to work on more than one branch, you'll have to `git p4 clone` once for each branch you want to submit to.

For creating or integrating branches, you'll have to use a Perforce client. Git-p4 can only sync and submit to existing branches, and it can only do it one linear changeset at a time. If you merge two branches in Git and try to submit the new changeset, all that will be recorded is a bunch of file changes; the metadata about which branches are involved in the integration will be lost.

Git and Perforce Summary

Git-p4 makes it possible to use a Git workflow with a Perforce server, and it's pretty good at it. However, it's important to remember that Perforce is in charge of the source, and you're only using Git to work locally. Just be really careful about sharing Git commits; if you have a remote that other people use, don't push any commits that haven't already been submitted to the Perforce server.

If you want to freely mix the use of Perforce and Git as clients for source control, and you can convince the server administrator to install it, Git Fusion makes using Git a first-class version-control client for a Perforce server.

Git and TFS

Git is becoming popular with Windows developers, and if you're writing code on Windows, there's a good chance you're using Microsoft's Team Foundation Server (TFS). TFS is a collaboration suite that includes defect and work-item tracking, process support for Scrum and others, code review, and version control. There's a bit of confusion ahead: TFS is the server, which supports controlling source code using both Git and their own custom VCS, which they've dubbed TFVC (Team Foundation Version Control). Git support is a somewhat new feature for TFS (shipping with the 2013 version), so all the tools that predate that refer to the version-control portion as "TFS," even though they're mostly working with TFVC.

If you find yourself on a team that's using TFVC but you'd rather use Git as your version-control client, there's a project for you.

Which Tool?

In fact, there are two: git-tf and git-tfs.

Git-tfs (found at http://git-tfs.com) is a .NET project, and (as of this writing) it only runs on Windows. To work with Git repositories, it uses the .NET bindings for libgit2, a library-oriented implementation of Git that is highly performant and allows a lot of flexibility with the guts of a Git repository. Libgit2 is not a complete implementation of Git, so to cover the difference git-tfs will actually call the command-line Git client for some operations, so there are no artificial limits on what it can do with Git repositories. Its support of TFVC features is very mature, since it uses the Visual Studio assemblies for operations with servers (however, this means you need a version of Visual Studio installed that includes access to TFVC; as of this writing, none of the free-of-charge versions of Visual Studio can connect with a TFS server).

Git-tf (whose home is at https://gittf.codeplex.com) is a Java project, and as such runs on any computer with a Java runtime environment. It interfaces with Git repositories through JGit (a JVM implementation of Git), which means it has virtually no limitations in terms of Git functions. However, its support for TFVC is limited as compared to git-tfs—it does not support branches, for instance.

So each tool has pros and cons, and there are plenty of situations that favor one over the other. We'll cover the basic usage of both of them in this book.

■ **Note** You'll need access to a TFVC-based repository to follow along with these instructions. These aren't as plentiful in the wild as Git or Subversion repositories, so you may need to create one of your own. Codeplex (https://www.codeplex.com) or Visual Studio Online (http://www.visualstudio.com) are both good choices for this.

Getting Started: git-tf

The first thing you do, just as with any Git project, is clone. Here's what that looks like with `git-tf`:

```
$ git tf clone https://tfs.codeplex.com:443/tfs/TFS13 $/myproject/Main project_git
```

The first argument is the URL of a TFVC collection, the second is of the form $/project/branch, and the third is the path to the local Git repository that is to be created (this last one is optional). Git-tf can only work with one branch at a time; if you want to make checkins on a different TFVC branch, you'll have to make a new clone from that branch.

This creates a fully functional Git repository:

```
$ cd project_git
$ git log --all --oneline --decorate
512e75a (HEAD, tag: TFS_C35190, origin_tfs/tfs, master) Checkin message
```

This is called a shallow clone, meaning that only the latest changeset has been downloaded. TFVC isn't designed for each client to have a full copy of the history, so `git-tf` defaults to only getting the latest version, which is much faster.

If you have some time, it's probably worth it to clone the entire project history, using the `--deep` option:

```
$ git tf clone https://tfs.codeplex.com:443/tfs/TFS13 $/myproject/Main \
  project_git --deep
Username: domain\user
Password:
Connecting to TFS...
Cloning $/myproject into /tmp/project_git: 100%, done.
Cloned 4 changesets. Cloned last changeset 35190 as d44b17a
$ cd project_git
$ git log --all --oneline --decorate
d44b17a (HEAD, tag: TFS_C35190, origin_tfs/tfs, master) Goodbye
126aa7b (tag: TFS_C35189)
8f77431 (tag: TFS_C35178) FIRST
0745a25 (tag: TFS_C35177) Created team project folder $/tfvctest via the \
        Team Project Creation Wizard
```

Notice the tags with names such as TFS_C35189; this is a feature that helps you know which Git commits are associated with TFVC changesets. This is a nice way to represent it, because you can see with a simple log command which of your commits is associated with a snapshot that also exists in TFVC. They aren't necessary (and in fact you can turn them off with `git config git-tf.tag false`)—git-tf keeps the real commit-changeset mappings in the .git/git-tf file.

Getting Started: git-tfs

Git-tfs cloning behaves a bit differently. Observe:

```
PS> git tfs clone --with-branches \
    https://username.visualstudio.com/DefaultCollection \
    $/project/Trunk project_git
Initialized empty Git repository in C:/Users/ben/project_git/.git/
C15 = b75da1aba1ffb359d00e85c52acb261e4586b0c9
```

```
C16 = c403405f4989d73a2c3c119e79021cb2104ce44a
Tfs branches found:
- $/tfvc-test/featureA
The name of the local branch will be : featureA
C17 = d202b53f67bde32171d5078968c644e562f1c439
C18 = 44cd729d8df868a8be20438fdeeefb961958b674
```

Notice the --with-branches flag. Git-tfs is capable of mapping TFVC branches to Git branches, and this flag tells it to set up a local Git branch for every TFVC branch. This is highly recommended if you've ever branched or merged in TFS, but it won't work with a server older than TFS 2010—before that release, "branches" were just folders, so git-tfs can't tell them from regular folders.

Let's take a look at the resulting Git repository:

```
PS> git log --oneline --graph --decorate --all
* 44cd729 (tfs/featureA, featureA) Goodbye
* d202b53 Branched from $/tfvc-test/Trunk
* c403405 (HEAD, tfs/default, master) Hello
* b75da1a New project
PS> git log -1
commit c403405f4989d73a2c3c119e79021cb2104ce44a
Author: Ben Straub <ben@straub.cc>
Date:   Fri Aug 1 03:41:59 2014 +0000

    Hello

    git-tfs-id: [https://username.visualstudio.com/DefaultCollection]$/myproject/Trunk;C16
```

There are two local branches, master and featureA, which represent the initial starting point of the clone (Trunk in TFVC) and a child branch (featureA in TFVC). You can also see that the tfs "remote" has a couple of refs too: default and featureA, which represent TFVC branches. Git-tfs maps the branch you cloned from to tfs/default, and others get their own names.

Another thing to notice is the git-tfs-id: lines in the commit messages. Instead of tags, git-tfs uses these markers to relate TFVC changesets to Git commits. This has the implication that your Git commits may have a different SHA-1 hash before and after they have been pushed to TFVC.

Git-tf[s] Workflow

■ **Note** Regardless of which tool you're using, you should set a couple of Git configuration values to avoid running into issues.

```
$ git config set --local core.ignorecase=true
$ git config set --local core.autocrlf=false
```

The obvious next thing you're going to want to do is work on the project. TFVC and TFS have several features that may add complexity to your workflow:

1. Feature branches that aren't represented in TFVC add a bit of complexity. This has to do with the very different ways that TFVC and Git represent branches.

2. Be aware that TFVC allows users to "checkout" files from the server, locking them so nobody else can edit them. This obviously won't stop you from editing them in your local repository, but it could get in the way when it comes time to push your changes up to the TFVC server.

3. TFS has the concept of "gated" checkins, where a TFS build-test cycle has to complete successfully before the checkin is allowed. This uses the "shelve" function in TFVC, which we don't cover in detail here. You can fake this in a manual fashion with `git-tf`, and `git-tfs` provides the `checkintool` command which is gate-aware.

In the interest of brevity, what we'll cover here is the happy path, which sidesteps or avoids most of these issues.

Workflow: git-tf

Let's say you've done some work, made a couple of Git commits on `master`, and you're ready to share your progress on the TFVC server. Here's our Git repository:

```
$ git log --oneline --graph --decorate --all
* 4178a82 (HEAD, master) update code
* 9df2ae3 update readme
* d44b17a (tag: TFS_C35190, origin_tfs/tfs) Goodbye
* 126aa7b (tag: TFS_C35189)
* 8f77431 (tag: TFS_C35178) FIRST
* 0745a25 (tag: TFS_C35177) Created team project folder $/tfvctest via the \
        Team Project Creation Wizard
```

We want to take the snapshot that's in the 4178a82 commit and push it up to the TFVC server. First things first: let's see if any of our teammates did anything since we last connected:

```
$ git tf fetch
Username: domain\user
Password:
Connecting to TFS...
Fetching $/myproject at latest changeset: 100%, done.
Downloaded changeset 35320 as commit 8ef06a8. Updated FETCH_HEAD.
$ git log --oneline --graph --decorate --all
* 8ef06a8 (tag: TFS_C35320, origin_tfs/tfs) just some text
| * 4178a82 (HEAD, master) update code
| * 9df2ae3 update readme
|/
* d44b17a (tag: TFS_C35190) Goodbye
* 126aa7b (tag: TFS_C35189)
* 8f77431 (tag: TFS_C35178) FIRST
* 0745a25 (tag: TFS_C35177) Created team project folder $/tfvctest via the \
        Team Project Creation Wizard
```

Looks like someone else is working, too, and now we have divergent history. This is where Git shines, but we have two choices of how to proceed:

1. Making a merge commit feels natural as a Git user (after all, that's what git pull does), and git-tf can do this for you with a simple git tf pull. Be aware, however, that TFVC doesn't think this way, and if you push merge commits your history will start to look different on both sides, which can be confusing. However, if you plan on submitting all of your changes as one changeset, this is probably the easiest choice.

2. Rebasing makes our commit history linear, which means we have the option of converting each of our Git commits into a TFVC changeset. Because this leaves the most options open, we recommend you do it this way; git-tf even makes it easy for you with git tf pull --rebase.

The choice is yours. For this example, we'll be rebasing:

```
$ git rebase FETCH_HEAD
First, rewinding head to replay your work on top of it...
Applying: update readme
Applying: update code
$ git log --oneline --graph --decorate --all
* 5a0e25e (HEAD, master) update code
* 6eb3eb5 update readme
* 8ef06a8 (tag: TFS_C35320, origin_tfs/tfs) just some text
* d44b17a (tag: TFS_C35190) Goodbye
* 126aa7b (tag: TFS_C35189)
* 8f77431 (tag: TFS_C35178) FIRST
* 0745a25 (tag: TFS_C35177) Created team project folder $/tfvctest via the \
          Team Project Creation Wizard
```

Now we're ready to make a checkin to the TFVC server. Git-tf gives you the choice of making a single changeset that represents all the changes since the last one (--shallow, which is the default) and creating a new changeset for each Git commit (--deep). For this example, we'll just create one changeset:

```
$ git tf checkin -m 'Updating readme and code'
Username: domain\user
Password:
Connecting to TFS...
Checking in to $/myproject: 100%, done.
Checked commit 5a0e25e in as changeset 35348
$ git log --oneline --graph --decorate --all
* 5a0e25e (HEAD, tag: TFS_C35348, origin_tfs/tfs, master) update code
* 6eb3eb5 update readme
* 8ef06a8 (tag: TFS_C35320) just some text
* d44b17a (tag: TFS_C35190) Goodbye
* 126aa7b (tag: TFS_C35189)
* 8f77431 (tag: TFS_C35178) FIRST
* 0745a25 (tag: TFS_C35177) Created team project folder $/tfvctest via the \
          Team Project Creation Wizard
```

There's a new TFS_C35348 tag, indicating that TFVC is storing the exact same snapshot as the 5a0e25e commit. It's important to note that not every Git commit needs to have an exact counterpart in TFVC; the 6eb3eb5 commit, for example, doesn't exist anywhere on the server.

That's the main workflow. There are a couple other considerations you'll want to keep in mind:

1. There is no branching. `Git-tf` can only create Git repositories from one TFVC branch at a time.

2. Collaborate using either TFVC or Git, but not both. Different `git-tf` clones of the same TFVC repository may have different commit SHA hashes, which will cause no end of headaches.

3. If your team's workflow includes collaborating in Git and syncing periodically with TFVC, only connect to TFVC with one of the Git repositories.

Workflow: git-tfs

Let's walk through the same scenario using `git-tfs`. Here are the new commits we've made to the master branch in our Git repository:

```
PS> git log --oneline --graph --all --decorate
* c3bd3ae (HEAD, master) update code
* d85e5a2 update readme
| * 44cd729 (tfs/featureA, featureA) Goodbye
| * d202b53 Branched from $/tfvc-test/Trunk
|/
* c403405 (tfs/default) Hello
* b75da1a New project
```

Now let's see if anyone else has done work while we were hacking away:

```
PS> git tfs fetch
C19 = aea74a0313de0a391940c999e51c5c15c381d91d
PS> git log --all --oneline --graph --decorate
* aea74a0 (tfs/default) update documentation
| * c3bd3ae (HEAD, master) update code
| * d85e5a2 update readme
|/
| * 44cd729 (tfs/featureA, featureA) Goodbye
| * d202b53 Branched from $/tfvc-test/Trunk
|/
* c403405 Hello
* b75da1a New project
```

Yes, it turns out our coworker has added a new TFVC changeset, which shows up as the new aea74a0 commit, and the tfs/default remote branch has moved.

As with git-tf, we have two fundamental options for how to resolve this divergent history:

1. Rebase to preserve a linear history.

2. Merge to preserve what actually happened.

In this case, we're going to do a "deep" checkin, where every Git commit becomes a TFVC changeset, so we want to rebase.

```
PS> git rebase tfs/default
First, rewinding head to replay your work on top of it...
Applying: update readme
Applying: update code
PS> git log --all --oneline --graph --decorate
* 10a75ac (HEAD, master) update code
* 5cec4ab update readme
* aea74a0 (tfs/default) update documentation
| * 44cd729 (tfs/featureA, featureA) Goodbye
| * d202b53 Branched from $/tfvc-test/Trunk
|/
* c403405 Hello
* b75da1a New project
```

Now we're ready to complete our contribution by checking in our code to the TFVC server. We'll use the rcheckin command here to create a TFVC changeset for each Git commit in the path from HEAD to the first tfs remote branch found (the checkin command would only create one changeset, sort of like squashing Git commits).

```
PS> git tfs rcheckin
Working with tfs remote: default
Fetching changes from TFS to minimize possibility of late conflict...
Starting checkin of 5cec4ab4 'update readme'
 add README.md
C20 = 71a5ddce274c19f8fdc322b4f165d93d89121017
Done with 5cec4ab4b213c354341f66c80cd650ab98dcf1ed, rebasing tail onto new TFS-commit...
Rebase done successfully.
Starting checkin of b1bf0f99 'update code'
 edit .git\tfs\default\workspace\ConsoleApplication1/ConsoleApplication1/Program.cs
C21 = ff04e7c35dfbe6a8f94e782bf5e0031cee8d103b
Done with b1bf0f9977b2d48bad611ed4a03d3738df05ea5d, rebasing tail onto new TFS-commit...
Rebase done successfully.
No more to rcheckin.
PS> git log --all --oneline --graph --decorate
* ff04e7c (HEAD, tfs/default, master) update code
* 71a5ddc update readme
* aea74a0 update documentation
| * 44cd729 (tfs/featureA, featureA) Goodbye
| * d202b53 Branched from $/tfvc-test/Trunk
|/
* c403405 Hello
* b75da1a New project
```

Notice how after every successful checkin to the TFVC server, git-tfs is rebasing the remaining work onto what it just did. That's because it's adding the git-tfs-id field to the bottom of the commit messages, which changes the SHA-1 hashes. This is exactly as designed, and there's nothing to worry about, but you should be aware that it's happening, especially if you're sharing Git commits with others.

TFS has many features that integrate with its version control system, such as work items, designated reviewers, gated checkins, and so on. It can be cumbersome to work with these features using only a command-line tool, but fortunately git-tfs lets you launch a graphical checkin tool very easily:

```
PS> git tfs checkintool
PS> git tfs ct
```

It looks a bit like this:

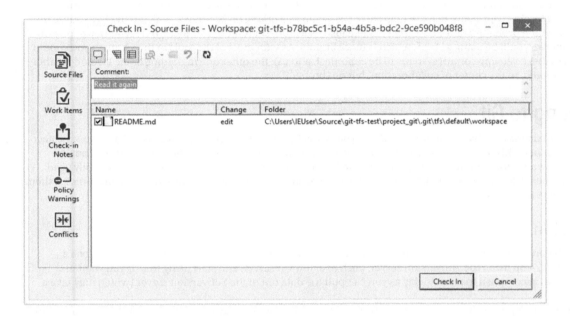

Figure 9-3. *The git-tfs checkin tool*

This will look familiar to TFS users, as it's the same dialog that's launched from within Visual Studio. Git-tfs also lets you control TFVC branches from your Git repository. As an example, let's create one:

```
PS> git tfs branch $/tfvc-test/featureBee
The name of the local branch will be : featureBee
C26 = 1d54865c397608c004a2cadce7296f5edc22a7e5
PS> git lga
* 1d54865 (tfs/featureBee) Creation branch $/myproject/featureBee
* ff04e7c (HEAD, tfs/default, master) update code
* 71a5ddc update readme
* aea74a0 update documentation
| * 44cd729 (tfs/featureA, featureA) Goodbye
| * d202b53 Branched from $/tfvc-test/Trunk
|/
* c403405 Hello
* b75da1a New project
```

Creating a branch in TFVC means adding a changeset where that branch now exists, and this is projected as a Git commit. Note also that git-tfs created the tfs/featureBee remote branch, but HEAD is still pointing to master. If you want to work on the newly-minted branch, you'll want to base your new commits on the 1d54865 commit, perhaps by creating a topic branch from that commit.

Git and TFS Summary

Git-tf and Git-tfs are both great tools for interfacing with a TFVC server. They allow you to use the power of Git locally, avoid constantly having to round-trip to the central TFVC server, and make your life as a developer much easier, without forcing your entire team to migrate to Git. If you're working on Windows (which is likely if your team is using TFS), you'll probably want to use git-tfs because its feature set is more complete, but if you're working on another platform, you'll be using git-tf, which is more limited. As with most of the tools in this chapter, you should choose one of these version-control systems to be canonical, and use the other one in a subordinate fashion—either Git or TFVC should be the center of collaboration, but not both.

Migrating to Git

If you have an existing codebase in another VCS but you've decided to start using Git, you must migrate your project one way or another. This section goes over some importers for common systems, and then demonstrates how to develop your own custom importer. You'll learn how to import data from several of the bigger professionally used SCM systems, because they make up the majority of users who are switching, and because high-quality tools for them are easy to come by.

Subversion

If you read the previous section about using git svn, you can easily use those instructions to git svn clone a repository; then, stop using the Subversion server, push to a new Git server, and start using that. If you want the history, you can accomplish that as quickly as you can pull the data out of the Subversion server (which may take a while).

However, the import isn't perfect; and because it will take so long, you may as well do it right. The first problem is the author information. In Subversion, each person committing has a user on the system who is recorded in the commit information. The examples in the previous section show schacon in some places, such as the blame output and the git svn log. If you want to map this to better Git author data, you need a mapping from the Subversion users to the Git authors. Create a file called users.txt that has this mapping in a format like this:

```
schacon = Scott Chacon <schacon@geemail.com>
selse = Someo Nelse <selse@geemail.com>
```

To get a list of the author names that SVN uses, you can run this:

```
$ svn log --xml | grep author | sort -u | \
  perl -pe 's/.*>(.*?)<.*/$1 = /'
```

That generates the log output in XML format, then keeps only the lines with author information, discards duplicates, strips out the XML tags. (Obviously this only works on a machine with grep, sort, and perl installed.) Then, redirect that output into your users.txt file so you can add the equivalent Git user data next to each entry.

You can provide this file to git svn to help it map the author data more accurately. You can also tell git svn not to include the metadata that Subversion normally imports, by passing --no-metadata to the clone or init command. This makes your import command look like this:

```
$ git-svn clone http://my-project.googlecode.com/svn/ \
    --authors-file=users.txt --no-metadata -s my_project
```

Now you should have a nicer Subversion import in your my_project directory. Instead of commits that look like this

```
commit 37efa680e8473b615de980fa935944215428a35a
Author: schacon <schacon@4c93b258-373f-11de-be05-5f7a86268029>
Date:    Sun May 3 00:12:22 2009 +0000

    fixed install - go to trunk

    git-svn-id: https://my-project.googlecode.com/svn/trunk@94 4c93b258-373f-11de-
    be05-5f7a86268029
```

they look like this:

```
commit 03a8785f44c8ea5cdb0e8834b7c8e6c469be2ff2
Author: Scott Chacon <schacon@geemail.com>
Date:    Sun May 3 00:12:22 2009 +0000

    fixed install - go to trunk
```

Not only does the Author field look a lot better, but the git-svn-id is no longer there, either.

You should also do a bit of post-import cleanup. For one thing, you should clean up the weird references that git svn set up. First you'll move the tags so they're actual tags rather than strange remote branches, and then you'll move the rest of the branches so they're local.

To move the tags to be proper Git tags, run

```
$ cp -Rf .git/refs/remotes/origin/tags/* .git/refs/tags/
$ rm -Rf .git/refs/remotes/origin/tags
```

This takes the references that were remote branches that started with remotes/origin/tags/ and makes them real (lightweight) tags.

Next, move the rest of the references under refs/remotes to be local branches:

```
$ cp -Rf .git/refs/remotes/* .git/refs/heads/
$ rm -Rf .git/refs/remotes
```

Now all the old branches are real Git branches and all the old tags are real Git tags. The last thing to do is add your new Git server as a remote and push to it. Here is an example of adding your server as a remote:

```
$ git remote add origin git@my-git-server:myrepository.git
```

Because you want all your branches and tags to go up, you can now run this:

```
$ git push origin --all
```

All your branches and tags should be on your new Git server in a nice, clean import.

Mercurial

Since Mercurial and Git have fairly similar models for representing versions, and since Git is a bit more flexible, converting a repository from Mercurial to Git is fairly straightforward, using a tool called "hg-fast-export", which you'll need a copy of:

```
$ git clone http://repo.or.cz/r/fast-export.git /tmp/fast-export
```

The first step in the conversion is to get a full clone of the Mercurial repository you want to convert:

```
$ hg clone <remote repo URL> /tmp/hg-repo
```

The next step is to create an author mapping file. Mercurial is a bit more forgiving than Git for what it will put in the author field for changesets, so this is a good time to clean house. Generating this is a one-line command in a bash shell:

```
$ cd /tmp/hg-repo
$ hg log | grep user: | sort | uniq | sed 's/user: *//' > ../authors
```

This will take a few seconds, depending on how long your project's history is, and afterwards the /tmp/authors file will look something like this:

```
bob
bob@localhost
bob <bob@company.com>
bob jones <bob <AT> company <DOT> com>
Bob Jones <bob@company.com>
Joe Smith <joe@company.com>
```

In this example, the same person (Bob) has created changesets under four different names, one of which actually looks correct, and one of which would be completely invalid for a Git commit. Hg-fast-export lets us fix this by adding ={new name and email address} at the end of every line we want to change, and removing the lines for any usernames that we want to leave alone. If all the usernames look fine, we won't need this file at all. In this example, we want our file to look like this:

```
bob=Bob Jones <bob@company.com>
bob@localhost=Bob Jones <bob@company.com>
bob jones <bob <AT> company <DOT> com>=Bob Jones <bob@company.com>
bob <bob@company.com>=Bob Jones <bob@company.com>
```

The next step is to create our new Git repository, and run the export script:

```
$ git init /tmp/converted
$ cd /tmp/converted
$ /tmp/fast-export/hg-fast-export.sh -r /tmp/hg-repo -A /tmp/authors
```

The -r flag tells hg-fast-export where to find the Mercurial repository we want to convert, and the -A flag tells it where to find the author-mapping file. The script parses Mercurial changesets and converts them into a script for Git's "fast-import" feature (which we'll discuss in detail a bit later on). This takes a bit (though it's much faster than it would be over the network), and the output is fairly verbose:

```
$ /tmp/fast-export/hg-fast-export.sh -r /tmp/hg-repo -A /tmp/authors
Loaded 4 authors
master: Exporting full revision 1/22208 with 13/0/0 added/changed/removed files
master: Exporting simple delta revision 2/22208 with 1/1/0 added/changed/removed files
master: Exporting simple delta revision 3/22208 with 0/1/0 added/changed/removed files
[...]
master: Exporting simple delta revision 22206/22208 with 0/4/0 added/changed/removed files
master: Exporting simple delta revision 22207/22208 with 0/2/0 added/changed/removed files
master: Exporting thorough delta revision 22208/22208 with 3/213/0 added/changed/removed files
Exporting tag [0.4c] at [hg r9] [git :10]
Exporting tag [0.4d] at [hg r16] [git :17]
[...]
Exporting tag [3.1-rc] at [hg r21926] [git :21927]
Exporting tag [3.1] at [hg r21973] [git :21974]
Issued 22315 commands
git-fast-import statistics:
---------------------------------------------------------------------
Alloc'd objects:     120000
Total objects:       115032 (    208171 duplicates                  )
      blobs  :        40504 (    205320 duplicates   26117 deltas of   39602 attempts)
      trees  :        52320 (      2851 duplicates   47467 deltas of   47599 attempts)
      commits:        22208 (         0 duplicates       0 deltas of       0 attempts)
      tags   :            0 (         0 duplicates       0 deltas of       0 attempts)
Total branches:         109 (         2 loads     )
      marks:         1048576 (     22208 unique     )
      atoms:           1952
Memory total:        7860 KiB
       pools:        2235 KiB
     objects:        5625 KiB
---------------------------------------------------------------------
pack_report: getpagesize()            =       4096
pack_report: core.packedGitWindowSize = 1073741824
pack_report: core.packedGitLimit     = 8589934592
pack_report: pack_used_ctr           =      90430
pack_report: pack_mmap_calls         =      46771
pack_report: pack_open_windows       =          1 /          1
pack_report: pack_mapped             =  340852700 /  340852700
---------------------------------------------------------------------

$ git shortlog -sn
   369  Bob Jones
   365  Joe Smith
```

That's pretty much all there is to it. All the Mercurial tags have been converted to Git tags, and Mercurial branches and bookmarks have been converted to Git branches. Now you're ready to push the repository up to its new server-side home:

```
$ git remote add origin git@my-git-server:myrepository.git
$ git push origin -all
```

Perforce

The next system you'll look at importing from is Perforce. As we discussed previously, there are two ways to let Git and Perforce talk to each other: git-p4 and Perforce Git Fusion.

Perforce Git Fusion

Git Fusion makes this process fairly painless. Just configure your project settings, user mappings, and branches using a configuration file (as discussed in the earlier "Git Fusion" section) and clone the repository. Git Fusion leaves you with what looks like a native Git repository, which is then ready to push to a native Git host if you desire. You could even use Perforce as your Git host if you like.

Git-p4

Git-p4 can also act as an import tool. As an example, we'll import the Jam project from the Perforce Public Depot. To set up your client, you must export the P4PORT environment variable to point to the Perforce depot:

```
$ export P4PORT=public.perforce.com:1666
```

■ **Note**   To follow along, you'll need a Perforce depot to connect with. We'll be using the public depot at public.perforce.com for our examples, but you can use any depot you have access to.

Run the git p4 clone command to import the Jam project from the Perforce server, supplying the depot and project path and the path into which you want to import the project:

```
$ git-p4 clone //guest/perforce_software/jam@all p4import
Importing from //guest/perforce_software/jam@all into p4import
Initialized empty Git repository in /private/tmp/p4import/.git/
Import destination: refs/remotes/p4/master
Importing revision 9957 (100%)
```

This particular project has only one branch, but if you have branches that are configured with branch views (or just a set of directories), you can use the --detect-branches flag to git p4 clone to import all the project's branches as well. See the "Branching" section for a bit more detail on this.

At this point you're almost done. If you go to the p4import directory and run git log, you can see your imported work:

```
$ git log -2
commit e5da1c909e5db3036475419f6379f2c73710c4e6
Author: giles <giles@giles@perforce.com>
Date:   Wed Feb 8 03:13:27 2012 -0800
```

    Correction to line 355; change </UL> to </OL>.

    [git-p4: depot-paths = "//public/jam/src/": change = 8068]

commit aa21359a0a135dda85c50a7f7cf249e4f7b8fd98
Author: kwirth <kwirth@perforce.com>
Date: Tue Jul 7 01:35:51 2009 -0800

    Fix spelling error on Jam doc page (cummulative -> cumulative).

    [git-p4: depot-paths = "//public/jam/src/": change = 7304]

You can see that git-p4 has left an identifier in each commit message. It's fine to keep that identifier there, in case you need to reference the Perforce change number later. However, if you'd like to remove the identifier, now is the time to do so—before you start doing work on the new repository. You can use git filter-branch to remove the identifier strings en masse:

```
$ git filter-branch --msg-filter 'sed -e "/^\[git-p4:/d"'
Rewrite e5da1c909e5db3036475419f6379f2c73710c4e6 (125/125)
Ref 'refs/heads/master' was rewritten
```

If you run git log, you can see that all the SHA-1 checksums for the commits have changed, but the git-p4 strings are no longer in the commit messages:

```
$ git log -2
commit b17341801ed838d97f7800a54a6f9b95750839b7
Author: giles <giles@giles@perforce.com>
Date:    Wed Feb 8 03:13:27 2012 -0800

    Correction to line 355; change </UL> to </OL>.

commit 3e68c2e26cd89cb983eb52c024ecdfba1d6b3fff
Author: kwirth <kwirth@perforce.com>
Date:    Tue Jul 7 01:35:51 2009 -0800

    Fix spelling error on Jam doc page (cummulative -> cumulative).
Your import is ready to push up to your new Git server.
TFS
```

If your team is converting their source control from TFVC to Git, you'll want the highest-fidelity conversion you can get. This means that, while we covered both git-tfs and git-tf for the interop section, we'll only be covering git-tfs for this part, because git-tfs supports branches, and this is prohibitively difficult using git-tf.

■ **Note**   This is a one-way conversion. The resulting Git repository won't be able to connect with the original TFVC project.

The first thing to do is map usernames. TFVC is fairly liberal with what goes into the author field for changesets, but Git wants a human-readable name and email address. You can get this information from the `tf` command-line client, like so:

```
PS> tf history $/myproject -recursive | cut -b 11-20 | tail -n+3 | uniq | sort > AUTHORS
```

This grabs all the changesets in the history of the project. The `cut` command ignores everything except characters 11-20 from each line (you'll have to experiment with the length of the fields to get these numbers right). The `tail` command skips the first two lines, which are field headers and ASCII-art underlines. The result of all this is piped to uniq to eliminate duplicates, and saved to a file named AUTHORS. The next step is manual; in order for `git-tfs` to make effective use of this file, each line must be in this format:

```
DOMAIN\username = User Name <email@address.com>
```

The portion on the left is the "User" field from TFVC, and the portion on the right side of the equal sign is the user name that will be used for Git commits.

Once you have this file, the next thing to do is make a full clone of the TFVC project you're interested in:

```
PS> git tfs clone --with-branches --authors=AUTHORS https://username.visualstudio.com/
DefaultCollection $/project/Trunk project_git
```

Next you'll want to clean the `git-tfs-id` sections from the bottom of the commit messages. The following command does that:

```
PS> git filter-branch -f --msg-filter 'sed "s/^git-tfs-id:.*$//g"' -- --all
```

That uses the `sed` command from the Git-bash environment to replace any line starting with `git-tfs-id:` with emptiness, which Git will then ignore.

Once that's all done, you're ready to add a new remote, push all your branches up, and have your team start working from Git.

A Custom Importer

If your system isn't one of the preceding, you should look for an importer online—quality importers are available for many other systems, including CVS, Clear Case, Visual Source Safe, even a directory of archives. If none of these tools works for you, you have a more obscure tool, or you otherwise need a more custom importing process, you should use `git fast-import`. This command reads simple instructions from stdin to write specific Git data. It's much easier to create Git objects this way than to run the raw Git commands or try to write the raw objects (see Chapter 10 for more information). This way, you can write an import script that reads the necessary information out of the system you're importing from and prints straightforward instructions to stdout. You can then run this program and pipe its output through `git fast-import`.

To quickly demonstrate, you'll write a simple importer. Suppose you work in current, you back up your project by occasionally copying the directory into a time-stamped back_YYYY_MM_DD backup directory, and you want to import this into Git. Your directory structure looks like this:

```
$ ls /opt/import_from
back_2014_01_02
back_2014_01_04
back_2014_01_14
back_2014_02_03
current
```

To import a Git directory, you need to review how Git stores its data. As you may remember, Git is fundamentally a linked list of commit objects that point to a snapshot of content. All you have to do is tell fast-import what the content snapshots are, what commit data points to them, and the order they go in. Your strategy will be to go through the snapshots one at a time and create commits with the contents of each directory, linking each commit back to the previous one.

As we did in Chapter 8, we'll write this in Ruby, because it's what we generally work with and it tends to be easy to read. You can write this example pretty easily in anything you're familiar with – it just needs to print the appropriate information to stdout. And, if you are running on Windows, this means you'll need to take special care to not introduce carriage returns at the end your lines – git fast-import is very particular about just wanting line feeds (LF) not the carriage return line feeds (CRLF) that Windows uses.

To begin, you'll change into the target directory and identify every subdirectory, each of which is a snapshot that you want to import as a commit. You'll change into each subdirectory and print the commands necessary to export it. Your basic main loop looks like this:

```
last_mark = nil

# loop through the directories
Dir.chdir(ARGV[0]) do
  Dir.glob("*").each do |dir|
    next if File.file?(dir)

    # move into the target directory
    Dir.chdir(dir) do
      last_mark = print_export(dir, last_mark)
    end
  end
end
```

You run print_export inside each directory, which takes the manifest and mark of the previous snapshot and returns the manifest and mark of this one; that way, you can link them properly. "Mark" is the fast-import term for an identifier you give to a commit; as you create commits, you give each one a mark that you can use to link to it from other commits. So, the first thing to do in your print_export method is generate a mark from the directory name:

```
mark = convert_dir_to_mark(dir)
```

You'll do this by creating an array of directories and using the index value as the mark, because a mark must be an integer. Your method looks like this:

```
$marks = []
def convert_dir_to_mark(dir)
  if !$marks.include?(dir)
    $marks << dir
  end
  ($marks.index(dir) + 1).to_s
end
```

Now that you have an integer representation of your commit, you need a date for the commit metadata. Because the date is expressed in the name of the directory, you'll parse it out. The next line in your print_export file is

```
date = convert_dir_to_date(dir)
```

where convert_dir_to_date is defined as

```
def convert_dir_to_date(dir)
  if dir == 'current'
    return Time.now().to_i
  else
    dir = dir.gsub('back_', '')
    (year, month, day) = dir.split('_')
    return Time.local(year, month, day).to_i
  end
end
```

That returns an integer value for the date of each directory. The last piece of meta-information you need for each commit is the committer data, which you hardcode in a global variable:

```
$author = 'John Doe <john@example.com>'
```

Now you're ready to begin printing out the commit data for your importer. The initial information states that you're defining a commit object and what branch it's on, followed by the mark you've generated, the committer information and commit message, and then the previous commit, if any. The code looks like this:

```
# print the import information
puts 'commit refs/heads/master'
puts 'mark :' + mark
puts "committer #{$author} #{date} -0700"
export_data('imported from ' + dir)
puts 'from :' + last_mark if last_mark
```

You hardcode the time zone (-0700) because doing so is easy. If you're importing from another system, you must specify the time zone as an offset. The commit message must be expressed in a special format:

```
data (size)\n(contents)
```

The format consists of the word data, the size of the data to be read, a newline, and finally the data. Because you need to use the same format to specify the file contents later, you create a helper method, export_data:

```
def export_data(string)
  print "data #{string.size}\n#{string}"
end
```

All that's left is to specify the file contents for each snapshot. This is easy, because you have each one in a directory—you can print out the deleteall command followed by the contents of each file in the directory. Git then records each snapshot appropriately:

```
puts 'deleteall'
Dir.glob("**/*").each do |file|
  next if !File.file?(file)
  inline_data(file)
end
```

■ **Note** Because many systems think of their revisions as changes from one commit to another, `fast-import` can also take commands with each commit to specify which files have been added, removed, or modified and what the new contents are. You could calculate the differences between snapshots and provide only this data, but doing so is more complex—you may as well give Git all the data and let it figure it out. If this is better suited to your data, check the `fast-import` man page for details about how to provide your data in this manner.

The format for listing the new file contents or specifying a modified file with the new contents is as follows:

```
M 644 inline path/to/file
data (size)
(file contents)
```

Here, 644 is the mode (if you have executable files, you need to detect and specify 755 instead), and `inline` says you'll list the contents immediately after this line. Your `inline_data` method looks like this:

```
def inline_data(file, code = 'M', mode = '644')
  content = File.read(file)
  puts "#{code} #{mode} inline #{file}"
  export_data(content)
end
```

You reuse the `export_data` method you defined earlier, because it's the same as the way you specified your commit message data.

The last thing you need to do is to return the current mark so it can be passed to the next iteration:

```
return mark
```

■ **Note** If you are running on Windows you'll need to make sure that you add one extra step. As mentioned before, Windows uses CRLF for new line characters while `git fast-import` expects only LF. To get around this problem and make git fast-import happy, you need to tell ruby to use LF instead of CRLF:

```
$stdout.binmode
```

That's it. Here's the script in its entirety:

```
#!/usr/bin/env ruby

$stdout.binmode
$author = "John Doe <john@example.com>"

$marks = []
def convert_dir_to_mark(dir)
    if !$marks.include?(dir)
        $marks << dir
    end
    ($marks.index(dir)+1).to_s
end
```

```ruby
def convert_dir_to_date(dir)
    if dir == 'current'
        return Time.now().to_i
    else
        dir = dir.gsub('back_', '')
        (year, month, day) = dir.split('_')
        return Time.local(year, month, day).to_i
    end
end

def export_data(string)
    print "data #{string.size}\n#{string}"
end

def inline_data(file, code='M', mode='644')
    content = File.read(file)
    puts "#{code} #{mode} inline #{file}"
    export_data(content)
end

def print_export(dir, last_mark)
    date = convert_dir_to_date(dir)
    mark = convert_dir_to_mark(dir)

    puts 'commit refs/heads/master'
    puts "mark :#{mark}"
    puts "committer #{$author} #{date} -0700"
    export_data("imported from #{dir}")
    puts "from :#{last_mark}" if last_mark

    puts 'deleteall'
    Dir.glob("**/*").each do |file|
        next if !File.file?(file)
        inline_data(file)
    end
    mark
end

# Loop through the directories
last_mark = nil
Dir.chdir(ARGV[0]) do
    Dir.glob("*").each do |dir|
        next if File.file?(dir)

        # move into the target directory
        Dir.chdir(dir) do
            last_mark = print_export(dir, last_mark)
        end
    end
end
```

If you run this script, you'll get content that looks something like this:

```
$ ruby import.rb /opt/import_from
commit refs/heads/master
mark :1
committer John Doe <john@example.com> 1388649600 -0700
data 29
imported from back_2014_01_02deleteall
M 644 inline README.md
data 28
# Hello

This is my readme.
commit refs/heads/master
mark :2
committer John Doe <john@example.com> 1388822400 -0700
data 29
imported from back_2014_01_04from :1
deleteall
M 644 inline main.rb
data 34
#!/bin/env ruby

puts "Hey there"
M 644 inline README.md
(...)
```

To run the importer, pipe this output through git fast-import while in the Git directory you want to import into. You can create a new directory and then run git init in it for a starting point, and then run your script:

```
$ git init
Initialized empty Git repository in /opt/import_to/.git/
$ ruby import.rb /opt/import_from | git fast-import
git-fast-import statistics:
---------------------------------------------------------------------
Alloc'd objects:       5000
Total objects:           13 (         6 duplicates                  )
      blobs  :            5 (         4 duplicates      3 deltas of          5 attempts)
      trees  :            4 (         1 duplicates      0 deltas of          4 attempts)
      commits:            4 (         1 duplicates      0 deltas of          0 attempts)
      tags   :            0 (         0 duplicates      0 deltas of          0 attempts)
Total branches:           1 (         1 loads     )
      marks:           1024 (         5 unique     )
      atoms:             2
Memory total:         2344 KiB
       pools:         2110 KiB
     objects:          234 KiB
```

```
------------------------------------------------------------------
pack_report: getpagesize()              =       4096
pack_report: core.packedGitWindowSize = 1073741824
pack_report: core.packedGitLimit        = 8589934592
pack_report: pack_used_ctr              =         10
pack_report: pack_mmap_calls            =          5
pack_report: pack_open_windows          =          2 /        2
pack_report: pack_mapped                =       1457 /     1457
------------------------------------------------------------------
```

As you can see, when it completes successfully, it gives you a bunch of statistics about what it accomplished. In this case, you imported 13 objects total for 4 commits into 1 branch. Now, you can run git log to see your new history:

```
$ git log -2
commit 3caa046d4aac682a55867132ccdfbe0d3fdee498
Author: John Doe <john@example.com>
Date:   Tue Jul 29 19:39:04 2014 -0700

    imported from current

commit 4afc2b945d0d3c8cd00556fbe2e8224569dc9def
Author: John Doe <john@example.com>
Date:   Mon Feb 3 01:00:00 2014 -0700

    imported from back_2014_02_03
```

There you go—a nice, clean Git repository. It's important to note that nothing is checked out—you don't have any files in your working directory at first. To get them, you must reset your branch to where master is now:

```
$ ls
$ git reset --hard master
HEAD is now at 3caa046 imported from current
$ ls
README.md main.rb
```

You can do a lot more with the fast-import tool—handle different modes, binary data, multiple branches and merging, tags, progress indicators, and more. A number of examples of more complex scenarios are available in the contrib/fast-import directory of the Git source code.

Summary

You should feel comfortable using Git as a client for other version-control systems, or importing nearly any existing repository into Git without losing data. In the next chapter, we'll cover the raw internals of Git so you can craft every single byte, if need be.

CHAPTER 10

■ ■ ■

Git Internals

You may have skipped to this chapter from a previous chapter, or you may have gotten here after reading the rest of the book—in either case, this is where we'll go over the inner workings and implementation of Git. We found that learning this information was fundamentally important to understanding how useful and powerful Git is, but others have argued to us that it can be confusing and unnecessarily complex for beginners. Thus, we've made this discussion the last chapter in the book so you could read it early or later in your learning process. We leave it up to you to decide.

Now that you're here, let's get started. First, if it isn't yet clear, Git is fundamentally a content-addressable filesystem with a VCS user interface written on top of it. You'll learn more about what this means in a bit.

In the early days of Git (mostly pre 1.5), the user interface was much more complex because it emphasized this filesystem rather than a polished VCS. In the last few years, the UI has been refined until it's as clean and easy to use as any system out there; but often, the stereotype lingers about the early Git UI that was complex and difficult to learn.

The content-addressable filesystem layer is amazingly cool, so I'll cover that first in this chapter; and then, you'll learn about the transport mechanisms and the repository maintenance tasks that you may eventually have to deal with.

Plumbing and Porcelain

This book covers how to use Git with 30 or so verbs such as checkout, branch, remote, and so on. But because Git was initially a toolkit for a VCS rather than a full user-friendly VCS, it has a bunch of verbs that do low-level work and were designed to be chained together UNIX style or called from scripts. These commands are generally referred to as "plumbing" commands, and the more user-friendly commands are called "porcelain" commands.

The book's first nine chapters deal almost exclusively with porcelain commands. But in this chapter, you'll be dealing mostly with the lower-level plumbing commands, because they give you access to the inner workings of Git, and help demonstrate how and why Git does what it does. Many of these commands aren't meant to be used manually on the command line, but rather to be used as building blocks for new tools and custom scripts.

When you run git init in a new or existing directory, Git creates the .git directory, which is where almost everything that Git stores and manipulates is located. If you want to back up or clone your repository, copying this single directory elsewhere gives you nearly everything you need. This entire chapter basically deals with the stuff in this directory. Here's what it looks like:

```
$ ls -F1
HEAD
config*
description
hooks/
info/
objects/
refs/
```

You may see some other files in there, but this is a fresh `git init` repository—it's what you see by default. The `description` file is only used by the GitWeb program, so don't worry about it. The `config` file contains your project-specific configuration options, and the `info` directory keeps a global exclude file for ignored patterns that you don't want to track in a `.gitignore` file. The `hooks` directory contains your client- or server-side hook scripts, which are discussed in detail in "Git Hooks" (Chapter 8).

This leaves four important entries: the `HEAD` and (yet to be created) `index` files, and the `objects` and `refs` directories. These are the core parts of Git. The `objects` directory stores all the content for your database, the `refs` directory stores pointers into commit objects in that data (branches), the `HEAD` file points to the branch you currently have checked out, and the `index` file is where Git stores your staging area information. You'll now look at each of these sections in detail to see how Git operates.

Git Objects

Git is a content-addressable filesystem. Great. What does that mean? It means that at the core of Git is a simple key-value data store. You can insert any kind of content into it, and it will give you back a key that you can use to retrieve the content again at any time. To demonstrate, you can use the plumbing command `hash-object`, which takes some data, stores it in your `.git` directory, and gives you back the key the data is stored as. First, you initialize a new Git repository and verify that there is nothing in the objects directory:

```
$ git init test
Initialized empty Git repository in /tmp/test/.git/
$ cd test
$ find .git/objects
.git/objects
.git/objects/info
.git/objects/pack
$ find .git/objects -type f
```

Git has initialized the objects directory and created `pack` and `info` subdirectories in it, but there are no regular files. Now, store some text in your Git database:

```
$ echo 'test content' | git hash-object -w --stdin
d670460b4b4aece5915caf5c68d12f560a9fe3e4
```

The -w tells `hash-object` to store the object; otherwise, the command simply tells you what the key would be. --stdin tells the command to read the content from stdin; if you don't specify this, `hash-object` expects a file path at the end. The output from the command is a 40-character checksum hash. This is the SHA-1 hash – a checksum of the content you're storing plus a header, which you'll learn about in a bit. Now you can see how Git has stored your data:

```
$ find .git/objects -type f
.git/objects/d6/70460b4b4aece5915caf5c68d12f560a9fe3e4
```

You can see a file in the `objects` directory. This is how Git stores the content initially—as a single file per piece of content, named with the SHA-1 checksum of the content and its header. The subdirectory is named with the first 2 characters of the SHA, and the filename is the remaining 38 characters.

You can pull the content back out of Git with the `cat-file` command. This command is sort of a Swiss army knife for inspecting Git objects. Passing -p to it instructs the `cat-file` command to figure out the type of content and display it nicely for you:

```
$ git cat-file -p d670460b4b4aece5915caf5c68d12f560a9fe3e4
test content
```

Now, you can add content to Git and pull it back out again. You can also do this with content in files. For example, you can do some simple version control on a file. First, create a new file and save its contents in your database:

```
$ echo 'version 1' > test.txt
$ git hash-object -w test.txt
83baae61804e65cc73a7201a7252750c76066a30
```

Then, write some new content to the file, and save it again:

```
$ echo 'version 2' > test.txt
$ git hash-object -w test.txt
1f7a7a472abf3dd9643fd615f6da379c4acb3e3a
```

Your database contains the two new versions of the file as well as the first content you stored there:

```
$ find .git/objects -type f
.git/objects/1f/7a7a472abf3dd9643fd615f6da379c4acb3e3a
.git/objects/83/baae61804e65cc73a7201a7252750c76066a30
.git/objects/d6/70460b4b4aece5915caf5c68d12f560a9fe3e4
```

Now you can revert the file back to the first version

```
$ git cat-file -p 83baae61804e65cc73a7201a7252750c76066a30 > test.txt
$ cat test.txt
version 1
```

or the second version:

```
$ git cat-file -p 1f7a7a472abf3dd9643fd615f6da379c4acb3e3a > test.txt
$ cat test.txt
version 2
```

But remembering the SHA-1 key for each version of your file isn't practical; plus, you aren't storing the filename in your system—just the content. This object type is called a blob. You can have Git tell you the object type of any object in Git, given its SHA-1 key, with cat-file -t:

```
$ git cat-file -t 1f7a7a472abf3dd9643fd615f6da379c4acb3e3a
blob
```

Tree Objects

The next type we'll look at is the tree, which solves the problem of storing the filename and also allows you to store a group of files together. Git stores content in a manner similar to a UNIX filesystem, but a bit simplified. All the content is stored as tree and blob objects, with trees corresponding to UNIX directory entries and blobs corresponding more or less to inodes or file contents. A single tree object contains one or more tree entries, each of which contains a SHA-1 pointer to a blob or subtree with its associated mode, type, and filename. For example, the most recent tree in a project may look something like this:

```
$ git cat-file -p master^{tree}
100644 blob a906cb2a4a904a152e80877d4088654daad0c859      README
100644 blob 8f94139338f9404f26296befa88755fc2598c289      Rakefile
040000 tree 99f1a6d12cb4b6f19c8655fca46c3ecf317074e0      lib
```

The master^{tree} syntax specifies the tree object that is pointed to by the last commit on your master branch. Notice that the lib subdirectory isn't a blob but a pointer to another tree:

```
$ git cat-file -p 99f1a6d12cb4b6f19c8655fca46c3ecf317074e0
100644 blob 47c6340d6459e05787f644c2447d2595f5d3a54b      simplegit.rb
```

Conceptually, the data that Git is storing is something like this:

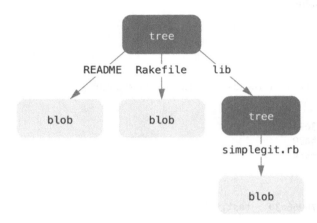

Figure 10-1. *Simple version of the Git data model*

You can fairly easily create your own tree. Git normally creates a tree by taking the state of your staging area or index and writing a series of tree objects from it. So, to create a tree object, you first have to set up an index by staging some files. To create an index with a single entry—the first version of your text.txt file—you can use the plumbing command update-index. You use this command to artificially add the earlier version of the test.txt file to a new staging area. You must pass it the --add option because the file doesn't yet exist in your staging area (you don't even have a staging area set up yet) and --cacheinfo because the file you're adding isn't in your directory but is in your database. Then, you specify the mode, SHA-1, and filename:

```
$ git update-index --add --cacheinfo 100644 \
   83baae61804e65cc73a7201a7252750c76066a30 test.txt
```

In this case, you're specifying a mode of 100644, which means it's a normal file. Other options are 100755, which means it's an executable file; and 120000, which specifies a symbolic link. The mode is taken from normal UNIX modes but is much less flexible—these three modes are the only ones that are valid for files (blobs) in Git (although other modes are used for directories and submodules).

Now, you can use the write-tree command to write the staging area out to a tree object. No -w option is needed—calling write-tree automatically creates a tree object from the state of the index if that tree doesn't yet exist:

```
$ git write-tree
d8329fc1cc938780ffdd9f94e0d364e0ea74f579
$ git cat-file -p d8329fc1cc938780ffdd9f94e0d364e0ea74f579
100644 blob 83baae61804e65cc73a7201a7252750c76066a30      test.txt
```

You can also verify that this is a tree object:

```
$ git cat-file -t d8329fc1cc938780ffdd9f94e0d364e0ea74f579
tree
```

You'll now create a new tree with the second version of test.txt and a new file as well:

```
$ echo 'new file' > new.txt
$ git update-index test.txt
$ git update-index --add new.txt
```

Your staging area now has the new version of test.txt as well as the new file new.txt. Write out that tree (recording the state of the staging area or index to a tree object) and see what it looks like:

```
$ git write-tree
0155eb4229851634a0f03eb265b69f5a2d56f341
$ git cat-file -p 0155eb4229851634a0f03eb265b69f5a2d56f341
100644 blob fa49b077972391ad58037050f2a75f74e3671e92    new.txt
100644 blob 1f7a7a472abf3dd9643fd615f6da379c4acb3e3a    test.txt
```

Notice that this tree has both file entries and also that the test.txt SHA is the "version 2" SHA from earlier (1f7a7a). Just for fun, you'll add the first tree as a subdirectory into this one. You can read trees into your staging area by calling read-tree. In this case, you can read an existing tree into your staging area as a subtree by using the --prefix option to read-tree:

```
$ git read-tree --prefix=bak d8329fc1cc938780ffdd9f94e0d364e0ea74f579
$ git write-tree
3c4e9cd789d88d8d89c1073707c3585e41b0e614
$ git cat-file -p 3c4e9cd789d88d8d89c1073707c3585e41b0e614
040000 tree d8329fc1cc938780ffdd9f94e0d364e0ea74f579    bak
100644 blob fa49b077972391ad58037050f2a75f74e3671e92    new.txt
100644 blob 1f7a7a472abf3dd9643fd615f6da379c4acb3e3a    test.txt
```

If you created a working directory from the new tree you just wrote, you would get the two files in the top level of the working directory and a subdirectory named bak that contained the first version of the test.txt file. You can think of the data that Git contains for these structures as being like this:

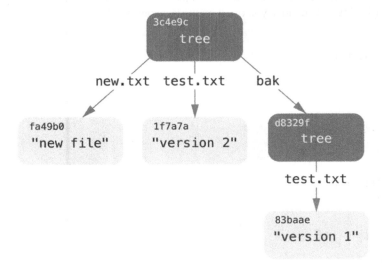

Figure 10-2. *The content structure of your current Git data*

Commit Objects

You have three trees that specify the different snapshots of your project that you want to track, but the earlier problem remains: you must remember all three SHA-1 values in order to recall the snapshots. You also don't have any information about who saved the snapshots, when they were saved, or why they were saved. This is the basic information that the commit object stores for you.

To create a commit object, you call commit-tree and specify a single tree SHA-1 and which commit objects, if any, directly preceded it. Start with the first tree you wrote:

```
$ echo 'first commit' | git commit-tree d8329f
fdf4fc3344e67ab068f836878b6c4951e3b15f3d
```

Now you can look at your new commit object with cat-file:

```
$ git cat-file -p fdf4fc3
tree d8329fc1cc938780ffdd9f94e0d364e0ea74f579
author Scott Chacon <schacon@gmail.com> 1243040974 -0700
committer Scott Chacon <schacon@gmail.com> 1243040974 -0700

first commit
```

The format for a commit object is simple: it specifies the top-level tree for the snapshot of the project at that point; the author/committer information (which uses your user.name and user.email configuration settings and a timestamp); a blank line, and then the commit message.

Next, you'll write the other two commit objects, each referencing the commit that came directly before it:

```
$ echo 'second commit' | git commit-tree 0155eb -p fdf4fc3
cac0cab538b970a37ea1e769cbbde608743bc96d
$ echo 'third commit'  | git commit-tree 3c4e9c -p cac0cab
1a410efbd13591db07496601ebc7a059dd55cfe9
```

Each of the three commit objects points to one of the three snapshot trees you created. Oddly enough, you have a real Git history now that you can view with the git log command, if you run it on the last commit SHA-1:

```
$ git log --stat 1a410e
commit 1a410efbd13591db07496601ebc7a059dd55cfe9
Author: Scott Chacon <schacon@gmail.com>
Date:   Fri May 22 18:15:24 2009 -0700

    third commit

 bak/test.txt | 1 +
 1 file changed, 1 insertion(+)

commit cac0cab538b970a37ea1e769cbbde608743bc96d
Author: Scott Chacon <schacon@gmail.com>
Date:   Fri May 22 18:14:29 2009 -0700
```

```
    second commit

 new.txt  | 1 +
 test.txt | 2 +-
 2 files changed, 2 insertions(+), 1 deletion(-)

commit fdf4fc3344e67ab068f836878b6c4951e3b15f3d
Author: Scott Chacon <schacon@gmail.com>
Date:   Fri May 22 18:09:34 2009 -0700

    first commit

 test.txt | 1 +
 1 file changed, 1 insertion(+)
```

Amazing. You've just done the low-level operations to build up a Git history without using any of the front end commands. This is essentially what Git does when you run the git add and git commit commands—it stores blobs for the files that have changed, updates the index, writes out trees, and writes commit objects that reference the top-level trees and the commits that came immediately before them. These three main Git objects – the blob, the tree, and the commit—are initially stored as separate files in your .git/objects directory. Here are all the objects in the example directory now, commented with what they store:

```
$ find .git/objects -type f
.git/objects/01/55eb4229851634a0f03eb265b69f5a2d56f341 # tree 2
.git/objects/1a/410efbd13591db07496601ebc7a059dd55cfe9 # commit 3
.git/objects/1f/7a7a472abf3dd9643fd615f6da379c4acb3e3a # test.txt v2
.git/objects/3c/4e9cd789d88d8d89c1073707c3585e41b0e614 # tree 3
.git/objects/83/baae61804e65cc73a7201a7252750c76066a30 # test.txt v1
.git/objects/ca/c0cab538b970a37ea1e769cbbde608743bc96d # commit 2
.git/objects/d6/70460b4b4aece5915caf5c68d12f560a9fe3e4 # 'test content'
.git/objects/d8/329fc1cc938780ffdd9f94e0d364e0ea74f579 # tree 1
.git/objects/fa/49b077972391ad58037050f2a75f74e3671e92 # new.txt
.git/objects/fd/f4fc3344e67ab068f836878b6c4951e3b15f3d # commit 1
```

If you follow all the internal pointers, you get an object graph something like this:

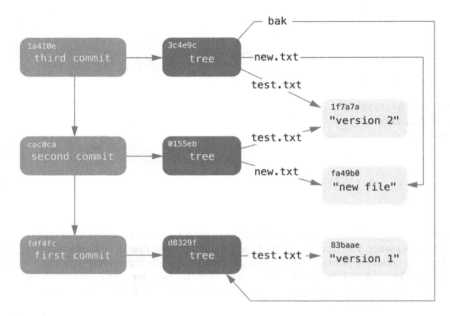

Figure 10-3. *All the objects in your Git directory*

Object Storage

We mentioned earlier that a header is stored with the content. Let's take a minute to look at how Git stores its objects. You'll see how to store a blob object—in this case, the string "what is up, doc?"—interactively in the Ruby scripting language.

You can start up interactive Ruby mode with the `irb` command:

```
$ irb
>> content = "what is up, doc?"
=> "what is up, doc?"
```

Git constructs a header that starts with the type of the object, in this case a blob. Then, it adds a space followed by the size of the content and finally a null byte:

```
>> header = "blob #{content.length}\0"
=> "blob 16\u0000"
```

Git concatenates the header and the original content and then calculates the SHA-1 checksum of that new content. You can calculate the SHA-1 value of a string in Ruby by including the SHA1 digest library with the `require` command and then calling `Digest::SHA1.hexdigest()` with the string:

```
>> store = header + content
=> "blob 16\u0000what is up, doc?"
>> require 'digest/sha1'
=> true
>> sha1 = Digest::SHA1.hexdigest(store)
=> "bd9dbf5aae1a3862dd1526723246b20206e5fc37"
```

Git compresses the new content with `zlib`, which you can do in Ruby with the zlib library. First, you need to require the library and then run `Zlib::Deflate.deflate()` on the content:

```
>> require 'zlib'
=> true
>> zlib_content = Zlib::Deflate.deflate(store)
=> "x\x9CK\xCA\xC9OR04c(\xCFH,Q\xC8,V(-\xDOQH\xC9O\xB6\a\x00_\x1C\a\x9D"
```

Finally, you'll write your zlib-deflated content to an object on disk. You'll determine the path of the object you want to write out (the first 2 characters of the SHA-1 value being the subdirectory name, and the last 38 characters being the filename within that directory). In Ruby, you can use the `FileUtils.mkdir_p()` function to create the subdirectory if it doesn't exist. Then, open the file with `File.open()` and write out the previously zlib-compressed content to the file with a `write()` call on the resulting file handle:

```
>> path = '.git/objects/' + sha1[0,2] + '/' + sha1[2,38]
=> ".git/objects/bd/9dbf5aae1a3862dd1526723246b20206e5fc37"
>> require 'fileutils'
=> true
>> FileUtils.mkdir_p(File.dirname(path))
=> ".git/objects/bd"
>> File.open(path, 'w') { |f| f.write zlib_content }
=> 32
```

That's it – you've created a valid Git blob object. All Git objects are stored the same way, just with different types – instead of the string blob, the header will begin with commit or tree. Also, although the blob content can be nearly anything, the commit and tree content are very specifically formatted.

Git References

You can run something like `git log 1a410e` to look through your whole history, but you still have to remember that 1a410e is the last commit in order to walk that history to find all those objects. You need a file in which you can store the SHA-1 value under a simple name so you can use that pointer rather than the raw SHA-1 value.

In Git, these are called "references" or "refs;" you can find the files that contain the SHA-1 values in the `.git/refs` directory. In the current project, this directory contains no files, but it does contain a simple structure:

```
$ find .git/refs
.git/refs
.git/refs/heads
.git/refs/tags
$ find .git/refs -type f
```

To create a new reference that will help you remember where your latest commit is, you can technically do something as simple as this:

```
$ echo "1a410efbd13591db07496601ebc7a059dd55cfe9" > .git/refs/heads/master
```

Now, you can use the head reference you just created instead of the SHA-1 value in your Git commands:

```
$ git log --pretty=oneline  master
1a410efbd13591db07496601ebc7a059dd55cfe9 third commit
cac0cab538b970a37ea1e769cbbde608743bc96d second commit
fdf4fc3344e67ab068f836878b6c4951e3b15f3d first commit
```

You aren't encouraged to directly edit the reference files. Git provides a safer command to do this if you want to update a reference called update-ref:

```
$ git update-ref refs/heads/master 1a410efbd13591db07496601ebc7a059dd55cfe9
```

That's basically what a branch in Git is: a simple pointer or reference to the head of a line of work. To create a branch back at the second commit, you can do this:

```
$ git update-ref refs/heads/test cac0ca
```

Your branch will contain only work from that commit down:

```
$ git log --pretty=oneline test
cac0cab538b970a37ea1e769cbbde608743bc96d second commit
fdf4fc3344e67ab068f836878b6c4951e3b15f3d first commit
```

Now, your Git database conceptually looks something like this:

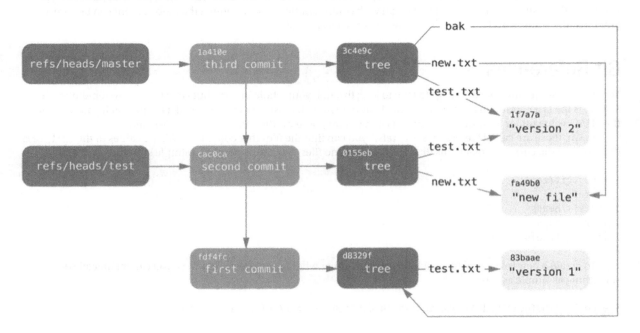

Figure 10-4. *Git directory objects with branch head references included*

When you run commands like git branch (branchname), Git basically runs that update-ref command to add the SHA-1 of the last commit of the branch you're on into whatever new reference you want to create.

The HEAD

The question now is, when you run git branch (branchname), how does Git know the SHA-1 of the last commit? The answer is the HEAD file.

The HEAD file is a symbolic reference to the branch you're currently on. By symbolic reference, we mean that unlike a normal reference, it doesn't generally contain a SHA-1 value but rather a pointer to another reference. If you look at the file, you'll normally see something like this:

```
$ cat .git/HEAD
ref: refs/heads/master
```

If you run git checkout test, Git updates the file to look like this:

```
$ cat .git/HEAD
ref: refs/heads/test
```

When you run git commit, it creates the commit object, specifying the parent of that commit object to be whatever SHA-1 value the reference in HEAD points to.

You can also manually edit this file, but again a safer command exists to do so: symbolic-ref. You can read the value of your HEAD via this command:

```
$ git symbolic-ref HEAD
refs/heads/master
```

You can also set the value of HEAD:

```
$ git symbolic-ref HEAD refs/heads/test
$ cat .git/HEAD
ref: refs/heads/test
```

You can't set a symbolic reference outside of the refs style:

```
$ git symbolic-ref HEAD test
fatal: Refusing to point HEAD outside of refs/
```

Tags

We just finished discussing Git's three main object types, but there is a fourth. The tag object is very much like a commit object – it contains a tagger, a date, a message, and a pointer. The main difference is that a tag object generally points to a commit rather than a tree. It's like a branch reference, but it never moves—it always points to the same commit but gives it a friendlier name.

As discussed in Chapter 2 there are two types of tags: annotated and lightweight. You can make a lightweight tag by running something like this:

```
$ git update-ref refs/tags/v1.0 cac0cab538b970a37ea1e769cbbde608743bc96d
```

That is all a lightweight tag is – a reference that never moves. An annotated tag is more complex, however. If you create an annotated tag, Git creates a tag object and then writes a reference to point to it rather than directly to the commit. You can see this by creating an annotated tag (-a specifies that it's an annotated tag):

```
$ git tag -a v1.1 1a410efbd13591db07496601ebc7a059dd55cfe9 -m 'test tag'
```

Here's the object SHA-1 value it created:

```
$ cat .git/refs/tags/v1.1
9585191f37f7b0fb9444f35a9bf50de191beadc2
```

Now, run the cat-file command on that SHA-1 value:

```
$ git cat-file -p 9585191f37f7b0fb9444f35a9bf50de191beadc2
object 1a410efbd13591db07496601ebc7a059dd55cfe9
type commit
tag v1.1
tagger Scott Chacon <schacon@gmail.com> Sat May 23 16:48:58 2009 -0700

test tag
```

Notice that the object entry points to the commit SHA-1 value that you tagged. Also notice that it doesn't need to point to a commit; you can tag any Git object. In the Git source code, for example, the maintainer has added their GPG public key as a blob object and then tagged it. You can view the public key by running this in a clone of the Git repository:

```
$ git cat-file blob junio-gpg-pub
```

The Linux kernel repository also has a non-commit-pointing tag object—the first tag created points to the initial tree of the import of the source code.

Remotes

The third type of reference that you'll see is a remote reference. If you add a remote and push to it, Git stores the value you last pushed to that remote for each branch in the refs/remotes directory. For instance, you can add a remote called origin and push your master branch to it:

```
$ git remote add origin git@github.com:schacon/simplegit-progit.git
$ git push origin master
Counting objects: 11, done.
Compressing objects: 100% (5/5), done.
Writing objects: 100% (7/7), 716 bytes, done.
Total 7 (delta 2), reused 4 (delta 1)
To git@github.com:schacon/simplegit-progit.git
   a11bef0..ca82a6d  master -> master
```

Then, you can see what the master branch on the origin remote was the last time you communicated with the server, by checking the refs/remotes/origin/master file:

```
$ cat .git/refs/remotes/origin/master
ca82a6dff817ec66f44342007202690a93763949
```

Remote references differ from branches (refs/heads references) mainly in that they're considered read-only. You can git checkout to one, but Git won't point HEAD at one, so you'll never update it with a commit command. Git manages them as bookmarks to the last known state of where those branches were on those servers.

Packfiles

Let's go back to the objects database for your test Git repository. At this point, you have 11 objects – 4 blobs, 3 trees, 3 commits, and 1 tag:

```
$ find .git/objects -type f
.git/objects/01/55eb4229851634a0f03eb265b69f5a2d56f341 # tree 2
.git/objects/1a/410efbd13591db07496601ebc7a059dd55cfe9 # commit 3
.git/objects/1f/7a7a472abf3dd9643fd615f6da379c4acb3e3a # test.txt v2
.git/objects/3c/4e9cd789d88d8d89c1073707c3585e41b0e614 # tree 3
.git/objects/83/baae61804e65cc73a7201a7252750c76066a30 # test.txt v1
.git/objects/95/85191f37f7b0fb9444f35a9bf50de191beadc2 # tag
.git/objects/ca/c0cab538b970a37ea1e769cbbde608743bc96d # commit 2
.git/objects/d6/70460b4b4aece5915caf5c68d12f560a9fe3e4 # 'test content'
.git/objects/d8/329fc1cc938780ffdd9f94e0d364e0ea74f579 # tree 1
.git/objects/fa/49b077972391ad58037050f2a75f74e3671e92 # new.txt
.git/objects/fd/f4fc3344e67ab068f836878b6c4951e3b15f3d # commit 1
```

Git compresses the contents of these files with zlib, and you're not storing much, so all these files collectively take up only 925 bytes. You'll add some larger content to the repository to demonstrate an interesting feature of Git. To demonstrate, we'll add the repo.rb file from the Grit library—this is about a 22K source code file:

```
$ curl https://raw.githubusercontent.com/mojombo/grit/master/lib/grit/repo.rb > repo.rb
$ git add repo.rb
$ git commit -m 'added repo.rb'
[master 484a592] added repo.rb
 3 files changed, 709 insertions(+), 2 deletions(-)
 delete mode 100644 bak/test.txt
 create mode 100644 repo.rb
 rewrite test.txt (100%)
```

If you look at the resulting tree, you can see the SHA-1 value your repo.rb file got for the blob object:

```
$ git cat-file -p master^{tree}
100644 blob fa49b077972391ad58037050f2a75f74e3671e92      new.txt
100644 blob 033b4468fa6b2a9547a70d88d1bbe8bf3f9ed0d5      repo.rb
100644 blob e3f094f522629ae358806b17daf78246c27c007b      test.txt
```

You can then use git cat-file to see how big that object is:

```
$ git cat-file -s 033b4468fa6b2a9547a70d88d1bbe8bf3f9ed0d5
22044
```

Now, modify that file a little, and see what happens:

```
$ echo '# testing' >> repo.rb
$ git commit -am 'modified repo a bit'
[master 2431da6] modified repo.rb a bit
 1 file changed, 1 insertion(+)
```

Check the tree created by that commit, and you see something interesting:

```
$ git cat-file -p master^{tree}
100644 blob fa49b077972391ad58037050f2a75f74e3671e92      new.txt
100644 blob b042a60ef7dff760008df33cee372b945b6e884e      repo.rb
100644 blob e3f094f522629ae358806b17daf78246c27c007b      test.txt
```

The blob is now a different blob, which means that although you added only a single line to the end of a 400-line file, Git stored that new content as a completely new object:

```
$ git cat-file -s b042a60ef7dff760008df33cee372b945b6e884e
22054
```

You have two nearly identical 22K objects on your disk. Wouldn't it be nice if Git could store one of them in full but then the second object only as the delta between it and the first?

It turns out that it can. The initial format in which Git saves objects on disk is called a "loose" object format. However, occasionally Git packs up several of these objects into a single binary file called a "packfile" in order to save space and be more efficient. Git does this if you have too many loose objects around, if you run the git gc command manually, or if you push to a remote server. To see what happens, you can manually ask Git to pack up the objects by calling the git gc command:

```
$ git gc
Counting objects: 18, done.
Delta compression using up to 8 threads.
Compressing objects: 100% (14/14), done.
Writing objects: 100% (18/18), done.
Total 18 (delta 3), reused 0 (delta 0)
```

If you look in your objects directory, you'll find that most of your objects are gone, and a new pair of files has appeared:

```
$ find .git/objects -type f
.git/objects/bd/9dbf5aae1a3862dd1526723246b20206e5fc37
.git/objects/d6/70460b4b4aece5915caf5c68d12f560a9fe3e4
.git/objects/info/packs
.git/objects/pack/pack-978e03944f5c581011e6998cd0e9e30000905586.idx
.git/objects/pack/pack-978e03944f5c581011e6998cd0e9e30000905586.pack
```

The objects that remain are the blobs that aren't pointed to by any commit—in this case, the "what is up, doc?" example and the "test content" example blobs you created earlier. Because you never added them to any commits, they're considered dangling and aren't packed up in your new packfile.

The other files are your new packfile and an index. The packfile is a single file containing the contents of all the objects that were removed from your filesystem. The index is a file that contains offsets into that packfile so you can quickly seek to a specific object. What is cool is that although the objects on disk before you ran the gc were collectively about 22K in size, the new packfile is only 7K. You've cut your disk usage by two-thirds by packing your objects.

How does Git do this? When Git packs objects, it looks for files that are named and sized similarly, and stores just the deltas from one version of the file to the next. You can look into the packfile and see what Git did to save space. The git verify-pack plumbing command allows you to see what was packed up:

```
$ git verify-pack -v .git/objects/pack/pack-978e03944f5c581011e6998cd0e9e30000905586.idx
2431da676938450a4d72e260db3bf7b0f587bbc1 commit 223 155 12
69bcdaff5328278ab1c0812ce0e07fa7d26a96d7 commit 214 152 167
80d02664cb23ed55b226516648c7ad5d0a3deb90 commit 214 145 319
43168a18b7613d1281e5560855a83eb8fde3d687 commit 213 146 464
092917823486a802e94d727c820a9024e14a1fc2 commit 214 146 610
702470739ce72005e2edff522fde85d52a65df9b commit 165 118 756
d368d0ac0678cbe6cce505be58126d3526706e54 tag    130 122 874
fe879577cb8cffcdf25441725141e310dd7d239b tree   136 136 996
d8329fc1cc938780ffdd9f94e0d364e0ea74f579 tree   36 46 1132
deef2e1b793907545e50a2ea2ddb5ba6c58c4506 tree   136 136 1178
d982c7cb2c2a972ee391a85da481fc1f9127a01d tree   6 17 1314 1 \
    deef2e1b793907545e50a2ea2ddb5ba6c58c4506
3c4e9cd789d88d8d89c1073707c3585e41b0e614 tree   8 19 1331 1 \
    deef2e1b793907545e50a2ea2ddb5ba6c58c4506
0155eb4229851634a0f03eb265b69f5a2d56f341 tree   71 76 1350
83baae61804e65cc73a7201a7252750c76066a30 blob   10 19 1426
fa49b077972391ad58037050f2a75f74e3671e92 blob   9 18 1445
b042a60ef7dff760008df33cee372b945b6e884e blob   22054 5799 1463
033b4468fa6b2a9547a70d88d1bbe8bf3f9ed0d5 blob   9 20 7262 1 \
    b042a60ef7dff760008df33cee372b945b6e884e
1f7a7a472abf3dd9643fd615f6da379c4acb3e3a blob   10 19 7282
non delta: 15 objects
chain length = 1: 3 objects
.git/objects/pack/pack-978e03944f5c581011e6998cd0e9e30000905586.pack: ok
```

Here, the 033b4 blob, which if you remember was the first version of your repo.rb file, is referencing the b042a blob, which was the second version of the file. The third column in the output is the size of the object in the pack, so you can see that b042a takes up 22K of the file, but that 033b4 only takes up 9 bytes. What is also interesting is that the second version of the file is the one that is stored intact, whereas the original version is stored as a delta—this is because you're most likely to need faster access to the most recent version of the file.

The really nice thing about this is that it can be repacked at any time. Git will occasionally repack your database automatically, always trying to save more space, but you can also manually repack at any time by running git gc by hand.

The Refspec

Throughout this book, we've used simple mappings from remote branches to local references, but they can be more complex. Suppose you add a remote like this:

```
$ git remote add origin https://github.com/schacon/simplegit-progit
```

It adds a section to your .git/config file, specifying the name of the remote (origin), the URL of the remote repository, and the refspec for fetching:

```
[remote "origin"]
        url = https://github.com/schacon/simplegit-progit
        fetch = +refs/heads/*:refs/remotes/origin/*
```

The format of the refspec is an optional +, followed by <src>:<dst>, where <src> is the pattern for references on the remote side and <dst> is where those references will be written locally. The + tells Git to update the reference even if it isn't a fast-forward.

In the default case that is automatically written by a git remote add command, Git fetches all the references under refs/heads/ on the server and writes them to refs/remotes/origin/ locally. So, if there is a master branch on the server, you can access the log of that branch locally via

```
$ git log origin/master
$ git log remotes/origin/master
$ git log refs/remotes/origin/master
```

They're all equivalent, because Git expands each of them to refs/remotes/origin/master.

If you want Git instead to pull down only the master branch each time, and not every other branch on the remote server, you can change the fetch line to

```
fetch = +refs/heads/master:refs/remotes/origin/master
```

This is just the default refspec for git fetch for that remote. If you want to do something one time, you can specify the refspec on the command line, too. To pull the master branch on the remote down to origin/mymaster locally, you can run

```
$ git fetch origin master:refs/remotes/origin/mymaster
```

You can also specify multiple refspecs. On the command line, you can pull down several branches like so:

```
$ git fetch origin master:refs/remotes/origin/mymaster \
         topic:refs/remotes/origin/topic
From git@github.com:schacon/simplegit
 ! [rejected]        master      -> origin/mymaster   (non fast forward)
 * [new branch]      topic       -> origin/topic
```

In this case, the master branch pull was rejected because it wasn't a fast-forward reference. You can override that by specifying the + in front of the refspec.

You can also specify multiple refspecs for fetching in your configuration file. If you want to always fetch the master and experiment branches, add two lines:

```
[remote "origin"]
        url = https://github.com/schacon/simplegit-progit
        fetch = +refs/heads/master:refs/remotes/origin/master
        fetch = +refs/heads/experiment:refs/remotes/origin/experiment
```

You can't use partial globs in the pattern, so this would be invalid:

```
fetch = +refs/heads/qa*:refs/remotes/origin/qa*
```

However, you can use namespaces (or directories) to accomplish something like that. If you have a QA team that pushes a series of branches, and you want to get the master branch and any of the QA team's branches but nothing else, you can use a config section like this:

```
[remote "origin"]
        url = https://github.com/schacon/simplegit-progit
        fetch = +refs/heads/master:refs/remotes/origin/master
        fetch = +refs/heads/qa/*:refs/remotes/origin/qa/*
```

If you have a complex workflow process that has a QA team pushing branches, developers pushing branches, and integration teams pushing and collaborating on remote branches, you can namespace them easily this way.

Pushing Refspecs

It's nice that you can fetch namespaced references that way, but how does the QA team get their branches into a qa/ namespace in the first place? You accomplish that by using refspecs to push.

If the QA team wants to push their master branch to qa/master on the remote server, they can run

```
$ git push origin master:refs/heads/qa/master
```

If they want Git to do that automatically each time they run git push origin, they can add a push value to their config file:

```
[remote "origin"]
        url = https://github.com/schacon/simplegit-progit
        fetch = +refs/heads/*:refs/remotes/origin/*
        push = refs/heads/master:refs/heads/qa/master
```

Again, this will cause a git push origin to push the local master branch to the remote qa/master branch by default.

Deleting References

You can also use the refspec to delete references from the remote server by running something like this:

```
$ git push origin :topic
```

Because the refspec is <src>:<dst>, by leaving off the <src> part, this basically says to make the topic branch on the remote nothing, which deletes it.

Transfer Protocols

Git can transfer data between two repositories in two major ways: the "dumb" protocol and the "smart" protocol. This section will quickly cover how these two main protocols operate.

The Dumb Protocol

If you're setting up a repository to be served read-only over HTTP, the dumb protocol is likely what will be used. This protocol is called "dumb" because it requires no Git-specific code on the server side during the transport process; the fetch process is a series of HTTP GET requests, where the client can assume the layout of the Git repository on the server.

■ **Note**   The dumb protocol is fairly rarely used these days. It's difficult to secure or make private, so most Git hosts (both cloud-based and on-premises) will refuse to use it. It's generally advised to use the smart protocol, which we describe a bit further on.

Let's follow the `http-fetch` process for the `simplegit` library:

```
$ git clone http://server/simplegit-progit.git
```

The first thing this command does is pull down the `info/refs` file. This file is written by the `update-server-info` command, which is why you need to enable that as a post-receive hook in order for the HTTP transport to work properly:

```
=> GET info/refs
ca82a6dff817ec66f44342007202690a93763949      refs/heads/master
```

Now you have a list of the remote references and SHAs. Next, you look for what the HEAD reference is so you know what to check out when you're finished:

```
=> GET HEAD
ref: refs/heads/master
```

You need to check out the `master` branch when you've completed the process. At this point, you're ready to start the walking process. Because your starting point is the `ca82a6` commit object you saw in the `info/refs` file, you start by fetching that:

```
=> GET objects/ca/82a6dff817ec66f44342007202690a93763949
(179 bytes of binary data)
```

You get an object back—that object is in loose format on the server, and you fetched it over a static HTTP GET request. You can zlib-uncompress it, strip off the header, and look at the commit content:

```
$ git cat-file -p ca82a6dff817ec66f44342007202690a93763949
tree cfda3bf379e4f8dba8717dee55aab78aef7f4daf
parent 085bb3bcb608e1e8451d4b2432f8ecbe6306e7e7
author Scott Chacon <schacon@gmail.com> 1205815931 -0700
committer Scott Chacon <schacon@gmail.com> 1240030591 -0700

changed the version number
```

Next, you have two more objects to retrieve—`cfda3b`, which is the tree of content that the commit we just retrieved points to; and `085bb3`, which is the parent commit:

```
=> GET objects/08/5bb3bcb608e1e8451d4b2432f8ecbe6306e7e7
(179 bytes of data)
```

That gives you your next commit object. Grab the tree object:

```
=> GET objects/cf/da3bf379e4f8dba8717dee55aab78aef7f4daf
(404 - Not Found)
```

Oops—it looks like that tree object isn't in loose format on the server, so you get a 404 response back. There are a couple of reasons for this—the object could be in an alternate repository, or it could be in a packfile in this repository. Git checks for any listed alternates first:

```
=> GET objects/info/http-alternates
(empty file)
```

If this comes back with a list of alternate URLs, Git checks for loose files and packfiles there—this is a nice mechanism for projects that are forks of one another to share objects on disk. However, because no alternates are listed in this case, your object must be in a packfile. To see what packfiles are available on this server, you need to get the objects/info/packs file, which contains a listing of them (also generated by update-server-info):

```
=> GET objects/info/packs
P pack-816a9b2334da9953e530f27bcac22082a9f5b835.pack
```

There is only one packfile on the server, so your object is obviously in there, but you'll check the index file to make sure. This is also useful if you have multiple packfiles on the server, so you can see which packfile contains the object you need:

```
=> GET objects/pack/pack-816a9b2334da9953e530f27bcac22082a9f5b835.idx
(4k of binary data)
```

Now that you have the packfile index, you can see if your object is in it—because the index lists the SHAs of the objects contained in the packfile and the offsets to those objects. Your object is there, so go ahead and get the whole packfile:

```
=> GET objects/pack/pack-816a9b2334da9953e530f27bcac22082a9f5b835.pack
(13k of binary data)
```

You have your tree object, so you continue walking your commits. They're all also within the packfile you just downloaded, so you don't have to do any more requests to your server. Git checks out a working copy of the master branch that was pointed to by the HEAD reference you downloaded at the beginning.

The Smart Protocol

The dumb protocol is simple but a bit inefficient, and it can't handle writing of data from the client to the server. The smart protocol is a more common method of transferring data, but it requires a process on the remote end that is intelligent about Git—it can read local data, figure out what the client has and needs, and generate a custom packfile for it. There are two sets of processes for transferring data: a pair for uploading data and a pair for downloading data.

Uploading Data

To upload data to a remote process, Git uses the send-pack and receive-pack processes. The send-pack process runs on the client and connects to a receive-pack process on the remote side.

SSH

For example, say you run git push origin master in your project, and origin is defined as a URL that uses the SSH protocol. Git fires up the send-pack process, which initiates a connection over SSH to your server. It tries to run a command on the remote server via an SSH call that looks something like this:

```
$ ssh -x git@server "git-receive-pack 'simplegit-progit.git'"
005bca82a6dff817ec66f4437202690a93763949 refs/heads/master report-status \
        delete-refs side-band-64k quiet ofs-delta \
        agent=git/2:2.1.1+github-607-gfba4028 delete-refs
003e085bb3bcb608e1e84b2432f8ecbe6306e7e7 refs/heads/topic
0000
```

The git-receive-pack command immediately responds with one line for each reference it currently has—in this case, just the master branch and its SHA. The first line also has a list of the server's capabilities (here, report-status, delete-refs, and some others, including the client identifier).

Each line starts with a 4-character hex value specifying how long the rest of the line is. Your first line starts with 005b, which is 91 in hex, meaning that 91 bytes remain on that line. The next line starts with 003e, which is 62, so you read the remaining 62 bytes. The next line is 0000, meaning the server is done with its references listing.

Now that it knows the server's state, your send-pack process determines what commits it has that the server doesn't. For each reference that this push will update, the send-pack process tells the receive-pack process that information. For instance, if you're updating the master branch and adding an experiment branch, the send-pack response may look something like this:

```
0085ca82a6dff817ec66f44342007202690a93763949  15027957951b64cf874c3557a0f3547bd83b3ff6 \
      refs/heads/master report-status
0067000000000000000000000000000000000000000000 cdfdb42577e2506715f8cfeacdbabc092bf63e8d \
      refs/heads/experiment
0000
```

Git sends a line for each reference you're updating with the line's length, the old SHA, the new SHA, and the reference that is being updated. The first line also has the client's capabilities. The SHA-1 value of all '0's means that nothing was there before—because you're adding the experiment reference. If you were deleting a reference, you would see the opposite: all '0's on the right side.

Next, the client sends a packfile of all the objects the server doesn't have yet. Finally, the server responds with a success (or failure) indication:

```
000Aunpack ok
```

HTTP(S)

This process is mostly the same over HTTP, though the handshaking is a bit different. The connection is initiated with this request:

```
=> GET http://server/simplegit-progit.git/info/refs?service=git-receive-pack
001f# service=git-receive-pack
000000ab6c5f0e45abd7832bf23074a333f739977c9e8188 refs/heads/master \
        report-status delete-refs side-band-64k quiet ofs-delta \
        agent=git/2:2.1.1~vmg-bitmaps-bugaloo-608-g116744e
0000
```

That's the end of the first client-server exchange. The client then makes another request, this time a POST, with the data that git-upload-pack provides.

```
=> POST http://server/simplegit-progit.git/git-receive/pack
```

The POST request includes the send-pack output and the packfile as its payload. The server then indicates success or failure with its HTTP response.

Downloading Data

When you download data, the fetch-pack and upload-pack processes are involved. The client initiates a fetch-pack process that connects to an upload-pack process on the remote side to negotiate what data will be transferred down.

SSH

If you're doing the fetch over SSH, fetch-pack instead runs something like this:

```
$ ssh -x git@server "git-upload-pack 'simplegit-progit.git'"
```

After fetch-pack connects, upload-pack sends back something like this:

```
00dfca82a6dff817ec66f44342007202690a93763949 HEADmulti_ack thin-pack \
        side-band side-band-64k ofs-delta shallow no-progress include-tag \
        multi_ack_detailed symref=HEAD:refs/heads/master \
        agent=git/2:2.1.1+github-607-gfba4028
003fca82a6dff817ec66f44342007202690a93763949 refs/heads/master
0000
```

This is very similar to what receive-pack responds with, but the capabilities are different. In addition, it sends back what HEAD points to (symref=HEAD:refs/heads/master) so the client knows what to check out if this is a clone.

At this point, the fetch-pack process looks at what objects it has and responds with the objects that it needs by sending "want" and then the SHA it wants. It sends all the objects it already has with "have" and then the SHA. At the end of this list, it writes "done" to initiate the upload-pack process to begin sending the packfile of the data it needs:

```
0054want ca82a6dff817ec66f44342007202690a93763949 ofs-delta
0032have 085bb3bcb608e1e8451d4b2432f8ecbe6306e7e7
0000
0009done
```

HTTP(S)

The handshake for a fetch operation takes two HTTP requests. The first is a GET to the same endpoint used in the dumb protocol:

```
=> GET $GIT_URL/info/refs?service=git-upload-pack
001e# service=git-upload-pack
000000e7ca82a6dff817ec66f44342007202690a93763949 HEADmulti_ack thin-pack \
    side-band side-band-64k ofs-delta shallow no-progress include-tag \
    multi_ack_detailed no-done symref=HEAD:refs/heads/master \
    agent=git/2:2.1.1+github-607-gfba4028
003fca82a6dff817ec66f44342007202690a93763949 refs/heads/master
0000
```

This is very similar to invoking `git-upload-pack` over an SSH connection, but the second exchange is performed as a separate request:

```
=> POST $GIT_URL/git-upload-pack HTTP/1.0
0032want 0a53e9ddeaddad63ad106860237bbf53411d11a7
0032have 441b40d833fdfa93eb2908e52742248faf0ee993
0000
```

Again, this is the same format as above. The response to this request indicates success or failure, and includes the packfile.

Protocols Summary

This section contains a very basic overview of the transfer protocols. The protocol includes many other features, such as `multi_ack` or `side-band` capabilities, but covering them is outside the scope of this book. We've tried to give you a sense of the general back-and-forth between client and server; if you need more knowledge than this, you'll probably want to take a look at the Git source code.

Maintenance and Data Recovery

Occasionally, you may have to do some cleanup—make a repository more compact, clean up an imported repository, or recover lost work. This section will cover some of these scenarios.

Maintenance

Occasionally, Git automatically runs a command called "auto gc." Most of the time, this command does nothing. However, if there are too many loose objects (objects not in a packfile) or too many packfiles, Git launches a full-fledged `git gc` command. The "gc" stands for garbage collect, and the command does a number of things: it gathers up all the loose objects and places them in packfiles, it consolidates packfiles into one big packfile, and it removes objects that aren't reachable from any commit and are a few months old.

You can run `auto gc` manually as follows:

```
$ git gc --auto
```

Again, this generally does nothing. You must have around 7,000 loose objects or more than 50 packfiles for Git to fire up a real `gc` command. You can modify these limits with the `gc.auto` and `gc.autopacklimit` config settings, respectively.

The other thing `gc` will do is pack up your references into a single file. Suppose your repository contains the following branches and tags:

```
$ find .git/refs -type f
.git/refs/heads/experiment
.git/refs/heads/master
.git/refs/tags/v1.0
.git/refs/tags/v1.1
```

If you run git gc, you'll no longer have these files in the refs directory. Git will move them for the sake of efficiency into a file named .git/packed-refs that looks like this:

```
$ cat .git/packed-refs
# pack-refs with: peeled fully-peeled
cac0cab538b970a37ea1e769cbbde608743bc96d refs/heads/experiment
ab1afef80fac8e34258ff41fc1b867c702daa24b refs/heads/master
cac0cab538b970a37ea1e769cbbde608743bc96d refs/tags/v1.0
9585191f37f7b0fb9444f35a9bf50de191beadc2 refs/tags/v1.1
^1a410efbd13591db07496601ebc7a059dd55cfe9
```

If you update a reference, Git doesn't edit this file but instead writes a new file to refs/heads. To get the appropriate SHA for a given reference, Git checks for that reference in the refs directory and then checks the packed-refs file as a fallback. However, if you can't find a reference in the refs directory, it's probably in your packed-refs file.

Notice the last line of the file, which begins with a ^. This means the tag directly above is an annotated tag and that line is the commit that the annotated tag points to.

Data Recovery

At some point in your Git journey, you may accidentally lose a commit. Generally, this happens because you force-delete a branch that had work on it, and it turns out you wanted the branch after all; or you hard-reset a branch, thus abandoning commits that you wanted something from. Assuming this happens, how can you get your commits back?

Here's an example that hard-resets the master branch in your test repository to an older commit and then recovers the lost commits. First, let's review where your repository is at this point:

```
$ git log --pretty=oneline
ab1afef80fac8e34258ff41fc1b867c702daa24b modified repo a bit
484a59275031909e19aadb7c92262719cfcdf19a added repo.rb
1a410efbd13591db07496601ebc7a059dd55cfe9 third commit
cac0cab538b970a37ea1e769cbbde608743bc96d second commit
fdf4fc3344e67ab068f836878b6c4951e3b15f3d first commit
```

Now, move the master branch back to the middle commit:

```
$ git reset --hard 1a410efbd13591db07496601ebc7a059dd55cfe9
HEAD is now at 1a410ef third commit
$ git log --pretty=oneline
1a410efbd13591db07496601ebc7a059dd55cfe9 third commit
cac0cab538b970a37ea1e769cbbde608743bc96d second commit
fdf4fc3344e67ab068f836878b6c4951e3b15f3d first commit
```

You've effectively lost the top two commits—you have no branch from which those commits are reachable. You need to find the latest commit SHA and then add a branch that points to it. The trick is finding that latest commit SHA—it's not like you've memorized it, right?

Often, the quickest way is to use a tool called git reflog. As you're working, Git silently records what your HEAD is every time you change it. Each time you commit or change branches, the reflog is updated. The reflog is also updated by the git update-ref command, which is another reason to use it instead of just writing the SHA value to your ref files, as we covered in "Git References". You can see where you've been at any time by running git reflog:

```
$ git reflog
1a410ef HEAD@{0}: reset: moving to 1a410ef
ab1afef HEAD@{1}: commit: modified repo.rb a bit
484a592 HEAD@{2}: commit: added repo.rb
```

Here we can see the two commits that we have had checked out, however there is not much information here. To see the same information in a much more useful way, we can run git log -g, which will give you a normal log output for your reflog.

```
$ git log -g
commit 1a410efbd13591db07496601ebc7a059dd55cfe9
Reflog: HEAD@{0} (Scott Chacon <schacon@gmail.com>)
Reflog message: updating HEAD
Author: Scott Chacon <schacon@gmail.com>
Date:   Fri May 22 18:22:37 2009 -0700

        third commit

commit ab1afef80fac8e34258ff41fc1b867c702daa24b
Reflog: HEAD@{1} (Scott Chacon <schacon@gmail.com>)
Reflog message: updating HEAD
Author: Scott Chacon <schacon@gmail.com>
Date:   Fri May 22 18:15:24 2009 -0700

        modified repo.rb a bit
```

It looks like the bottom commit is the one you lost, so you can recover it by creating a new branch at that commit. For example, you can start a branch named recover-branch at that commit (ab1afef):

```
$ git branch recover-branch ab1afef
$ git log --pretty=oneline recover-branch
ab1afef80fac8e34258ff41fc1b867c702daa24b modified repo a bit
484a59275031909e19aadb7c92262719cfcdf19a added repo.rb
1a410efbd13591db07496601ebc7a059dd55cfe9 third commit
cac0cab538b970a37ea1e769cbbde608743bc96d second commit
fdf4fc3344e67ab068f836878b6c4951e3b15f3d first commit
```

Cool—now you have a branch named recover-branch that is where your master branch used to be, making the first two commits reachable again. Next, suppose your loss was for some reason not in the reflog—you can simulate that by removing recover-branch and deleting the reflog. Now the first two commits aren't reachable by anything:

```
$ git branch -D recover-branch
$ rm -Rf .git/logs/
```

Because the reflog data is kept in the .git/logs/ directory, you effectively have no reflog. How can you recover that commit at this point? One way is to use the git fsck utility, which checks your database for integrity. If you run it with the --full option, it shows you all objects that aren't pointed to by another object:

```
$ git fsck --full
Checking object directories: 100% (256/256), done.
Checking objects: 100% (18/18), done.
dangling blob d670460b4b4aece5915caf5c68d12f560a9fe3e4
dangling commit ab1afef80fac8e34258ff41fc1b867c702daa24b
dangling tree aea790b9a58f6cf6f2804eeac9f0abbe9631e4c9
dangling blob 7108f7ecb345ee9d0084193f147cdad4d2998293
```

In this case, you can see your missing commit after the string "dangling commit." You can recover it the same way, by adding a branch that points to that SHA.

Removing Objects

There are a lot of great things about Git, but one feature that can cause issues is the fact that a git clone downloads the entire history of the project, including every version of every file. This is fine if the whole thing is source code, because Git is highly optimized to compress that data efficiently. However, if someone at any point in the history of your project added a single huge file, every clone for all time will be forced to download that large file, even if it was removed from the project in the very next commit. Because it's reachable from the history, it will always be there.

This can be a huge problem when you're converting Subversion or Perforce repositories into Git. Because you don't download the whole history in those systems, this type of addition carries few consequences. If you did an import from another system or otherwise find that your repository is much larger than it should be, here is how you can find and remove large objects.

Be warned: this technique is destructive to your commit history. It rewrites every commit object since the earliest tree you have to modify to remove a large file reference. If you do this immediately after an import, before anyone has started to base work on the commit, you're fine—otherwise, you have to notify all contributors that they must rebase their work onto your new commits.

To demonstrate, you'll add a large file into your test repository, remove it in the next commit, find it, and remove it permanently from the repository. First, add a large object to your history:

```
$ curl https://www.kernel.org/pub/software/scm/git/git-2.1.0.tar.gz > git.tgz
$ git add git.tgz
$ git commit -m 'add git tarball'
[master 7b30847] add git tarball
 1 file changed, 0 insertions(+), 0 deletions(-)
 create mode 100644 git.tgz
```

Oops—you didn't want to add a huge tarball to your project. Better get rid of it:

```
$ git rm git.tgz
rm 'git.tgz'
$ git commit -m 'oops - removed large tarball'
[master dadf725] oops - removed large tarball
 1 file changed, 0 insertions(+), 0 deletions(-)
 delete mode 100644 git.tgz
```

Now, gc your database and see how much space you're using:

```
$ git gc
Counting objects: 17, done.
Delta compression using up to 8 threads.
Compressing objects: 100% (13/13), done.
Writing objects: 100% (17/17), done.
Total 17 (delta 1), reused 10 (delta 0)
```

You can run the count-objects command to quickly see how much space you're using:

```
$ git count-objects -v
count: 7
size: 32
in-pack: 17
packs: 1
size-pack: 4868
prune-packable: 0
garbage: 0
size-garbage: 0
```

The `size-pack` entry is the size of your packfiles in kilobytes, so you're using almost 5MB. Before the last commit, you were using closer to 2K—clearly, removing the file from the previous commit didn't remove it from your history. Every time anyone clones this repository, they will have to clone all 5MB just to get this tiny project, because you accidentally added a big file. Let's get rid of it.

First you have to find it. In this case, you already know what file it is. But suppose you didn't; how would you identify what file or files were taking up so much space? If you run `git gc`, all the objects are in a packfile; you can identify the big objects by running another plumbing command called `git verify-pack` and sorting on the third field in the output, which is file size. You can also pipe it through the `tail` command because you're only interested in the last few largest files:

```
$ git verify-pack -v .git/objects/pack/pack-29...69.idx \
  | sort -k 3 -n \
  | tail -3
dadf7258d699da2c8d89b09ef6670edb7d5f91b4 commit 229 159 12
033b4468fa6b2a9547a70d88d1bbe8bf3f9ed0d5 blob   22044 5792 4977696
82c99a3e86bb1267b236a4b6eff7868d97489af1 blob   4975916 4976258 1438
```

The big object is at the bottom: 5MB. To find out what file it is, you'll use the `rev-list` command, which you used briefly in 'Enforcing a Specific Commit-Message Format' (Chapter 8). If you pass `--objects` to `rev-list`, it lists all the commit SHAs and also the blob SHAs with the file paths associated with them. You can use this to find your blob's name:

```
$ git rev-list --objects --all | grep 82c99a3
82c99a3e86bb1267b236a4b6eff7868d97489af1 git.tgz
```

Now, you need to remove this file from all trees in your past. You can easily see what commits modified this file:

```
$ git log --oneline -- git.tgz
dadf725 oops - removed large tarball
7b30847 add git tarball
```

You must rewrite all the commits downstream from 7b30847 to fully remove this file from your Git history. To do so, you use `filter-branch`, which you used in "Rewriting History" (Chapter 7) :

```
$ git filter-branch --index-filter \
  'git rm --cached --ignore-unmatch git.tgz' -- 7b30847^..
Rewrite 7b30847d080183a1ab7d18fb202473b3096e9f34 (1/2)rm 'git.tgz'
Rewrite dadf7258d699da2c8d89b09ef6670edb7d5f91b4 (2/2)
Ref 'refs/heads/master' was rewritten
```

The `--index-filter` option is similar to the `--tree-filter` option used in "Rewriting History" (Chapter 7), except that instead of passing a command that modifies files checked out on disk, you're modifying your staging area or index each time.

Rather than remove a specific file with something like `rm file`, you have to remove it with `git rm --cached`—you must remove it from the index, not from disk. The reason to do it this way is speed—because Git doesn't have to check out each revision to disk before running your filter, the process can be much, much faster. You can accomplish the same task with `--tree-filter` if you want. The `--ignore-unmatch` option to `git rm` tells it not to error out if the pattern you're trying to remove isn't there. Finally, you ask `filter-branch` to rewrite your history only from the 6df7640 commit up, because you know that is where this problem started. Otherwise, it will start from the beginning and will unnecessarily take longer.

Your history no longer contains a reference to that file. However, your reflog and a new set of refs that Git added when you did the `filter-branch` under `.git/refs/original` still do, so you have to remove them and then repack the database. You need to get rid of anything that has a pointer to those old commits before you repack:

```
$ rm -Rf .git/refs/original
$ rm -Rf .git/logs/
$ git gc
Counting objects: 15, done.
Delta compression using up to 8 threads.
Compressing objects: 100% (11/11), done.
Writing objects: 100% (15/15), done.
Total 15 (delta 1), reused 12 (delta 0)
```

Let's see how much space you saved.

```
$ git count-objects -v
count: 11
size: 4904
in-pack: 15
packs: 1
size-pack: 8
prune-packable: 0
garbage: 0
size-garbage: 0
```

The packed repository size is down to 8K, which is much better than 5MB. You can see from the size value that the big object is still in your loose objects, so it's not gone; but it won't be transferred on a push or subsequent clone, which is what is important. If you really wanted to, you could remove the object completely by running `git prune` with the `--expire` option:

```
$ git prune --expire now
$ git count-objects -v
count: 0
size: 0
in-pack: 15
packs: 1
size-pack: 8
prune-packable: 0
garbage: 0
size-garbage: 0
```

Environment Variables

Git always runs inside a bash shell, and uses a number of shell environment variables to determine how it behaves. Occasionally, it comes in handy to know what these are, and how they can be used to make Git behave the way you want it to. This isn't an exhaustive list of all the environment variables Git pays attention to, but we'll cover the most useful.

Global Behavior

Some of Git's general behavior as a computer program depends on environment variables.

GIT_EXEC_PATH determines where Git looks for its sub-programs (like git-commit, git-diff, and others). You can check the current setting by running git --exec-path.

HOME isn't usually considered customizable (too many other things depend on it), but it's where Git looks for the global configuration file. If you want a truly portable Git installation, complete with global configuration, you can override HOME in the portable Git's shell profile.

PREFIX is similar, but for the system-wide configuration. Git looks for this file at $PREFIX/etc/gitconfig.

GIT_CONFIG_NOSYSTEM, if set, disables the use of the systemwide configuration file. This is useful if your system config is interfering with your commands, but you don't have access to change or remove it.

GIT_PAGER controls the program used to display multi-page output on the command line. If this is unset, PAGER will be used as a fallback.

GIT_EDITOR is the editor Git launches when the user needs to edit some text (a commit message, for example). If unset, EDITOR will be used.

Repository Locations

Git uses several environment variables to determine how it interfaces with the current repository.

GIT_DIR is the location of the .git folder. If this isn't specified, Git walks up the directory tree until it gets to ~ or /, looking for a .git directory at every step.

GIT_CEILING_DIRECTORIES controls the behavior of searching for a .git directory. If you access directories that are slow to load (such as those on a tape drive, or across a slow network connection), you may want to have Git stop trying earlier than it might otherwise, especially if Git is invoked when building your shell prompt.

GIT_WORK_TREE is the location of the root of the working directory for a non-bare repository. If not specified, the parent directory of $GIT_DIR is used.

GIT_INDEX_FILE is the path to the index file (non-bare repositories only).

GIT_OBJECT_DIRECTORY can be used to specify the location of the directory that usually resides at .git/objects.

GIT_ALTERNATE_OBJECT_DIRECTORIES is a colon-separated list (formatted like /dir/one:/dir/two:...) which tells Git where to check for objects if they aren't in GIT_OBJECT_DIRECTORY. If you happen to have a lot of projects with large files that have the exact same contents, this can be used to avoid storing too many copies of them.

Pathspecs

A "pathspec" refers to how you specify paths to things in Git, including the use of wildcards. These are used in the .gitignore file, but also on the command-line (git add *.c).

GIT_GLOB_PATHSPECS and GIT_NOGLOB_PATHSPECS control the default behavior of wildcards in pathspecs. If GIT_GLOB_PATHSPECS is set to 1, wildcard characters act as wildcards (which is the default); if GIT_NOGLOB_PATHSPECS is set to 1, wildcard characters only match themselves, meaning something like *.c would only match a file named *.c, rather than any file whose name ends with .c. You can override this in individual cases by starting the pathspec with :(glob) or :(literal), as in :(glob)*.c.

GIT_LITERAL_PATHSPECS disables both of the preceding behaviors; no wildcard characters will work, and the override prefixes are disabled as well.

GIT_ICASE_PATHSPECS sets all pathspecs to work in a case-insensitive manner.

Committing

The final creation of a Git commit object is usually done by `git-commit-tree`, which uses these environment variables as its primary source of information, falling back to configuration values only if these aren't present.

`GIT_AUTHOR_NAME` is the human-readable name in the "author" field.

`GIT_AUTHOR_EMAIL` is the email for the "author" field.

`GIT_AUTHOR_DATE` is the timestamp used for the "author" field.

`GIT_COMMITTER_NAME` sets the human name for the "committer" field.

`GIT_COMMITTER_EMAIL` is the email address for the "committer" field.

`GIT_COMMITTER_DATE` is used for the timestamp in the "committer" field.

`EMAIL` is the fallback email address in case the `user.email` configuration value isn't set. If this isn't set, Git falls back to the system user and host names.

Networking

Git uses the curl library to do network operations over HTTP, so `GIT_CURL_VERBOSE` tells Git to emit all the messages generated by that library. This is similar to doing `curl -v` on the command line.

`GIT_SSL_NO_VERIFY` tells Git not to verify SSL certificates. This can sometimes be necessary if you're using a self-signed certificate to serve Git repositories over HTTPS, or you're in the middle of setting up a Git server but haven't installed a full certificate yet.

If the data rate of an HTTP operation is lower than `GIT_HTTP_LOW_SPEED_LIMIT` bytes per second for longer than `GIT_HTTP_LOW_SPEED_TIME` seconds, Git will abort that operation. These values override the `http.lowSpeedLimit` and `http.lowSpeedTime` configuration values.

`GIT_HTTP_USER_AGENT` sets the user-agent string used by Git when communicating over HTTP. The default is a value such as git/2.0.0.

Diffing and Merging

`GIT_DIFF_OPTS` is a bit of a misnomer. The only valid values are -u<n> or --unified=<n>, which controls the number of context lines shown in a `git diff` command.

`GIT_EXTERNAL_DIFF` is used as an override for the `diff.external` configuration value. If it's set, Git will invoke this program when `git diff` is invoked.

`GIT_DIFF_PATH_COUNTER` and `GIT_DIFF_PATH_TOTAL` are useful from inside the program specified by `GIT_EXTERNAL_DIFF` or `diff.external`. The former represents which file in a series is being diffed (starting with 1), and the latter is the total number of files in the batch.

`GIT_MERGE_VERBOSITY` controls the output for the recursive merge strategy. The allowed values are as follows:

- 0 outputs nothing, except possibly a single error message.

- 1 shows only conflicts.

- 2 also shows file changes.

- 3 shows when files are skipped because they haven't changed.

- 4 shows all paths as they are processed.

- 5 and above show detailed debugging information.

The default value is 2.

Debugging

Want to really know what Git is up to? Git has a fairly complete set of traces embedded, and all you need to do is turn them on. The possible values of these variables are as follows:

- "true," "1," or "2"—the trace category is written to stderr.

- An absolute path starting with /—the trace output will be written to that file.

GIT_TRACE controls general traces, which don't fit into any specific category. This includes the expansion of aliases and delegation to other sub-programs.

```
$ GIT_TRACE=true git lga
20:12:49.877982 git.c:554              trace: exec: 'git-lga'
20:12:49.878369 run-command.c:341      trace: run_command: 'git-lga'
20:12:49.879529 git.c:282              trace: alias expansion: lga => 'log' '--graph'
                                       '--pretty=oneline' '--abbrev-commit' '--decorate' '--all'
20:12:49.879885 git.c:349              trace: built-in: git 'log' '--graph' '--pretty=oneline'
                                       '--abbrev-commit' '--decorate' '--all'
20:12:49.899217 run-command.c:341      trace: run_command: 'less'
20:12:49.899675 run-command.c:192      trace: exec: 'less'
```

GIT_TRACE_PACK_ACCESS controls tracing of packfile access. The first field is the packfile being accessed; the second is the offset within that file:

```
$ GIT_TRACE_PACK_ACCESS=true git status
20:10:12.081397 sha1_file.c:2088       .git/objects/pack/pack-c3fa...291e.pack 12
20:10:12.081886 sha1_file.c:2088       .git/objects/pack/pack-c3fa...291e.pack 34662
20:10:12.082115 sha1_file.c:2088       .git/objects/pack/pack-c3fa...291e.pack 35175
# [...]
20:10:12.087398 sha1_file.c:2088       .git/objects/pack/pack-e80e...e3d2.pack 56914983
20:10:12.087419 sha1_file.c:2088       .git/objects/pack/pack-e80e...e3d2.pack 14303666
On branch master
Your branch is up-to-date with 'origin/master'.
nothing to commit, working directory clean
```

GIT_TRACE_PACKET enables packet-level tracing for network operations.

```
$ GIT_TRACE_PACKET=true git ls-remote origin
20:15:14.867043 pkt-line.c:46          packet:          git< # service=git-upload-pack
20:15:14.867071 pkt-line.c:46          packet:          git< 0000
20:15:14.867079 pkt-line.c:46          packet:          git<
97b8860c071898d9e162678ea1035a8ced2f8b1f HEAD\0multi_ack thin-pack side-band side-band-64k ofs-
delta shallow no-progress include-tag multi_ack_detailed no-done symref=HEAD:refs/heads/master
agent=git/2.0.4
20:15:14.867088 pkt-line.c:46          packet:          git<
0f20ae29889d61f2e93ae00fd34f1cdb53285702 refs/heads/ab/add-interactive-show-diff-func-name
20:15:14.867094 pkt-line.c:46          packet:          git<
36dc827bc9d17f80ed4f326de21247a5d1341fbc refs/heads/ah/doc-gitk-config
# [...]
```

GIT_TRACE_PERFORMANCE controls logging of performance data. The output shows how long each particular git invocation takes.

```
$ GIT_TRACE_PERFORMANCE=true git gc
20:18:19.499676 trace.c:414              performance: 0.374835000 s: git command: 'git' 'pack-refs'
                                         '--all' '--prune'
20:18:19.845585 trace.c:414              performance: 0.343020000 s: git command: 'git' 'reflog'
                                         'expire' '--all'
Counting objects: 170994, done.
Delta compression using up to 8 threads.
Compressing objects: 100% (43413/43413), done.
Writing objects: 100% (170994/170994), done.
Total 170994 (delta 126176), reused 170524 (delta 125706)
20:18:23.567927 trace.c:414              performance: 3.715349000 s: git command: 'git' 'pack-
objects' '--keep-true-parents' '--honor-pack-keep' '--non-empty' '--all' '--reflog' '--unpack-
unreachable=2.weeks.ago' '--local' '--delta-base-offset' '.git/objects/pack/.tmp-49190-pack'
20:18:23.584728 trace.c:414              performance: 0.000910000 s: git command: 'git' 'prune-packed'
20:18:23.605218 trace.c:414              performance: 0.017972000 s: git command: 'git' 'update-
                                         server-info'
20:18:23.606342 trace.c:414              performance: 3.756312000 s: git command: 'git' 'repack'
                                         '-d' '-l' '-A' '--unpack-unreachable=2.weeks.ago'
Checking connectivity: 170994, done.
20:18:25.225424 trace.c:414              performance: 1.616423000 s: git command: 'git' 'prune'
                                         '--expire' '2.weeks.ago'
20:18:25.232403 trace.c:414              performance: 0.001051000 s: git command: 'git' 'rerere' 'gc'
20:18:25.233159 trace.c:414              performance: 6.112217000 s: git command: 'git' 'gc'
```

GIT_TRACE_SETUP shows information about what Git is discovering about the repository and environment it's interacting with.

```
$ GIT_TRACE_SETUP=true git status
20:19:47.086765 trace.c:315              setup: git_dir: .git
20:19:47.087184 trace.c:316              setup: worktree: /Users/ben/src/git
20:19:47.087191 trace.c:317              setup: cwd: /Users/ben/src/git
20:19:47.087194 trace.c:318              setup: prefix: (null)
On branch master
Your branch is up-to-date with 'origin/master'.
nothing to commit, working directory clean
```

Miscellaneous

GIT_SSH, if specified, is a program that is invoked instead of ssh when Git tries to connect to an SSH host. It is invoked like $GIT_SSH [username@]host [-p <port>] <command>. Note that this isn't the easiest way to customize how ssh is invoked; it won't support extra command-line parameters, so you'd have to write a wrapper script and set GIT_SSH to point to it. It's probably easier just to use the ~/.ssh/config file for that.

GIT_ASKPASS is an override for the core.askpass configuration value. This is the program invoked whenever Git needs to ask the user for credentials, which can expect a text prompt as a command-line argument, and should return the answer on stdout. (See "Credential Storage" in Chapter 7 for more on this subsystem.)

GIT_NAMESPACE controls access to namespaced refs, and is equivalent to the --namespace flag. This is mostly useful on the server side, where you may want to store multiple forks of a single repository in one repository, only keeping the refs separate.

GIT_FLUSH can be used to force Git to use non-buffered I/O when writing incrementally to stdout. A value of 1 causes Git to flush more often, a value of 0 causes all output to be buffered. The default value (if this variable is not set) is to choose an appropriate buffering scheme depending on the activity and the output mode.

GIT_REFLOG_ACTION lets you specify the descriptive text written to the reflog. Here's an example:

```
$ GIT_REFLOG_ACTION="my action" git commit --allow-empty -m 'my message'
[master 9e3d55a] my message
$ git reflog -1
9e3d55a HEAD@{0}: my action: my message
```

Summary

You should have a pretty good understanding of what Git does in the background and, to some degree, how it's implemented. This chapter has covered a number of plumbing commands—commands that are lower level and simpler than the porcelain commands you've learned about in the rest of the book. Understanding how Git works at a lower level should make it easier to understand why it's doing what it's doing and also to write your own tools and helping scripts to make your specific workflow work for you.

Git as a content-addressable filesystem is a very powerful tool that you can easily use as more than just a VCS. We hope you can use your newfound knowledge of Git internals to implement your own cool application of this technology and feel more comfortable using Git in more advanced ways.

APPENDIX A

■ ■ ■

Git in Other Environments

If you read through the whole book, you've learned a lot about how to use Git at the command line. You can work with local files, connect your repository to others over a network, and work effectively with others. But the story doesn't end there; Git is usually used as part of a larger ecosystem, and the terminal isn't always the best way to work with it. Now we'll take a look at some of the other kinds of environments where Git can be useful, and how other applications (including yours) work alongside Git.

Graphical Interfaces

Git's native environment is in the terminal. New features show up there first, and only at the command line is the full power of Git completely at your disposal. But plain text isn't the best choice for all tasks; sometimes a visual representation is what you need, and some users are much more comfortable with a point-and-click interface.

It's important to note that different interfaces are tailored for different workflows. Some clients only expose a carefully curated subset of Git functionality, in order to support a specific way of working that the author considers effective. When viewed in this light, none of these tools can be called "better" than any of the others; they're simply more fit for their intended purpose. Also note that there's nothing these graphical clients can do that the command-line client can't; the command-line is still where you'll have the most power and control when working with your repositories.

gitk and git-gui

When you install Git, you also get its visual tools, `gitk` and `git-gui`.

`gitk` is a graphical history viewer. Think of it like a powerful GUI shell over `git log` and `git grep`. This is the tool to use when you're trying to find something that happened in the past, or visualize your project's history.

Gitk is easiest to invoke from the command-line. Just cd into a Git repository, and type:

```
$ gitk [git log options]
```

Gitk accepts many command-line options, most of which are passed through to the underlying `git log` action. Probably one of the most useful is the `--all` flag, which tells `gitk` to show commits reachable from any ref, not just `HEAD`. `gitk`'s interface looks like this:

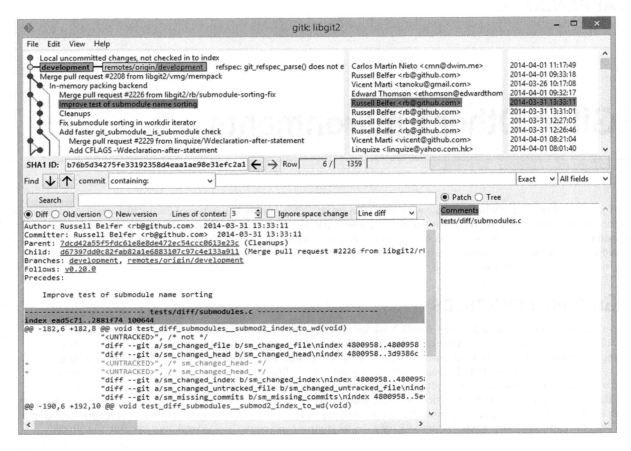

Figure A-1. *The gitk history viewer*

On the top is something that looks a bit like the output of git log --graph; each dot represents a commit, the lines represent parent relationships, and refs are shown as colored boxes. The yellow dot represents HEAD, and the red dot represents changes that are yet to become a commit. At the bottom is a view of the selected commit; the comments and patch on the left, and a summary view on the right. In between is a collection of controls used for searching history.

git-gui, on the other hand, is primarily a tool for crafting commits. It, too, is easiest to invoke from the command line:

```
$ git gui
```

And it looks something like this:

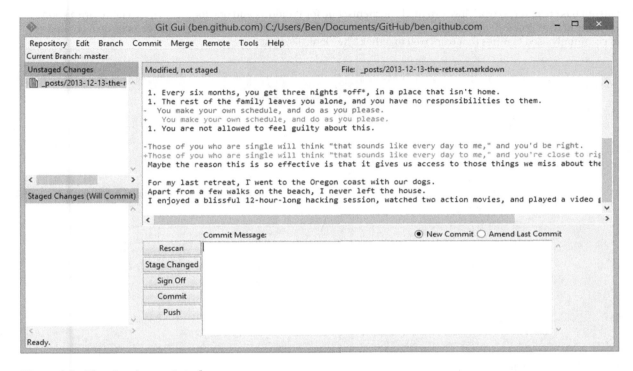

Figure A-2. *The git-gui commit tool*

On the left is the index; unstaged changes are on top, staged changes on the bottom. You can move entire files between the two states by clicking on their icons, or you can select a file for viewing by clicking on its name.

At top right is the diff view, which shows the changes for the currently-selected file. You can stage individual hunks (or individual lines) by right-clicking in this area.

At the bottom right is the message and action area. Type your message into the text box and click "Commit" to do something similar to `git commit`. You can also choose to amend the last commit by choosing the "Amend" radio button, which updates the "Staged Changes" area with the contents of the last commit. Then you can simply stage or unstage some changes, alter the commit message, and click "Commit" again to replace the old commit with a new one.

`gitk` and `git-gui` are examples of task-oriented tools. Each of them is tailored for a specific purpose (viewing history and creating commits, respectively), and omit the features not necessary for that task.

GitHub for Mac and Windows

GitHub has created two workflow-oriented Git clients: one for Windows and one for Mac. These clients are a good example of workflow-oriented tools—rather than expose all of Git's functionality, they instead focus on a curated set of commonly used features that work well together. They look like this:

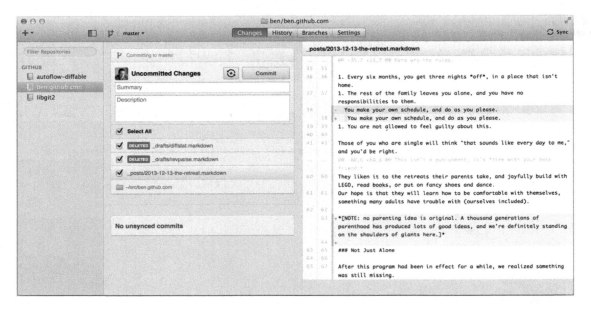

Figure A-3. *GitHub for Mac*

Figure A-4. *GitHub for Windows*

They are designed to look and work very much alike, so we'll treat them like a single product in this chapter. We won't be doing a detailed rundown of these tools (they have their own documentation), but a quick tour of the "changes" view (which is where you'll spend most of your time) is in order.

On the left is the list of repositories the client is tracking; you can add a repository (either by cloning or attaching locally) by clicking the "+" icon at the top of this area.

In the center is a commit-input area, which lets you input a commit message, and select which files should be included. (On Windows, the commit history is displayed directly below this; on Mac, it's on a separate tab.)

On the right is a diff view, which shows what's changed in your working directory, or which changes were included in the selected commit.

The last thing to notice is the "Sync" button at the top-right, which is the primary way you interact over the network.

■ **Note**   You don't need a GitHub account to use these tools. While they're designed to highlight GitHub's service and recommended workflow, they will happily work with any repository, and do network operations with any Git host.

Installation

GitHub for Windows can be downloaded from `https://windows.github.com`, and GitHub for Mac from `https://mac.github.com`. When the applications are first run, they walk you through all the first-time Git setup, such as configuring your name and email address, and both set up sane defaults for many common configuration options, such as credential caches and CRLF behavior.

Both are "evergreen"—updates are downloaded and installed in the background while the applications are open. This helpfully includes a bundled version of Git, which means you probably won't have to worry about manually updating it again. On Windows, the client includes a shortcut to launch Powershell with Posh-Git, which we'll talk more about later in this appendix.

The next step is to give the tool some repositories to work with. The client shows you a list of the repositories you have access to on GitHub, and can clone them in one step. If you already have a local repository, just drag its directory from the Finder or Windows Explorer into the GitHub client window, and it will be included in the list of repositories on the left.

Recommended Workflow

Once it's installed and configured, you can use the GitHub client for many common Git tasks. The intended workflow for this tool is sometimes called the "GitHub Flow." We cover this in more detail in "The GitHub Flow" (Chapter 6), but the general gist is that (a) you'll be committing to a branch, and (b) you'll be syncing up with a remote repository fairly regularly.

Branch management is one of the areas where the two tools diverge. On Mac, there's a button at the top of the window for creating a new branch:

Figure A-5. *"Create Branch" button on Mac*

On Windows, this is done by typing the new branch's name in the branch-switching widget:

Figure A-6. *Creating a branch on Windows*

Once your branch is created, making new commits is fairly straightforward. Make some changes in your working directory, and when you switch to the GitHub client window, it shows you which files changed. Enter a commit message, select the files you'd like to include, and click the "Commit" button (Ctrl-enter or ⌘-enter).

The main way you interact with other repositories over the network is through the "Sync" feature. Git internally has separate operations for pushing, fetching, merging, and rebasing, but the GitHub clients collapse all these into one multi-step feature. Here's what happens when you click the Sync button:

1. `git pull --rebase`. If this fails because of a merge conflict, fall back to `git pull --no-rebase`.

2. `git push`.

This is the most common sequence of network commands when working in this style, so squashing them into one command saves a lot of time.

Summary

These tools are very well-suited for the workflow they're designed for. Developers and non-developers alike can be collaborating on a project within minutes, and many of the best practices for this kind of workflow are baked into the tools. However, if your workflow is different, or you want more control over how and when network operations are done, we recommend you use another client or the command line.

Other GUIs

There are a number of other graphical Git clients, and they run the gamut from specialized, single-purpose tools all the way to apps that try to expose everything Git can do. The official Git website has a curated list of the most popular clients at http://git-scm.com/downloads/guis. A more comprehensive list is available on the Git wiki site, at https://git.wiki.kernel.org/index.php/Interfaces,_frontends,_and_tools#Graphical_Interfaces.

Git in Visual Studio

Starting with Visual Studio 2013 Update 1, Visual Studio users have a Git client built directly into their IDE. Visual Studio has had source-control integration features for quite some time, but they were oriented toward centralized, file-locking systems, and Git was not a good match for this workflow. Visual Studio 2013's Git support has been separated from this older feature, and the result is a much better fit between Studio and Git.

To locate the feature, open a project that's controlled by Git (or just `git init` an existing project), and select View ➤ Team Explorer from the menu. You'll see the "Connect" view, which looks a bit like this:

Figure A-7. *Connecting to a Git repository from Team Explorer*

Visual Studio remembers all the projects you've opened that are Git-controlled, and they're available in the list at the bottom. If you don't see the one you want there, click the "Add" link and type in the path to the working directory. Double-clicking one of the local Git repositories leads you to the Home view, which looks like Figure A-8. This is a hub for performing Git actions; when you're writing code, you'll probably spend most of your time in the Changes view, but when it comes time to pull down changes made by your teammates, you'll use the Unsynced Commits and Branches views.

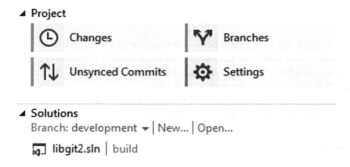

Figure A-8. *The Home view for a Git repository in Visual Studio*

Visual Studio now has a powerful task-focused UI for Git. It includes a linear history view, a diff viewer, remote commands, and many other capabilities. For complete documentation of this feature (which doesn't fit here), go to http://msdn.microsoft.com/en-us/library/hh850437.aspx.

Git in Eclipse

Eclipse ships with a plugin called Egit, which provides a fairly-complete interface to Git operations. It's accessed by switching to the Git Perspective (Window ➤ Open Perspective ➤ Other…, and select Git).

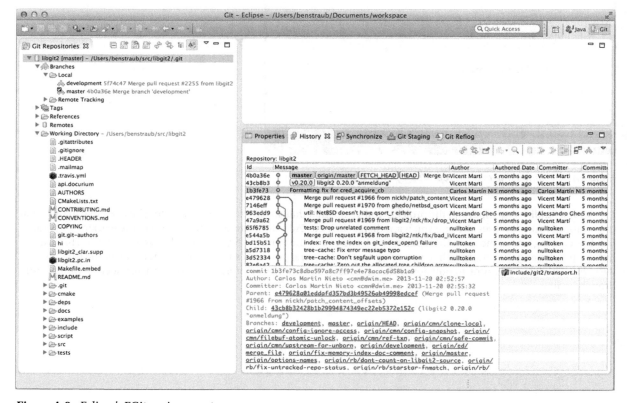

Figure A-9. *Eclipse's EGit environment*

EGit comes with plenty of great documentation, which you can find by going to Help ➤ Help Contents, and choosing the EGit Documentation node from the contents listing.

Git in Bash

If you're a Bash user, you can tap into some of your shell's features to make your experience with Git a lot friendlier. Git actually ships with plugins for several shells, but it's not turned on by default.

First, you need to get a copy of the contrib/completion/git-completion.bash file out of the Git source code. Copy it somewhere handy, like your home directory, and add this to your .bashrc:

```
. ~/git-completion.bash
```

Once that's done, change your directory to a git repository, and type:

```
$ git chec<tab>
```

...and Bash will auto-complete to git checkout. This works with all of Git's subcommands, command-line parameters, and remotes and ref names where appropriate.

It's also useful to customize your prompt to show information about the current directory's Git repository. This can be as simple or complex as you want, but there are generally a few key pieces of information that most people want, like the current branch and the status of the working directory. To add these to your prompt, just copy the contrib/completion/git-prompt.sh file from Git's source repository to your home directory, add something like this to your .bashrc:

```
. ~/git-prompt.sh
export GIT_PS1_SHOWDIRTYSTATE=1
export PS1='\w$(__git_ps1 " (%s)")\$ '
```

The \w means print the current working directory, the \$ prints the $ part of the prompt, and __git_ps1 " (%s)" calls the function provided by git-prompt.sh with a formatting argument. Now your bash prompt will look like this when you're anywhere inside a Git-controlled project

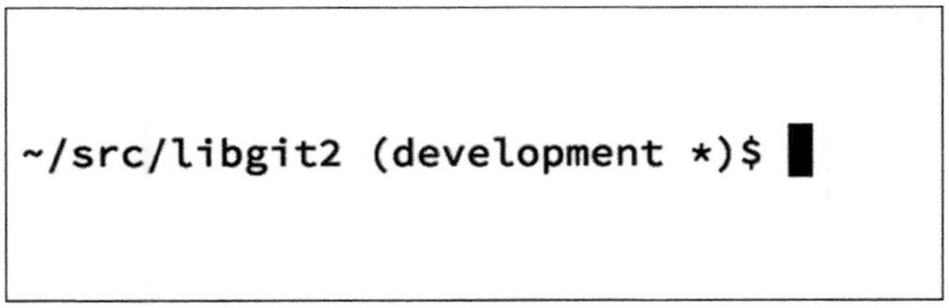

Figure A-10. *Customized bash prompt*

Both of these scripts come with helpful documentation; take a look at the contents of git-completion.bash and git-prompt.sh for more information.

Git in Zsh

Git also ships with a tab-completion library for Zsh. Just copy contrib/completion/git-completion.zsh to your home directory and source it from your .zshrc. Zsh's interface is a bit more powerful than Bash's:

```
$ git che<tab>
check-attr         -- display gitattributes information
check-ref-format   -- ensure that a reference name is well formed
checkout           -- checkout branch or paths to working tree
checkout-index     -- copy files from index to working directory
cherry             -- find commits not merged upstream
cherry-pick        -- apply changes introduced by some existing commits
```

Ambiguous tab-completions aren't just listed; they have helpful descriptions, and you can graphically navigate the list by repeatedly hitting Tab. This works with Git commands, their arguments, and names of things inside the repository (like refs and remotes), as well filenames and all the other things Zsh knows how to tab-complete.

Zsh happens to be fairly compatible with Bash when it comes to prompt customization, but it allows you to have a right-side prompt as well. To include the branch name on the right side, add these lines to your ~/.zshrc file:

```
setopt prompt_subst
. ~/git-prompt.sh
export RPROMPT=$'$(__git_ps1 "%s")'
```

This results in a display of the current branch on the right-hand side of the terminal window, whenever your shell is inside a Git repository. It looks a bit like this:

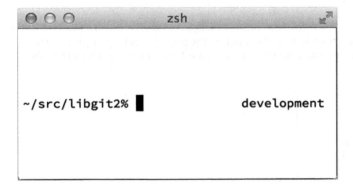

Figure A-11. *Customized zsh prompt*

Zsh is powerful enough that there are entire frameworks dedicated to making it better. One of them is called "oh-my-zsh", and it can be found at https://github.com/robbyrussell/oh-my-zsh. oh-my-zsh's plugin system comes with powerful git tab-completion, and it has a variety of prompt themes, many of which display version-control data. Figure A-12 is just one example of what can be done with this system.

Figure A-12. *An example of an oh-my-zsh theme*

Git in Powershell

The standard command-line terminal on Windows (cmd.exe) isn't really capable of a customized Git experience, but if you're using Powershell, you're in luck. A package called Posh-Git (https://github.com/dahlbyk/posh-git) provides powerful tab-completion facilities, as well as an enhanced prompt to help you stay on top of your repository status. It looks like this:

Figure A-13. *Powershell with Posh-Git*

If you've installed GitHub for Windows, Posh-Git is included by default, and all you have to do is add these lines to your profile.ps1 (which is usually located in C:\Users\<username>\Documents\WindowsPowerShell):

```
. (Resolve-Path "$env:LOCALAPPDATA\GitHub\shell.ps1")
. $env:github_posh_git\profile.example.ps1
```

If you're not a GitHub for Windows user, just download a Posh-Git release from (https://github.com/dahlbyk/posh-git), and uncompress it to the WindowsPowershell directory. Then open a Powershell prompt as the administrator, and do this:

```
> Set-ExecutionPolicy RemoteSigned -Scope CurrentUser -Confirm
> cd ~\Documents\WindowsPowerShell\posh-git
> .\install.ps1
```

This adds the proper line to your profile.ps1 file, and Posh-Git will be active the next time you open your prompt.

Summary

You've learned how to harness Git's power from inside the tools that you use during your everyday work, and also how to access Git repositories from your own programs.

■ ■ ■

Embedded Git in Your Applications

If your application is for developers, chances are good that it could benefit from integration with source control. Even non-developer applications, such as document editors, could potentially benefit from version-control features and Git's model works very well for many different scenarios.

If you need to integrate Git with your application, you have essentially three choices: spawning a shell and using the Git command-line tool, Libgit2, and JGit.

Command-line Git

One option is to spawn a shell process and use the Git command-line tool to do the work. This has the benefit of being canonical, and all Git's features are supported. This also happens to be fairly easy, as most runtime environments have a relatively simple facility for invoking a process with command-line arguments. However, this approach does have some downsides.

One is that all the output is in plain text. This means that you'll have to parse Git's occasionally changing output format to read progress and result information, which can be inefficient and error-prone.

Another is the lack of error recovery. If a repository is corrupted somehow, or the user has a malformed configuration value, Git will simply refuse to perform many operations.

Yet another is process management. Git requires you to maintain a shell environment on a separate process, which can add unwanted complexity. Trying to coordinate many of these processes (especially when potentially accessing the same repository from several processes) can be quite a challenge.

Libgit2

Another option at your disposal is to use Libgit2. Libgit2 is a dependency-free implementation of Git, with a focus on having a nice API for use within other programs. You can find it at http://libgit2.github.com.

First, let's take a look at what the C API looks like. Here's a whirlwind tour:

```
// Open a repository
git_repository *repo;
int error = git_repository_open(&repo, "/path/to/repository");

// Dereference HEAD to a commit
git_object *head_commit;
error = git_revparse_single(&head_commit, repo, "HEAD^{commit}");
git_commit *commit = (git_commit*)head_commit;
```

```
// Print some of the commit's properties
printf("%s", git_commit_message(commit));
const git_signature *author = git_commit_author(commit);
printf("%s <%s>\n", author->name, author->email);
const git_oid *tree_id = git_commit_tree_id(commit);

// Cleanup
git_commit_free(commit);
git_object_free(head_commit);
git_repository_free(repo);
```

The first couple of lines open a Git repository. The `git_repository` type represents a handle to a repository with a cache in memory. This is the simplest method, for when you know the exact path to a repository's working directory or `.git` folder. There's also the `git_repository_open_ext,` which includes options for searching, `git_clone` and friends for making a local clone of a remote repository, and `git_repository_init` for creating an entirely new repository.

The second chunk of code uses `rev-parse` syntax (see "Branch References" in Chapter 7 for more on this) to get the commit that HEAD eventually points to. The type returned is a `git_object` pointer, which represents something that exists in the Git object database for a repository. `git_object` is actually a "parent" type for several different kinds of objects; the memory layout for each of the "child" types is the same as for `git_object`, so you can safely cast to the right one. In this case, `git_object_type(commit)` would return `GIT_OBJ_COMMIT`, so it's safe to cast to a `git_commit` pointer.

The next chunk shows how to access the commit's properties. The last line here uses a `git_oid` type; this is Libgit2's representation for a SHA-1 hash.

From this sample, a couple of patterns have started to emerge:

- If you declare a pointer and pass a reference to it into a Libgit2 call, that call will probably return an integer error code. A 0 value indicates success; anything less is an error.

- If Libgit2 populates a pointer for you, you're responsible for freeing it.

- If Libgit2 returns a `const` pointer from a call, you don't have to free it, but it will become invalid when the object it belongs to is freed.

- Writing C is a bit painful.

That last one means it isn't very probable that you'll be writing C when using Libgit2. Fortunately, there are a number of language-specific bindings available that make it fairly easy to work with Git repositories from your specific language and environment. Let's take a look at the preceding example written using the Ruby bindings for Libgit2, which are named Rugged, and can be found at `https://github.com/libgit2/rugged`.

```
repo = Rugged::Repository.new('path/to/repository')
commit = repo.head.target
puts commit.message
puts "#{commit.author[:name]} <#{commit.author[:email]}>"
tree = commit.tree
```

As you can see, the code is much less cluttered. Firstly, Rugged uses exceptions; it can raise things like `ConfigError` or `ObjectError` to signal error conditions. Secondly, there's no explicit freeing of resources, because Ruby is garbage-collected. Let's take a look at a slightly more complicated example: crafting a commit from scratch:

```
blob_id = repo.write("Blob contents", :blob) (1)
```

```
index = repo.index
index.read_tree(repo.head.target.tree)
index.add(:path => 'newfile.txt', :oid => blob_id) (2)

sig = {
    :email => "bob@example.com",
    :name => "Bob User",
    :time => Time.now,
}

commit_id = Rugged::Commit.create(repo,
    :tree => index.write_tree(repo), (3)
    :author => sig,
    :committer => sig, (4)
    :message => "Add newfile.txt", (5)
    :parents => repo.empty? ? [] : [ repo.head.target ].compact, (6)
    :update_ref => 'HEAD', (7)
)

commit = repo.lookup(commit_id) (8)
```

1. Create a new blob, which contains the contents of a new file.

2. Populate the index with the head commit's tree, and add the new file at the path newfile.txt.

3. This creates a new tree in the ODB, and uses it for the new commit.

4. We use the same signature for both the author and committer fields.

5. The commit message.

6. When creating a commit, you have to specify the new commit's parents. This uses the tip of HEAD for the single parent.

7. Rugged (and Libgit2) can optionally update a reference when making a commit.

8. The return value is the SHA-1 hash of a new commit object, which you can then use to get a commit object.

The Ruby code is nice and clean, but because Libgit2 is doing the heavy lifting, this code will run pretty fast, too. If you're not a rubyist, we touch on some other bindings in the section "Other Bindings."

Advanced Functionality

Libgit2 has a couple of capabilities that are outside the scope of core Git. One example is pluggability: Libgit2 allows you to provide custom "backends" for several types of operation, so you can store things in a different way than stock Git does. Libgit2 allows custom backends for configuration, ref storage, and the object database, among other things.

Let's take a look at how this works. The code that follows is borrowed from the set of backend examples provided by the Libgit2 team (which can be found at https://github.com/libgit2/libgit2-backends). Here's how a custom backend for the object database is set up:

```
git_odb *odb;
int error = git_odb_new(&odb); (1)

git_repository *repo;
error = git_repository_wrap_odb(&repo, odb); (2)
```

```
git_odb_backend *my_backend;
error = git_odb_backend_mine(&my_backend, /*...*/); (3)

error = git_odb_add_backendodb, my_backend, 1); (4)
```

■ **Note**   Errors are captured, but not handled. We hope your code is better than ours.

---

1. Initialize an empty object database (ODB) "frontend," which will act as a handle to the real ODB.

2. Construct a git_repository around the empty ODB.

3. Initialize a custom ODB backend

4. Set the repository to use the custom backend for its ODB.

But what is this git_odb_backend_mine thing? Well, that's your own ODB implementation, and you can do whatever you want in there, so long as you fill in the git_odb_backend structure properly. Here's what it could look like:

```
typedef struct {
    git_odb_backend parent;

    // Some other stuff
    void *custom_context;
} my_backend_struct;

int git_odb_backend_mine(git_odb_backend **backend_out, /*...*/)
{
    my_backend_struct *backend;

    backend = calloc(1, sizeof (my_backend_struct));

    backend->custom_context = ...;

    backend->parent.read = &my_backend__read;
    backend->parent.read_prefix = &my_backend__read_prefix;
    backend->parent.read_header = &my_backend__read_header;
    // ...

    *backend_out = (git_odb_backend *) backend;

    return GIT_SUCCESS;
}
```

The subtlest constraint here is that my_backend_struct's first member must be a git_odb_backend structure; this ensures that the memory layout is what the Libgit2 code expects it to be. The rest of it is arbitrary; this structure can be as large or small as you need it to be.

The initialization function allocates some memory for the structure, sets up the custom context, and then fills in the members of the parent structure that it supports. Take a look at the include/git2/sys/odb_backend.h file in the Libgit2 source for a complete set of call signatures; your particular use case will help determine which of these you'll want to support.

Other Bindings

Libgit2 has bindings for many languages. Here we show a small example using a few of the more complete bindings packages as of this writing; libraries exist for many other languages, including C++, Go, Node.js, Erlang, and the JVM, all in various stages of maturity. The official collection of bindings can be found by browsing the repositories at https://github.com/libgit2. The code we'll write will return the commit message from the commit eventually pointed to by HEAD (sort of like git log -1).

LibGit2Sharp

If you're writing a .NET or Mono application, LibGit2Sharp (https://github.com/libgit2/libgit2sharp) is what you're looking for. The bindings are written in C#, and great care has been taken to wrap the raw Libgit2 calls with native-feeling CLR APIs. Here's what our example program looks like:

```
new Repository(@"C:\path\to\repo").Head.Tip.Message;
```

For desktop Windows applications, there's even a NuGet package that will help you get started quickly.

objective-git

If your application is running on an Apple platform, you're likely using Objective-C as your implementation language. Objective-Git (https://github.com/libgit2/objective-git) is the name of the Libgit2 bindings for that environment. The example program looks like this:

```
GTRepository *repo =
    [[GTRepository alloc] initWithURL:[NSURL fileURLWithPath: @"/path/to/repo"] error:NULL];
NSString *msg = [[[repo headReferenceWithError:NULL] resolvedTarget] message];
```

Objective-git is fully interoperable with Swift, so don't fear if you've left Objective-C behind.

pygit2

The bindings for Libgit2 in Python are called Pygit2, and can be found at http://www.pygit2.org/. Our example program:

```
pygit2.Repository("/path/to/repo") # open repository
    .head.resolve()                # get a direct ref
    .get_object().message          # get commit, read message
```

Further Reading

Of course, a full treatment of Libgit2's capabilities is outside the scope of this book. If you want more information on Libgit2 itself, there's API documentation at https://libgit2.github.com/libgit2, and a set of guides at https://libgit2.github.com/docs. For the other bindings, check the bundled README and tests; there are often small tutorials and pointers to further reading there.

APPENDIX C

■ ■ ■

Git Commands

Throughout the book we have introduced dozens of Git commands and have tried hard to introduce them within something of a narrative, adding more commands to the story slowly. However, this leaves us with examples of usage of the commands somewhat scattered throughout the whole book.

In this appendix, we'll go through all the Git commands we addressed throughout the book, grouped roughly by what they're used for. We'll talk about what each command very generally does and then point out where in the book you can find us having used it.

Setup and Config

There are two commands that are used quite a lot, from the first invocations of Git to common every day tweaking and referencing, the config and help commands.

git config

Git has a default way of doing hundreds of things. For a lot of these things, you can tell Git to default to doing them a different way, or set your preferences. This involves everything from telling Git what your name is to specific terminal color preferences or what editor you use. There are several files this command will read from and write to so you can set values globally or down to specific repositories.

The git config command has been used in nearly every chapter of the book.

- In 'First-Time Git Setup' (Chapter 1), we used it to specify our name, email address and editor preference before we even got started using Git.

- In 'Git Aliases' (Chapter 2), we showed how you could use it to create shorthand commands that expand to long option sequences so you don't have to type them every time.

- In 'Rebasing' (Chapter 3), we used it to make --rebase the default when you run git pull.

- In 'Credential Storage' (Chapter 7), we used it to set up a default store for your HTTP passwords

- Finally, basically the entirety of 'Git Configuration' (Chapter 8) is dedicated to the command.

git help

The git help command is used to show you all the documentation shipped with Git about any command. While we're giving a rough overview of most of the more popular ones in this appendix, for a full listing of all of the possible options and flags for every command, you can always run git help <command>.

We introduced the git help command in 'Getting Help' (Chapter 1), and showed you how to use it to find more information about the git shell in 'Setting Up The Server' (Chapter 4).

Getting and Creating Projects

There are two ways to get a Git repository. One is to copy it from an existing repository on the network or elsewhere and the other is to create a new one in an existing directory.

git init

To take a directory and turn it into a new Git repository so you can start version controlling it, you can simply run `git init`.

- We talk briefly about how you can change the default branch from "master" in 'Remote Branches' (Chapter 3).

- We use this command to create an empty bare repository for a server in 'Putting the Bare Repository on the Server' (Chapter 4).

- Finally, we go through some of the details of what it actually does behind the scenes in 'Plumbing and Porcelain' (Chapter 10).

git clone

The git clone command is actually something of a wrapper around several other commands. It creates a new directory, goes into it and runs git init to make it an empty Git repository, adds a remote (git remote add) to the URL that you pass it (by default named origin), runs a git fetch from that remote repository and then checks out the latest commit into your working directory with git checkout.

The git clone command is used in dozens of places throughout the book, but we'll just list a few interesting places.

- It's basically introduced and explained in 'Git Cloning' (Chapter 2), where we go through a few examples.

- In 'Git on the Server' (Chapter 4), we look at using the `--bare` option to create a copy of a Git repository with no working directory.

- In 'Bundling' (Chapter 7), we use it to unbundle a bundled Git repository.

- Finally, in 'Cloning a Project with Submodules' (Chapter 7) we learn the `--recursive` option to make cloning a repository with submodules a little simpler.

Though it's used in many other places through the book, these are the ones that are somewhat unique or where it is used in ways that are a little different.

Basic Snapshotting

For the basic workflow of staging content and committing it to your history, there are only a few basic commands.

git add

The `git add` command adds content from the working directory into the staging area (or "index") for the next commit. When the `git commit` command is run, by default it only looks at this staging area, so `git add` is used to craft what exactly you would like your next commit snapshot to look like.

This command is an incredibly important command in Git and is mentioned or used dozens of times in this book. We'll quickly cover some of the unique uses that can be found.

- We first introduce and explain git add in detail in 'Tracking New Files' (Chapter 2).

- We mention how to use it to resolve merge conflicts in 'Basic Merge Conflicts' (Chapter 3).

- We go over using it to interactively stage only specific parts of a modified file in 'Interactive Staging' (Chapter 7).

- Finally, we emulate it at a low level in 'Tree Objects' (Chapter 10), so you can get an idea of what it's doing behind the scenes.

git status

The git status command will show you the different states of files in your working directory and staging area. Which files are modified and unstaged and which are staged but not yet committed. In it's normal form, it also will show you some basic hints on how to move files between these stages.

We first cover status in 'Checking the Status of Your Files' (Chapter 2), both in its basic and simplified forms. While we use it throughout the book, pretty much everything you can do with the git status command is covered there.

git diff

The git diff command is used when you want to see differences between any two trees. This could be the difference between your working environment and your staging area (git diff by itself), between your staging area and your last commit (git diff --staged), or between two commits (git diff master branchB).

- We first look at the basic uses of git diff in 'Viewing Your Staged and Unstaged Changes' (Chapter 2), where we show how to see what changes are staged and which are not yet staged.

- We use it to look for possible whitespace issues before committing with the --check option in 'Commit Guidelines' (Chapter 5).

- We see how to check the differences between branches more effectively with the git diff A...B syntax in 'Determining What Is Introduced' (Chapter 5).

- We use it to filter out whitespace differences with -w and how to compare different stages of conflicted files with --theirs, --ours and --base in 'Advanced Merging' (Chapter 7).

- Finally, we use it to effectively compare submodule changes with --submodule in 'Starting with Submodules' (Chapter 7).

git difftool

The git difftool command simply launches an external tool to show you the difference between two trees in case you want to use something other than the built in git diff command.

git commit

The `git commit` command takes all the file contents that have been staged with `git add` and records a new permanent snapshot in the database and then moves the branch pointer on the current branch up to it.

- We first cover the basics of committing in 'Committing Your Changes' (Chapter 2). There we also demonstrate how to use the -a flag to skip the `git add` step in daily workflows and how to use the -m flag to pass a commit message in on the command line instead of firing up an editor.

- In 'Undoing Things' (Chapter 2) we cover using the --amend option to redo the most recent commit.

- In 'Branches in a Nutshell' (Chapter 3), we go into much more detail about what `git commit` does and why it does it like that.

- We looked at how to sign commits cryptographically with the -s flag in 'Signing Commits' (Chapter 7).

- Finally, we take a look at what the git commit command does in the background and how it's actually implemented in 'Commit Objects' (Chapter 10).

git reset

The `git reset` command is primarily used to undo things, as you can possibly tell by the verb. It moves around the HEAD pointer and optionally changes the `index` or staging area and can also optionally change the working directory if you use --hard. This final option makes it possible for this command to lose your work if used incorrectly, so make sure you understand it before using it.

- We first effectively cover the simplest use of `git reset` in 'Unstaging a Staged File' (Chapter 2), where we use it to unstage a file we had run `git add` on.

- We then cover it in quite some detail in 'Reset Demystified' (Chapter 7), which is entirely devoted to explaining this command.

- We use `git reset --hard` to abort a merge in 'Aborting a Merge' (Chapter 7), where we also use `git merge --abort`, which is a bit of a wrapper for the `git reset` command.

git rm

The git rm command is used to remove files from the staging area and working directory for Git. It is similar to git add in that it stages a removal of a file for the next commit.

- We cover the `git rm` command in some detail in 'Removing Files' (Chapter 2), including recursively removing files and only removing files from the staging area but leaving them in the working directory with --cached.

- The only other differing use of git rm in the book is in 'Removing Objects' (Chapter 10) where we briefly use and explain the --ignore-unmatch when running `git filter-branch`, which simply makes it not error out when the file we are trying to remove doesn't exist. This can be useful for scripting purposes.

git mv

The git mv command is a thin convenience command to move a file and then run git add on the new file and git rm on the old file. We only briefly mention this command in 'Moving Files' (Chapter 2).

git clean

The git clean command is used to remove unwanted files from your working directory. This could include removing temporary build artifacts or merge conflict files. We cover many of the options and scenarios in which you might used the clean command in 'Cleaning Your Working Directory' (Chapter 7).

Branching and Merging

There are just a handful of commands that implement most of the branching and merging functionality in Git.

git branch

The git branch command is actually something of a branch management tool. It can list the branches you have, create a new branch, delete branches and rename branches.

- Most of Chapter 3 is dedicated to the branch command and it's used throughout the entire chapter. We first introduce it in 'Creating a New Branch' and we go through most of it's other features (listing and deleting) in 'Branch Management'.

- In 'Tracking Branches' we use the git branch -u option to set up a tracking branch.

- Finally, we go through some of what it does in the background in 'Git References' (Chapter 10).

git checkout

The git checkout command is used to switch branches and check content out into your working directory.

- We first encounter the command in 'Switching Branches' (Chapter 3) along with the git branch command.

- We see how to use it to start tracking branches with the --track flag in "Tracking Branches" (Chapter 3).

- We use it to reintroduce file conflicts with --conflict=diff3 in "Checking Out Conflicts" (Chapter 7).

- We go into closer detail on its relationship with git reset in "Reset Demystified" (Chapter 7).

- Finally, we go into some implementation detail in "The HEAD" (Chapter 10).

git merge

The `git merge` tool is used to merge one or more branches into the branch you have checked out. It will then advance the current branch to the result of the merge.

- The `git merge` command was first introduced in 'Basic Branching' (Chapter 3). Though it is used in various places in the book, there are very few variations of the `merge` command — generally just `git merge <branch>` with the name of the single branch you want to merge in.

- We covered how to do a squashed merge (where Git merges the work but pretends like it's just a new commit without recording the history of the branch you're merging in) at the very end of 'Forked Public Project' (Chapter 5).

- We went over a lot about the merge process and command, including the `-Xignore-all-whitespace` command and the `--abort` flag to abort a problem merge in 'Advanced Merging' (Chapter 7).

- We learned how to verify signatures before merging if your project is using GPG signing in 'Signing Commits' (Chapter 7).

- Finally, we learned about Subtree merging in 'Subtree Merging' (Chapter &).

git mergetool

The `git mergetool` command simply launches an external merge helper in case you have issues with a merge in Git.

We mention it quickly in "Basic Merge Conflicts" (Chapter 3) and go into detail on how to implement your own external merge tool in "External Merge and Diff Tools" (Chapter 8).

git log

The `git log` command is used to show the reachable recorded history of a project from the most recent commit snapshot backwards. By default it will only show the history of the branch you're currently on, but can be given different or even multiple heads or branches from which to traverse. It is also often used to show differences between two or more branches at the commit level.

This command is used in nearly every chapter of the book to demonstrate the history of a project.

- We introduce the command and cover it in some depth in "Viewing the Commit History" (Chapter 2). There we look at the `-p` and `--stat` option to get an idea of what was introduced in each commit and the `--pretty` and `--oneline` options to view the history more concisely, along with some simple date and author filtering options.

- In "Creating a New Branch" (Chapter 3) we use it with the `--decorate` option to easily visualize where our branch pointers are located and we also use the `--graph` option to see what divergent histories look like.

- In "Private Small Team" (Chapter 5) and "Commit Ranges" (Chapter 7) we cover the `branchA..branchB` syntax to use the git log command to see what commits are unique to a branch relative to another branch. In "Commit Ranges" we go through this fairly extensively.

- In "Merge Log" and "Triple Dot" (Chapter 7) we cover using the `branchA...branchB` format and the `--left-right` syntax to see what is in one branch or the other but not in both. In "Merge Log" we also look at how to use the `--merge` option to help with merge conflict debugging as well as using the `--cc` option to look at merge commit conflicts in your history.

- In "Git Notes" we use the `--notes=` option to display notes inline in the log output, and in "RefLog Shortnames" (Chapter 7) we use the `-g` option to view the Git reflog through this tool instead of doing branch traversal.

- In "Searching" (Chapter 7) we look at using the `-S` and `-L` options to do fairly sophisticated searches for something that happened historically in the code such as seeing the history of a function.

- In "Signing Commits" (Chapter 7) we see how to use `--show-signature` to add a validation string to each commit in the `git log` output based on if it was validly signed or not.

git stash

The `git stash` command is used to temporarily store uncommitted work in order to clean out your working directory without having to commit unfinished work on a branch. This is basically entirely covered in "Stashing and Cleaning" (Chapter 7).

git tag

The `git tag` command is used to give a permanent bookmark to a specific point in the code history. Generally this is used for things like releases.

- This command is introduced and covered in detail in "Tagging" (Chapter 2) and we use it in practice in "Tagging Your Releases" (Chapter 5).

- We also cover how to create a GPG signed tag with the `-s` flag and verify one with the `-v` flag in "Signing Your Work" (Chapter 7).

Sharing and Updating Projects

There are not very many commands in Git that access the network, nearly all of the commands operate on the local database. When you are ready to share your work or pull changes from elsewhere, there are a handful of commands that deal with remote repositories.

git fetch

The `git fetch` command communicates with a remote repository and fetches down all the information that is in that repository that is not in your current one and stores it in your local database.

- We first look at this command in "Fetching and Pulling from Your Remotes" (Chapter 2) and we continue to see examples of it use in "Remote Branches" (Chapter 3).

- We also use it in several of the examples in "Contributing to a Project" (Chapter 5).

- We use it to fetch a single specific reference that is outside of the default space in "Pull Request Refs" (Chapter 6) and we see how to fetch from a bundle in "Bundling" (Chapter 7).

- We set up highly custom refspecs in order to make `git fetch` do something a little different than the default in "Getting Notes" and "The Refspec" (Chapter 10).

git pull

The `git pull` command is basically a combination of the `git fetch` and `git merge` commands, where Git will fetch from the remote you specify and then immediately try to merge it into the branch you're on.

- We introduce it quickly in "Fetching and Pulling from Your Remotes" (Chapter 2) and show how to see what it will merge if you run it in "Inspecting a Remote" (Chapter 2).

- We also see how to use it to help with rebasing difficulties in "Rebase when you Rebase" (Chapter 3).

- We show how to use it with a URL to pull in changes in a one-off fashion in "Checking Out Remote Branches" (Chapter 5).

- Finally, we very quickly mention that you can use the `--verify-signatures` option to it in order to verify that commits you are pulling have been GPG signed in "Signing Commits" (Chapter 7).

git push

The `git push` command is used to communicate with another repository, calculate what your local database has that the remote one does not, and then pushes the difference into the other repository. It requires write access to the other repository and so normally is authenticated somehow.

- We first look at the `git push` command in "Pushing to Your Remotes" (Chapter 2). Here we cover the basics of pushing a branch to a remote repository. In "Pushing" (Chapter 3) we go a little deeper into pushing specific branches and in "Tracking Branches" (Chapter 3) we see how to set up tracking branches to automatically push to. In "Deleting Remote Branches" (Chapter 3) we use the `--delete` flag to delete a branch on the server with `git push`.

- Throughout "Contributing to a Project" (Chapter 5) we see several examples of using git push to share work on branches through multiple remotes.

- We see how to use it to share tags that you have made with the `--tags` option in "Sharing Tags" (Chapter 2).

- In "Publishing Submodule Changes" (Chapter 7) we use the `--recurse-submodules` option to check that all of our submodules work has been published before pushing the superproject, which can be really helpful when using submodules.

- In "Other Client Hooks" (Chapter 8) talk briefly about the `pre-push` hook, which is a script we can setup to run before a push completes to verify that it should be allowed to push.

- Finally, in "Pushing Refspecs" (Chapter 10) we look at pushing with a full refspec instead of the general shortcuts that are normally used. This can help you be very specific about what work you wish to share.

git remote

The `git remote` command is a management tool for your record of remote repositories. It allows you to save long URLs as short handles, such as "origin" so you don't have to type them out all the time. You can have several of these and the git remote command is used to add, change and delete them.

- This command is covered in detail in "Working with Remotes" (Chapter 2), including listing, adding, removing and renaming them.

- It is used in nearly every subsequent chapter in the book too, but always in the standard `git remote add <name> <url>` format.

git archive

The `git archive` command is used to create an archive file of a specific snapshot of the project. We use `git archive` to create a tarball of a project for sharing in "Preparing a Release" (Chapter 5).

git submodule

The `git submodule` command is used to manage external repositories within a normal repositories. This could be for libraries or other types of shared resources. The submodule command has several sub-commands (add, update, sync, etc) for managing these resources. This command is only mentioned and entirely covered in "Submodules" (Chapter 7).

Inspection and Comparison

git show

The `git show` command can show a Git object in a simple and human readable way. Normally you would use this to show the information about a tag or a commit.

- We first use it to show annotated tag information in "Annotated Tags" (Chapter 2).

- Later we use it quite a bit in "Revision Selection" (Chapter 7) to show the commits that our various revision selections resolve to.

- One of the more interesting things we do with git show is in "Manual File Re-merging" (Chapter 7) to extract specific file contents of various stages during a merge conflict.

git shortlog

The `git shortlog` command is used to summarize the output of `git log`. It will take many of the same options that the `git log` command will but instead of listing out all of the commits it will present a summary of the commits grouped by author. We showed how to use it to create a nice changelog in "The Shortlog" (Chapter 5).

git describe

The `git describe` command is used to take anything that resolves to a commit and produces a string that is somewhat human-readable and will not change. It's a way to get a description of a commit that is as unambiguous as a commit SHA but more understandable.

We use `git describe` in "Generating a Build Number" (Chapter 5) and "Preparing a Release" (also in Chapter 5) to get a string to name our release file after.

Debugging

Git has a couple of commands that are used to help debug an issue in your code. This ranges from figuring out where something was introduced to figuring out who introduced it.

git bisect

The `git bisect` tool is an incredibly helpful debugging tool used to find which specific commit was the first one to introduce a bug or problem by doing an automatic binary search. It is fully covered in "Binary Search" (Chapter 7) and is only mentioned in that section.

git blame

The `git blame` command annotates the lines of any file with which commit was the last one to introduce a change to each line of the file and what person authored that commit. This is helpful in order to find the person to ask for more information about a specific section of your code. It is covered in "File Annotation" (Chapter 7) and is only mentioned in that section.

git grep

The `git grep` command can help you find any string or regular expression in any of the files in your source code, even older versions of your project. It is covered in "Git Grep" (Chapter 7) and is only mentioned in that section.

Patching

A few commands in Git are centered around the concept of thinking of commits in terms of the changes they introduce, as thought the commit series is a series of patches. These commands help you manage your branches in this manner.

git cherry-pick

The `git cherry-pick` command is used to take the change introduced in a single Git commit and try to re-introduce it as a new commit on the branch you're currently on. This can be useful to only take one or two commits from a branch individually rather than merging in the branch that takes all the changes. Cherry picking is described and demonstrated in "Rebasing and Cherry Picking Workflows" (Chapter 5).

git rebase

The `git rebase` command is basically an automated cherry-pick. It determines a series of commits and then cherry-picks them one by one in the same order somewhere else.

- Rebasing is covered in detail in "Rebasing" (Chapter 3) including covering the collaborative issues involved with rebasing branches that are already public.

- We use it in practice during an example of splitting your history into two separate repositories in "Replace" (Chapter 7), using the --onto flag as well.

- We go through running into a merge conflict during rebasing in "Rerere" (Chapter 7).

- We also use it in an interactive scripting mode with the -i option in "Changing Multiple Commit Messages" (Chapter 7).

git revert

The `git revert` command is essentially a reverse git cherry-pick. It creates a new commit that applies the exact opposite of the change introduced in the commit you're targeting, essentially undoing or reverting it. We use this in "Reverse the Commit" (Chapter 7) to undo a merge commit.

Email

Many Git projects, including Git itself, are entirely maintained over mailing lists. Git has a number of tools built into it that help make this process easier, from generating patches you can easily email to applying those patches from an email box.

git apply

The `git apply` command applies a patch created with the `git diff` or even `GNU diff` command. It is similar to what the patch command might do with a few small differences. We demonstrate using it and the circumstances in which you might do so in "Applying Patches from Email" (Chapter 5).

git am

The git am command is used to apply patches from an email inbox, specifically one that is mbox formatted. This is useful for receiving patches over email and applying them to your project easily.

- We covered usage and workflow around git am in "Applying a Patch with am" (Chapter 5) including using the `--resolved`, `-i` and `-3` options.

- There are also a number of hooks you can use to help with the workflow around `git am` and they are all covered in "Email Workflow Hooks" (Chapter 8).

- We also use it to apply patch formatted GitHub Pull Request changes in "Email Notifications" (Chapter 6).

git format-patch

The `git format-patch` command is used to generate a series of patches in mbox format that you can use to send to a mailing list properly formatted. We go through an example of contributing to a project using the `git format-patch` tool in "Public Project Over Email" (Chapter 5).

git send-email

The `git send-email` command is used to send patches that are generated with `git format-patch` over email. We go through an example of contributing to a project by sending patches with the `git send-email` tool in "Public Project Over Email" (Chapter 5).

git request-pull

The `git request-pull` command is simply used to generate an example message body to email to someone. If you have a branch on a public server and want to let someone know how to integrate those changes without sending the patches over email, you can run this command and send the output to the person you want to pull the changes in.

We demonstrate how to use `git request-pull` to generate a pull message in "Forked Public Project" (Chapter 5).

External Systems

Git comes with a few commands to integrate with other version control systems.

git svn

The `git svn` command is used to communicate with the Subversion version control system as a client. This means you can use Git to checkout from and commit to a Subversion server. This command is covered in depth in "Git and Subversion" (Chapter 9).

git fast-import

For other version control systems or importing from nearly any format, you can use `git fast-import` to quickly map the other format to something Git can easily record. This command is covered in depth in "A Custom Importer" (Chapter 9).

Administration

If you're administering a Git repository or need to fix something in a big way, Git provides a number of administrative commands to help you out.

git gc

The `git gc` command runs "garbage collection" on your repository, removing unnecessary files in your database and packing up the remaining files into a more efficient format. This command normally runs in the background for you, though you can manually run it if you wish. We go over some examples of this in "Maintenance" (Chapter 10).

git fsck

The `git fsck` command is used to check the internal database for problems or inconsistencies. We only quickly use this once in "Data Recovery" (Chapter 10) to search for dangling objects.

git reflog

The `git reflog` command goes through a log of where all the heads of your branches have been as you work to find commits you may have lost through rewriting histories.

- We cover this command mainly in "RefLog Shortnames" (Chapter 7), where we show normal usage to and how to use `git log -g` to view the same information with `git log` output.

- We also go through a practical example of recovering such a lost branch in "Data Recovery" (Chapter 10).

git filter-branch

The `git filter-branch` command is used to rewrite loads of commits according to certain patterns, like removing a file everywhere or filtering the entire repository down to a single subdirectory for extracting a project.

- In "Removing a File from Every Commit" (Chapter 7) we explain the command and explore several different options such as `--commit-filter`, `--subdirectory-filter` and `--tree-filter`.

- In "Git-p4" (Chapter 9) and "TFS" (Chapter 9) we use it to fix up imported external repositories.

Plumbing Commands

There were also quite a number of lower level plumbing commands that we encountered in the book.

- The first one we encounter is `ls-remote` in "Pull Request Refs" (Chapter 6) which we use to look at the raw references on the server.

- We use `ls-files` in Chapter 7, in "Manual File Re-merging", "Rerere" and "The Index", to take a more raw look at what your staging area looks like.

- We also mention `rev-parse` in "Branch References" (Chapter 7) to take just about any string and turn it into an object SHA.

- However, most of the low level plumbing commands we cover are in Chapter 10, which is more or less what the chapter is focused on. We tried to avoid use of them throughout most of the rest of the book.

Index

Get the eBook for only $10!

Now you can take the weightless companion with you anywhere, anytime. Your purchase of this book entitles you to 3 electronic versions for only $10.

This Apress title will prove so indispensible that you'll want to carry it with you everywhere, which is why we are offering the eBook in 3 formats for only $10 if you have already purchased the print book.

Convenient and fully searchable, the PDF version enables you to easily find and copy code—or perform examples by quickly toggling between instructions and applications. The MOBI format is ideal for your Kindle, while the ePUB can be utilized on a variety of mobile devices.

Go to www.apress.com/promo/tendollars to purchase your companion eBook.

Printed by Books on Demand, Germany